THE GROVER E. MURRAY STUDIES IN THE AMERICAN SOUTHWEST

ALSO IN THE SERIES

Agaves, Yuccas, and Their Kin: Seven Genera of the Southwest, by Jon L. Hawker

Between Two Rivers: Photographs and Poems Between the Brazos and the Rio Grande, by Jerod Foster and John Poch

Brujerías: Stories of Witchcraft and the Supernatural in the American Southwest and Beyond, by Nasario García

Cacti of Texas: A Field Guide, by A. Michael Powell, James F. Weedin, and Shirley A. Powell

Cacti of the Trans-Pecos and Adjacent Areas, by A. Michael Powell and James F. Weedin

Cowboy Park: Steer-Roping Contests on the Border, by John O. Baxter

Dance All Night: Those Other Southwestern Swing Bands, Past and Present, by Jean A. Boyd

Dancin' in Anson: A History of the Texas Cowboys' Christmas Ball, by Paul H. Carlson

Deep Time and the Texas High Plains: History and Geology, by Paul H. Carlson

"Don't Count the Tortillas: The Art of Texas Mexican Cooking, by Adán Medrano

Equal Opportunity Hero: T.J. Patterson's Service to West Texas, by Phil Price

Finding the Great Western Trail, by Sylvia Gann Mahoney

From Texas to San Diego in 1851: The Overland Journal of Dr. S. W. Woodhouse, Surgeon-Naturalist of the Sitgreaves Expedition, edited by Andrew Wallace and Richard H. Hevly

Grasses of South Texas: A Guide to Identification and Value, by James H. Everitt, D. Lynn Drawe, Christopher R. Little, and Robert I. Lonard

A Kineño's Journey: On Learning, Family, and Public Service, by Lauro F. Cavazos, with Gene B. Preuss

Kit Carson and the First Battle of Adobe Walls: A Tale of Two Journeys, by Alvin R. Lynn

In the Shadow of the Carmens: Afield with a Naturalist in the Northern Mexican Mountains, by Bonnie Reynolds McKinney

Javelinas: Collared Peccaries of the Southwest, by Jane Manaster

Land of Enchantment Wildflowers: A Guide to the Plants of New Mexico, by LaShara J. Nieland and Willa F. Finley

Little Big Bend: Common, Uncommon, and Rare Plants of Big Bend National Park, by Roy Morey

Lone Star Wildflowers: A Guide to Texas Flowering Plants, by LaShara J. Nieland and Willa F. Finley

My Wild Life: A Memoir of Adventures within America's National Parks, by Roland H. Wauer

Myth, Memory, and Massacre: The Pease River Capture of Cynthia Ann Parker, by Paul H. Carlson and Tom Crum

Pecans: The Story in a Nutshell, by Jane Manaster

Picturing a Different West: Vision, Illustration, and the Tradition of Austin and Cather, by Janis P. Stout

Plants of Central Texas Wetlands, by Scott B. Fleenor and Stephen Welton Taber

Seat of Empire: The Embattled Birth of Austin, Texas, by Jeffrey Stuart Kerr

Texas, New Mexico, and the Compromise of 1850: Boundary Dispute and Sectional Crisis, by Mark J. Stegmaier

Texas Quilts and Quilters: A Lone Star Legacy, by Marcia Kaylakie with Janice Whittington

Truly Texas Mexican: A Native Culinary Heritage in Recipes, by Adán Medrano

The Wineslinger Chronicles: Texas on the Vine, by Russell D. Kane

1 - PLATERESQUE
ANTICIPATION - The early spring of a style

2 - HIGH RENAISSANCE
DETERMINATION - The stern dictates of Philip II

3 - BAROQUE
EXULTATION - Freedom from Philip's commands

4 - CHURRIGUERESQUE
EXUBERANCE - It reached its height in Mexico.

For the Neo-Classic repeat the High Renaissance but call it RESIGNATION

OPUS IN BRICK AND STONE

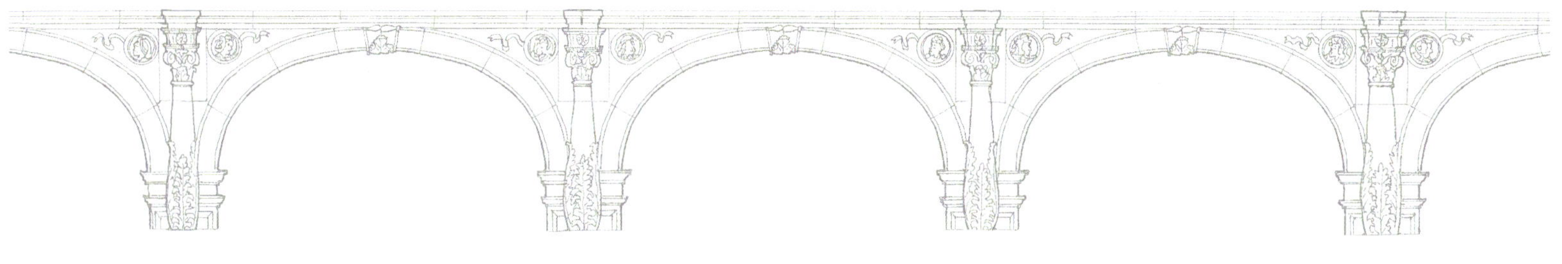

The Architectural and Planning Heritage of Texas Tech University

BRIAN H. GRIGGS

Foreword by Richard L. Kagan

TEXAS TECH UNIVERSITY PRESS

Unless otherwise noted in Appendix C, illustrations and photographs by Brian H. Griggs.

Publication made possible by The CH Foundation and Parkhill, Smith & Cooper.

This book is typeset in Galliard by Copperline Book Services.
The paper used in this book meets the minimum requirements of ANSI/NISO Z39.48-1992 (R1997). ∞

Designed by April Leidig

Cover photograph courtesy Texas Tech University

Frontispiece: "The Plateresque [style was the] ANTICIPATION—The early spring of a [Renaissance] style."—Trent Elwood Sanford, Yale University, 1947.

Library of Congress Cataloging-in-Publication Data
Names: Griggs, Brian H., author.
Title: Opus in brick and stone : the architectural and planning heritage of Texas Tech University / Brian H. Griggs.
Description: Lubbock, TX : Texas Tech University Press, 2019. |
Series: Grover E. Murray studies in the American Southwest |
Includes bibliographical references and index. | Summary: "An in-depth visual history of the Texas Tech University System's Spanish Renaissance architectural style, including comparisons with its historic design inspirations"— Provided by publisher.
Identifiers: LCCN 2019032072 | ISBN 9781682830444 (cloth)
Subjects: LCSH: Texas Tech University—Buildings. | Watkin, William Ward, 1886-1952. | Architecture, Spanish—Texas—Lubbock. | Renaissance revival (Architecture)—Texas—Lubbock. | Lubbock (Tex.)—Buildings, structures, etc.
Classification: LCC LD5314 .G75 2019 | DDC 378.764/847—dc23
LC record available at https://lccn.loc.gov/2019032072

Printed in China

20 21 22 23 24 25 26 27 28 | 9 8 7 6 5 4 3 2 1

Texas Tech University Press
Box 41037
Lubbock, Texas 79409-1037 USA

800.832.4042

ttup@ttu.edu
www.ttupress.org

For Jaime, Will, Emilie, and KaLee

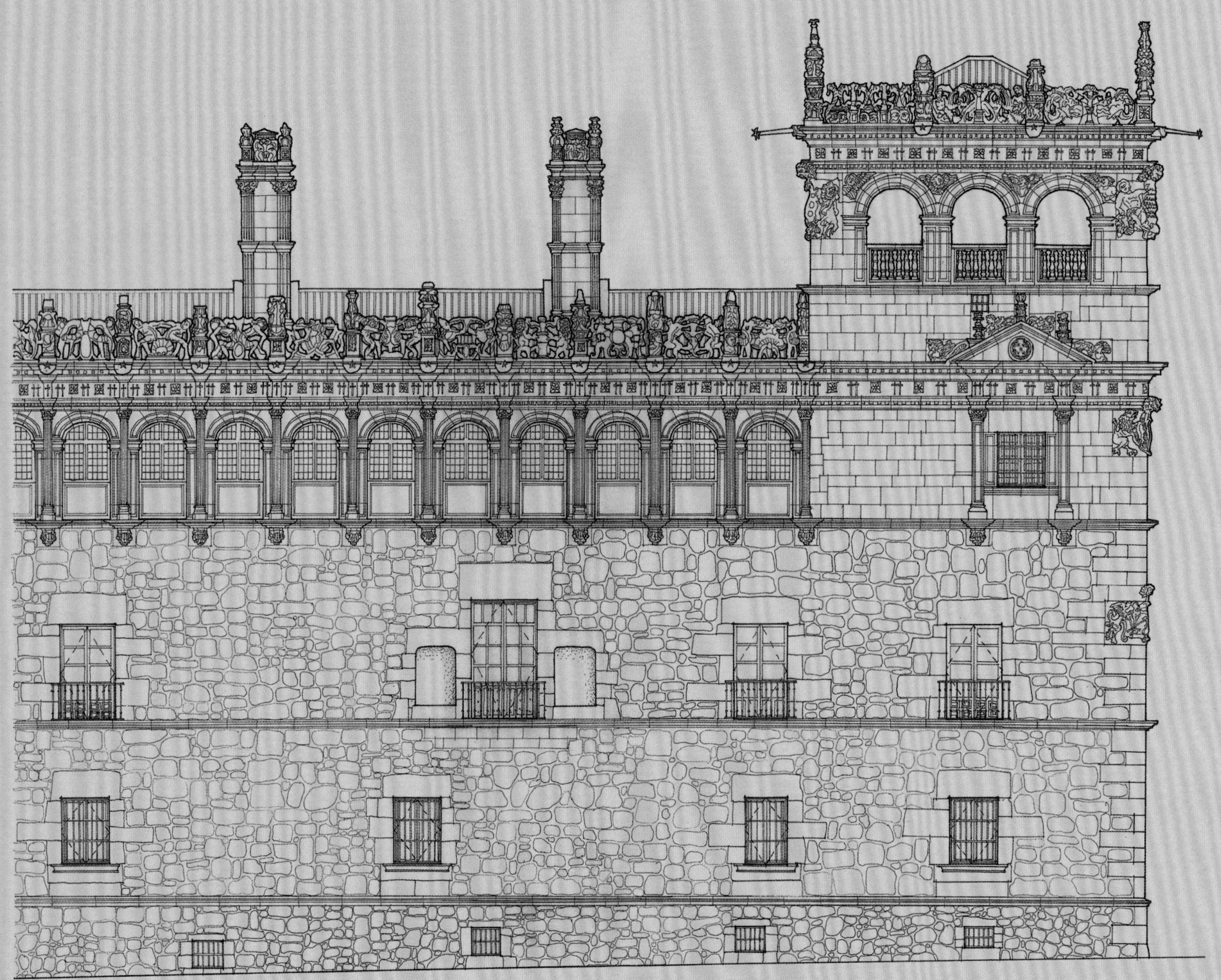

CONTENTS

FOREWORD

I HAVE A VIVID MEMORY of my first visit to the campus of Texas Tech University. It was at the end of March 2016, a moment when I was in the midst of preparing a book devoted to changes in the image of Spain and Spanish culture in the United States. I already knew that the façade of TTU's Administration Building was modeled upon the Renaissance-cum-Plateresque façade of the Colegio Mayor de San Ildefonso, centerpiece of the University of Alcalá de Henares, but specifically traveled to Lubbock in order to have a firsthand look. What I did not know—and this was a real surprise—is that several of TTU's original buildings, notably the Chemistry Building, parts of which resembled Salamanca's elegant Palacio del Monterrey, were also built in Spanish style. Why these design choices? What was William Ward Watkin, the architect responsible for the original architectural plan of what was then called Texas Technological College, thinking when he set out to design a campus in the style of Renaissance Spain?

As a historian who has dedicated much of his life to the history of early modern Spain, and the author of a book on the history of its universities, I understood that the curriculum of Alcalá de Henares, founded in 1508, differed radically from Spain's existing universities. The latter emphasized professional studies in law, theology, and medicine; Alcalá privileged humanistic studies of a Renaissance bent. The elaborate façade of the Colegio Mayor de San Ildefonso reflected that forward-looking curriculum. Rather than employ the more traditional Gothic style, the college's architects, Luis de Vega and Rodrigo de Hontañón, opted for something more novel, namely a design combining the solidity and symmetry of Italian Renaissance architecture with decorative surface ornaments characteristic of Spain's then emergent Plateresque (or Isabelline) style. These ornaments included figures of Minerva, goddess of wisdom and learning, along with a large heraldic shield of its reigning monarch, Emperor Charles V, whose possessions embraced Spain's rapidly expanding empire in the Americas. In this respect, San Ildefonso's façade spoke to Spain's glorious future as opposed to its medieval past.

Texas Technological College, founded in 1923, was equally forward looking, albeit in ways markedly different from Alcalá. Whereas the latter emphasized the liberal arts and humanities, TTC's founders specifically sought to encourage study in technological, manufacturing, and agricultural subjects and to "to elevate the ideals, enrich the lives, and increase the capacity of the people for democratic self-government." With such aims in mind, Watkin might have easily landed upon any one of a variety of architectural styles in which to build the new campus. At the time, university architects opted for buildings designed in various neoclassical or revivalist styles, including Beaux-Arts classical (Columbia), neo-Georgian (Johns Hopkins), neo-Gothic (Chicago and Princeton), Romanesque revival (UCLA), or in the case of the original administrative building at Rice, neo-Byzantine. No architect, however, had ever elected to build a campus in a style that harked back directly to Spain, a country Americans traditionally linked with the Inquisition, religious intolerance, and intellectual backwardness as opposed to innovative learning and thought.

The rationale for this decision, and as this richly illustrated volume lucidly explains, is connected to what Griggs terms an architectural

"Spanish wave" that rippled across much of the United States in the wake of the Spanish American War of 1898. Prior to that conflict Americans generally regarded Spain as a backward country that merited little in the way of admiration or respect. Gradually, however, cracks in that image emerged. Starting in the 1830s, popular writers such as Washington Irving and Henry Wadsworth Longfellow presented Spain in a new, softer, more romantic light. If hooded Inquisitors symbolized America's traditional image of Spain, Carmen, together with guitar-strumming gypsies and dashing matadors, symbolized the one Irving endeavored to create. Adding further to this changing image was William H. Prescott, the famed historian who credited Spaniards for bringing civilization and religion to the New World. Soon other writers highlighted the civilizing role of Spaniards in North America, especially in California, Texas, and other parts of the Southwest, none more passionately than transplanted New Englander–cum–Los Angelino, Charles Lummis. In his best-selling *The Spanish Pioneers* (1st ed., 1890) Lummis praised Spaniards for their "humane and progressive spirit" while also reminding his readers that "Had there not been no Spain four hundred years ago, there would be no United States today. . . . There would be no Los Angeles, no San Francisco, no San Diego, and almost certainly no American state west of Kansas . . . from first to last."

To be sure, the war precipitated in large part by anti-Spanish propaganda disseminated in the so-called Yellow Press, temporarily darkened Spain's emergent halo, but in keeping with the idea of "forgive and forget," that cloud lifted as memories of the charge of Cuba's San Juan Hill started to fade. At that point Irving's romanticized Spain joined forces with Lummis's notion of the country as a force for good, enabling Americans to embrace Spanish culture to an extent never before possible. The trend began in California and other parts of the Southwest, where it was coupled with a growing nostalgia for an older, simpler, and overly romanticized way of life associated with region's Spanish past. But such ideas quickly spread to other parts of the country and contributed directly to the start of what I have designated the "Spanish craze," which was essentially a mania or vogue for all things Spanish—in literature as well as music, cinema, fashion, and more, among them the original nickname—Matadors—of TTU's football team. The craze—Griggs's wave—was especially pronounced in architecture, where what became known as Spanish-colonial or Spanish-revival architecture became all the rage—in California, Florida, Texas, and other parts of the country that could arguably claim a Spanish heritage, but also in others that could not, among them Arkansas, Illinois, Maryland, and New York. Critics even suggested that the Spanish-revival style, with its roots in the colonial period, was quintessentially American and understood in terms of "dignity," "honesty," and "sincerity," attributes that writers such as Alexis de Tocqueville and Mark Twain had previously used to describe the essence of the American character. From this perspective, the architectural Spanish wave Griggs outlines in this important book was less a tsunami, generated from afar, but rather more like a geyser, gushing forth up from caverns deep within American soil. For this reason, it was even suggested that the country should adopt Spanish revival as its national architectural style.

William Ward Watkin's 1924 decision to design TTC's campus in traditional Spanish style belonged to this trend. Further justification derived from the state's Spanish origins and enshrined in the remnants of such Spanish frontier missions as San Antonio, San José, and San Juan Capistrano. Yet as Griggs explains, Watkin learned about the importance of the new Spanish style from his mentor, Ralph Cram, an architect who had himself "discovered" the glories of traditional Spanish architecture, especially that of the Plateresque, during a prolonged trip to Spain as part of a broader European pilgrimage in search of the best case studies of Cram's beloved Gothic style. The odd part of the story is that Watkin, unlike Cram, never visited Spain prior to preparing his plans for the TTC campus. Rather, he based his designs on what he had seen in books such as Andrew Noble Prentice, *Renaissance Architecture and Ornament in Spain* (1st ed., 1888), together with *Spanish Architecture of the Sixteenth Century* (1917), the work of two American writers Arthur and Mildred Stapley Byne. A visit to Spain came later; by then, however, TTC's Spanish-themed campus was already under construction.

Yet for all its importance, TTC's Spanish wave, like all waves, soon ebbed. As this volume demonstrates, interest in traditional Spanish architecture—Griggs labels it the last neo-classical revival in the United States—evaporated in the course of depression and negative publicity generated by Spain's bloody and bitterly divisive civil war of 1936–39. In the interim, other, more forward-looking styles of modern architecture came to the fore, a trend reflected in buildings erected starting during the 1930s and in subsequent decades. More recently, however, and in keeping with Watkin's original design scheme, the university's authorities have shown renewed interest in Spanish-revival architecture, or what is now euphemistically referred to as SpanRen, which has appeared in the guise of the design of Kent Hance Chapel, completed in 2012, as well as in the Seeds Innovation Center, a building whose entrance is modeled after that of a hospital built in the northern Spanish city of Burgos in 1526.

To be honest, I only learned about these new SpanRen buildings in the pages that follow as I never saw them firsthand, either during my initial 2016 visit to TTU or in the course of another in the spring of 2017 when I presented a lecture on the Spanish craze to a large (and mercifully attentive) audience in the University Library. In keeping with my own historical interests, I did not stray very far from those parts of the campus that Watkin designed and are now officially designated as the Texas Technical College Historic District and part of the National Register of Historic Places. Yet the university's turn (or return) to SpanRen is one I both welcome and applaud, as it not only aligns with so much of Texas's early history but also with the culture of the state's emergent Hispanic population. From my perspective, it also captures something of the spirit of what the famed nineteenth-century US poet, Walt Whitman, labeled the "Spanish element in our nationality." Writing in 1883, Whitman recognized that the "splendor and sterling value" of that "element" was underappreciated, almost invisible in fact, but he prophetically suggested that it would eventually "emerge in broadest flow and permanent action." Watkin's original master plan for TTC's campus, together with TTU's renewed embrace of SpanRen, is proving the great poet right.

Richard L. Kagan
Johns Hopkins University

ACKNOWLEDGMENTS

THE SAGA OF THIS BOOK began with a visit to a dying Chicago bookstore in July 2009. Within the antiquarian stacks of the Prairie Avenue Bookstore, which was sadly slated to close that September—was a tattered copy of the Andrew Noble Prentice's *Renaissance Architecture and Ornament in Spain*. Though I did not realize it at the time, within that massive, beautiful book were many of the very drawings that inspired the architecture of Texas Technological College, and a realization that Tech's architectural heritage was far from fully known. Prentice's book, along with the writings of Arthur and Mildred Stapley Byne, Paul Venable Turner, Stephen Fox, and others would provide invaluable insight into Spanish architecture, campus planning, and the history of both within Texas. A month later, after a visit with Nolan and Betty Barrick, followed by Mr. Barrick's agreement that time was nigh for a more comprehensive story about Tech's architecture, I resolved to undertake this project. Without his support, and a number of priceless interviews with him prior to his death in 2013, many crucial nuggets of Texas Tech's history would likely be lost today. Even then, I half-believed this project to be a ridiculous undertaking. If not for the fervent encouragement of particularly my parents, friends, and colleagues like Mike Baker and Richard Minckler, I likely would not have pursued this book further.

Fort Worth architect Ames Fender and his mother, Mildred Hedrick Fender (daughter of Wyatt Hedrick), were most kind to make time for an invaluable interview in late 2009. Some further truly precious insight about Wyatt Hedrick and the Koeppe family came about thanks to a priceless interview with E. Paul Koeppe and his wife in August 2013. Further invaluable insight on Wyatt Hedrick, his firm, and the Koeppe family was provided thanks to author and historian Debbie Lyles. Interviews with input from a myriad other architects and design professionals—Bill Cartwright, David Messersmith, Stephen Faulk, Bill Adling, Eric Williams, Al York, Gary Ferguson, Jim Doche, and Joe McKay to name a few—provided much light to this story. Former AIA College of Fellows Chancellors Ronald Skaggs and Jack DeBartolo went far in dusting off the largely unknown, but fascinating story of the Tech Medical School. Other interviews such as a treasured visit with former Tech football back Lonnie "Primo" McCurry in late 2009, Bill McMillan Jr. in 2011, and a phone interview with retired newspaper journalist Frances Hallam Hurt in 2012 each uncovered pieces to this story. Particular thanks is due to former Chancellor John Montford and former regent Debbie Montford, who were kind enough to entertain an interview in San Antonio in July 2016. For years, people around Texas Tech joked that Associate Vice Chancellor Theresa Drewell "knew where all of the bodies were buried" from her three decades-plus of work at Facilities Planning and Construction (FP&C). Many hours interviewing her, followed by a constant peppering of phone calls and correspondence with her in the months and years after, proved that perception correct. In addition, interviews with the three previous vice chancellors for FP&C—Doug Mann, Mike Ellicott, and Michael Molina—each provided invaluable insight in the maelstrom of growth in the system era. In particular to Vice Chancellor Billy Breedlove and the FP&C leadership and staff in general—namely John Russell and Todd Hardin—my sincerest thanks for their support on many fronts. Likewise, my thanks to Assistant Vice President for Operations Sean Childers, as well as Brenda Bullard, James Thornton, and the Engineering Services team at the Texas Tech Physical Plant—most particularly to Ray Perez, who endured years of my pestering him for drawings or information about existing buildings.

For the countless visits to the Southwest Special Collection at Texas Tech, I would be remiss without thanking Lynn Whitfield, Randy Vance, and the scores of student staffing the reading room, whom I invariably pestered for over six years with requests for photocopies, holds, and pull requests. Special thanks are owed to Lee Pecht and the Woodson Research Center team at Rice University, as well as Nancy Sparrow at the Alexander Architectural Archives at University of Texas-Austin. In addition, gratitude is due to Mike Kelly and the Committee of One Hundred at Balboa Park, the San Diego History Center, the Oregon Historical Society, the staff of the Julia Ideson Library, the Pecan Valley Genealogical Society, the Stanford University Archives, Sara Schumacher at the Texas Tech Architecture Library, the Special Collections Research Center at the University of Chicago, the Schaffer Library at Union College, and the Gledhill Library at the Santa Barbara Historical Museum for their assistance. Particular thanks are also due to Micah Parzen, Jody Forrest, Mark Lonn, and many others at the San Diego Museum of Man for allowing me three precious days in March 2017 to document Bertram Goodhue's Spanish masterpiece.

Research and writing this book came at a pivotal time of my life—a period of joyous upheaval beginning with my move from Lubbock to Amarillo in 2011, and shortly thereafter meeting and later marrying my beloved wife, Jaime, followed by the birth of our son Will in 2015, our daughter Emilie in 2017, and the serendipitous opportunity to informally adopt our oldest "daughter"—KaLee French. Words cannot express my thanks to Jaime for her support, patience, and understanding during an already challenging chapter in our lives. Likewise, this book would not have been possible without the unwavering support of my colleagues and fellow principals at Parkhill, Smith & Cooper. Beginning with Mary Crites and Mike Moss, as well as Joe Rapier, Greg Billman, and many others, PSC's support was quite simply unparalleled. In particular, I must singularly thank Dan Hart for his mentorship, feedback, and unswerving support. Likewise, many others at Texas Tech provided valued seeds of encouragement, namely Jim and John White, Clifton Ellis, and Dr. James Brink in the Honors College to name a few.

In March 2013, I had first approached Texas Tech University seeking a partnership to complete the Opus project, which eventually led to a 2015 phone call from TTU Press Editor-in-Chief Joanna Conrad. Joanna has been a patient, persistent, and capable counterpart, from contract negotiation, logistics, and of course in her prime editorial role. Words cannot express enough my gratitude to her, as well as Press Director Brian Ott, the great work of Lisa Stallings and April Leidig at Longleaf Services, and many others. Furthermore, sincere gratitude is due to The CH Foundation, whose generous 2017 grant made design and production of Opus ultimately possible. Brian Ott's efforts in securing the contribution of Dr. Richard Kagan as to write the foreword to this project warrants particular note. I cannot say thanks enough to Dr. Kagan—one of the foremost Hispanicists and historians on Habsburg-era Spain—for his enthusiastic involvement in this project. Kagan's writings on Spain, along with those of John Huxtable Elliott, Hugh Thomas, and Albert Frederick Calvert, proved crucial to providing an architect-turned-novice Hispanicist some much-needed insight on a complex nation and its history.

Finally, most complicated to the Opus project was the travel to Spain in fall 2017 to document the *estilo plateresco* works that inspired Texas Tech. Without the assistance of Ralston Dorn, TTU Class of 2009, an old friend and fellow Eagle Scout from earlier days in North Dallas, that trip would have assuredly been less successful. Despite Ralston's constant smart-aleck humor, his Spanish fluency saved the day on more than one occasion with Spanish representatives.

Special thanks must be extended to the offices of His Excellency, Don Carlos Fitz-James Stuart y Martínez de Irujo, the Duke of Alba de Tormes, and the Fundación Casa de Alba, in particular José Andrés

Miguel Benito; managing director of the Palacio de Monterrey, archivist Álvaro Romero Sánchez-Arjona, and architect José Javier Lopez Martín of REARASA, S.A. in Zamora. Likewise, Dr. Javier Rivera Blanco and the office of Rector Dr. Fernando Galván of the Universidad de Alcalá, as well as José Luis González Sánchez, architect to the bishop of the Diocese of Alcalá de Henares, were beyond helpful in our visit to Alcalá. Julián García Sánchez and Victor Parrilla of the Cabildo Catedral de Sigüenza provided us with invaluable assistance and information during our visit to Sigüenza, while the office of the Secretary General, Heritage Director Eduardo Azofra Agustín, and the staff of the Colegio Arzobispo Fonseca made our efforts to document the beautiful architecture at the Universidad de Salamanca possible. Thanks is extended to the staff of the Diputación de Ávila for their patience and friendliness during our visit to the Torreón de los Guzmanes, and particular thanks must be extended to Jesús Tudela Nieves and Sarai Herrera of the Cabildo Catedral de Córdoba, as well as Arquitectos Ruiz, Rebollo y Herrero of Córdoba, whose information, drawings, and a priceless tour of the Torre del Alminar and Cathedral shed precious light on one of Spain's greatest landmarks. Words cannot fully express my appreciation and love for a nation whose architectural heritage made Texas Tech possible, but I will try:

España, siempre tendrás mi amor. Para mi, fue una experiencia inolvidable.

Amarillo, Texas, 2019

INTRODUCTION

IN THE FALL OF 1944, Winston Churchill addressed the House of Commons in a plea for funding to rebuild a blitz-ravaged London. Churchill's words articulated the importance of architecture in society: "We shape our buildings; thereafter, they shape us." Winston Churchill could have as easily been speaking about the architecture of Texas Tech.

It is difficult to imagine any college or university that has been more profoundly shaped by its architecture than Texas Tech University. On October 1, 1925, when Texas Technological College opened, it was a new institution situated at the edge of the Great American Desert. For students, faculty, and administration, there was no better stimulus for the beginnings of a heritage. The school colors, the original mascot, the names of the newspaper and yearbook, the Victory Bells (ringing out from the Administration Building after successes of athletic teams and other pursuits), the Carol of Lights (the holiday lighting ceremony), and the very seal of the institution (designed by the original campus architect) represent a mere sampling of the burgeoning tradition that owes its inspiration to the architectural fabric of the first campus buildings. Many have admired Texas Tech's architecture. Few have grasped its impact.

A great deal has been written of the general history of Texas Tech, and in particular the athletics history of the university, but comparatively little of the institution's architecture. Even descriptions contemporaneous with Tech's founding years failed to properly comprehend the style; often loosely describing it as "mission-style" architecture. The seemingly quaint pastiche of red clay tile, buff-blend brick, and stone with Spanish detailing belies a far richer, more colorful history that produced Spain's *estilo plateresco,* and the story of how a Pennsylvania-born Houston architect would stumble upon the style nearly a century ago. That discovery proved visionary given that Plateresque Spanish Renaissance architecture is a style so well adapted to the South Plains of Texas, and is a style in itself indicative of the ethos of the typical Texas Tech Red Raider. The estilo plateresco emerged from the stark, rugged lands of Castile and Andalusia—lands that bear striking similarities to the arid climes of West Texas. Even today, north of Seville, hectares upon hectares of cotton fields grow, while hours to the north, the flat landscape and prominent grain elevator that mark the small town of Peñaranda de Bracamonte—located between Salamanca and Ávila—gives the *municipio* an uncanny resemblance to the likes of Hale Center or Dimmitt. The hills of Arapiles, south of Salamanca, where the Duke of Wellington and his Anglo-Portugese army defeated the French in 1812, resembles the rolling hills between Lamesa and Patricia, and squat mesas dotting the landscape south of Memphis, Texas. It was in these dusty, arid regions of Castilian and Andalusian Spain where an eclectic Spanish architectural renaissance flourished in the first half of the sixteenth century.

Beginning with the writing of former Tech College Architect and Architecture Department chair Nolan Barrick in the 1980s, Red Raiders began to learn of the more specific case studies of sixteenth-century Spain that had inspired Texas Tech, in particular the architecture of Alcalá de Henares and Salamanca. A facet of this story explores that Spanish inspiration with greater depth. This narrative

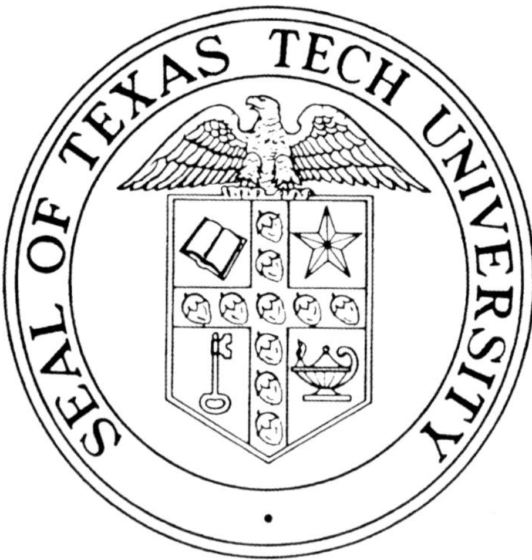

The seal of Texas Tech University, William Ward Watkin, designer, 1924 (revised by institution name change, 1969).

will also highlight more discoveries in research that links other rich sources of Plateresque architecture in Spanish communities like Ávila and Sigüenza, and more recent and proximate sources like San Antonio and San Diego. That architectural vernacular proved not only to be visually defining but has also attracted and influenced the scores of plain-spoken, hard-working, understated, and overachieving students, faculty, and alumni, who have built Texas Tech into the world-class institution it is today.

THE STORY OF the inspiration, planning, design, construction, and coming-of-age of the Texas Tech University campus and its architecture is very much a classical drama. Emerging from the demands of a proud group of West Texans who were simply advocating for a regional institution of higher education to call their own, Texas Technological College emerged first into law in 1923, and then in physical form west of Lubbock two-and-a-half years later. The battle for funding and sustaining Texas Tech in the early years has proven a familiar prologue for the same battles that Tech—now a university system—faces today as the political epicenter of statewide interests remain within the eastern half of Texas. In a state that had yet to develop much of an economic or architectural pedigree in 1923, it was the selection of William Ward Watkin as design architect and Wyatt C. Hedrick as the architect-of-record that would prove fortuitous even before its doors opened for classes.

It was Watkin's proposed architectural style for the new West Texas college that remains today a remarkable choice. This story delves into not only the formative understanding of that style—the *estilo plateresco*—itself a complex and nuanced style, but its manifold origins emerging in the rise of imperial Spain, its introduction into American architecture, and the early progenitors of its use such as Watkin mentors Ralph Adams Cram and Bertram Grosvenor Goodhue. It is within that substory that we learn that the design and early construction of Texas Technological College was one of a number of crest points atop the tidal wave of the last great Beaux-Arts revivalist architectural movement in American history—the *Spanish revival.*

The drama of Texas Tech's history—both institutional and architectural—was one of ebbs and flows. After seven initially fruitful years of growth, Tech faced a series of infractions that nearly marked the end of the college—the death of its inaugural president, the Great Depression, the departure of William Ward Watkin from design work at Tech following family tragedy, and years of suffocating austerity in state funding. Even after the college recovered from the trauma of the 1930s, it faced disruption and upheaval from the conscription and training demands of the Second World War. It was only after the war that Tech began a steady trajectory of enrollment and facility growth that helped to transition its place as a rural college into a more broadly respected Texas college. That growth was not easily integrated into the established Beaux-Arts–inspired plan of the campus. Wyatt Hedrick and his team executed noble efforts in adhering to Watkin's original master plan with mixed results, but the design of new facilities in a Spanish Renaissance–revival style had become both cost prohibitive and *démodé*. Milquetoast attempts at adhering to Tech's Plateresque

Agricultural fields west of Peñaranda de Bracamonte, Castile and León, 2017.

roots gave way to various experiments with "blended" modernism, followed by a brief period of mid-rise and high-rise Brutalism. The products of that period are generally unpopular among the Tech faithful. That public sentiment, though, is commonly underinformed with the realities of the day. The architects and administrators who presided over these developments faced incredible enrollment growth, severe funding limitations, and the opportunity to address needs thanks in large part to the highly urban-influenced auspices of the national Higher Education Act. Their decisions through that period were driven by more than design sensibilities.

Just as university leadership began to rediscover the intrinsic beauty of their original architectural heritage, Texas Tech experienced malaise in the form of stagnant enrollment growth and declining funding that resulted in little change between 1975 and 1995. A series of transformative events would propel Texas Tech from this period into some two decades of phenomenal growth. Entry into a new athletics conference, the establishment of a university system, the influx of two entire generations—first xennial, and then millennial students—and a meteoric increase in fundraising and research have rocketed Texas Tech University into the forefront of American higher education.

Throughout this rollercoaster narrative of the relatively brief life of this West Texas institution, there is a fundamental question this story seeks to answer: What is Plateresque? This alien word, largely unknown even to the most diehard Tech aficionado, represents one of four distinctive phases of the Spanish Renaissance, named for the style's ornamental resemblance to Spanish silver jewelry—*plata*. The Spanish Renaissance (1492–1580) was a period of profound transformation in which a collection of dissimilar Iberian kingdoms, free from seven centuries of Islamic rule, unified themselves through the marriage of the queen of Castile and king of Aragon, and rapidly ascended into the upper echelons of sixteenth-century European geopolitics with the aid of growing wealth and power gained in part from their discoveries in the Western Hemisphere.

While Spain is home to a great many historical architectural styles—the Romanesque, the Gothic, Moorish, and the hyperbolized Churrigueresque among others—one style that turn-of-the-century Anglo-American architects and writers gravitated to for its stately beauty, its stunning ornament, and mélange influences of other styles and cultures was the estilo plateresco. It was a style that, when established, lasted for barely six decades before its banishment in Spanish society, but later reemerged as a nineteenth-century neoclassical beacon of design inspiration within the Spanish-speaking world and eventually the United States some 350 years later. The works of Andrew Noble Prentice, Albert Frederick Calvert, and Arthur and Mildred Stapley Byne, and the early design advocacy of architects Ralph Adams Cram and Bertram Grosvenor Goodhue served to spark renewed interest in the Plateresque during the Beaux-Arts era. Even then, recognition of the opportunities of mating Spanish design and planning principles with Thomas Jefferson's brilliant vision for the distinctly American university campus—the Academical Village—did not arise from collegiate case studies, but rather from the curious post-Victorian fad of the world's fair. Remarkably, Texas Tech University's planning heritage owes more to a host of past world's fair events in Chicago, Portland, and San Diego than anything else.

This is an unorthodox telling of an architectural history. It is the remarkable range of seemingly random (and sometimes ridiculous) events in history that have led to the present-day campus plan and architecture of Texas Tech University that has proven so fascinating. *Opus in Brick and Stone* is an appreciation for the victories, failures, human foibles, and the remarkable way historical events have affected the course of design at Texas Tech. Who could have ever conceived that a whiskey advertisement in *Life* magazine, a world's fair in San Diego, or the design of an embassy building in New Delhi, India could have so profoundly shaped the humble beginnings of this West Texas college? That this place, then, would go on to positively shape so many lives since is awe-inspiring.

TECH'S ARCHITECTURAL HISTORY has not received its due. Texas Tech is more prone to associations with dust storms, the flatness of its terrain, and as a place where tumbleweeds outnumber trees a-hundred-to-one. What little objective historical assessment has been made regarding the Tech campus has critiqued its plan as being less sophisticated than, say, Cram, Goodhue, and Ferguson's 1909 plan for Rice University. Other critiques have been aimed at the overly broad expanses of Watkin's original plan for Tech—namely the Broadway Mall and Engineering Key. While these observations are not entirely without merit, a careful review of events, drawings, and correspondence of the day reveals that Tech's campus plan and design is also the result of thoughtful, logical, regionalist-minded decisions made by Watkin, Wyatt Hedrick, and Tech administrators.

The selection of Lubbock as home to Texas Technological College was driven by regional considerations rather than by the overt, natural beauty of its surroundings. This story spotlights a people creating a

Looking west overhead of the Court of Honor at the World's Columbian Exposition, 1893. World's fairs like this in Chicago would have profound impact on both urban and campus planning in the United States.

place of idyllic beauty with architecture where natural idyllic beauty was hard to find. Lubbock's beauty is not as obvious as the settings for other great institutions: the rolling forests of Chapel Hill, the mountainside waterfall gorge of Ithaca, the mountainous backdrop of Seattle, or Pacific coastal views of Malibu. This story is one of building place upon the *tabula rosa* of the South Plains.

The Texas Tech campus is not a perfect creation. Established with limited funding and without the advantages of land-grant endowments that other public institutions enjoy, Texas Tech has thrived nonetheless. "Doing more with less" is not only a reality at Texas Tech: it is a point of pride. Former military barracks abounded on campus for four decades to stand in for the envisioned Spanish-revival buildings planned by William Ward Watkin in the 1920s. The present-day President's Office served as the college's library for fourteen painful years. Tech's Medical School—now the Health Sciences Center—was first relegated to converted dormitory space until cobbled-together funding could be garnered to construct a purpose-built complex. Only recently has Tech begun to enjoy the comparative luxuries of planning and designing the facilities worthy of a Carnegie Foundation Tier One institution. And yet, even now, there remain remnants of Tech's humble and wayward years: an unfortunate sea of asphalt parking adjacent to the iconic Administration Building; the continued problems of low campus density coupled with urges to continue building at the campus periphery, and a handful of unloved facilities mostly of the modernist era. The campus of Texas Tech is like Gilbert Stuart's *Athenaeum*—the artist's unfinished 1796 portrait of George Washington that inspired Washington's dollar bill portrait—incomplete but recognized with distinction. That work retains rough edges that somehow contribute to a remarkable composition.

Even in Texas Tech's rough edges, and maybe even because of them, there is a persistent beauty of plan and architecture. The purpose of this accounting is to more deeply appreciate—by those who both shaped and were shaped by—what it took to come to this place. This is the story of the *Opus in Brick and Stone.*

OPUS IN BRICK AND STONE

MAP OF THE
SOUTH CENTRAL STATES.
By A. von Steinwehr.
Jewett & Chandler.
West of Washington.
West of Greenwich.
PUBLIC LANDS
KANSAS
MISSOURI
KENTUCKY
INDIAN TERRITORY
CHEYENNES AND ARRAPAHOES
CHEROKEE COUNTRY
CREEK COUNTRY
CHICKASAW NATION
CHOCTAW NATION
NEW MEXICO
Llano Estacado
(barren Table land)
TEXAS
MEXICO
GULF OF MEXICO
AUSTIN
LITTLE ROCK
BATON ROUGE
JACKSON
San Antonio
Galveston
Houston
Brownsville
Matamoras
Red R.
Canadian R.
Rio Grande
Pecos R.
1000 Square Miles.
Scale of Statute Miles.

PART I

BIRTH

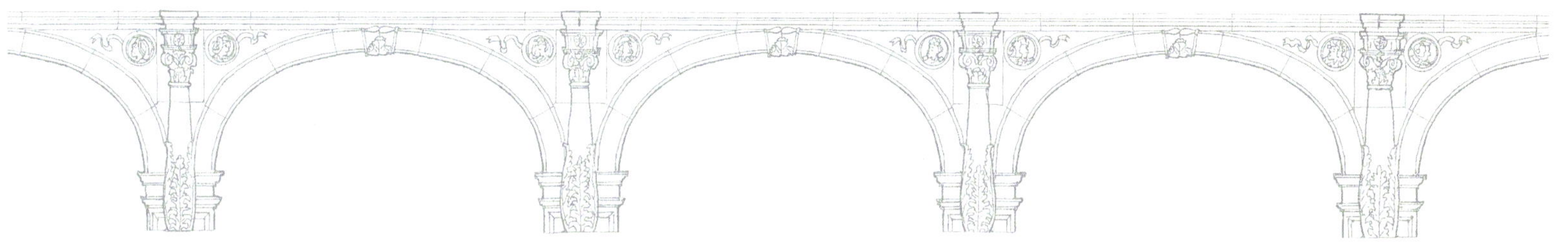

The whole country from the head waters of the Red, Brazos and Colorado Rivers to the Rio Pecos is a sterile and barren plain without water or Timber producing only a few stinted shrubs which are insufficient to sustain animal life.

—J. H. Colton and Company, circa 1854 annotation describing the Llano Estacado found in the "General Map Showing Countries Surveyed by the United States and Mexican Boundary Commission in the Years 1850–1853."

I

WHAT IF?

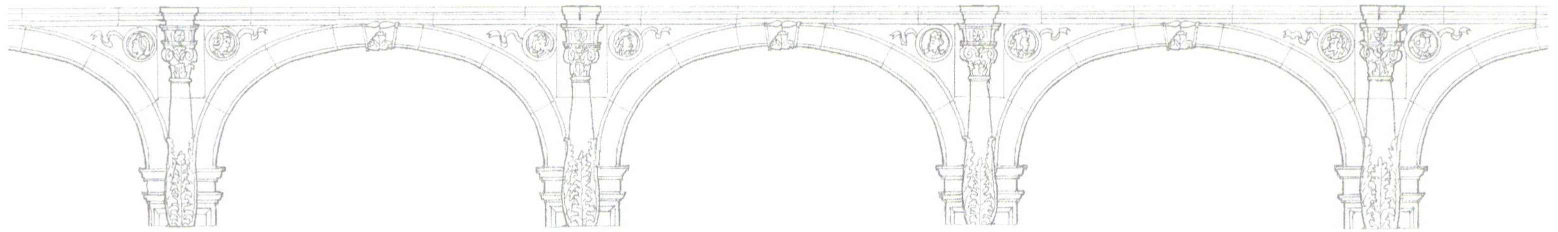

MONDAY, MARCH 31, 1952, was another busy day at the Shamrock Hotel, the monstrous art deco–stylized behemoth located at the southwest corner of Main and West Holcombe in south Houston. Regardless of its eclectic and obsolescent style, it was still one of the great Houston hotels, and its proximity to the nearby William M. Rice Institute for the Advancement of Literature, Science and Art, known today as Rice University, made it a frequented lunch destination for a longtime member of Rice's faculty, an architect named William Ward Watkin. Albeit gaudy and outmoded, the Shamrock still held sentiment to the old architect. Three years earlier—on Saint Patrick's Day 1949, the opening night for the Shamrock—Watkin was invested as a Fellow in the American Institute of Architects during the AIA's National Convention that was also being held there. Today, he was meeting someone for lunch at the Shamrock's Cork Club—perhaps to partake of their well-regarded Irish stew.[1]

As he was leaving the Shamrock, Watkin suddenly fell in the portal of one of the Shamrock's bright brass revolving doors, as a rotating door leaf badly crushed his kneecap to the gasps and screams of people nearby. An ambulance rushed the tall, thin, chisel-faced architect to the sleek new Methodist Hospital nearby—ironically a building that Watkin himself had recently designed.[2] Watkin's leg was operated on immediately, and while the surgery initially appeared to be a success, during the coming days and weeks of convalescing in the hospital, it became clear that Watkin's leg was not healing properly. An infection in his knee led to the formation of septicemia, first in his leg and later spreading into his body over the next two months. Eighty-five days after the accident at the Shamrock, with his family at his side, William Ward Watkin died.

The *Houston Chronicle* ran a fitting obituary about the late architect.[3] Tributes were written of Watkin's design accomplishments—Houston's first art museum, many of the city's great churches, homes, and of course many great buildings on the Rice campus. He was extolled for his gentlemanly demeanor, his devotion to his family, his profession, and the Rice Institute. In particular, references were made to William Ward Watkin's contribution to higher education, in college

The Shamrock Hotel, undated. Wyatt C. Hedrick, architect. It is remarkable how a Houston hotel would so profoundly impact the architectural history of Texas Tech.

and university commissions he had completed spanning from Alpine in the Big Bend region to Canyon in the Panhandle, and of course in the Bayou City. The *Chronicle* made particular reference that Watkin had been instrumental in the design of Texas Technological College in Lubbock. Sadly, news of the great architect's passing never reached Lubbock, so local newspapers ran no obituaries about the man, and Red Raiders of the day never learned of the passing of the man who had singularly defined so much of the heritage that in itself defined Texas Tech.

The unexpected passing of William Ward Watkin was a profound and ironic event in Texas Tech history, especially asking the rhetorical question "*What if?*" "What ifs" had long intermingled the history of and around Texas Tech. Had the political chicanery of Governor James Ferguson survived scrutiny in 1917, Texas Tech would never have come into existence in the first place, and West Texas A&M College—Tech's legislative vision that eventually evolved to become Texas Tech with Senate Bill 103 in 1923—would reside today in Abilene. (West Texas A&M College should not be confused with the present-day West Texas A&M University in Canyon; formerly known as West Texas State University. The West Texas Chamber of Commerce had since 1913 proposed a "West Texas A&M," either as a branch- or stand-alone institution.) The tragic crash of a T-38 training jet in St. Louis, Missouri in 1966 killing two NASA Gemini Astronauts—Charles Bassett and Elliot See—both slated to fly Gemini IX that June, had a profound impact on space exploration history.[4] Their deaths prompted a flight reassignment allowing veteran James Lovell and rookie Edwin E. "Buzz" Aldrin to become backup crew to Gemini IX, and the two would fly Gemini XII five months later. Some speculation has been made that if not for the 1966 crash, Charlie Bassett—a 1960 electrical engineering graduate of Texas Technological College—would likely have been named a pilot of a subsequent Apollo moon flight in 1969 or 1970.[5] If so, one of only a dozen humans to walk on the Moon to date would have been a Texas Tech alumnus.

The creation of Tech's iconic trademarked logo—the Double T—was a direct result of the founding name of the institution: Texas Technological College. Ironically, by the 1960s, disillusionment of Tech's institutional name led to a bitter and controversy-filled battle to rename the institution, with names like the Texas University of Arts, Science, and Technology, University of the Southwest, and student body–favorite Texas State University under consideration.[6] The universal public affinity of the Double T is widely credited with saving Tech—both in identity and literal name—and had the logo of the school been different, the name Texas Tech would not exist today.

Likewise, seminal events in the architectural and planning history of Texas Tech made for a cavalcade of intriguing what-if potentialities. Watkin's premature departure from the pivotal role of design architect at Texas Tech in 1929 resulted from a tragic death—his first wife, Annie Ray, from pancreatic cancer while on vacation in France

(*Left*) William Ward Watkin, circa early 1920s.
(*Right*) Ralph Adams Cram, architect, undated.

that year.[7] At that time, much of Watkin's Spanish-inspired vision for Texas Technological College remained unbuilt, most notably his vision for a great commencement hall—at times referred to as the "Hall of Texas" or "Alamo Commencement Hall"—intended to anchor the western vista of the campuses' Broadway axis. Watkin attempted to re-enter the arena of design at Tech during World War II, but the developmental evolution of the Texas Technological College campus from the Great Depression onward had been totally wrested from his influence. The greatest irony of all was that Watkin's former student, former employee, and son-in-law, Nolan Barrick, would coincidentally assume the dual role of campus architect and head of the Architecture Department of the School of Engineering at Texas Tech only a year after Watkin's death. Barrick's arrival came after the fall from grace of longtime campus architect Wyatt C. Hedrick and his firm, who had partnered with Watkin in the first years of the college, and who had largely dominated architectural design at Tech in the decades after. Had the freakish accident at the Shamrock not happened, Barrick's arrival at Tech would have almost certainly marked Watkin's return to the campus he was so instrumental in designing, begging the question as to what Watkin-era visions might have become reality in the 1950s. Barrick maintained a close mentor-protégé relationship with his one-time professor and boss, and in all likelihood would have at least consulted Watkin on his prior vision of the original campus master plan for Tech.[8] Watkin's knowledge of the Tech Plan would have aided Barrick in counteracting the devolution of the Lubbock campus in the early 1950s, as it became lost in the clutter of a growing Lubbock street grid and myriad temporary buildings that had invaded the campus fabric. Had Watkin lived, architectural development on the Texas Tech campus may very well have unfolded in a totally different manner.

WILLIAM WARD WATKIN had the challenge of designing a master plan for Texas Technological College different than many prior Beaux-Arts–era planning endeavors. Architectural programming, understanding the quantitative science of spatial needs in higher education, was a science at best in its embryonic stage. Should agricultural sciences facilities be located near textile engineering, or should the library be located near the engineering buildings? What will the anticipated enrollment of a college to be situated within a relatively unknown and sparsely populated region of Texas? Correspondence indicates that there was a strong relationship that existed between Tech President Paul Horn, Board Chair Amon Carter, and Watkin, providing much of the programmatic insight needed to ultimately develop the Tech master plan. What he developed in many regards paralleled the notable shift then underway in national planning trends, as compared to the Rice plan, for example, that Watkin was involved in creating just fifteen years earlier. Whereas the Rice plan featured a core pedestrian mall devoid of automobile access, the Texas Tech plan of 1924 was designed with the automobile in mind. This pivotal difference would have profound impacts upon Texas Tech only three decades later.

Blanco Canyon, near Floydada, Texas, undated. Modern-day archaeological analysis has confirmed Coronado, or at least part of his party, traveled through and camped in this canyon, not forty miles from Lubbock.

Watkin's premature death in 1952 was not the only event that would have had a profound impact upon Texas Tech. In all reality, credit was not entirely due to the Rice professor for the ingenious decision to propose the Spanish Renaissance style as the vernacular of choice for the new West Texas institution. Ralph Adams Cram, the Boston architect and principal of Cram & Ferguson—then one of the most influential higher education design firms in the country—was already partnered with Watkin on a separate project, a new central library in downtown Houston. While Watkin's original Italianate proposal for the library prior to Cram's entrance into the project was handsome, it was Cram who instead urged Watkin to look to Spain for architectural inspiration in honor of the history of Texas.[9] Given it was a style Watkin had never dabbled in, had it not been for Cram's design intervention coinciding with Watkin's teaming with Wyatt Hedrick and L. W. Robert for the Tech commission, the architectural design of Texas Technological College, and quite likely the advance of the Spanish-revival architectural movement—the last of the Beaux-Arts movements—may never have happened.

Perhaps most ridiculous of all stories that ultimately shaped the architectural and planning heritage of Texas Tech lay in the events and fallout from the Saint Patrick's Day 1949 opening of the Shamrock Hotel. Of the two seminal architects who so critically shaped Texas Tech in its fragile early life, the Shamrock notably damaged the reputation of one, and killed the other. The famous March 1949 opening was a focal point in the space-time continuum of Texas architecture—the day when future AIA Gold Medalist Fay Jones would first meet his future mentor Frank Lloyd Wright, the night when a little girl would kick Wright in the shin in defense of Wyatt Hedrick's honor, and a spectacle that would inspire Edna Ferber to later write the novel *Giant*. Aside from the tragic revolving door accident that killed William Ward Watkin, had Wyatt Hedrick's firm not designed the Shamrock, Hedrick likely would not have been asked to appear in an otherwise harmless national whiskey advertisement that ultimately banned the architect from roles at Baylor and then at Texas Tech.[10] His departure, Watkin's death, the coming surge in construction, and the combined tidal wave of modernism and the automobile would forever impact the design of Texas Tech with consequences still being counteracted even today.

Moreover, the very establishment of the *estilo plateresco* on the heels of the Reconquista and Columbus's arrival in the West Indies is in itself collection of coincidences with what-if ramifications to the vernacular heritage of Texas Tech. The combination of *Mudéjar* craftsmanship, influences of the Italian Renaissance, and a flamboyant and prosperous royal family and noble class of Spain—the *hidalguia*—and numerous other factors made the Plateresque style possible not only for the Spanish culture, but also for Texas Tech University five centuries later. Even the coincidences of European exploration of the New World made Watkin's and Hedrick's decision to adopt the Plateresque style at Texas Tech that much more apropos. It only made sense that the architecture of Salamanca—the hometown

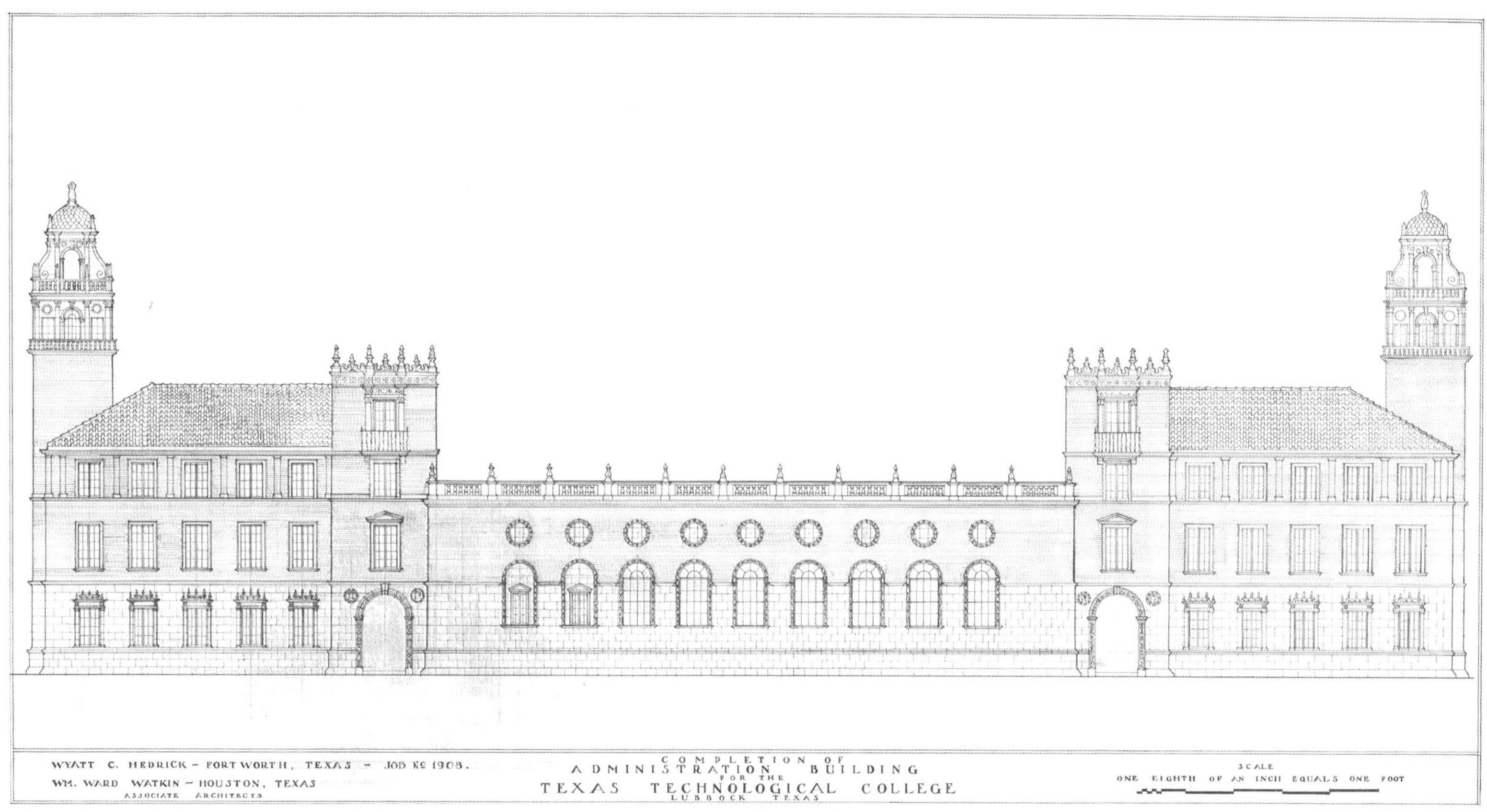

Proposed south elevation of the failed 1926–1927 expansion bid to the Administration Building, featuring an indoor pool and gymnasium (center), and two additional carillon towers.

of conquistador Francisco Vázquez de Coronado y Luján—would inspire the architecture of an institution less than fifty miles from where Coronado and his expedition camped in 1541.

The year 1959 had been a momentous one for Texas Tech and a year of many what-ifs. Contentious deliberation raged over the placement of a badly needed new Library Building. Had college librarian R. C. Janeway and *Lubbock Avalanche-Journal* editor Charles A. Guy had their way, the new library would have ultimately been located in the middle of Memorial Circle,[11] but thankfully intervention by Nolan Barrick halted implementation of that disastrous plan. That year also marked the year when the new Computer Sciences and Nuclear Engineering Building was to be constructed at the northwest corner of the Texas Tech Engineering Key. The original design included a functioning Argonaut-class nuclear training reactor, whose scope was cut at the last minute due to the loss of federal grant funding. Had the reactor survived, the structure and curriculum of the College of Engineering would be greatly different today.

Farther to the north, the then twelve-year-old Clifford B. and

Detail photograph of the Mudéjar-inspired artesonado ceiling of the Capilla de San Ildefonso, Universidad de Alcalá.

Audrey Jones Stadium facility's future was in doubt. Three years earlier, Southwest Conference leadership had finally tendered the invitation Texas Tech had fought three decades for, but it included certain caveats. To meet conference standards, Jones Stadium needed to either expand to provide a minimum of forty thousand seats or build a new stadium with the same or greater capacity. It was not the first time that the future of Tech's football stadium was in question. In late 1935, despite heavy lobbying by Tech President Bradford Knapp to gain federal New Deal funding for an earthen-berm venue nearly identical in seating capacity to the eventual 1947 plan for Jones Stadium, a PWA grant was refused.[12] Had the 1935 stadium been built, Tech would have been in even more challenging straits upon having joined the SWC, as Tech's 1935 earthen-bermed stadium concept would have been incapable of the novel expansion scheme that was eventually used to expand Jones Stadium in 1959. In one of the little-known ironies of Tech football lore, it would take the ingenious idea of a former Texas A&M quarterback to save Jones Stadium from premature demise.

What would have happened had Amon Carter and Paul Horn convinced the Texas State Legislature to fund an expansion of the Administration Building in 1927? Despite Watkin's pleas not to proceed with the plan on the grounds that the resulting Administration Building would be an awkward hodgepodge of academic, recreational, and office spaces, Horn needed a number of key campus facilities as soon as possible, namely a more permanent library, general classroom space, and a college gymnasium. Watkin's and Hedrick's offices toiled between 1926 and 1927 for an expansion plan for the Administration Building to become a "square donut" plan enclosing a cloistered courtyard, much akin to the Colegio Mayor de San Ildefonso Complex at the Universidad de Alcalá that inspired the Administration façade. A basketball gymnasium and an indoor swimming pool would anchor the south end of the complex, while east and west wings would feature additional classrooms and a more permanent library space. Had the 1927 plan been funded, the Administration Building would have featured four identical carillon towers at its corners, producing an "El Escorial"-like building form as a seat of leadership for the emerging Texas Technological College.[13]

2

1492

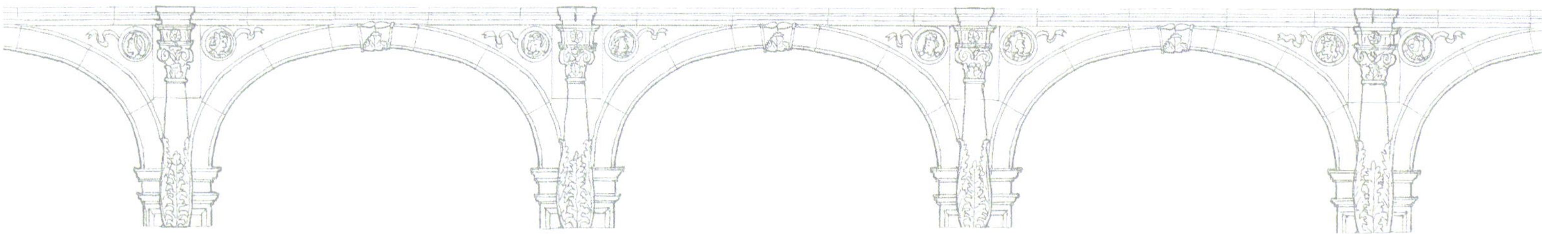

THE YEAR 1492 DAWNED and Europe was in a state of turmoil. Although nearly a century and a half had passed since the black plague had cut down half of the population of Europe, people across the continent had little to look forward to in the new year. For the Catholic Church and those nations that claimed themselves as part of Christendom, the outlook hinged between uncertain and bleak. Constantinople—the final bastion of the Byzantine Empire and vital gateway between Asia and Europe—had finally succumbed to the besieging armies of Sultan Mehmed II nearly four decades earlier. With the fall of Constantinople, cities ranging from Venice to Vienna now lay within striking distance of the Ottoman Empire. After four centuries of blood-spilt attempts, European monarchs had long since abandoned hopes of recapturing Jerusalem as they were far more content investing resources into the more profitable endeavor of invading, usurping, and pillaging their own continental adversaries. Europe was an unquestionable mess.

But then there was Spain.

Yet, in 1492, Spain did not even exist. Spaniards did not regard themselves as Spaniards. The Iberian Peninsula approached the sixteenth century as at best a loose conglomeration of royal states that spoke four distinct languages and even more dialects. The people of central and western Spain considered themselves Castilians, as they were subjects of the Crown of Castile and Leon. The people of eastern Spain, the Aragonese, proclaimed their loyalty to King Ferdinand of Aragon.[1] The people of present-day southern Spain—Andalusia—were a mixed cadre, some of whom were loyal to Catholic Castile, but many of whom were Muslims, remnants of a decaying Nasrid Dynasty that seven centuries earlier had commanded the Iberian emirate of Al-Andalus. It was not until 1469, when Ferdinand married Queen Isabella of Castile, that there was any even cursory sense of unification across Spanish lands. The people of Barcelona in the east certainly did not consider themselves united with the people of Badajoz in the west—a sociopolitical matter where regional

The Capitulation of Granada, by Francisco Pradilla y Ortiz, 1882. The fall of the Nasrid Dynasty in Spain and the end of the Reconquista was one of many seminal events in 1492 that not only marked the transition into Spain's imperial era, but also coincided with the arrival of the Spanish Renaissance.

nationalism in places like Catalonia remains today a source of intense national debate. But national unity would be only one of many fortuitous by-products of the events of 1492.

For Ferdinand and Isabella, the armies of Castile, Leon, and Aragon began on a high note in 1492. On the morning of January 2, 1492, the Catholic monarchs arrived on horseback with their entourages in the plain below Granada in Andalusia.[2] Opposite the Catholic monarchs arrived the last emir of an Islamic territory on the Iberian Peninsula, Muhammad XII, better known in history as Boabdil. Boabdil came to establish terms of an armistice agreed to late in the previous year. Granada—Boabdil's last stronghold—was surrendered to Ferdinand and Isabella, and the emir, his family, administration, and army were forced into exile in North Africa. Despite the fundamental objective of the Reconquista, the Catholic monarchs had agreed to very favorable terms for the tens of thousands of Muslims—the Mudéjar population—who would likely to remain in Spanish lands once Boabdil and his government left. Included within the Mudéjar population was a sizeable corps of stonemasons, carpenters, polychromists, glaziers, and ironworkers skilled in the building trades of Mudéjar architecture who remained behind to serve their new Christian chieftains. The stylistic infusion was noticeable, as Castilians and Leonese, who had come to prefer the use of dense gray granite and the warm, golden Piedra de Villamayor in their buildings, readily incorporated the Mudéjar use of brick—including unique styles like ornate corbeling or the quoin paneling of the *enjabalgadura* style[3]—in their architecture as well. Spanish architect builders of the day—*maestros mayores*—now designed their chapels and cathedrals beyond the waning Gothic style to include prominent telescoping carillon towers in the Mudéjar vein, just as residents of these communities centuries before built minarets in the same fashion as part of the mosques that once resided there.

However much of Spain remained a sociocultural melting pot,

Example of the Mudéjar-inspired enjabalgadura masonry style, found on the east façade of the Colegio de San Ildefonso, Universidad de Alcalá.

academic pursuits were underway in 1492 to exact one component of Castilian culture as an instrument of national power. Antonio de Nebrija—a linguist, mathematician, and historian to the Spanish Court—had that August published a fascinating compendium of what no other culture in Europe had for their native language—a guide to properly speaking it. It was titled *Gramática de la Lengua Castellana*, and despite its landmark place in history, Queen Isabella was bewildered at first as to its importance. While presiding over court, the queen was handed a copy of Nebrija's work only to ask, "What is it for?" Hernando de Talavera, the Bishop of Ávila gave a prophetic response that foretold the next three centuries of Spanish history, "Language, Your Majesty, is the perfect instrument of empire."[4] Spain would soon need such an instrument.

On October 12, 1492, a party led by Cristóbal Colón—known also by his Anglicized name Christopher Columbus—came ashore on the island of Guanahani, in the present-day Bahamas.[5] In the coming months, Columbus's expedition would encounter a multitude of Caribbean islands, including present-day Cuba, Haiti, and the Dominican Republic, before returning to Spain the following spring. Although Columbus only returned with a handful of natives, and not the trade route to Asia promised to the Portuguese king or the wealth that he had promised the Catholic monarchs, the history of Western Civilization, and certainly of Spain, would be forever altered. Another quarter century would pass before Spanish explorers, mariners, and a cadre of young Spanish nobility—*conquistadores*—would seek out, explore, conquer, pillage, and in many cases destroy territories that would soon be claimed by the Spanish Crown. By the sixteenth century, millions of gold and silver ducats in treasure would arrive annually from the new Spanish territories in the Western Hemisphere. This cache of wealth ensured that the sixteenth century—the *Siglo de Oro*, or "Golden Century"—would belong to Spain. To absorb such an influx of wealth, the Spanish economy; namely the Spanish currency system, had to modernize.

In 1492, the Spanish currency system was a confusing mess. The Spanish currency laws of the period—the System of 1475—was a

Landing of Columbus (1846), by John Vanderlyn (1775–1852), United States Capitol.

Obverse and reverse details of a Spanish peso a ocho, 1776 minting, featuring Charles III. Imperial seal features the twin "Pillars of Hercules"—the left of the two that would later inspire the iconic dollar sign, which is highlighted for visibility.

purely weight-based system based on the comparative value of copper, silver, and gold. The most common Spanish coin of the era—the *maravedi*, relatively equal to two American pennies—exchanged at a rate of thirty maravedis to the primary silver coin of the realm—the *real*. Twelve and one-half reales equaled the rate of a single gold *ducat*. Some regions and businesses continued to use other larger or older Spanish gold coins of the period, like the *castellano* and the *excelente*, which had totally different exchange rates.[6] It was a confusing system to say the least. In 1492, advisors to the Corte Real presented a *guldengroschen* for inspection by the Catholic monarchs—a new, large Austrian silver coin that would profoundly influence global currency, along with the German *thaler* (pronounced "tall-er") and the Dutch *daalder* (pronounced "doll-ders").[7] In time, both coins would inspire a new word that one day would become the monetary standard for United States—the dollar. By 1497, Spanish minters developed their own version of the guldengroschen that would revolutionize Spanish currency—the *peso a ocho* (or pieces of eight).

It was actually silver, not gold, that would become the predominant precious metal currency in the Spanish Kingdom in the sixteenth century. The capture of territories such as Mexico and Peru unlocked Spanish access to some of the richest silver mines the world had ever seen; but in 1492, the only known process to refine silver required immersing raw silver in a bath of mercury. Spain possessed one of the world's largest cinnabar mines at Almadén, where cinnabar, a ruby-like crystal rich in mercury, provided Spain a huge global advantage in silver production. The Spanish Crown would import one hundred pounds of silver into Spain for every one of gold during the *Siglo de oro*.[8] For Spain, the sixteenth century should have been called the *Siglo de plata*. The prevalence of silver found its way into the Spanish upper and middle classes, where ornate silver jewelry would become popular well into the nineteenth century. This fashion trend appears to have been what inspired Spanish historians to first fashion the term estilo plateresco, or a "style like silver jewelry." The first reference to the nomenclature was made by Renaissance essayist Cristóbal de Villalón in 1539 when describing an ornament on the Cathedral of León,[9] and later applied by the noted chronicler of Seville—Diego Ortiz de

Third floor detail of the main façade of the Colegio de San Ildefonso, Universidad de Alcalá, displaying a large imperial seal of Charles V, completed 1543.

Zúñiga—a century later.[10] The florid Arabesques and embellishments carved into Castilian stone or fashioned into iron *rejas* on the buildings of the era resembled the work of silversmiths, or *platero*, of the day. We know that architectural style today as the Plateresque style.

It would be 1497 before Spain enacted currency reforms that would shift the centerpiece of their currency system to this new and larger silver coin that would exchange at a rate equal to eight of the older silver reales. The resulting peso a ocho led to the converse Anglicized moniker "bit"—equaling one-eighth of a peso a ocho. Spanish economic dominance in South and Central America and the Caribbean

Tomb of a hidalgo located in the Capilla de San Juan y Santa Catalina, Sigüenza Cathedral, completed 1511. This is an ideal example of the transitional mélange seen in Spain during the Renaissance era—in this case a combination of Isabelline ornament and Italianate sculpture.

remained a pillar of regional economic stability well into the nineteenth century, a reality not lost on the fledgling government of the United States, who in the Coinage Act of 1792 instructed the United States Mint to produce silver dollars equal in size and purity to the peso a ocho.[11] Spanish currency was such an influence upon the American currency and banking system that Congress permitted actual Spanish dollars to be used as legal US currency as late as 1857. The dollar sign itself is a fragment of Spanish Imperial heraldry—specifically the right-hand pillar of Hercules found within the imperial seal found on Spanish dollars from 1575 onward.[12] The "bit"—however impractical at twelve-and-a-half cents it might be—still remains an informal part of American life today. One particular chant illustrates that best: "Two bits, four bits, six bits, a dollar . . . . All for the Raiders—stand up and holler!"

Heraldry had long been an instrument of personal, family, and national pride in Spain, and the importance of heraldic symbolism would become even more prevalent in Spain after 1492. Ferdinand and Isabella had instituted a system of royal privileges and subsidy to the Spanish nobility—the *hidalguía*—including tax exemption, royal appointments, and deeds and titles to lands.[13] The resulting national furor sent Spaniards nationwide seeking claims of noble lineage in vain searches to claim their peerage as an *hidalgo*, while existing noble families proceeded to intermarry and strengthen their position within the Corte Real. In a broader sense, the growing influence of the hidalguía and likewise the Spanish Crown had a tangible visual impact on national culture. There was a growing trend to affix the royal seal of state on more than just coinage. Documents, uniforms, and, in particular, buildings were now marked with the national coat of arms. Some hidalguía who would host the visiting Catholic monarchs during a royal travel proceeded to have the seal of state carved outside the window of the bedroom where the king and queen had once slept. Spanish hidalguía were keen to carve their family crests upon their homes or any private, public, or church project they funded with their patronage. Particularly in Castile and Andalusia, homes and patronages of the houses of Maldonado, Fonseca, Ulloa, Diaz,

East ambulatory façade, Catedral de Santa María de la Sede, Sevilla, completed 1528. This is an excellent example of a predominantly Gothic structure with flying buttresses and tracery, whose ambulatory exterior was completed with Plateresque detailing.

Mendoza, Zúñiga, and many others could be readily identified by the flamboyant *escudos* carved in stone over doorways or building corners. The Palacio de Monterrey in Salamanca—long the palace home to the royal-appointed Duke of Monterrey—would by the seventeenth century feature on its façades the shields of no less than eight different noble families who at one time occupied the palace.[14]

By edict, any building financed by the Spanish Royal Treasury required the royal coat of arms ensconced upon its façade. When the new Spanish King Charles—the Flemish-born Spanish monarch—was elected Holy Roman emperor as Charles V in 1519, Spain's coat of arms ballooned to a massive size, featuring two Corinthian columns referred to as the "Pillars of Hercules," and backed by the Habsburg double-headed eagle of the Holy Roman Empire. Proud Spanish maestro mayores were all too eager to emblazon the monstrous new seal upon the façade of Plateresque buildings of the era. A massive Imperial Spanish seal equal to three stories in height was set in stone over the Puerta de Bisagra, an entry gate to the city of Toledo in Castile, while a smaller eleven-foot-high version of the royal seal was installed over the entrance to the Colegio Mayor de San Ildefonso at the Universitas Complutensis in Alcalá de Henares—today the Universidad de Alcalá (and the inspiration for Texas Tech's Administration Building's north façade). Not only had the Spanish obsession with heraldry become an inextricable component of their Renaissance-era architecture, it would remain an integral element of architectural identity well into Spain's neoclassical era at the start of the twentieth century.

In late July 1492, Roderic Llançol i de Borja, archbishop of the Aragonese coastal city of Valencia, was elected pontiff as Pope Alexander VI.[15] Borja, best remembered in history by the Italianization of his name—Borgia—was known for a range of habits including corruption, nepotism, and political scheming during his time in papacy. In 1494, Ferdinand I of Naples died, and was succeeded by his ineffectual son Alfonso II. Sensing Neapolitan weakness, Charles VIII, king of France, marched an army into Italy intending to seize the Kingdom of Naples. Pope Alexander now faced the likelihood that the Vatican was now threatened by the approaching French, who would likely march through Rome en route to Naples. In response, Alexander led the rise of the League of Venice that ultimately repeled the French threat—an alliance of Venetians, Austrians, Neapolitans, Milanese, and Sicilian forces. But it was the addition of the Kingdom of Spain that would tip the balance of fortune invariably in the league's favor.

Fresh from completion of the Reconquista, the armies of Castile and Aragon were shipped to southern Italy in 1494 to engage the French in the first of a series of proxy wars between Spain and foreign invaders over the next five decades. With the Spanish Army came their military commanders, mostly hidalguía, who remained in Italy during a time when the European Renaissance was nearing its climax. Spanish hidalguía already had a well-known preference for Italian artistry, as the Castilian aristocracy regularly commissioned Italian artisans to design and carve their tombs.[16] This preference would have an indelible influence on Spanish stonework for the era, as Spanish masters like Alonso González de Berruguete, who himself studied in Rome under Michelangelo,[17] would largely adopt Italian influences. Spanish hidalguía in Italy would often transport Italian artisans back to Spain after the war to complete further commissions there. War brought the unintended effect of accelerating Spain's entry into the broader European Renaissance, in both art and architecture. Italian artists and builders would not lead the Spanish Renaissance, but rather added another key ingredient into the mélange of stylistic elements that defined much of sixteenth-century Spanish architecture.

For those larger chapel and cathedral projects underway in 1492, such as cathedrals at Seville or Toledo, the Gothic style—a style that was on the decline elsewhere on the continent—in Spain continued to reign supreme. Accordingly, in the years immediately prior to the Spanish Renaissance, a hybrid style still possessing many Gothic elements known as the *Isabelline* style briefly appeared in Spain. Highly florid, but still bearing much of the aesthetic patterns of the Gothic era, buildings like the Palacio del Infantado in Guadalajara and much of the exterior of buildings at the Universidad de Salamanca were built in this style.

Regardless of which architectural style was in vogue, Spain's small cadre of talented maestro mayores were a patrilineal group. Fathers who designed and began construction of large commissions often mentored their sons who likewise would complete projects following their father's passing. Such was the case with Juan de Egas and his son Enrique, or Juan Gil de Hontañon and his son Rodrigo, who completed his father's Gothic commissions even as he designed and built projects in the newer estilo plateresco.[18] This form of apprenticeship ensured that stylistic elements from earlier styles, namely the Gothic and intermediate Isabelline styles, continued to appear in later Renaissance-era works. Distinctive elements of Spain's Gothic era, notably the tracery-inspired stone filigree that sat atop building eaves, or the floral-encrusted stone finials that crowned the buttress towers of cathedrals, were readily adapted and incorporated into more modern Isabelline and Plateresque compositions. Further, these maestro

The Torre del Alminar (Bell Tower) to the Mezquita-Catedral de Córdoba, as seen from the Patio de los Naranjos.

mayores often relied upon the same Mudéjar craftsmen for the fabrication of wood doors; the renowned ironwork grilles, or *rejería*, of Spain; polychrome tile details; and the *techos artesonados*—the incredibly ornate wood-coffered ceilings which crowned many Spanish interior spaces of the period.

Only later, in the latter half of the sixteenth century, did Spanish architecture shift away from the Plateresque to a more staid direction. With the assent of the austere Spanish king (and Holy Roman emperor) Philip II, royal court architects Juan Bautista de Toledo, Juan de Herrera, and other contemporaries cast aside decades of national flamboyance and practically banished all ornament from Spanish architecture. Applying their Italian training to the establishment of a mathematically precise style, a sober puristera of Renaissance architecture in Spain would be enforced up until the end of the century.

IN CÓRDOBA, once a premiere city in the emirate of Al-Andalus—now Andalusia—the Cathedral of Our Lady of the Assumption had once been a hypostyle hall mosque until the city fell into Castilian hands relatively early during the Reconquista in 1236. The stunningly beautiful Moorish-styled, red-and-cream-colored *voussoir* arches that defined the converted cathedral's interiors had largely remained as Catholic clergy incorporated additions in the Plateresque, and later Baroque and Churrigueresque styles. The result is a richly eclectic complex, in which baroque choir stalls and Churrigueresque altars sit only a short distance from an ornate gilded *mihrab*. Over time, this conversion effort extended outside beyond the famed Patio de los Naranjos—the orange tree-gridded courtyard north of the cathedral—to the former minaret of Sultan Abd al-Rahmán III dating back to 951, which stood watch over the city. Begun in 1593 by maestro mayor Hernan Ruiz II,[19] the old minaret, which was damaged by an earthquake four years earlier, was stripped of its Moorish detailing (or in some cases, entombed in new construction) and rebuilt in a hybrid combination of Plateresque and baroque motifs. It would take over seventy years and the work of three other maestros mayores before the former minaret was completed into a new tower over five stories taller than before,[20] and topped with a statue of the archangel San Rafael. Ruiz and his successors completed the belfry conversion in the telescoping tower style popular in Spain in that era. In its new role, the rebuilt tower in Córdoba would be known alternatively as the Torre del Alminar or the Torre Campanario—the Tower of Bells.

The estilo plateresco very much owed its creation to the events of 1492—events that were far broader in scope than the arrival of a Genovese navigator to an island in the Caribbean. In fact, had the events of 1492 not unfolded as they did, beyond the obvious and immediate impact upon European and Western Civilization in general, it is likely that this truly unique, beautiful and intriguing architectural style never would have come to be. Had that been the case, the architectural style and resulting heritage of a particular university situated in the South Plains of West Texas would likewise have been a vastly different story as well.

3

WESTERN INSPIRATION

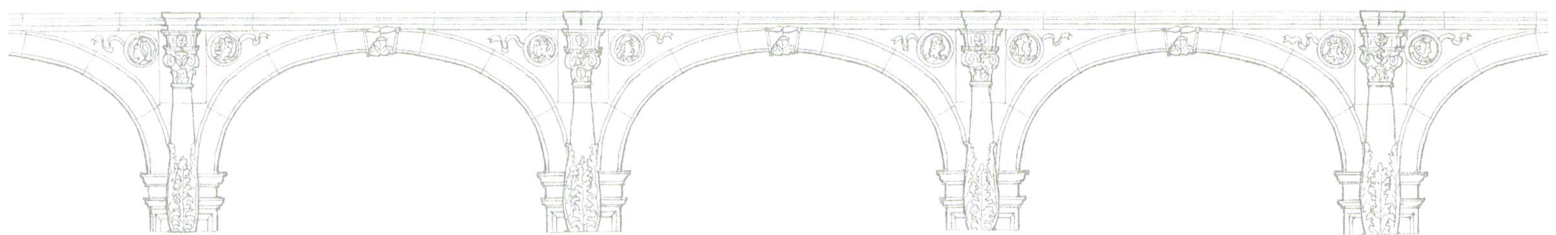

On cue, a band broke into "Hail Columbia!" as Vice President Charles Fairbanks and Speaker of the House Joseph G. Cannon emerged from the Portland Hotel to rousing applause. It was the morning of June 1, 1905, and the two VIPs were visiting Portland, Oregon, for the opening of a World's Fair.[1] The Portland Fair—known officially as the Lewis and Clark Centennial American Pacific Exposition and Oriental Fair—was one of many expositions across America held between the last decade of the nineteenth century up to World War I. Beginning with the seminal 1893 World's Columbian Exposition in Chicago, the American public was exposed to the Beaux-Arts–stylized fantasy world of the City Beautiful, replete with whitewashed neoclassical buildings, immaculate lawns, lush gardens, and every pavilion hall stuffed with a plethora of new technologies and products few had seen before. World's Fairs first exposed America to Cracker Jack popcorn, Campbell's condensed soup, and the Buffalo wing, as well as Ferris wheels, wireless telegraphy, and, later, television. Fairs and expositions changed American history. On September 6, 1901, a Polish-American anarchist, Leon Czolgosz, shot President William McKinley in the Temple of Music at the Pan-American Exposition in Buffalo, New York. McKinley succumbed to his wounds eight days later, leading to the succession of Theodore Roosevelt as the twenty-sixth President of the United States. Perhaps it was the events in Buffalo four years earlier that left Roosevelt leery about attending the opening of the Portland Fair, opting to send subordinates instead.

The day before his assassination, McKinley gave what would be his final speech to the crowds attending the Buffalo World's Fair, illustrating what World's Fairs had become to America:

> Expositions are the timekeepers of progress. They record the world's advancement. They stimulate the energy, enterprise, and intellect of the people, and quicken human genius. They go into the home. They broaden and brighten the daily life of the people. They open mighty storehouses of information to the student.

View looking over the water of Guild's Lake north to the US Government Pavilion; Lewis and Clark Centennial Exposition, Portland, Oregon, 1905.

> Every exposition, great or small, has helped to some onward step. Comparison of ideas is always educational, and as such instructs the brain and hand of man.[2]

McKinley was correct in more ways than one. Despite designs that varied between majestic and gaudy, the kitschy or sublime, the City Beautiful movement, as Daniel Burnham had coined it, indelibly generated both a commercial, societal, and environmental impact upon American society. Fairs embodied the vision of what an American city, or perhaps even the built fabric of college campuses, could aspire to be. Expositions in Chicago, Omaha, Buffalo, Saint Louis, Portland, Norfolk, Seattle, and elsewhere so vividly contrasted from the ugliness of urban tenements, grimy streets, noise, and congestion of the turn-of-the-century American city. But the average world's fair was not a lasting monument, as most buildings consisted of wood framing coated by plaster of Paris mixed with straw and then whitewashed for good measure. After fairs ended, local populations and businesses had grown, and gate revenue had been collected, organizers were content with demolishing their idyllic white cities. The visiting public for the most part, never knew differently.

America's real cities proved intractable canvases for architects like Burnham to realize permanent City Beautiful visions, but aside from fairs and exhibitions, college and university campuses proved to be the most readily available canvases in that era to work with. America was already exposed to the idyllic possibilities of an axially ordinated and logically thought campus plan, first with Joseph-Jacques Ramée's vision for Union College in Schenectady, New York, in 1813, followed by Thomas Jefferson's vision for the Academical Village at the University of Virginia four years later, and later case studies like McKim, Mead & White's urban plan for Columbia University. The architects and planners of fairs and exhibitions were often the same people competing for university planning commissions of the same period. Frederick Law Olmsted, de facto founder of the landscape architectural profession in the United States and master planner for New York City's Central Park, not only designed the landscapes of the 1893 World's Columbian Exposition in Chicago, but also collaborated with architect Charles A. Coolidge in the 1888 master plan for the new Leland Stanford Jr. University in Palo Alto, California. Though Coolidge's design for Stanford was still strongly influenced by the Romanesque-revival style preferred by his former employer and colleague Henry Hobson Richardson, Stanford's early architecture included many elements of unquestionable Spanish influence,[3] including colonnaded cloisters, red clay tiled roofs, and exposed wood-beam ceilings. Stanford demonstrated the idyllic potential that lies in the combined forces in architecture, landscape architecture, and planning on a college campus.

Fairs themselves had a direct, indelible impact on American campus planning. The same year as the World's Columbian Exposition

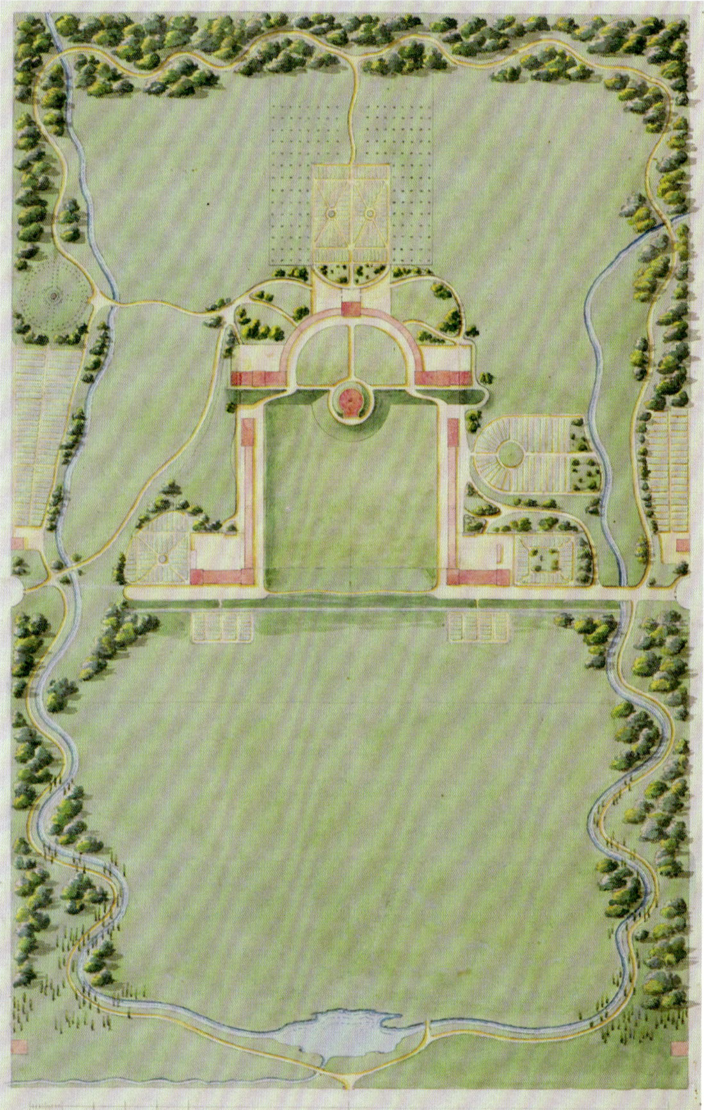

Proposed campus plan for Union College, Schenectady, New York, 1813; Joseph Jacques Ramée, architect. Preceding Jefferson's plan for the University of Virginia by four years. Union College was the first comprehensively planned college in US history, and bears formative similarities to the Court of Honor quadrangle designed at Texas Tech.

Aerial rendering of the proposed quadrangle plan for Leland Stanford Jr. University, Palo Alto, California, 1886; Shepley, Rutan & Coolidge, architects, with Frederick Law Olmsted, landscape architect.

View looking north down the Columbia Court, Lewis and Clark Centennial Exposition, 1905.

Axonometric drawing illustrating the layout of the US Government Building Complex, including exhibit buildings, twin carillon towers, and peristyle colonnades; James Knox Taylor, architect, 1905.

opened, Henry Ives Cobb completed his Oxbridge-inspired master plan for the adjacent University of Chicago. In time, Cobb's plan for the university would be as much shaped by the massive nearby Midway Park—the former Midway Plaisance grounds of the world's fair converted after 1893 into green space. Emmanuel Louis Masqueray's design for the Louisiana Purchase Exposition in Saint Louis in 1904 would grow into what is today Washington University. In 1909, an exposition plan developed by the Olmsted Brothers—the sons of the late Frederick Law Olmsted—became the Alaska-Yukon-Pacific Exposition in Seattle, Washington. The unique triangulated-axis plan for the exposition would become the epicenter of the University of Washington campus built over the fair site after its closing. Sited at that epicenter so as to frame a view south toward Mount Rainier, the central circular pool and Drumheller Fountain remains today a beloved icon to the UW campus. Even modern Olympic games—in many ways predecessors to the expositions of a century ago—have become the equivalent of twenty-first–century City Beautiful planning and design. The last three Olympiads held in the United States—the 1984 Summer Games in Los Angeles, the 1996 Summer Games in Atlanta, and the 2002 Winter Games in Salt Lake City—each profoundly shaped the modern campuses of host universities to those events—the University of Southern California, the Georgia Institute of Technology, and the University of Utah, respectively.

Grounds plan of the Panama-California Exposition, San Diego, 1915. Primary elements of the exposition situated upon the plateau east of Cabrillo Canyon were centered around a linear prado and the rectilinear Plaza de Panama.

IN JUNE 1905, Fairbanks and Cannon arrived by coach at another white city constructed along the banks of the Willamette River in northwest Portland. The Lewis and Clark Fair was another product

Bertram Grosvenor Goodhue, photograph undated.

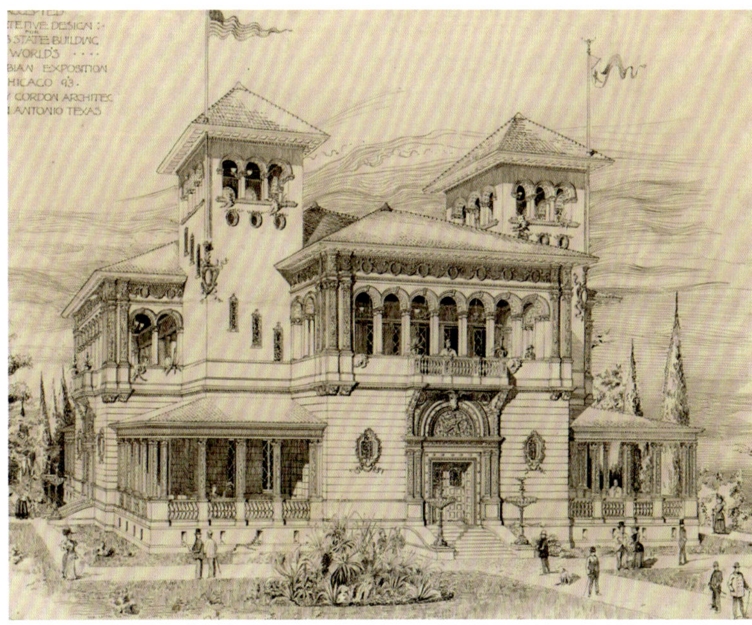

(*Above*) Rendering of the Texas State Building at the World's Columbian Exposition, Chicago, 1893. Gordon & Laub, architects.

of John and Frederick Law Olmsted Jr., with fair architecture designed by the Oregon firm of Whidden & Lewis. Architect Ion Lewis had suggested a different architectural style than the typical Greco-Roman neoclassical style that had dominated American fair architecture for the last twelve years. Rather, opting instead for the "Spanish Renaissance" style,[4] a curious choice for the Pacific Northwest, but likely a doff to the Spanish exploration of the northwestern coast in the late eighteenth century. Though the whitewashed façade finish remained, along with Spanish finials and either red clay tile or red corrugated roofs, which made for an awkward mélange, it was an important departure in exposition design from past case studies. Fairbanks and Cannon arrived onto the fair's central plaza—The Columbia Court—and looking to the north across the dredged former swamp renamed as Guild's Lake,[5] they observed a causeway-connected island on which sat the focal point of the fair—the US Government Building. Designed by James Knox Taylor—architect of the US Treasury Building in Washington, DC—the Government Building,[6] aside from the fifteen-foot-thick Douglas fir columns of the exposition's Forestry Building, was easily the most fascinating architectural work featured at the Lewis and Clark Fair.

The US Government Building consisted of two identical Spanish-styled towers flanking the main colonnade entry façade of the complex with a pair of radiating curved arcades connecting to flanking exhibit buildings. The towers bore a resemblance to both the famed Giralda of the Catedral de Sevilla as well as the tower of the Church of Santa María la Mayor in Ronda, Spain—the same carillon that would inspire the twin towers to William Randolph Hearst's Casa Grande in California, as well as W. L. Bradshaw's 1931 tower design for Lubbock High School. It was the first campuswide application of such a style in the United States, highlighting the design potential resulting from combining Beaux-Arts planning principles and Spanish design vernacular.

Spanish-revival architecture was still a new and unfamiliar sight in American architecture at the turn of the century. While the vast majority of buildings at the World's Columbian Exposition featured Greco-Roman-revival motifs, two states—California and Texas—featured distinctive Spanish-inspired fair pavilions instead. California's large, Spanish-colonial revival pavilion reflected a position as terminus of the national westward expansion and a growing economy. Texas, on the other hand, was still largely regarded as a sleepy, backwoods state—an enigmatic place largely unknown to Easterners. Not far from the California Building was the Texas Pavilion, designed by noted Texas architect James Riely Gordon of the Texas firm Gordon & Laub—best known for his numerous Romanesque-revival county courthouses, and who would later design the Arizona state capitol. Curiously, the original Gordon & Laub pavilion proposal was not Spanish at all, but rather Italianate with a broad dome situated over the main exhibition hall. Lead fair architect Daniel Burnham selected Gordon & Laub's proposal, only to reject their design submission, and summoned Gordon to Chicago in late 1891 for consultations on what would emerge as a completely different Texas State Building design.[7]

Completed in February 1892, the revised Texas State Building design was handsome and Plateresque—a remarkable development given neither architect had ever visited Spain and no English-written publication yet existed on Spanish Renaissance architecture. The building ornament was undoubtedly drawn from the flamboyant era of the Spanish Renaissance, with Arabesque panels and Corinthian capitals adorning columns and pilasters, while the building retained an irregular, but still harmonious rhythm of various windows and openings. Burnham's interjection had transformed the Texas State Building into an unqualified success that garnered a medal from the Fair Commission for the building's use of Spanish design motifs.[8]

THE 1905 PORTLAND FAIR and Gordon's 1893 Texas State Building remained outliers in an era worn down by whitewashed neoclassicism. By the eve of the World War I, expositions themselves had become fiscally questionable ventures, as less than half of US fairs barely broke even in revenue, regardless of their economic development value to American cities.[9] But there was one exception. Named for the missionary Saint Didacus, who ironically hailed from the city of Alcalá de Henares, San Diego was in 1909 little more than a small, quiet town of thirty-nine thousand on the Southern California coastline, largely unknown on the national or global radar. In 1868, San Diego city leaders set aside 1,400 acres—a massive tract of land for a city its size—as a city park for public use. Prominent New York City landscape architect Samuel Parsons Jr. was hired by local business leaders in 1902 to master plan the park[10] and transform the semiarid Sonoran landscape into a lush paradise, but it would require a grand event to fund a landscaping transformation the size of Parson's vision for City Park. The city did have one thing to boast—one of the finest natural harbors on the West Coast, and the closest Pacific US harbor to the largest construction project in world history at that time: the Panama Canal.

Cities on both coasts showed interest in establishing another world's fair to celebrate the opening of the Panama Canal. San Diego was quick to join the competition, envisioning the city park as an ideal fair site and renaming the park Balboa Park in honor of Spanish explorer Vasco Núñez de Balboa—the first European to transit the Isthmus of Panama. New Orleans and San Francisco had designs

Present-day view looking south across the Laguna de las Flores at the Panama-California Exposition, San Diego; Bertram Grosvenor Goodhue, architect, with Carleton Winslow, associate architect, 1914–1915.

Postcard photograph of the Plaza de Panama looking northeast towards buildings at the Panama-California Exposition, 1915. One of the two east flanking towers to the Prado—the Palacio de Monterrey-inspired Electricity Building (right) would inspire William Ward Watkin in a building framing concept for his Court of Honor at Texas Technological College.

for a similar exposition as well—two large, influential US cities that could easily crowd little San Diego out of contention. But thanks to influential pro–San Diego representatives in Congress, a joint-California contingent from San Francisco and San Diego was brokered to ward off the Louisiana delegation. San Francisco was determined to demonstrate that they had rebuilt their city from the ashes and rubble of the 1906 earthquake and thus received a lion's share position. San Diego would host a fair, but the San Francisco fair was to be the official Bureau International des Expositions–sanctioned event—to be named the Panama-Pacific International Exposition (PPIE). San Diego was permitted to hold a smaller regional exposition, but it would be limited to state pavilions and foreign exhibits from Central and South America only.[11] To add further challenge, San Diego would not receive federal funding for the exposition, which led citizens to finance the exposition by referendum vote in favor of $5 million in public financing—a tremendous sum for a city of their size in 1912.[12] Little did San Diegans realize that their exposition would become the most successful and enduring exposition in American history and would serve as the premiere case study for the last great revivalist movement in American architecture. It would also forever define the future design of Texas Tech University.

The architect finally selected for the San Diego Fair had neither the pedigree nor experience of the majority of his peers, having achieved advancement through humble beginnings as a draftsman and by his gifted skills in drawing that few if any in his profession possessed. His name was Bertram Grosvenor Goodhue.

Goodhue was the penultimate delineator, producing tremendous perspectival drawings as early as his preteenage years. In 1891, a twenty-two-year-old Goodhue boldly entered into a national design competition for the new Episcopal Cathedral in Dallas winning the project outright.[13] Goodhue traveled via train to Dallas to consult with the bishop of the Episcopal Church to begin work, but rather than returning home following the meeting, Goodhue instead traveled south into Mexico for his first international journey. It was a journey that Goodhue later recollected in his book *Mexican Memories*. In particular, he was mesmerized by the frenetic, luxuriant ornament found in Mexican churches and civic architecture, as well as the juxtaposition between the ornate entries and details of their Churrigueresque architecture, while the balance of façades featured a stately simplicity with relatively little ornament. Goodhue returned to the United States in late 1891 and shortly after joined the firm of Cram and Wentworth,[14] forever inspired by his Mexican journey, but unaware of its lasting impact upon the Spanish-revival architecture movement in the United States.

Awaiting at Cram and Wentworth in Boston was another young architect who would first serve as Goodhue's employer, then later colleague and partner. Five years older than Goodhue, the thin, chiseled-faced, bespectacled Ralph Adams Cram was both similar and vastly different than Goodhue. Cram too was a product of the apprenticeship system, rather than the educated aristocracy of graduates from higher institutions of architecture like L'Ecole des Beaux-Arts. Both were romantics and appreciated architectural styles prevalent in the Northeast—particularly the Gothic-revival style. The firm—later renamed Cram, Goodhue, and Ferguson—was winning notable design commissions, such as the master plan commissions for United States Military Academy at West Point in 1901, Sweet Briar College in Virginia, and later Princeton University. Both architects possessed a lesser-known albeit deep interest in the Spanish styles of revivalist architecture that were only just becoming more appreciated by American architects. Cram's love emerged from his obsessive search of the perfect examples of Gothic architecture in Europe, and few realized that some of Europe's finest Gothic architecture resides in Spain.[15] It was while visiting there that Cram first experienced the *estilo plateresco*. In January 1923, Ralph Adams Cram wrote an introduction for his California colleague Winsor Soule in the book *Spanish Farm Houses and Minor Public Buildings*, in which he extolled his praise for Spanish architecture: "Spanish architecture is incomparable, Moorish, Romanesque, Gothic, Plateresque, Rococo; and whatever its source or genre is transformed by Spanish temperament into something quite racial and unique."[16]

Goodhue too had been mystified by Spanish-revival architecture from his experiences in Mexico. He had arguably completed more Spanish-revival work than most American architects of the day, thanks to a 1905 commission to design the Anglican Pro-Cathedral of Santísima Trinidad in Havana, followed by a 1911 commission for a Spanish Renaissance–revival hotel for Canal Zone visitors in Colon, Panama. By the beginning of the 1910s however, Cram and Goodhue found themselves butting heads more frequently on projects, and sometimes outright competing against each other in competitions and schematic design proposals. Such was the case with the 1909 commission for the master plan of the William M. Rice Institute in Houston. By this time, Goodhue had moved to New York City to form an office there, while Cram and chief draftsman Frank Ferguson continued in Boston. It was also during this period that two young recent graduates joined their firm—Carleton Winslow, an École des Beaux-Arts graduate who had joined Goodhue's New York staff in 1907, and a University of Pennsylvania graduate who joined Cram's Boston team in 1908. His name was William Ward Watkin.

It had taken heavy politicking by Bertram Goodhue to wrest the San Diego fair commission away from Irving Gill and the Olmsted Brothers, who had originally won the commission and had begun to develop plans for the exposition as early as late 1910. Goodhue personally traveled to San Diego in 1911 to persuade the exposition committee of his familiarity of the Spanish-revival styles and his unequaled value to the project.[17] His lobbying worked, and both Gill and the Olmsted Brothers withdrew from the project in 1912. Fair leaders recognized from the outset the importance of a Spanish theme to the exposition grounds and buildings, and Goodhue's proposal, particularly when presented through his immense delineation skills, presented a radical shift from two decades of neoclassical world's fair planning.

Drawing from his enchanting travels in Mexico, Goodhue proposed an aesthetic scheme for the exposition that combined the flamboyance of Churrigueresque ornament with the simple stuccoed forms of the mission-revival style seen in Alta California architecture. Central to Goodhue's plan for Balboa Park was a linear axial boulevard—El Prado—which would span the nearby Cabrillo Canyon with a clean, monolithic concrete arched bridge connecting visitors west of the canyon in San Diego with the exposition grounds to the east. Colonnaded exhibition buildings would not serve as formative "islands" in the San Diego exposition plan as in past fairs like in Chicago or Portland. Rather, there would only be a handful of primary open malls which interconnected a handful of Spanish-inspired plazas, while individual buildings were congregated in a more Spanish-inspired method of cloistered organization and bounded with colonnaded arcades to form gardens replete with quick-blooming flowers, acacias, and a variety of fruit trees. Goodhue recoiled at the thought of the San Diego fair being another white city, proposing instead a warmer range of beige and cream hues to the buildings reflective of the exhibition's Latin themes. His feelings toward prior neoclassical white cities were made clear in the foreword to his and Carleton Winslow's 1916 book, *The Architecture and the Gardens of the San Diego Exposition*:

> To house such enormous congeries of exhibits enormous groups of buildings have become necessary, and so all local, ethnic, and fitting character has been lost, and the architectural scheme and style, following the "easiest way," has taken on a rather colourless classic character with rows of columns, triumphal arches, courts of honors, and the like.[18]

While most of the exposition buildings would still be built in the temporary method of wood framing and plaster-and-staff applique, the very character of the Panama-California Exposition would be totally different from any previous fair in American history.

One building in the exposition stood out: the California State Building, a basilica-like ferroconcrete domed hall anchoring the eastern end of El Prado. The California State Building towered over the exposition, and at that time, San Diego in general, with its polychrome tile-clad dome and its baroque-inspired telescoping bell tower. Goodhue envisioned an entry façade to the California pavilion replete with incredibly ornate detailing, with representations of Spanish and European notables from early Californian history situated between pairs of ornate *estípites* so common to the Churrigueresque style. Goodhue drew heavily from his travels in Mexico, as the entry façade to the California State Building bears an uncanny resemblance to the Templo de La Valenciana (also known as the Iglesia de San Cayetano) near Guanajuato. Built during 1765–1788 at the foot of one of Mexico's most fruitful silver mines that had helped fuel Spain's Siglo de Oro, La Valenciana's composition includes a Churriguereque-detailed main entry façade.[19] Meanwhile, the California State Building's sizeable dome was inspired by a similar dome at the Church of Santa Prisca de Taxco. Even the Mudéjar geometric patterning of the wood entry doors into the Iglesia de San Cayetano are remarkably similar to the entry doors to the California State Building's main entrance.

Despite Goodhue's leadership in the design of the exhibition plan and the California State Building, design of many of the smaller buildings fell to Carleton Winslow, who moved to San Diego in 1913 as project field supervisor. Other exposition buildings and the very elegantly executed Laguna de las Flores reflecting pool situated between El Prado and the Botanical Building Greenhouse are all attributed to Winslow. Framing the eastern entry onto the Plaza de Panama, a pair of distinctive towers designed by Winslow were unmistakably inspired by Rodrigo Gil de Hontañon's iconic Palacio de Monterrey Tower form in Salamanca. Though the Panama-California Exposition was smaller in comparison to PPIE, the general design and harmonious integration of buildings and landscape would prove a far superior composition.

At 3:00 a.m. on New Year's Day 1915, President Woodrow Wilson awoke at the White House to press a telegraph button linked by relay to San Diego, where in the dark night, thousands burst into cheer as Wilson's signal simultaneously illuminated thousands of electric lights lining the arcades and buildings of the exposition.[20] The Panama-California Exposition was now open to the public and would prove to be one of the most successful world's fairs in US history, albeit not even being an official world's fair; 3.7 million visitors would attend

A pivotal source of inspiration in the neoclassical Spanish-revival era, the iconic corner tower of the Palacio de Monterrey, Salamanca. Rodrigo Gil de Hontañon, maestro mayor, completed 1539.

the exposition over the next two years.[21] To the north, the much larger Panama-Pacific International Exposition, though successful, was more akin to another white city, and failed to match the public praise heaped on San Diego. In large part due to the war in Europe, the PPIE was never able to gain international interest to the degree hoped by organizers, and upon its closing in late 1915, many of the international exhibits and staff—unable to return to Europe due to the Great War—instead moved to San Diego to take advantage of the success there. With steady continued business, fair organizers kept Balboa Park open into the next year, and in March 1916, the fair was rebranded the Panama-California International Exposition.[22] San Diego had built a world's fair after all.

4

WYATT, BILLY, AND CHIP

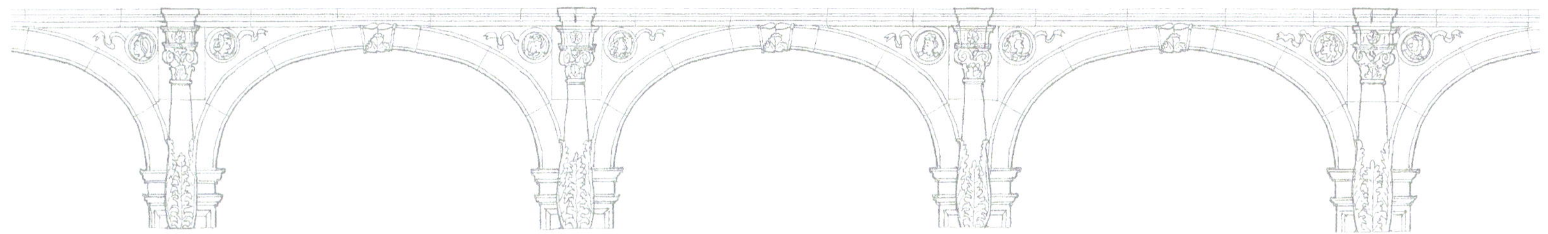

A ROOF REPAIR CREW had been dispatched on the morning of Wednesday, March 25, 1914, with gasoline torches onto the roof of the main building of the new West Texas State Normal College in Canyon. (The institution would later undergo a number of name changes over the next century, including being renamed West Texas State University in 1963. Thirty years later, West Texas State would join the Texas A&M University System and become West Texas A&M University.)[1] Handsome but eclectic, the College Main was a neoclassical argyle brick-clad building that was at the time the most substantial college building in the region between Fort Worth and Albuquerque. Whether it was the wind, carelessness, or both, by that afternoon the building labeled the "Pride of the Panhandle" was a pyre of flames whose column of black smoke was clearly visible from Amarillo fifteen miles to the north. Hundreds of students and Canyon residents gathered on the south lawn, helplessly watching as their school burned to the ground.

In the days and weeks following the disaster, an exposé unfolded where the public learned that replacing the $100,000 building in Canyon would prove difficult. All state-owned buildings were required by law to be insured, but the state comptroller reported to the press that the indemnity payout for the insurance policy on the College Main had mysteriously disappeared, leaving West Texas Normal with the only option to build a ramshackle set of temporary wood cabins to replace their former flagship building. Over a year would pass before Austin appropriated funds so that West Texas State Normal College could build a replacement and when that came to pass, they needed an architect to design it.[2]

Once funding was available in the summer of 1915, William Ward Watkin found himself on a Santa Fe train riding north through West Texas to Canyon. At thirty-one, Watkin's meteoric rise as an architect had taken him from childhood in the woods of Pennsylvania through Philadelphia, Boston, and then to Houston. None of that prepared him for the austere landscape of West Texas. Traveling with Watkin was Austin-based architect George Endress, who regularly partnered in joint ventures with Watkin, to meet with West Texas State Normal leadership on the design of a replacement for the former College Main.

Fire destroys the original College Main Building at West Texas State Normal College, Canyon, Texas on March 25, 1914. The disaster proves influential to the later site city selection and architectural design of Texas Tech, with the subsequent scandals and impeachment of Governor Ferguson, and William Ward Watkin's first visit to West Texas.

A young William Ward Watkin, during his final year of matriculation at the University of Pennsylvania, 1908.

The Canyon commission was one of many that Endress and Watkin would secure in their five-year partnership, including collegiate work spanning from Alpine to Denton.[3] Unbeknownst to Endress, Watkin was rapidly becoming one of the most experienced collegiate design architects in all of Texas. Watkin sat and gazed out at the largely flat, featureless prairie, which had only begun to be touched by the well and plow. Much of West Texas—then still devoid of power lines, rows of wind-breaking trees, and center pivots—appeared much like the brusque landscape first encountered by Salamanca-native Francisco Vázquez de Coronado y Luján in his visit through the Texas Panhandle some 372 years earlier.[4] Watkin then remained largely unaware of the region's Spanish-colonial history or of the unique beauty the Spanish-revival styles of architecture could provide during the popular Beaux-Arts neoclassicism of the day.

The son of Northamptonshire immigrants, William Ward Watkin was born in 1886 in Massachusetts, later growing up in the small ironworking town of Danville, Pennsylvania. Though having lost his father when only six, Watkin matriculated through school with great success and later balanced his high school education alongside summer employment with a local architect named J. H. Brugler. Brugler planted the idea in Watkin's mind not only of a future in architecture,[5] but also recommended the University of Pennsylvania as a place of study for the promising young man. Watkin arrived in Philadelphia coincidentally just as Penn welcomed a new professor of architecture from Lyon, France. Though still a relative unknown in architectural circles upon his arrival in 1903, Paul Philippe Cret would in the coming decades become a crucial force in advancing Beaux-Arts planning and design, including his 1931 master plan for the University of Texas at Austin, and the design of UT's iconic clock tower.

But Cret's arrival at the University of Pennsylvania School of Architecture would prove invaluable to the young Watkin, whose early interests in architecture leaned heavily toward the Gothic style. It is arguable that the architecture of Texas Tech itself indirectly owes thanks to Cret's influence in Watkin's life. Cret eventually

and the Polytechnic College of Pennsylvania—both of which the board would visit in early 1924.[27]

It was also in late 1923—on Thanksgiving Day—that the board of directors selected a new president of Texas Technological College. Paul Whitfield Horn, a Missouri native, Methodist Sunday school teacher, and president of Southwestern University in Georgetown, Texas may not have been the board's first choice, but the gaunt-faced but affable Horn accepted the post with workmanlike zeal. Horn's selection would prove fortuitous to the architectural outcomes of Texas Tech, as Paul Horn and William Ward Watkin would develop a strong working relationship of mutual respect—a relationship that would have profound impacts upon the architectural heritage of Texas Tech even today. Horn arrived by train to Lubbock on December 6, and after being welcomed by city leaders, adjourned with Hedrick and Watkin to the most overpriced plot of ground in Lubbock history to walk the site and discuss ideas for a new college.[28] In an act of legislative stupidity, Senate Bill 103 declared that no more than $150,000 of the $1 million endowment for the college could be set for the cost of the land acquisition. Most of the land that would become Texas Technological College was then part of the Spade Ranch, owned by the Ellwood brothers formerly of Illinois. Shrewdness was a well-known trait among the Ellwood clan, as the brothers' father, Isaac, had amassed a fortune as an original patent holder and marketer of barbed wire.[29] The state of Texas paid dearly for that shrewdness as the board paid over $75,000 over the stipulated land acquisition limit,[30] essentially guaranteeing that two thousand acres of land west of Lubbock sold for more than four times its market value. That bilking likely cost the college at least two new Plateresque-clad buildings when it opened two years later.

Watkin, Hedrick, and Horn drove out to the grassy land then west of Lubbock and peered out on the flat, featureless landscape. A recent project Watkin was undertaking with his Boston mentor Ralph Adams Cram had opened his eyes to a style largely absent from the repertoire of Texas architecture, but one that Watkin felt was ideally suited for the new Texas Technological College. But it would require convincing—perhaps not to Horn or Hedrick—but to Carter and the new college board to adopt this new style at Tech. A testament to his congenial nature, Hedrick would often address letters sent to both Watkin and Robert as "Dear Billy and Chip." [31] There would be many letters, telegrams, and phone calls to pass between them, as the three men now had just only twenty months not only to design but also to oversee completion of construction of an entire college campus from scratch.

The clock was now ticking.

5

ARMISTICE DAY

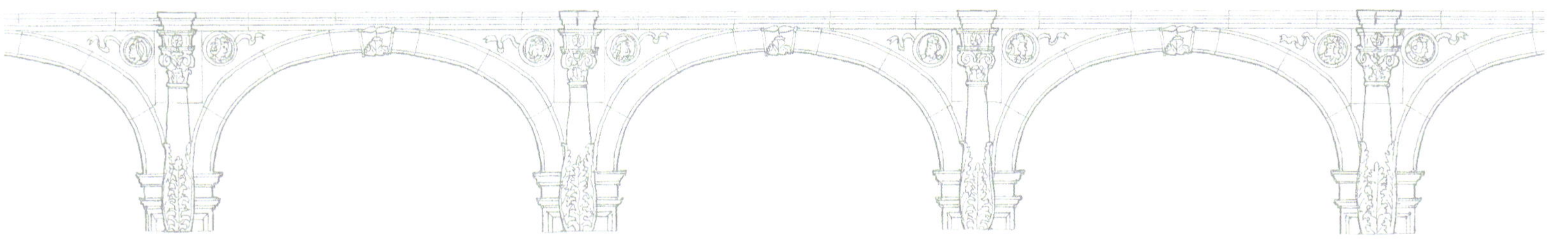

It was the worst time to be sick with the flu, but the tall, slender William Ward Watkin—whose academic responsibilities in 1924 included serving as Rice's athletic secretary—had left for New Orleans to meet with none other than John Heisman to discuss the future trophy-namesake's interest in becoming Rice's new football coach.[1] Watkin was wearing too many hats, and after returning from New Orleans, he resigned himself to stay in Houston and recuperate as he dictated a letter to Tech Board Chairman Amon Carter. Watkin had been pressing both his design team and the new Texas Tech leadership for a unique style for the new campus—a style yet to be seen en masse in Texas. Despite the state's indisputable Spanish heritage, Texans had been slow in adopting Spanish-revival architecture styles in its regional aesthetic. The prevailing architecture of Houston, Dallas, Fort Worth, and even San Antonio—home to the Alamo and a handful of other eighteenth-century Spanish missions—had been dominated since the Civil War with other prevailing styles: second empire, Romanesque-revival, Victorian, and a host of neoclassical themes. But Watkin had a plan to convince everyone that Spain was the ideal vernacular for this new college.

In accordance with Watkin's letter, on February 24, 1924, Hedrick's elder ailing partner, architect Carl Staats met Paul Horn in the Santa Fe Rail Station in Lubbock and boarded a train to Albuquerque to connect with the Chief bound for San Diego.[2] In Watkin's letter telegraphed on the 23rd, he wanted both Horn and a representative from Hedrick's team to "see the splendid Spanish architecture of Goodhue" at Balboa Park[3]—the former site of the 1915 Panama-California Exposition. Nearly a decade after the fair's opening, almost all of Goodhue and Winslow's original exposition buildings were standing and in use, with shops and restaurants still turning a profit.

What these men, accustomed to the arid climes of West Texas, found when they arrived at Balboa Park dazzled the imagination. Fruit trees filled the gardens, pleached acacia trees lined the Prado, and a grand ten-story Spanish belfry framed views to the west. Though the architecture of the exposition was in fact Churrigueresque—the style

An Afternoon Stroll, by Colin Campbell Cooper, 1916. Cooper visited Balboa Park in 1916 and plein-air painted the architecture and grounds of the Panama-California International Exposition extensively, providing an impressionistic view of the grounds as the Tech delegation would observe them eight years later.

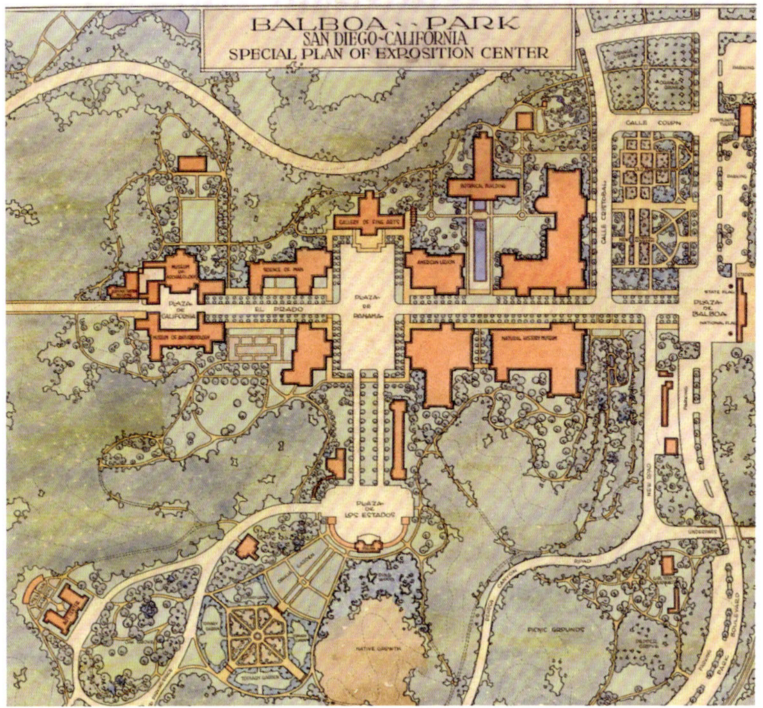

Post-1925 color plan of the Balboa Park exposition grounds, largely reflective of the layout of the grounds when the Tech delegation visited in early 1924.

Watkin's fall 1922 Italianate design proposal, developed in concert with Houston architect Louis A. Glover, for the Julia Ideson Library. Prior to the Library Board having brought Ralph Adams Cram on board, the thought of designing in a Spanish-revival style had not been considered by Watkin, let alone most Texas architects on projects of the period.

Goodhue first experienced in Mexico and fell in love with three decades earlier—the differences between Churrigueresque and Plateresque were barely perceptible to the layperson. No notes or correspondence outline Horn and Staats's opinion of what they saw that day, but minutes from the next two board of directors meetings clearly indicate that Watkin's stylistic suggestion had won through.[4]

But unlike the Churrigueresque-detailed buildings of Balboa Park, William Ward Watkin had another particular style in mind for the new Texas Tech campus—a style that owed its inspiration to Watkin's mentor and former employer in Boston. Beginning in 1920, Watkin had prepared a fundraising concept rendering for a potential new library for the city of Houston. Watkin's Italianate, single-story design was handsome and received notable attention, but when Watkin—in association with local architect Louis Glover—were retained in late 1922 as local associate architects to the library project,[5] the Library Board of Trustees named none other than Cram and Ferguson of Boston as design architects to the project. An opportunity of inspiration presented itself. Upon Cram's entry into the project, he advised the client and his old protégé Watkin to incorporate a style inspired by "the Spanish Colonial work in Texas," which was readily received by all involved.[6] Cram, in his fervent passion for seeking out the finest in Gothic architecture across Europe, had in the process encountered the warm and enchanting work of the estilo plateresco alongside the Gothic cathedrals he sought in Toledo, Seville, Burgos, and elsewhere. For both Cram and Watkin, this was the first venture into a style that Watkin in particular would find worthwhile uses for in commissions elsewhere in Texas.

Cram's suggestion to his Houston protégé for an ideal style for the Julia Ideson Library not only opened the door to introducing a Spanish idiom at Texas Tech, but more important, convinced Watkin that

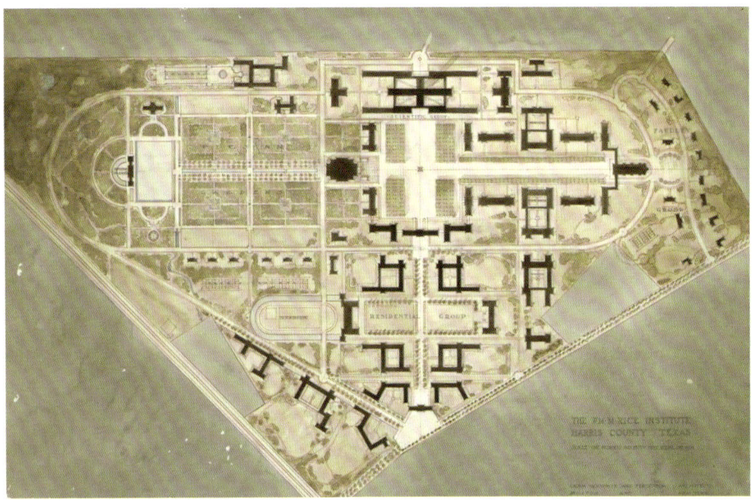

Goodhue's alternative proposed general plan for the Rice Institute, dated October 5, 1909. This plan, reflective of Goodhue's fondness of large central Spanish-inspired plazas, and the prado of Balboa Park, would profoundly influence Watkin fifteen years later in the design of the Tech general plan.

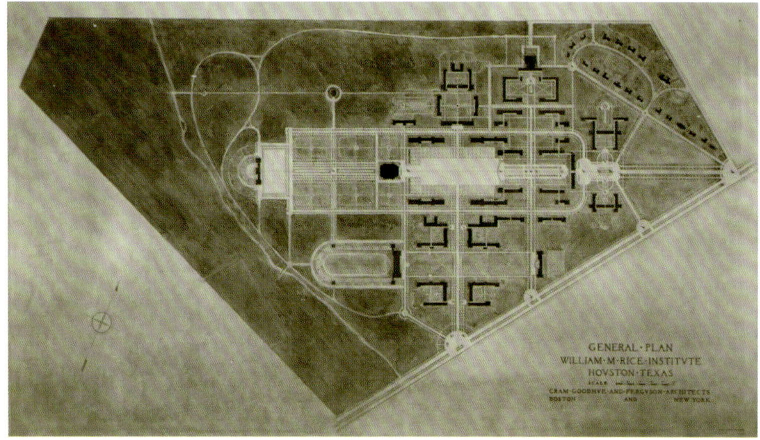

Final General Plan of the Rice Institute, reflecting a compromise between Cram's more monastic concept, Goodhue's more Spanish scheme, and feedback from Rice leadership. Interestingly, this plan was personally produced by William Ward Watkin prior to Watkin leaving Boston to be dispatched by Cram, Goodhue & Ferguson to serve as field representative during construction of the institute in 1910.

the more mannerist Plateresque would be elegantly better suited for Tech than the organic, frenetic Churrigueresque style that visitors observed in San Diego. With board support, Watkin and Hedrick were now released to design both the campus plan and buildings posthaste. The college board had committed to unveiling the campus design to the public at the West Texas Chamber of Commerce meeting on May 15,[7] giving Watkin barely two months to complete a master plan and elevations. While Watkin's office was busy with the design, Hedrick's office pushed through a myriad of pressing pragmatic matters—how to route fuel oil rail service from the nearby Santa Fe Rail Line, whose easement ran through the new Tech campus, and gathering case studies of successful academic buildings elsewhere from newly hired faculty and administrators to evaluate their programs and layouts.

Watkin's design efforts focused first on the Administration Building, the initial centerpiece of campus earmarked with a $350,000 budget[8] of the $775,000 appropriation remaining, and then to the campus plan en masse. As for the latter, fifteen years prior, when Watkin was still at Cram, Goodhue & Ferguson, development of a campus plan of the Rice Institute involved a collegial competition between Cram and Goodhue—a contest between a vision for a more densely cloistered building grouping proposed by Cram, and a larger, more broadly spaced collection of buildings proposed by Goodhue. Though Cram had already began developing plan concepts for Rice President Edgar Odell Lovett, Goodhue's office nonetheless produced an alternative plan to Cram's—first in September 1909, and then revised and submitted on October 5, which bore clear resemblance to planning strategies utilized in Goodhue's later 1914 plan for the San Diego Exposition.[9] Goodhue's Rice concept included a grand central plaza similar in scale to the Plaza de Panama in San Diego, with Prado-like malls extending out and framed by surrounding academic

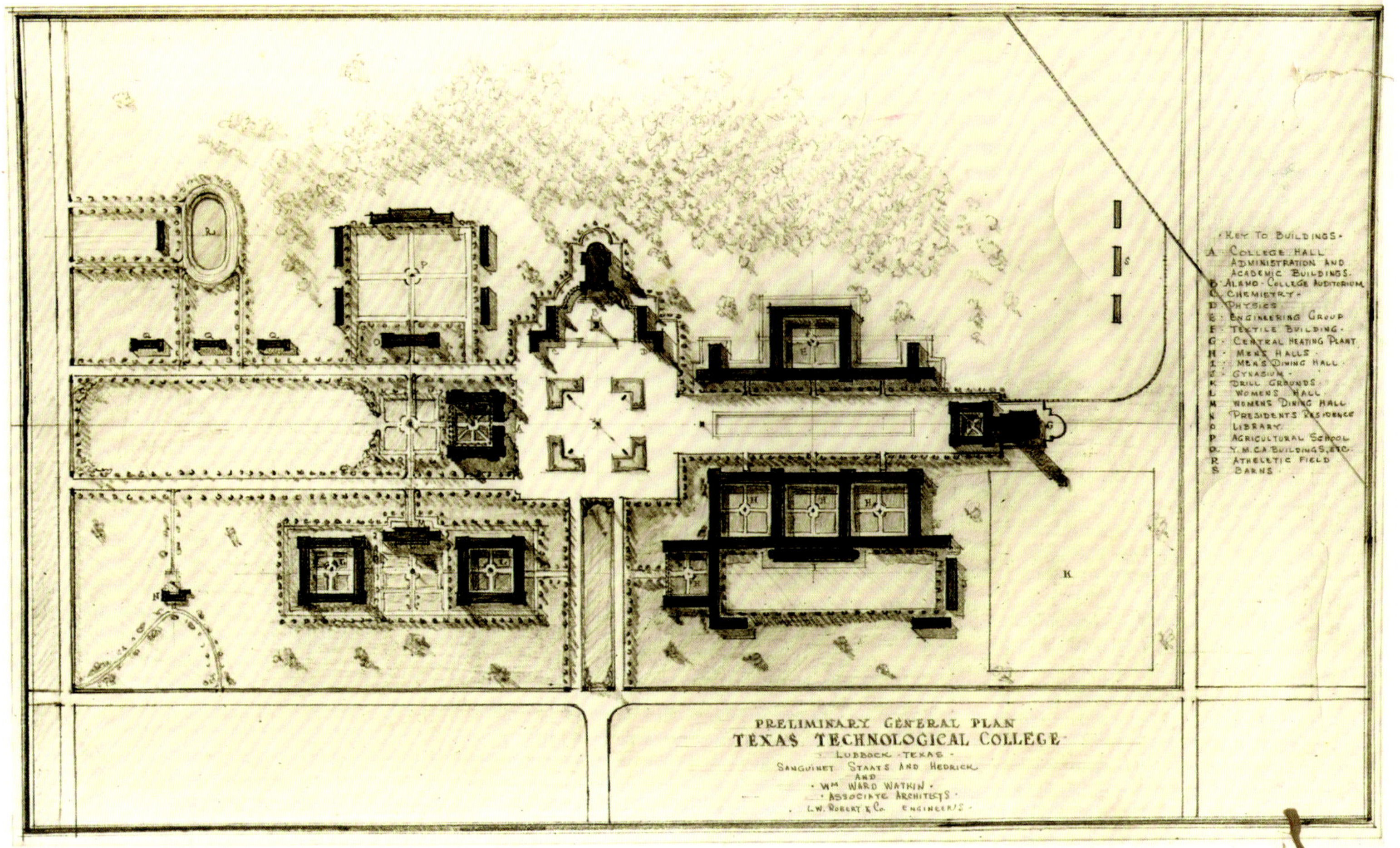

Watkin's Preliminary General Plan for Texas Technological College in Lubbock, as presented to the West Texas Chamber of Commerce in Brownwood on May 15, 1924.

or student-life buildings. In the Rice plan, academic space, library space, and administrative functions were juxtaposed with other functions such as student housing, athletics, and faculty housing, but were defined by the large central plaza acting as a hinge between two perpendicular mall axes. Goodhue's fall 1909 scheme contained a main east-west axis defined by a great auditorium, crossed by a north-south axis connecting scientific academic buildings to the north to a main entrance off Main Street to the south.[10] It was Goodhue's concept for the Rice campus that had in retrospect a hugely inspirational impact upon Watkin's later plan concept for Texas Tech.

Adapting Goodhue's Rice plan to climatic and vegetative limitations of West Texas would not come without a challenge. The open

Lovett Hall, the Rice Institute [today Rice University], Houston, Texas, illustrating its distinctive and influential salle-porte that would inspire Tech's Administration Building, completed 1912, Cram, Goodhue & Ferguson, architects.

green spaces in Goodhue's Rice plan were notably longer and broader than Cram's final iteration and more compact plan for the new Houston school. The same could be said for the Panama-California Exposition, though the cooler coastal climate in San Diego and Goodhue's profuse use of colonnaded arcades provided respite from the California sun. Elsewhere, the oppressive heat and humidity of Houston could be checked in part thanks to growing conditions that could cultivate shade trees of every kind, and the Rice plan had called for copious quantities of trees, as well as scores of colonnaded arcades bounding malls and plazas. But Lubbock was another matter.

In Lubbock, Watkin faced a dilemma that pitted two totally inverse planning factors against each other. The land parcel for Texas Technological College was nearly two thousand acres[11]—enough to fit five Panama-California Expositions or eight Rice Institutes on it, and still have unused land for agricultural learning purposes like crop farming and herd management. Developing an overly broad and sprawling campus plan could be an easy temptation—a trap that the college would inevitably fall into three decades later. The hot, dry climate of West Texas, punctuated by winters of biting cold wind, demanded a compact plan, but Watkin's plan remained broad in nature. In a way, Watkin's recommendation for a Spanish-revival campus was an ideal solution, as Spanish building massing and urban planning strategies were ideally adapted to the bioclimatic conditions of Castile and Andalusia—both remarkably similar to Lubbock. Watkin provided an explanation for his broad plan for Tech in interviews with the *Houston Chronicle* in September 1924:

> So the greatest difficulty faced by the modern architect is how to get the charming seclusion of the older schools with the circulation necessary for large enrollments and necessary automobile traffic. In looking at the general plan of the new Texas Technological College . . . one sees a rather daring solution of the difficulty.[12]

In Watkin's decision, grass and shade trees would be difficult to cultivate in the South Plains, certainly compared to San Diego or Houston. With only a fraction of the endowment needed to fully build out Watkin's emerging vision for Tech, students, faculty, and the public would have to contend with a sparsely vegetated and incomplete plan for years, if not decades ahead.

It was during this design stage that synergy began to emerge between Watkin and Horn, the Episcopalian classicist architect and the Methodist Sunday school teacher. Hedrick likewise found a strong interaction in Amon Carter, as communications between the two belied a fidgety concern regarding the timeliness of Watkin's team in completing of the plan and architectural concepts.[13] This came to a head on May 10 when Hedrick cabled Watkin advising him of completion status.[14] Watercolors had barely dried on presentation boards as the master plan concept and elevations were express couriered by train to Paul Horn at the West Texas Chamber of Commerce meeting in Brownwood the night before the presentation on the May 15.[15] Fittingly, the chamber of commerce—one of the strongest Tech boosters since the beginning—would be first to see the new design. As best and simply reported in the *Brownwood Bulletin,* the plan was "Heartily endorsed." [16]

With the design approved, it had come time for Watkin's team, as well as Sanguinet, Staats & Hedrick, and soon L.W. Robert & Company to begin coordinating design and production for working drawings—not an easy task in the world of circa-1924 communications. With Watkin lay the greatest strain. He still had refinements to make to the campus plan prior to submitting drawings to Fort Worth, where Hedrick's team, notably lead by Sanguinet, Staats & Hedrick designer Hermann Koeppe and his draftsmen, feverishly transformed preliminary drawings into a set of working drawings and specifications for bidding. The challenge for Hedrick's team was that no one at Hedrick's office had ever detailed a Plateresque Spanish Renaissance-revival building. It was for that reason that once any Tech project had bid, in a peculiar arrangement, Watkin's team produced detailed design drawings specifically for the stone fabricators and ironworkers, whose florid stone detailing and rejería—the Spanish ironwork—would be the most ornate components of the buildings at Tech. Weeks before the Brownwood presentation, Watkin's office had already shipped to Fort Worth concept drawings for the first building of the college group—the Administration Building. In an illustration of the frightening pace of the project, Koeppe and a herd of draftsmen at Hedrick's office had little more than three weeks to complete the drawings and specifications for Texas Tech's most iconic building.[17]

Author's conjectural elevation of what the Alamo Commencement Hall could have looked like based on general plan massing and shadows noted in the May 1924 Preliminary General Plan. Evidence indicates that Watkin envisioned a structure notably larger than the resulting 1951 Science Building built in its place.

THE CONCEPT PRESENTED in Brownwood on May 15, with only minor later modifications, would come to be known as the "Watkin Plan." Aligned to the Lubbock arterial roadway known as Broadway, Watkin's plan featured a broadened Broadway-aligned, paired-drive

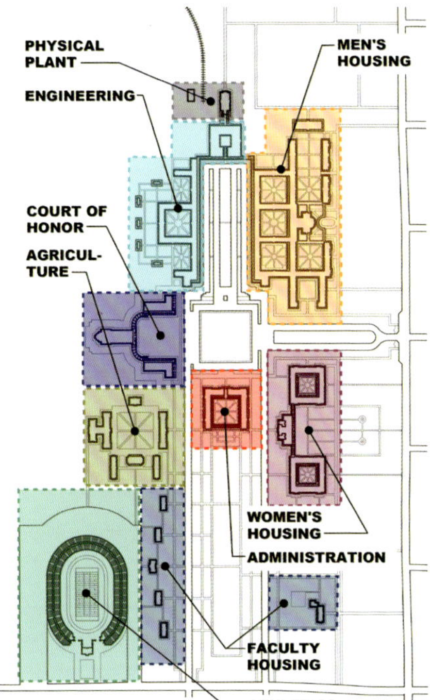

Building type district organization of the proposed Texas Technological College General Plan, 1924.

open mall extending west and terminating in a great plaza akin to the Plaza de Panama at San Diego and Goodhue's central plaza vision for Rice. The plaza was bound on two sides—by the Administration Building to the south and a proposed elevated Court of Honor to the west. This Court of Honor—intended to be elevated seven feet above the general grade of the campus—likely served as a solution to the monotonous flatness of the site. The building was approached from the central plaza via a broad boundary of approaching stairs, smaller in scale but not entirely unlike Charles McKim's design for the stairway approach to the Low Memorial Library at Columbia University. The actual cloister of buildings planned to frame the Court of Honor consisted of a chemistry laboratory to the south, a physics laboratory to the north, with both connected by peristyle arcades to a college auditorium to the west. Alternatively referred to in later media and correspondence as the "Hall of Texas" or "Alamo Memorial Hall,"[18] Watkin had drawn from Goodhue's unheeded suggestion at Rice of an auditorium for commencement-type events. Correspondence provides an impression that early sketches from Watkin may have existed of the basilica-like auditorium, and even the shadow cast by the hall in the master plan drawing bears this out. It can be discerned that the proposed auditorium would have two flanking entry façade towers, and the central apex tower of the basilica was at least twice the height of the hall itself. Unfortunately, any such sketches, if they existed, have been lost to history. The Science Building designed on the Auditorium site by Hermann Koeppe's son, Emmett Earl Koeppe, twenty-seven years later has since become a beloved part of the Tech landscape, but evidence suggests those familiar with Watkin's vision expected more substance than what the Science Building provided. One assessment came from Paul Horn's daughter Ruth Horn Andrews in her 1956 treatise *The First Thirty Years*: "At the end of the campus drive leading out of Lubbock's splendid wide street, appropriately called Broadway, there stands not the envisioned Hall of Texas but a squatty structure of anomalous design denominated the Science Building."[19]

The grand plaza south of the Court of Honor would serve as a hinge to a longer perpendicular axis aligned between the Administration Building and a mall consisting of engineering laboratories and housing for male students to the north. The Administration Building and salle-porte passageway was another nod to Cram, reflective of Rice's Administration Building—known as Lovett Hall. For visitors within the grand plaza or the north engineering and men's housing district (today the Engineering Key), Watkin's plan did exactly as it was intended, much like Goodhue's prior visions—use a framework of buildings to visually bind the campus in all directions. Given the stark, featureless landscape, which existed west of Lubbock, this was imperative. Watkin's design in terms of functional organization was straightforward and parochial. Texas Technological College would have four quadrants—engineering in the northwest, agricultural science and athletics in the southwest, and residential and student life activities east of the Engineering Key, with men's residences to the north and women housing south of Broadway. Symbolic of the chaste governance of coeducational institutions of the day, women's housing and dining resided in a sequestered location between the Administration Building and President's House. Watkin's concept for the administrative block formed a single cloistered compound with a salle-porte at the north end, a single-story arcade at the south end, and in a nod to Juan de Herrera and Pedro Machuca's El Escorial—the Spanish imperial palace and monastery—a collection of not two, but four carillon towers at the four corners of the building.

Housing units, laboratories, and the Administration Building were organized not in rectilinear blocks as seen in so many Cram-designed master plans like Rice and Princeton. Rather, the Tech plan incorporated cloistered grids of courtyards surrounded by narrow cross-section building units much like seen at Balboa Park. These arcaded "square donuts" could be regularly found in the Plateresque architecture of Spain—the Colegio de San Gregorio in Valladolid and the Colegio Mayor Fonseca in Salamanca being only two examples. Even if the broad malls prove to be too vast for the hot, arid Lubbock climate, Watkin's proposed collection of interspersed gardens and cloistered courtyards would still provide students and visitors a relief from the elements.

Pending the outcome on bids for the Administration Building, Texas Tech had less than $500,000 in funds for the construction of the remaining facilities, including a textile engineering laboratory, a home economics building, and an agricultural block of buildings including an instructional building, barn, and judging pavilion.[20] Horn received from his counterpart at the Iowa State College in Ames (today known as Iowa State University), Dr. Raymond Pearson, drawings of their dairy judging pavilion[21]—an elongated octagonal space. Tech's new dean of agriculture, A. H. Leidigh had recommended the Iowa State case study, which Watkin readily adapted to be moderately larger and finished with a Spanish-revival clay tile roof and stucco façade. On other fronts, on March 10, Hedrick sent a letter to the

The corner tower form and massing of the Monastery and Royal Palace of El Escorial, northwest of Madrid; Juan de Herrera and Pedro de Machuca, maestros mayores, completed 1603. The four-corner tower scheme and cloister plan of the Spanish Imperial Palace bears fascinating similarity to Watkin's plan for the Administration Building.

The Old Dairy Barn, Iowa State Agricultural College (today Iowa State University), built 1921–1922. This building served as inspiration for Tech's Livestock Judging Pavilion.

Present-day view looking north through the carpanel-arched salle-porte of the Administration Building at Texas Tech.

Atcheson, Topeka & Santa Fe Railroad requesting the railroad bear the cost of constructing a siding off the Lubbock-Seagraves Line that bounded the campus.[22] Arguing that regular shipments of fuel oil to the college would provide the railroad with continuous carrying cost revenue that would pay for the spur, Hedrick and the college board learned in May that the Santa Fe Railroad was not persuaded, resulting in yet another cost bleeding away a diminishing endowment.

The Torre del Alminar, Mosque-Cathedral of Córdoba would become Watkin's eventual source of inspiration for the Administration Building's carillon towers.

Before the Administration Building could be let to bid, Hedrick was required by the State Board of Control to submit college drawings and specifications for review by W. R. Hendrickson, the state building inspector. Hendrickson submitted a brief review response to Hedrick on June 12, objecting to the use of wood veneer exterior doors in lieu of solid wood doors, and the specification of "cement stone," known today as cast stone.[23] In reality, Watkin's intricate Plateresque detailing envisioned for Tech buildings could never be achieved with cast stone technology of the day, and cast stone of that era did not weather well, so the objection proved fortuitous. Hendrickson recommended: "use natural stone in place of manufactured stone. Stone from Leuders, Jones County, is first class stone; grey in color; easily worked and short haul. The difference in cost is worth the price." Events over the next year would test Hendrickson's claim of a "short haul," but regardless of the cost consequences, the opening sentence of his letter best described the Administration Building: "The Main building is a beautiful design, and very elaborate."

THE ARCHITECTURE OF Texas Tech University quite simply begins and ends with the Administration Building. In this building, one discovers the depth of the Plateresque heritage of the campus, the cost of intricate Spanish-revival architecture, the genius of Watkin, the execution of Hedrick, but likewise the budgetary limitations and unrealized hopes of what could have been. Watkin was able to channel both recently experienced aesthetic concepts derived from his work with Ralph Adams Cram on the Houston Library along with yet-unused case studies drawn directly from sixteenth-century Spain. Albeit borrowing formative elements from Rice's Lovett Hall and some aesthetic components from Cram's emerging design of the Julia Ideson Library, the Administration Building would emerge as a new and different case study. While Cram's design for the Houston Library exposed Watkin and his office to a formative understanding of Spanish-revival building massing, it is important to note that Cram and Ferguson's contract for the library was limited to quarter-inch drawings—the balance of drawings and specifications fell to Watkin and Glover.[24] Watkin's team had already begun developing design details for what would become the Julia Ideson Library, and those details would likewise prove invaluable in charting the details for Tech's Administration Building.

The Administration Building would be a three-story building without a basement, with three floors of offices, general classroom space, and a stopgap library space for the college until a formal standalone library could be built. With a $350,000 construction budget, the initial Administration Building phase would be limited to the north wing, with extending ells and an enclosing arcade planned for later construction. In the meantime, the south façade corners would be finished with simple brick gable end walls as a temporary measure. Watkin's initial sketches from early spring 1924 included relatively squat tower forms positioned on the east and west ends of the north wing, but the final design incorporated more prominent belfries of curious origin.[25] Neither Arthur Byne nor other architectural writers of the period documented the bell tower at the Cathedral of Our Lady of the Assumption, the former mosque of incredible beauty in Córdoba. That tower, the Torre del Alminar (also known as the Torre Campanario), was documented extensively in Albert Frederick Calvert's extensive writings on Spain and in the travel sketchbooks published by the Boston Architectural Society,[26] to which Watkin likely had access. The iconic Torre had been converted in stages from an Islamic minaret into a Renaissance-era carillon tower beginning in 1593 by Hernan Ruiz III, and continued through 1664 by other maestros mayores.[27] Watkin's placement of openings, balustrades, finials, and buttresses in his carillon design was an unmistakable reference to the Córdoba landmark.

In the Julia Ideson Library design, Cram turned to Rodrigo Gil de Hontañon's circa-1537 design for the main façade to the Colegio Mayor de San Ildefonso at the Universidad Complutense in Alcalá. The writings of Byne, Whittlesey, and Prentice had placed great emphasis on the façade in Alcalá de Henares as a seminal example of the Renaissance aesthetic.[28] But where the central façade at Houston was

Present-day view of the northeast cloister façade of the Colegio Mayor Fonseca; Universidad de Salamanca. Considered one of the finest of the Plateresque-era cloisters in Spain, the ground-floor colonnade provided Watkin with vital inspiration for the Administration Building's south colonnade.

Present-day view of the north façade of the Texas Tech Administration Building, demonstrating similar massing, ordering, pilaster configuration, and ornament.

designed as condensed, square frontispiece iteration of the façade in Alcalá, Watkin adopted on the Administration Building at Tech a north entry façade that was more formatively representative of the Alcalá case study. The Lubbock façade differed from the Alcalá case study in large part due to fenestration into a pair of monumental interior stairways that flanked the central salle-porte of the Administration Building, requiring midrise arched windows at the intermediate landings of the stairwells.

As a twentieth-century regionalistic adaptation of the estilo plateresco, Watkin substituted the *heráldica real y hidalguía* of Spain with Texas vernacular—notably the seals of the six nations of Texas's past and present history. In fact, extremely similar detailing adorns both the Administration Building and the Ideson Library, where the same canted shields bearing the US and Texan seals of state appearing on the center parapet pediment to the Administration Building also appear within an aedicule arch on the Ideson Library façade. In an odd bit of irony, given that construction of the Ideson Library began in fact *after* construction of the Administration Building, details drawn at Tech may very well have been adapted for use on the Ideson Library.

It is also in the Administration Building that Watkin's selection of specific materials and colors are, in retrospect, appropriate to the South Plains. The use of Leuders limestone provided a light, contrasting palette ideal for articulating fine detailing, as compared to the coarse appearance of straked-face buff-blend of brick set in joints of very loosely tooled mortar. All of the brick masonry on the Administration Building would be laid in Flemish bond, so as to interlock into the structural clay tile of the building's exterior walls. As a brick masonry detail, upper floor panels of brick masonry would be framed with soldier and rowlock courses on all sides as a subtle

Present-day view of the northeast cloister facadefaçade of the Colegio Mayor Fonseca; Universidad de Salamanca. Considered one of the finest of the Plateresque-era cloisters in Spain, the ground-floor colonnade provided Watkin with vital inspiration for the Administration Building's south colonnade.

ornamental add. A terra cotta blend of barrel-form clay tile was, for such a Spanish-revival building, a given, and would be trimmed with copper flashing at eaves, gutters, and downspouts. This palette would oddly enough be selected less than a year later on the Julia Ideson Library as well, save that the canary-cream color selected for window mullion paint on Administration was substituted with a dark umber brown color in Houston. (This trim color is known today as "Texas Tech Ivory," and due to the university system's insistence to adopt and adhere to a common color that is used heavily for window and trim work, both Pantone and the Central European Color Standard (RAL) have assigned internationally recognized IDs for this color.)

In June, the board of directors received bids for the Administration Building, as well as the President's House to be situated at the southeast corner of campus. The cost premium of Leuders limestone was apparent as the college awarded a construction contract to Ramey Brothers of El Paso for $371,383.[29] Watkin's intention to clad the Administration Building in ornate Plateresque stonework had its consequences as the low-qualified stonework bidder, Bedford-Carthage Stone Company of Houston, who owned one of the three quarries in Leuders, was awarded the dressed stonework subcontract for $73,000. Nearly one-dollar-in-five being spent on the Administration Building was for stone veneer. Ramey Brothers commenced construction work on July 1, 1924, with a contractual construction completion date of May 1, 1925.[30] While the stone detailing was extravagant, no one anticipated what headaches would emerge because of the cream-gray limestone being quarried from outside of Leuders.

Later that fall, Watkin completed the final master plan, with revisions limited to the agricultural quadrangle to include Leidigh's Iowa-inspired livestock judging pavilion, a revised rail spur and power plant configuration, including a $3,038 rail switch and spur that Texas Tech was paying the Santa Fe Railroad to get fuel into campus.[31] Well received by the public, and run not only in Lubbock newspapers and the *Star-Telegram,* but even the *Houston Chronicle* plastered the college plan across the front page of their September 14th edition, claiming "[the] School will be most beautiful in state"[32]—a bold

Looking northeast toward the south colonnade of the Administration Building at Texas Tech, as inspired by the Colegio Mayor Fonseca in Salamanca.

(*Left*) Designing stone details as an aesthetic joke on the architect was nothing new in Beaux Arts–era design. Completed a year prior to the Tech master plan, staff at Watkin's office included a caricature of Watkin into a pilaster capital on the Rice Chemistry Building.

(*Right*) In an early 1980s interview, former Watkin employee Ruth Young Magonigle confirmed that the above flanking faces on the arabesques astride the south salle-porte arch at Administration were intended as a humorous caricature of Watkin.

prognostication for a city home to the Rice Institute. If Tech were to become beautiful, Watkin and his staff had to first feverishly complete detail drawings to colonnades, pilasters, Arabesques, and a bevy of other ornate stone elements on the Administration Building for the stone carvers at Leuders. Bedford-Carthage was beginning to run behind on delivering stone to Lubbock as early as August 9,[33] and even that stone consisted of the simple base courses of the building. Carvers had yet to even begin any of the most intricate detailing.

The cornerstone laying ceremony to the Texas Technological College Administration Building held on Armistice Day, November 11, 1924.

SOMETIME IN LATE SUMMER 1924, a young man arrived in Lubbock. Young, stocky, and handsome, William G. McMillan was of all things a former football star at Texas A&M, having defeated the hated Texas Longhorns the year before as a senior starting quarterback for the Aggies.[34] McMillan had been hired on a contractor's timekeeper for the construction of the seven-story Hotel Lubbock[35]—one of many new projects underway across a booming Lubbock. Planned to become Lubbock's tallest building and later renamed as the Pioneer Hotel, it was another neoclassical design by Sanguinet, Staats & Hedrick—one of many Edwardian-styled high-rises designed by the Fort Worth firm. With a degree in business administration, McMillan liked Lubbock but was discontent with his new job and moved quickly to make acquaintances in hopes of bigger plans for his future

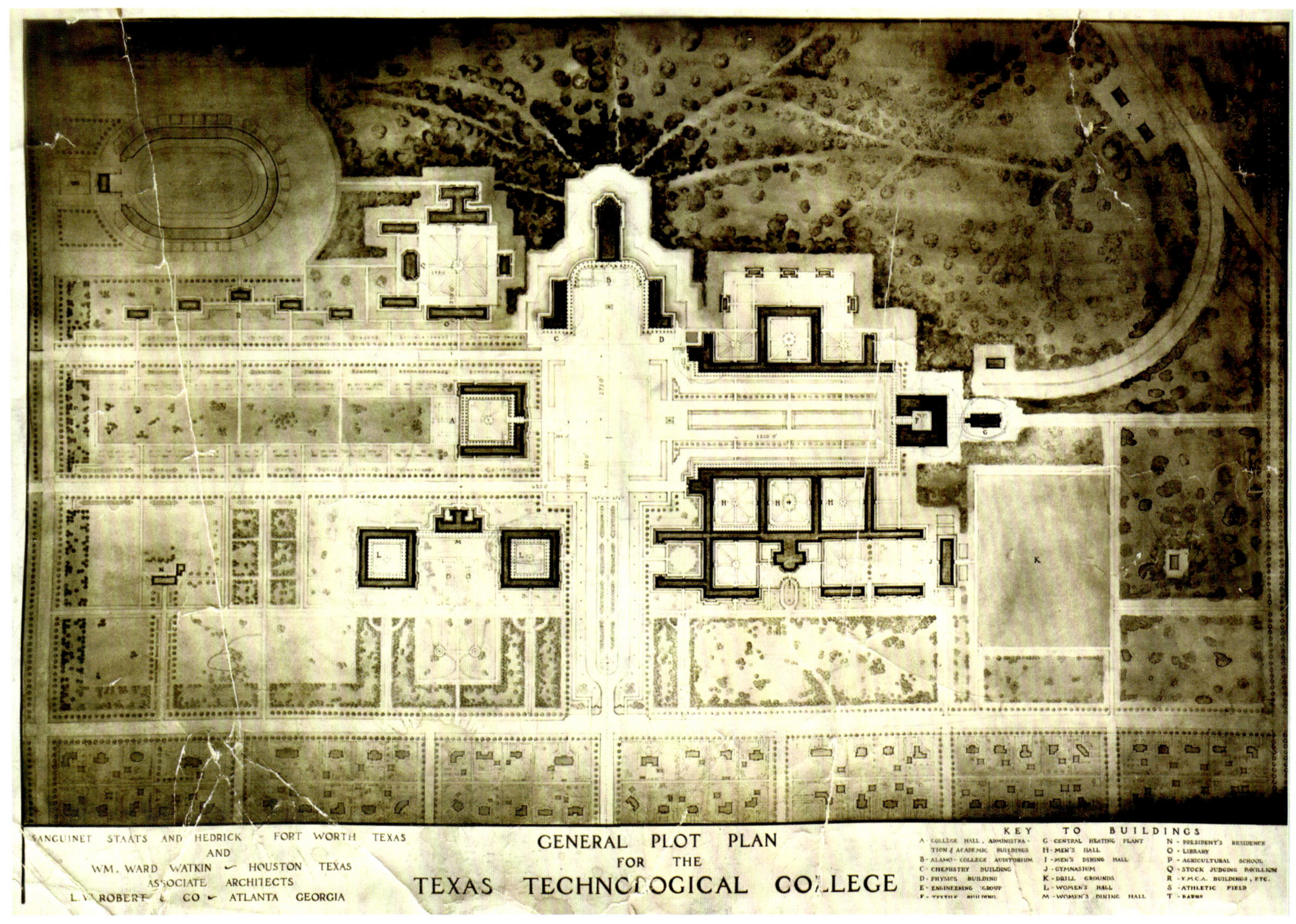

Final General Plan for the campus of Texas Technological College, as completed by William Ward Watkin, fall 1924.

career. It might take time, but young Bill McMillan was determined to run his own contracting business one day.

BACK AT TECH, attention had now solidly shifted toward the remaining buildings, including the Livestock Judging Pavilion and the Textile Engineering Building. With Hedrick's office finished with drawings and specifications for both buildings, it was at this moment that the college affirmed their faith in Watkin's broad campus plan, and the board approved siting both buildings exactly where the campus plan dictated[36]—over a thousand feet away from the Administration Building. Many people now had placed their faith in Watkin's plan, whether or not realizing that years would pass where the campus would appear barren and spotty. Three weeks after those projects were let, college leadership held a cornerstone-laying ceremony for the Administration Building on the sixth anniversary of Armistice Day—November 11, 1924 which honored the end of the Great War. Governor Neff attended, along with other political and academic luminaries, all of whom arrived in Lubbock to see the raw ferroconcrete skeleton of the Administration Building towering over the west Lubbock plains, replete with steel frames now in place for the two bell towers. Any question as to public sentiment toward the college became confirmed when approximately twenty thousand people—nearly two times the population of Lubbock at the time—attended the ceremony.[37] Watkin, unable to attend, relayed his sentiments in a letter to Paul Horn four days later: "The expressions of confidence in the school's future as I read them from Governor Neff's speech . . . show that the vision of the school's possibilities is gradually taking a definite hold, and I think [the school] has a splendid future ahead of it."[38]

6

START WALKING

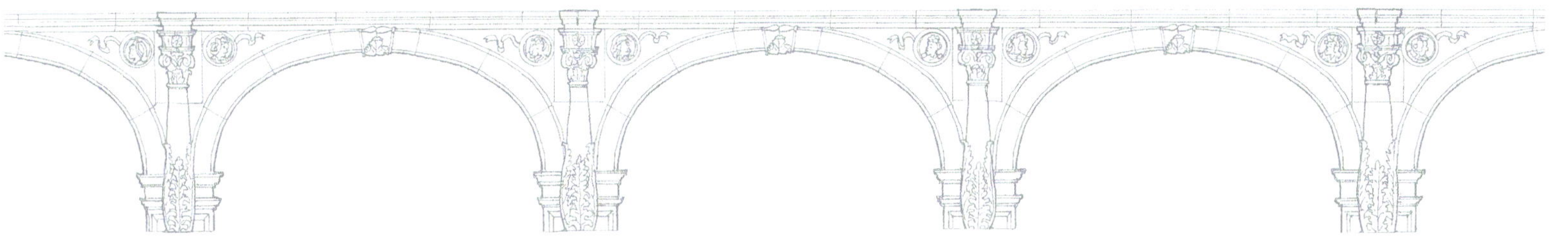

Everyone was becoming exasperated with the delivery of stone to the Administration Building. Bedford-Carthage had promised two carloads per week beginning after August 9, 1924, with all of the Leuders stone to be on site in Lubbock by New Year's Day 1925.[1] Watkin's draftsmen had burned the midnight oil completing shop drawings for the fabricators in Leuders, but were nonetheless a month-and-a-half late completing all of them,[2] though their tardiness was not entirely their doing. Watkin patiently corresponded with Horn into December 1924, as the president had originally hoped to have a single inspirational quote carved along the south frieze overhead of the south court colonnade. Watkin suggested in a December 15 letter that the width of the frieze warranted listing individual names in lieu of Horn's original desire for a continuous quote, and that perhaps enshrining the names of fifteen Texas heroes would be appropriate.[3] Horn settled on a compromise, opting instead for engraving the names fifteen noted individuals in science, art, literature, statecraft, and mathematics.[4] One of the names—that of Michelangelo di Lodovico Buonarroti Simoni—was ultimately carved in the split surname form that was common of the day: "MICHEL ANGELO." Horn also relayed quotations for the north façade—two quotes to be set in the entablature over the *arco carpanel* of the salle-porte. Horn's first choice came from Solomon's Proverbs: "Righteousness exalteth a nation; but sin is a reproach to any people" (Proverbs 14: 34). The other was a well-worn quote by the second president of the Texas Republic Mirabeau Lamar—a quote that had already appeared on other buildings statewide, most notably Henry Trost's neoclassical El Paso High School[5] and the State Capitol:[6] "A cultivated mind is the guardian genius of a democracy."

It was around this same time they were determining engraved verbiage that Watkin also developed at Horn's request a design for the seal of the college. Following some minor revisions submitted by Horn, the seal would include five key elements: a lamp symbolizing "school," a key representing "home," a star representative of the "state," and a book representing "church"; all situated in a quadrant shield grasped by the talons of an eagle representing the United States.[7] In a bit of regional vernacular design, the quadrants of the

The carved Lueders stone product for the seal of Texas Technological College, designed by William Ward Watkin with consultation by Paul W. Horn, 1924 and 1925.

shield would be divided by a commandment cross of ten cotton bolls. (A "commandment cross" in heraldry is a reference to a dividing cross to a shield filled with ten heraldic elements representing those Ten Commandments found in Exodus:20. In heraldry, these are often divided between four horizontal elements representing those commandments that exist between God and man, and six vertical elements representing those commandments established between man and fellowman.) Watkin hurriedly completed the final seal for the board of directors's approval, along with Horn's engravings, all of which were approved at the January 6, 1925 board meeting.[8] Once approved, Watkin's office rushed drawings of the seal to Bedford-Carthage, who needed the seal design for the pair of seals to be set over the north

One of many quarry pits outside of Lueders, Texas. One USGS report in 1951 described the Oolitic limestone quarried at Lueders to be the second-finest stone available from any quarry in the United States.

salle-porte. It was also during this shop drawing phase that members of Watkin's staff continued a humorous Beaux-Arts–era tradition of sneaking carved caricatures of design architects into neoclassical stone building detailing. Around the same time at Princeton, conspiring draftsmen and stone carvers had slipped a bespectacled representation of Ralph Adams Cram onto a keystone crocket over an arch of the new Cram-designed University Chapel.[9] Paul Horn and other Tech leaders were likely unaware that Watkin's draftsperson Ruth Young had slipped a pair of flanking profiles of William Ward Watkin onto an Arabesque situated astride the south salle-porte arch to the Administration Building.[10] Staff had already detailed a more expansive caricature of Watkin over a column capital at the new Chemistry Building project at Rice.[11] But the seals and caricature busts were but minor details overshadowed by the myriad issues Leuders was battling in completing their massive fabrication order for the new college.

Bedford-Carthage was charged to fabricate over four thousand tons of ornate dressed limestone alone for the Administration Building, representing the most ornate composition of carved stone ever placed on a Texas building west of the Brazos to date. Leuders did have railroad service into Abilene in 1924, but quarry craftsmen could not complete the detailed carving fast enough to fill rail cars to meet freight quota. Bedford-Carthage could not afford the high

Likely late spring or early summer 1925 photograph of mason and construction labor in front of the Administration Building north façade. Note the horse-drawn cart loaded with dressed balusters to the right.

President's House, undated. Sanguinet, Staats & Hedrick, architects.

Texas Tech's Livestock Judging Pavilion, photograph dated shortly after completion in 1925.

Students at work in one of the textile machinery halls of the Textile Engineering Building at Texas Tech, undated.

expense of shipping partial loads by rail to Lubbock,[12] leaving them no choice but to resort to a dated, but available solution. Stone pieces were packed into crates and loaded onto horse-, mule-, and ox-drawn carts to make the 170-mile trek from Leuders to Lubbock. The Lubbock Chamber of Commerce had been quick to boast their new city nickname as "The Hub City"—a reference to the myriad roads that spoked into Lubbock, but conveniently failed to note in marketing media that most of these roads into the city in 1924 were little more than dirt ruts. In fact, with practically no state or federal highway system in place in the 1920s, Texans had to rely on a loose network of quasi-privately funded roads that crisscrossed the state. The High Plains Air-Line—a mostly dirt road between Fort Worth and Lubbock that had no bridge crossings at the western forks of the Brazos River, happened to run near Leuders.[13] Cart teams made the near two-week round trip up and down the Air-Line to Lubbock to unload the scant few tons of stone that horses and oxen could manageably carry. At this rate, it would take months for Leuders to complete their order—nearly six extra months in fact.[14]

Concern among the board continued to build regarding the stone delay. Drywall as a building material existed in 1925, but was a novelty alternative available in East Coast locales, and not in Lubbock. Rather, the commonplace finish for interior wall and ceiling finishing

Southwick Hall at the Lowell Technical Institute (now the University of Massachusetts—Lowell); one of the most comprehensive textile training facilities in the United States in the early twentieth century and visited by a delegation from Texas Tech in early 1924.

was plaster-and-lath construction, but interior gypsum plaster required having a near totally sealed building envelope, which was still impossible at the Administration Building as brick could not be laid or windows installed while much of the stone veneer of the building sat undressed in a quarry in Leuders.

Elsewhere, Ramey's work on the President's House and Livestock Judging Pavilion were moving along splendidly, and Dr. and Mrs. Horn and their daughter moved into their home—the college's first completed building—on February 19.[15] Watkin had envisioned a relatively spartan and more Spanish-colonial design for the two-story President's House, which demonstrated his vision for a more complex hierarchy to aesthetics employed between academic and residential architecture at Tech. The President's House, clad with clay tile roofs, was largely a stucco mass with limited detail, and, if anything, resembled a design more akin to the Spanish-colonial-revival work of George Washington Smith in California. To the west, the Livestock Judging Pavilion—an elongated octagon in plan with a clay tile–clad hip roof divided into a lower roof and upper lantern with clerestory windows—likewise reflected Watkin's intent to apply lesser detail and ornament to secondary campus buildings. The pavilion, though a "secondary" building at a cost of $34,722.20,[16] was completed and accepted in late March. Without a college gymnasium in 1925, the enlarged version of the Iowa State Pavilion would prove invaluable in holding Tech's first basketball matches.

Even without the plodding delays on the Administration Building to contend with, spring 1925 was an unceasing whirlwind of activity in Lubbock, Fort Worth, Houston, and now Atlanta. Chip Roberts's team, though involved early on analyzing peer textile engineering institutions that were visited in 1924, were now designing Tech's textile laboratories and production plants, as well as some of the civil and mechanical engineering components of the campus physical plant. Robert's office was in consultation with East Coast millinery plant manufacturers in late 1924 establishing a textile plant equipment scope for training in the production of finished cotton and woolen fabric goods. Based on a December 10, 1924, outlay issued to the Tech Board of Directors, Roberts estimated that cotton ginning, delinting, testing equipment, wool carding and production, spinning, weaving, fabric design, dyeing and bleaching, and knitting and mercerizing machinery would cost the college an additional $102,790[17]—funds the college would have to request from the state legislature. That mass of equipment would be housed in laboratory bays of the new two-story, 28,130-square-foot Textile Engineering Building situated at the north end of the yet-to-be-named Engineering Key.

The Textile Engineering Building represented a handsome compromise between the ornate detail of the Administration Building and the second tier of stucco-clad buildings envisioned by Watkin for ancillary roles on the Tech campus. It was a very "California" building in the vein of those exhibition halls found at Balboa Park in which detail and ornament was concentrated at entries, but with Texas brick substituted in lieu of stucco for the comparably simple exterior treatment to the balance of the building. The $85,500 building was generally loved by everyone, with Paul Horn having once stated

Present-day view of central south salle-porte façade to the Textile Engineering Building (today Industrial Engineering)—perhaps the most Churrigueresque of Tech buildings. Note the engaged scallop shells ringing the salle-porte arch, as well as the cotton bales inset and flanking the second-floor window.

of it, "I think that in some respects this is the handsomest building we are to have." [18] Textile Engineering's Alta California appearance may explain in part Horn and others' habit during this period of describing Tech's architecture as "mission-style." [19] Stonework was limited only to minor details in the springlines of its south colonnade and the circumference of the building's parapet, as well of course as the ornate main entry façade. Situated at its centerline to the salle-porte centerline of the Administration Building some 1,534 feet to the south, the Textile Administration Building too had a salle-porte arch intended to connect through the building north to a future engineering courtyard, and further northward to the college's future power plant building.

The plan for Textile Engineering—yet another "square donut" did not owe its inspiration as much from Castilian planning principles, but rather from the plan and textile hall configurations of Southwick Hall at the Lowell Technical Institute in Massachusetts. Built in 1903, Southwick too had a main entry salle-porte, and so provided

The Churrigueresque-revival central entry façade to the California State Building at Balboa Park.

Designed by San Diego architect William Templeton Johnson, the west façade to the United States Pavilion at the Ibero-American Exposition at Sevilla (1929) joins the California State Building and Textile Engineering as the three known scallop shell-arched buildings of the Beaux-Arts era.

Roberts and Watkin with a straightforward case study to blend a successful East Coast case study with Spanish-revival planning strategies at Tech. But Textile Engineering's beautiful entry was a direct inspiration of Goodhue's masterpiece façade of the California State Building (today known as the San Diego Museum of Man). The Textile Engineering façade is perhaps one of the less Plateresque components of the Tech campus—the frenetic undulation found around its entry feature is more commensurate of Churrigueresque architecture—the style Goodhue and Winslow had largely adopted in San Diego. The centerpiece to Textile Engineering is beautiful both in proportion and ornament with two pairs of Arabesque-clad Corinthian-engaged columns flanking a profusely detailed archway. Even the salle-porte stone arch itself was clad in an *arcature*—a collection of fifteen recessed conches—each carefully carved by Leuders craftsmen. The conch arcature was a uniquely neoclassical concept envisioned by Goodhue for the California State Building façade, and as best known has only repeated twice—here at Texas Tech, and on the entry façade to San Diego architect William Templeton Johnson's United States Pavilion at the Ibero-American Exposition of 1929 in Sevilla. Watkin had designed a protruding balcony over the archway beset with a *reja* railing, but it was in the pair of inset conches that flanked the second floor central window where Watkin incorporated a bit of circa-1924 regionalism with each conch featuring a carved stone cotton bale set to highlight the intended use of the building. Watkin would have had access to drawings of the California State Building façade—both a monograph of Goodhue's work and his drawings existed at the time, and elevations of the façade appeared in an *Architectural Record* article in 1915.[20] It was one of the few sources of inspiration at Tech that Watkin would not draw from Spain and further illustrated the importance of Balboa Park as an inspirational case study in both plan and aesthetic strategy at Texas Tech.

BY MAY, the exterior of Textile Engineering was nearing completion, and Robert's office was completing textile machinery delivery

Undated image of Textile Engineering, illustrating the simpler Spanish colonial-revival details of her colonnade and façade work.

Masonry progress on Administration finally making headway mid-1925. The brick-clad gable walls south of the carillon towers were intended as short-term cladding, though they would remain for over twenty-five years.

Portion of the artesonado ceiling of the atrium to the Julia Ideson Library, Houston. Cram's library design would be admittedly constructed on a more luxuriant budget, allowing for the richly ornate Spanish Mudéjar ceiling.

Example of the entry doorway to the carillon towers of the Administration Building, inspired by works at Sigüenza Cathedral.

and field installation instructions for the contractor. Back in Atlanta, Chip Roberts welcomed an architecture student from his own alma mater Georgia Tech onto his staff as a draftsman. It is very likely that the new hire worked on the Tech commission in some fashion, as final machinery shop drawings were reviewed by Robert's office that June. An Alabama native, at some point in college, the new employee had acquired the nickname "Skeet," as too many Southerners had difficulty with correctly pronouncing his Welsh given name.[21] Though thirty-four years would pass until he himself would be designing hundreds of thousands of square feet of buildings on the Texas Tech campus, little did anyone know what an important name in Texas architecture, or the architecture of Texas Tech for that matter, Llewellyn Pitts would one day be.

WHAT WOULD a Texas college be without football? In April 1925, Paul Horn's search for a football coach was underway. Horn went so far as to reach out to famed Notre Dame coach Knute Rockne for advice, and Rockne was kind enough to send some recommendations back to Horn.[22] After deliberating, both the Tech president and board of directors agreed during their April 19 meeting on a former Vanderbilt lettermen and later Southern Methodist University head coach—Ewing Young Freeland. Freeland's dual coaching experience in football and baseball made him that much more valuable as he could coach both programs, serve as athletic director, and all at the cost of a single faculty member. Freeland, nicknamed "Big 'Un" by those who knew him—accepted, and he and his wife Sammye arrived from Dallas that summer, and were quickly impressed with the emerging campus. Sammye in particular was taken in by Tech's Spanish architectural character, suggesting to her husband that the College mascot should be the "Matador,"[23] and likewise use the colors red and black in honor of the archetypal hero of the Spanish bullring. Freeland passed his wife's recommendation on to President Horn. Sammye Freeland's suggestion likely solved a prickly problem with Horn and the board of directors, as Amon Carter had been keen on naming the Texas Tech mascot Dogies, in honor of a calf whose mother had died but doggedly survived by fending for itself. Carter had gone so far as to use the *Star-Telegram* as a bully pulpit by publicly shopping the mascot idea in an editorial.[24] A helpless calf as a mascot did not inspire fear in a state where one major state university already had an adult cow for a mascot. So Horn and the board eagerly accepted Sammye Freeland's architecturally inspired suggestion for discussion later that summer in executive session.[25]

With only dirt and 2 × 10 planks, students, faculty, and guests assemble in front of the Administration Building on October 1, 1925, for commencement of classes.

THE ADMINISTRATION BUILDING was finally nearing completion. By September, final stone shipments for the Carillon Towers and twin interior stairways arrived from Leuders. The Administration Building featured four stairways—two more modestly detailed stucco-and-tile stairs situated within the Carillon Towers, as well as two central grand stairways discharging into the salle-porte. The latter pair had afforded Watkin the rare opportunity in the Tech commission to incorporate Plateresque interior detailing, in which the Houston architect modeled Tech's stairs from maestro mayor Alonso de Covarrubias's seminal circa-1524 stairway connecting the library to the interior patio at the Palacio Arzobispal in Alcalá de Henares.[26] Covarrubias's stair had been carefully documented in the building section by Arthur Byne and Mildred Stapley in their 1917 book *Spanish Architecture of the Sixteenth Century*.[27] Watkin would design similarly scaled and ornamented balusters and newel posts to the Alcála case study, but any hopes to incorporate an *artesonado* ceiling similar to what Cram had planned for the central gallery of the Julia Ideson Library, and the stunning *techo artesonado* crowning Covarrubias's Palacio Arzobispal stair had been dashed. In the fifteenth and sixteenth centuries, Mudéjar carpenters were renowned for their skill for using what paltry resources of Spanish timber were available in Castile and Andalusia, and intricately crafted repetitive geometrically patterned ceilings out of many smaller pieces of wood, often without ever using a single nail. Known to the Spanish as techos artesonados, the craft had originated from Moorish maestros mayores who fashioned complex geometrically patterned artesonado ceilings and adorned them with rich colors and gold inlay. But with the Administration Building's budget spiraling due to change orders beyond $434,000,[28] Horn and the board simply wanted their flagship building done. Hedrick's own drawings for the stairs from the previous year only indicated a simple moulding-edged plaster ceiling. For such a distinctive element of the estilo plateresco, it was unfortunate that no artesonado ceilings had been incorporated into the early Tech campus.

Even without artesonado ceilings, the Administration Building was a trove of Plateresque-revival design and detailing whose handsome composition was finally becoming appreciated as final touches were completed. Rejería, custom wrought iron grille-work, arrived that summer for installation at small ornamental windows, carillon stairs, and transom windows at entries along the building's south colonnade. Situated above the Sigüenza Cathedral-inspired side entrances at the base of the two carillon towers, Watkin had amended Hedrick's construction drawings to include two identical second-floor stairwell rose windows, issuing fabrication drawings to Leuders in early 1925 for an elongated rose window whose rejas were inspired by the Churrigueresque-styled sacristy window to the Mission San José y San Miguel de Aguayo in San Antonio (built 1720–1768). Even as the rose window rejas were installed, Watkin could not make the train trip to Lubbock to observe completion status on the new campus and buildings, as he was departing with his family for a summer sabbatical in Spain on the recommendation of his mentor Ralph Adams Cram. Watkin would visit many sites across Castile and Andalusia, including the Cathedral/Mosque and Torre del Alminar in Córdoba.[29]

Even with additional state emergency funds, Texas Technological College was barely able to reach an operational status when the doors of the college opened for its first fall semester. Though buildings were ready, books and furnishings were in place, and Chip Robert's textile mill machinery was operational, the breakneck race to completion still left the new Lubbock campus a diamond in the rough at best. The board of directors had ordered the final $20,000 in campus funds liquidated to pay for any remaining roads, paths, or building work that Horn and his staff deemed crucial to complete before convocation.[30] At 10:00 a.m. on Thursday, October 1, when convocation assembly was held north of the Administration Building, the best the college could muster for event seating was to run 2 x 10 lumber planks across to make benches for attendees.[31] Only a handful of trees existed on campus—mostly existing elms and mulberries—and practically no grass was planted around any of the new buildings. Sidewalks were practically nonexistent, which did not help matters for the estimated eight thousand visitors in attendance as it rained later on Convocation Day. Texas Technological College possessed no dormitories, no street lights, no stadium, and ran its bookstore out of a converted two-story wood shack. Tech now had six operational primary buildings, of which only three—Administration, Home Economics, and Textile Engineering—represented the more ornate high Spanish Renaissance vision of the new college. But boosterism and constant headlining by Amon Carter in the *Star-Telegram* presented a statewide impression that an oasis equal to the Alhambra had emerged on the plains west of Lubbock. Carter even ordered the *Star-Telegram* to run full-page ads in rival newspapers like the *Morning Avalanche* in Lubbock or the *Amarillo Daily News* extolling the new college.[32] Within two weeks after the opening of classes for the fall semester—on October 15, 1925—Texas Technological College reported to the State Board of Control that 910 students had enrolled at the new school,[33] far more than anyone, even the propagandizing Carter, had ever hoped for. To Paul Horn, the enrollment news was a vindication of massive proportions that for the time being would quell the naysaying from the eastern half of the state about Texas Tech.

As the story goes, Pat Neff—who had signed Senate Bill 103 into law in 1923 and had only recently stepped down from his governorship, may have had less faith in Texas Tech being a success. Carter and his allies had generated such a furor for a West Texas college platform that Neff's support in 1923 for Tech was a political mandate. Neff, likely at the Armistice Day 1924 cornerstone laying ceremony, confided his personal opinions in confidence to Horn, that "if even a thousand students were to enroll at Tech, [Neff] would personally walk to Lubbock." The moment of humor was not lost on a satisfied Paul Whitfield Horn eleven months later when he received the enrollment report. Horn dictated to his secretary a brief telegram to be cabled to Pat Neff's home in Waco.[34]

It read simply: "Start walking."

PART II

SURVIVAL

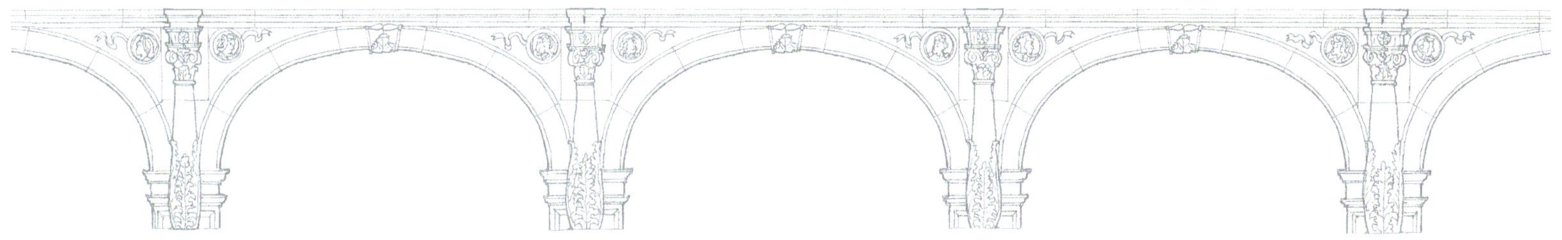

No great institution is ever built alone upon money, or the brick, the stone and the steel which money can buy. More, it is built upon the brains and sinew and the blood of men who alone can make of a thing of masonry a lasting contribution to civilization.

—Editorial tribute to the late Dr. Bradford Knapp, second president of Texas Technological College. *Sunday Avalanche-Journal,* June 12, 1938.

(*Opposite top*) Undated aerial photograph of the Texas Technological College campus, looking south toward campus and town.

(*Opposite bottom*) In the embryonic years of Texas Tech, teaching crop fields existed in areas that are today part of the campus core.

7

A SPANISH TRIUMPH

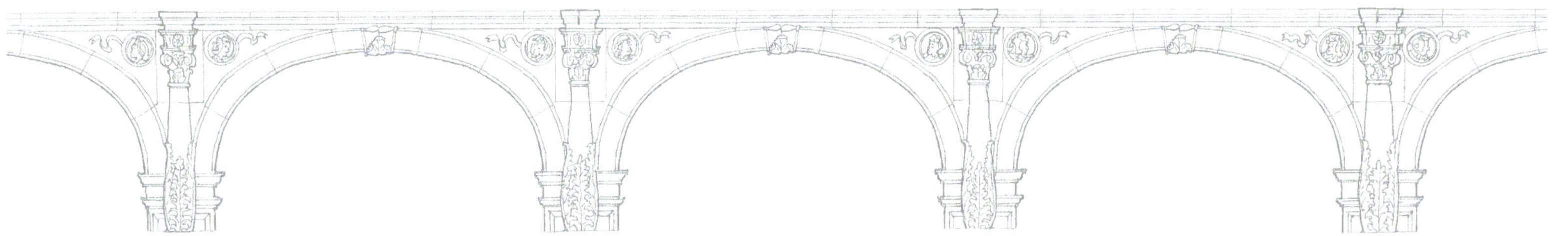

AT 6:43 A.M. ON MONDAY, JUNE 29, 1925, resounder terminals across the Southern Pacific Railroad's telegraph network fell silent at stations across Southern California. The Southern Pacific Line already had in the 1920s one of the finest telegraphic networks in the United States (a network that decades later would divest from the Southern Pacific and become its own telecom company—then known as the Southern Pacific Railroad Internal Network Telecommunications system, or SPRINT).[1] The reason for the failure became clear in coastal towns northwest of Los Angeles moments later as tremors alerted to an earthquake having just occurred. After a short repair effort, only one station on the line remained off the network signaling the likely epicenter of the quake at Santa Barbara.

Though the earthquake only lasted nineteen seconds,[2] a fraction in comparison to the forty-two-second quake that had devastated San Francisco in 1906, the magnitude 6.8 tremor nonetheless laid ruin to Santa Barbara. Thankfully, most residents were still at home waking up for the day, with few occupying any of the multistory buildings in the city center—the Victorian and neoclassical hotels, office buildings, and businesses that failed—leaving the city center in rubble. Above the city, the 720-foot-long Sheffield Dam, a new earthen dam that retained forty-five-million gallons of Santa Barbara's water supply became the first dam in American history to fail during an earthquake. Excessively sandy soil under the dam succumbed to liquefaction, sending a land-borne tsunami of earth, water, and debris charging downhill toward the city. The potential repeat of structural fires two decades earlier in San Francisco was largely spared as utility workers quickly shut down electrical power to the city and shut off the city's natural gas supply. Remarkably, only thirteen people would perish.

The nation was transfixed by the Santa Barbara disaster, as police, relief aid, and medical care providers rushed from throughout the region to the stricken city. The next day, the Santa Barbara *Morning Press* shouted from the front page the intentions of the community:

California led the nation, and perhaps much of the world into the final revivalist architectural movement—the Spanish-revival movement. Particularly catalytic to that movement was Balboa Park, where neoclassical or Victorian architecture was cast aside in lieu of Spanish themes. Here, in 1915, a new Spanish-revival Union Station awaits opening as the Victorian-era Southern Pacific Rail Terminal is ingloriously torn down.

"CITY TO REBUILD AT ONCE!"[3] What few realized at the time was that out of the rubble of the 1925 Santa Barbara earthquake was a final, seminal catalyst in initiating the last great neoclassical revival movement in the United States—the Spanish-revival movement. In fact, neoclassicism and the revivalist era were already singing their swan songs. A month before the Santa Barbara earthquake, yet another world's fair had opened in Paris, but not an event in any way resembling the neoclassical white cities of the past. The L'Exposition Internationale des Arts Décoratifs et Industriels Modernes was an event designed specifically to showcase the latest in modern art, architecture, and fashion styles emerging from the ashes of the Great War. An abbreviation of the fair's name would become the lasting moniker of the resulting design movement that it would spawn—art deco. For the remainder of the decade, Spanish-revival architecture was practically the only revivalist style still considered en vogue given the sudden and rapid proliferation of the art deco movement.

Santa Barbara was already an economically strong and diverse community in 1925—oil had been recently discovered along the Santa Barbara coastline, and the community had been the birthplace to the motion picture and aviation industries. This prosperity provided the needed capital and urgency to rebuild Santa Barbara into a Spanish-colonial-stylized paradise. Relatively little architecture in Santa Barbara constructed prior to the 1925 earthquake was built in the now-ubiquitous Spanish-colonial revival style commonplace in Southern California. Neoclassical, second empire, Romanesque-revival, Victorian, and more exotic Moorish-revival prevailed throughout the city prior to the disaster. It was the work of recently arrived architects like George Washington Smith who demonstrated what the Spanish-colonial-revival style could provide if adapted en masse to a variety of building types, including schools, businesses, and single- and multifamily homes. Local organizations like the Community Art Association, a newly formed nongovernmental body of local citizens captivated with Santa Barbara's historic past, proposed efforts to further embrace a unified Spanish style in the city's reconstruction. In response, the city formed two committees that had review authority over all new construction, and much like Juan de Herrera 350 years earlier, exercised draconian authority in enforcing a Spanish-revival style to any project that crossed their desk.

In short time, the destroyed storefronts and façades throughout the city center transformed into idyllic whitewashed stucco façades with colonnaded esplanades, stone-clad entrances, and red clay tile roofs, while rebuilt neighborhoods likewise transformed into Spanish-hued enclaves. A new Spanish-colonial-revival centerpiece county courthouse designed by William Mooser III was completed in 1929 to national acclaim, replete with custom rejería, Spanish tile floors with polychrome inlay, and artesonado wood ceilings. The grand transformation caught the attention of national newspapers, as well as architectural publications of the period, namely *Architectural*

William Mooser's iconic City Hall Building for Santa Barbara, completed in 1929, represented a seminal example of the citywide Spanish-colonial revival rebuilding efforts.

Forum, *Architectural Record*, and a growing new California-based publication—John C. Brasfield's *The Architectural Digest*. Though not yet the Condé Nast–owned symbol of en vogue residential design it is today, when established in 1920, Brasfield intended the magazine as little more than a booster piece for California architecture, in particular targeting distribution in newsstands at rail stations whose lines served the West and Southwest. Given *The Architectural Digest* highlighted California architecture, it could not be helped that the vast majority of architecture showcased in the magazine was Spanish revival.[5] Though to Brasfield and the public were unaware, *Architectural Digest* became a germinator for spreading interest in Spanish-revival architecture across the nation.

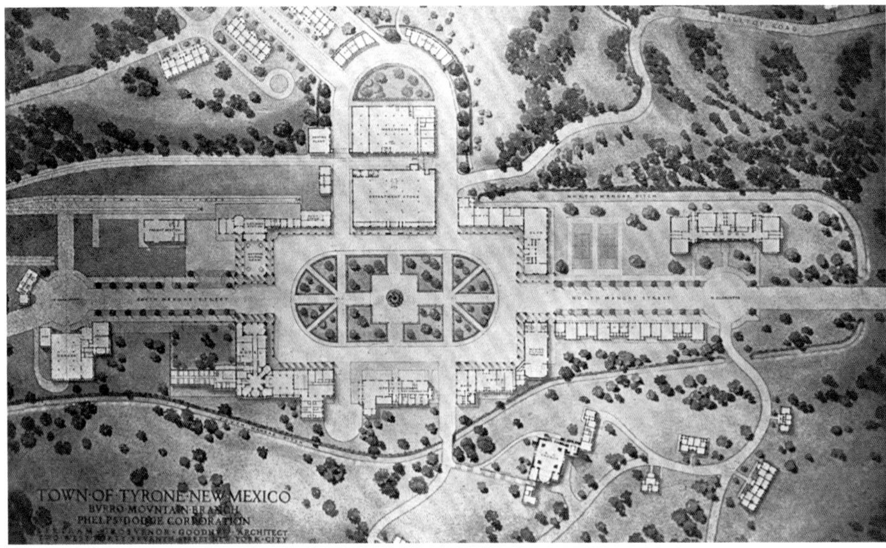

Nestled in the Burro Mountains of southwestern New Mexico, Bertram Goodhue's master plan for the mining community of Tyrone retained Spanish-styled features common to his plans, such as a large central rectilinear plaza connected to linear prado-like malls.

If Goodhue's exposition design in San Diego had primed the pump of interest toward Spanish-revival architecture, the reconstruction of post-earthquake Santa Barbara propelled the movement into overdrive. Spanish-revival architecture had been with rare exception, by the end of the World War I, a limited, regional movement captured largely by those areas of the country where Spanish historical influence had prevailed. Even then, interest in Spanish idioms was mixed, and in many areas of Texas, Florida, and California, practically nonexistent. Balboa Park's continued existence and prosperity after 1916, as well as the overall economic prosperity throughout California where the movement was strongest, kept a brightly lit pilot light burning and ready to ignite a larger national movement. Many of the opportunities to expand the Spanish-revival movement in the United States emerged directly from San Diego as a result.

Edith Douglas, the wife of Phelps-Dodge Mining Company general manager Walter Douglas, became enchanted with Goodhue's Balboa Park design when she visited the Panama-California Exposition in 1915. Walter Douglas, however, was far more concerned with locating US sources of copper while a war raged in Europe. Phelps-Dodge had scouted rich copper deposits in the Burro Mountains, just south of Silver City, New Mexico, and spurred by his wife's suggestion, Douglas hired Goodhue to design a Spanish-revival city for his miners and families. Goodhue's design for what became the town of Tyrone, New Mexico—his only foray into civic urban planning—was an elegant blend of Churrigueresque-revival and Spanish-colonial-revival architecture, intermixing the symmetry of a Beaux-Arts–inspired plan into the irregular plan of the scrub-covered valleys of the Burro Mountains. Goodhue's city plan even featured yet another smaller domed church and carillon tower. Tyrone had been so sufficiently built out per Goodhue's plans that by 1917, four thousand people lived there, and by 1920 it was the seventh-largest city in New Mexico.[6] Tyrone joined a growing chorus of California projects and planned communities like Ajo, Arizona,[7] which heralded a Spanish-revival wave that would sweep across much of the western United States.

But that wave had yet to hit Texas, and despite the Lone Star State's

Battle Hall main (east) elevation, University of Texas at Austin; Cass Gilbert, architect, 1911.

The peculiar forms of the Atascosa County Courthouse, Jourdanton, Texas, undated.

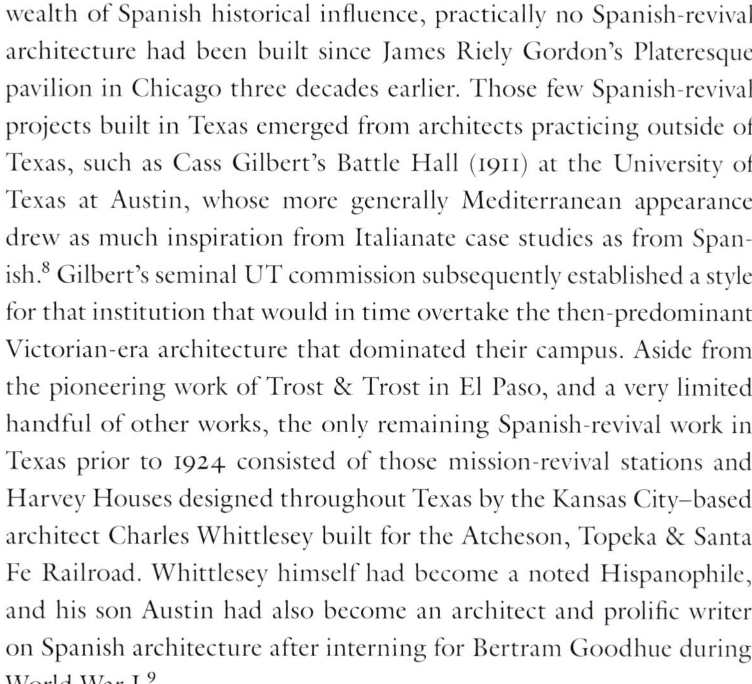

wealth of Spanish historical influence, practically no Spanish-revival architecture had been built since James Riely Gordon's Plateresque pavilion in Chicago three decades earlier. Those few Spanish-revival projects built in Texas emerged from architects practicing outside of Texas, such as Cass Gilbert's Battle Hall (1911) at the University of Texas at Austin, whose more generally Mediterranean appearance drew as much inspiration from Italianate case studies as from Spanish.[8] Gilbert's seminal UT commission subsequently established a style for that institution that would in time overtake the then-predominant Victorian-era architecture that dominated their campus. Aside from the pioneering work of Trost & Trost in El Paso, and a very limited handful of other works, the only remaining Spanish-revival work in Texas prior to 1924 consisted of those mission-revival stations and Harvey Houses designed throughout Texas by the Kansas City–based architect Charles Whittlesey built for the Atcheson, Topeka & Santa Fe Railroad. Whittlesey himself had become a noted Hispanophile, and his son Austin had also become an architect and prolific writer on Spanish architecture after interning for Bertram Goodhue during World War I.[9]

It is debatable as to the reason for Texas being such a late bloomer in the Spanish-revival movement. A combination of potential racial overtones coupled with a dogged insistence by Texas politicians and businessmen to embrace anything East Coast–like to demonstrate that Texas possessed both sophistication and a growing economy were most likely the culprits as to the lag. However, one pragmatic reason for the delay may simply have been that the predominant Spanish style of the day—the California mission style—was at best an awkward combination with what was and remains today Texas' most prevalent exterior building veneer—brick. Few buildings combined the Spanish-revival style and veneer, and those that did, such as Francis Wilson's 1911 Casa del Desierto—a Santa Fe station and Harvey House in Barstow, California, and the circa-1912 Atascosa County Courthouse in Jourdanton, Texas,[10] appear as odd conglomerations that were not repeated elsewhere. Higher-profile architectural case studies such as the Julia Ideson Library and Texas Technological College were necessary to finally burst the dam that unleashed a tidal wave of Spanish-revival design in Texas. Interestingly enough, 1925 would be the year in which the glass ceiling shattered, likely due to the media exposure

Built at the foot of a mountain visited by Spanish explorer Hernando de Soto, the Spanish-revival-styled Arlington Hotel in Hot Springs, Arkansas, undated.

Originally built for the Panama-California Exposition as the Southern Counties Building and designed by Goodhue protege Carleton Winslow, the San Diego City Auditorium at Balboa Park, would until its 1925 destruction serve as a seminal inspiration to a score of Spanish-revival civic buildings throughout Texas.

Texas Tech, the Julia Ideson Library, and other projects received in newspaper headlines across the state.

A national phenomenon emerged with Spanish motifs appearing across a myriad of building types, scales, and forms. The world's first indoor self-storage facility—the Hollywood Storage Company Building—a forerunner to thousands of such facilities that exist today—was completed in Los Angeles in 1925 as a twelve-story blend of Plateresque and Churrigueresque-revival styles.[11] Hollywood Storage may have also been the most opulent self-storage facility ever conceived, with lavish rejería security grilles, polychrome tile ceilings, and marble inlay floors. In Birmingham, Alabama, the nineteen-story Thomas Jefferson Hotel became for a time the tallest Spanish-revival building on earth and the only hotel ever equipped with a rooftop mooring mast to anchor visiting zeppelins. Spanish-revival apartment buildings were springing up in Washington, DC. Spanish-revival homes were popping up across the Midwest. The eleven-story Spanish-revival Arlington Hotel was built in 1924 at the head of Bathhouse Row in the resort town of Hot Springs, Arkansas, quickly becoming a favorite getaway for the likes of Babe Ruth and Al Capone. Back in California, only a year after the Texas Tech delegation's visit to San Diego, Bertram Goodhue's former US Government Pavilion at the north end of the Plaza de Panama at Balboa Park was razed to make way for the new Plateresque-inspired San Diego Museum of Art designed by William Templeton Johnson—highlighted by a central two-story façade entablature inspired by the iconic entrance façade at the Universidad de Salamanca.[12] Two blocks to the east of Johnson's new museum, Carleton Winslow's former California Southern Counties Building, later repurposed by the city of San Diego as their Civic Auditorium, burned to the ground on the night of November 25, 1925—ironically, only hours before it was slated to host the

City Hall and Auditorium, Sweetwater, Texas, Page Brothers, architects, 1926.

Highland Park City Hall, Lang & Witchell, architects, 1924.

Firefighter's Ball.[13] Johnson was commissioned once again to design the Plateresque-inspired Natural History Museum built over the site of the former auditorium, which was completed in 1932. But, even after its fiery demise, little did anyone know that the former Civic Auditorium had proven a vital source to a number of Texas architects who had already used the auditorium as a case study for a fleet of new Spanish-revival buildings in Texas.

Winslow's Southern Counties Building was a fascinating combination of the formative mass of a two-story exhibition hall merged with a pair of low domed towers connecting to a cloistered entry courtyard. Though it is not clear how Texas architects emerged upon the San Diego case study, the building proved the eureka solution to Spanish-revival architecture in Texas, as now tax-revenue-flush cities and towns in the mid-1920s embarked in a building spree of city halls, auditoria, and convention facilities modeled after the late San Diego Auditorium. And for the first time, these facilities were being designed by Texas architects. In 1926, Atlee B. and Robert M. Ayres, along with Willis & Jackson designed the San Antonio Municipal Auditorium.[14] The Page brothers of Austin would design a similar Romanesque-revival facility in Sweetwater the same year, followed by a single-towered version of the same building type in Mexia a year later. Dallas firm Lang and Witchell had designed a handsome dome tower-capped Spanish-baroque city hall for the borough of Highland Park in 1924,[15] and then

One of the tallest Plateresque-revival buildings in the world, the Hotel Cortez (formerly the Hotel Orndorff), Trost & Trost, architects, 1925.

engaged in a rivalry with local competitors Fooshee and Cheek, where the former had designed a grand new Plateresque/Churrigueresque-blended city hall and auditorium in downtown Wichita Falls[16] overshadowing Fooshee and Cheek's Spanish-Colonial Amarillo Auditorium built the year before. Fooshee and Cheek responded with their 1929 Spanish-revival-themed Highland Park Shopping Village, still a premiere and posh retail venue for Dallas-area residents today.[17] Even Lubbock-based architects jumped into the mix, as Peters, Strange & Bradshaw would design a similar twin-towered auditorium for Big Spring in 1930.[18] Texas was becoming dotted with Spanish-stylized civic centers, each bearing some similarity to Winslow's now lost San Diego case study, and the mass of Spanish-inspired civic work elevated statewide interest in the style to every building type and form.

Hotels, high-rises, banking institutions, and retail establishments began to spring up across Texas—some adorned with the more pedestrian mission-revival style, but mostly designed with the higher Spanish detailing of the Plateresque or Churrigueresque styles. In 1925, El Paso firm Trost & Trost designed the world's largest Plateresque-revival building—the eleven-story Hotel Orndorff situated on El Paso's downtown square. Renamed later as the Hotel Cortez, the $1.5 million monster (over $350 million in present day costs)[19] featured an ornate ground floor and *piano nobile* whose exterior was clad in a mix of arched windows and Arabesque pilasters reminiscent of the façade of the Monastery of San Marcos in León. Criticized for its relatively bare upper floors in comparison to the ornate stone work that adorned the lower three floors, the Cortez demonstrated the dilemma of applying Spanish Renaissance–revival styling to high-rise buildings—a question Texas Tech would one day face. The Trosts completed two other Spanish-revival hotels in 1926: the Spanish-baroque-detailed El Paisano Hotel in Marfa, followed with the Spanish colonial-revival Las Lomas in Junction, which demonstrated how ideally suited the Spanish-revival style was for smaller-scale structures. Wyatt Hedrick too entered the Spanish-revival foray, now equipped with a plethora of Plateresque details that a keen Herman Koeppe had learned from collaborating with Watkin on the Texas Tech project.

Built in 1926, Sanguinet, Staats & Hedrick designed the Fort Worth Club—a twelve-story mix of Plateresque- and Churrigueresque-revival detail situated in downtown Fort Worth. A favorite locale to accommodate Will Rogers when visiting his good friend Amon Carter,[20] The Fort Worth Club was in fact just another Sanguinet & Staats "C-shaped" high-rise adapted with a Spanish-revival aesthetic. Two years later, Hedrick's team applied similar motifs to an adaptation of the successful Hot Springs Arlington Hotel plan for the Baker Hotel in Mineral Wells—a smaller Texas iteration of the Arkansas health resort town located west of Fort Worth. Completed in 1929, the Baker featured an araeostyle-colonnaded piano nobile surrounding three sides of the hotel situated over a ground-level floor of retail shops. The hotel featured Spanish reja–infilled rosette portholes along with stair-approached arched grand entry similar to the Arlington but finished with more distinctive Spanish detailing. Around that same time, Hedrick, in partnership with Houston architect R. D. Gottlieb under the venture Hedrick & Gottlieb, completed a number of Spanish Renaissance–revival buildings in Houston, including offices for the Gulf Publishing Company in 1928 and the 1929 Federal Land Bank.[21] Even beyond Texas and the United States, neoclassical Spanish-revival architecture was being built en masse from Puerto Rico to Mexico, and from South America to across Spain herself. In 1929 alone, the Spanish government, under the leadership of dictator Miguel Primo de Rivera, funded not one, but two world's fairs in Sevilla and Barcelona—the last Beaux-Arts fairs of their kind. In Sevilla alone, the massive and ornate *Plaza de España* built for the Ibero-American Exposition—itself a giant peristyled court not unlike the Texas Tech Court of Honor—nearly bankrupted the national treasury.

William Ward Watkin too was busy, not only with continued teaching responsibilities at Rice, but also with new commissions including schools and residences in Spanish idioms as well. Houston's Julia Ideson Library, which opened in 1926, was such a success that when the city retained Kansas City planning firm Hare & Hare months before the library's opening, the council adamantly ordered all buildings of their future civic plaza—including their new city hall—designed in the same architectural theme as the Ideson's Plateresque style.[22] Texas's economic prosperity brought the state to not only national attention, but also global attention, resulting in a request directed to Watkin in 1927 from the *Times of London* for an article describing the building boom as well as the architectural styles proliferating in the state.[23] Watkin expounded romantically about the architecture of Texas's former Spanish missions and their influence on Texas architecture, as well as the architecture of Spain inspiring buildings now rising across the state. While his description was partially accurate, Watkin's essay failed to note the almost total absence of the style from modern Texas architecture only three years earlier. Watkin was also asked in 1928 to pen an article for the new magazine *The American School and University* on the design of the campus and Plateresque-revival architecture of Texas Technological College,[24] the first national recognition the college would receive.

Tech's spring 1927 semester would close with news that Amon Carter was resigning as chairman of the board of directors. Far more comfortable with the role of editorial armchair quarterback, the past four years had worn Carter thin. Carter confided with friends that he had come to loathe the minutia of governance for a college three hundred miles away, coupled with endless boostering, meetings, and in particular, bitter bickering with lawmakers in Austin.[25] Carter believed the fledgling college could survive on its own now, and recommended Clifford Jones, who succeeded Carter as chairman on April 18.[26]

Board chairman or not, one favorite annual form of marketing for Amon Carter was giving Christmas gifts, as the newspaper tycoon would ship thousands of dollars in foodstuffs and baubles to politicians, businessmen, friends, and movie stars every year. Boxes of Texas pecans, handmade cowboy boots, Stetson hats, vicuna coats, melons, and other goods served as unspoken messages as to both the importance of a person or whether they stood in favor with Carter.[27] The ultimate gift in the Carter Christmas gift hierarchy was a live turkey, delivered by courier along with a personal letter signed by Harold Hough—also known by his radio moniker "Hired Hand"—the radio personality of Carter's newly bought Fort Worth radio station, WBAP. A few weeks before Carter's resignation on Christmas Eve 1926, Paul and Maud Horn were enjoying a holiday evening at the President's House, when interrupted by a knock at the door. Horn opened the front door to find a courier manhandling a cage holding the largest turkey the President of Texas Technological College had ever seen.[28] Horn was flabbergasted, as it was common knowledge that the sumptuous thirty-pound gobblers were Carter's choicest gift for the likes of governors and President Calvin Coolidge.[29] There was at least one reason Amon Carter had faith that Texas Technological College would survive and thrive. Paul Horn was doing a damn fine job.

8

NO BED TO SLEEP IN

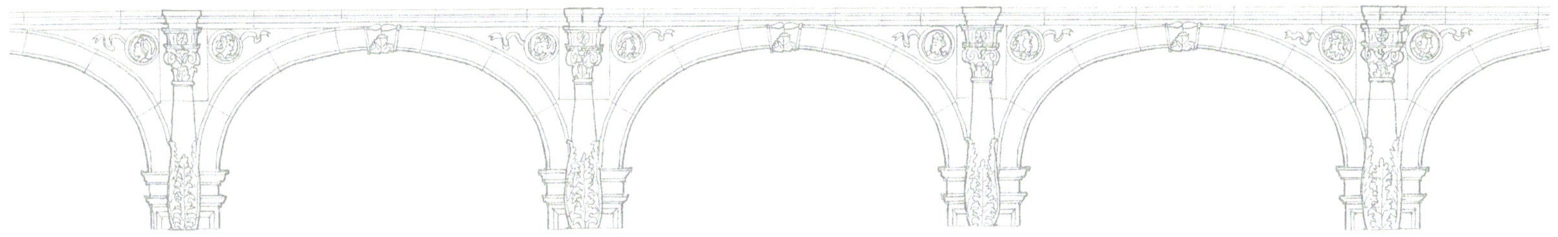

By FALL 1928, Texas Technological College had nearly doubled from its inaugural enrollment,and now boasted a new Graduate School with two students enrolled.[1] In the span of three years, Tech had skyrocketed to the position of being the second-largest public higher education institution in the state of Texas, even eclipsing Texas A&M College—the same institution that had rebuffed West Texas proposals for a branch institution in 1923. The argument that West Texas needed a seat of higher learning had proven true, though enrollment figures did not easily sway the state legislature or Governor Dan Moody for more money. Moody, a conservative Democrat, was more interested in upgrading Texas's ramshackle roads, reforming state prisons from medieval conditions, and restoring public trust from the graft and corruption of the Ferguson era than funding colleges and universities. Texas Tech was not a Morrill Land Grant-modeled institution, and thus lacked the fiscal resources of the Permanent University Fund that UT and A&M enjoyed. Three sources of revenue could fund implementation of Tech's master plan. The first—college revenue—was in 1928 minimal if nonexistent, as Tech collected no housing income, and tuition revenue barely broke even against operating costs and faculty salaries. The second source of funding was private donations. While a lifeblood to universities today, they were uncommon in the 1920s, and rarer still in West Texas. That left legislative funding, either through budget appropriation or implementing an ad valorem tax, which Moody was not at all interested in entertaining.

Tech still lacked roads across much of the campus. Its library consisted of two office-sized rooms in the Administration Building, and a stucco-clad, sparrow-infested wood barn doubled as the intramural gymnasium and basketball fieldhouse. President Horn did not dare request funding from the State Legislature for so lavish a luxury as Watkin's vision for a commencement hall. Coach Freeland lamented the lack of a gymnasium of any kind, as all of his teams had to dress in an old former tractor garage before games.[2] Watkin's and Hedrick's offices had prepared drawings in 1926 for a Plateresque-detailed gym whose high cost and low priority as compared to unmet academic facility needs ensured a place in back of the line.

Tech's first library, today part of the space occupied in the Administration Building by the President's Office, took up space only twice the size of the space visible in this photograph.

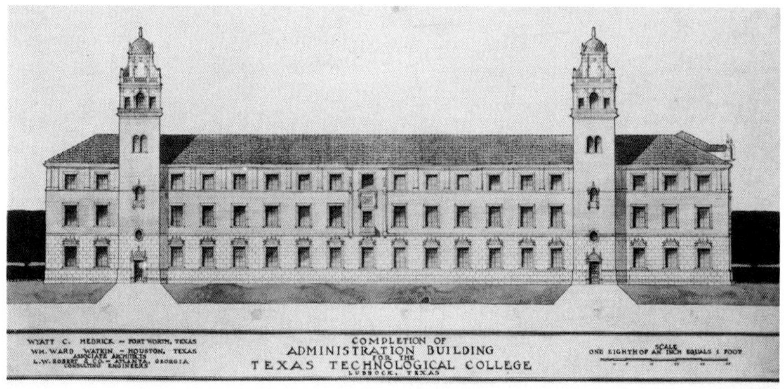

Proposed east elevation denoting the proposed expansion of the Administration Building, as proposed to the Texas Legislature in 1927.

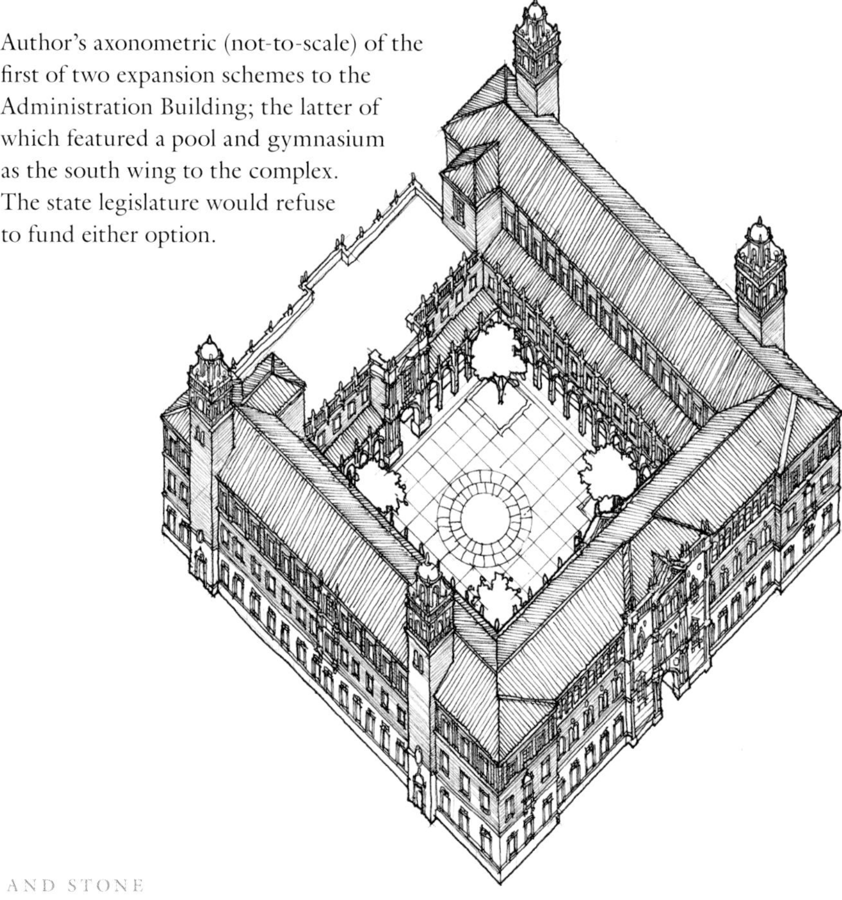

Author's axonometric (not-to-scale) of the first of two expansion schemes to the Administration Building; the latter of which featured a pool and gymnasium as the south wing to the complex. The state legislature would refuse to fund either option.

And then there was student housing, which too was nonexistent at Texas Tech. Even prior to the Great Depression, the challenge of finding beds for nearly two thousand students was daunting for Horn and his staff. A handful of "approved" privately owned dormitories existed near campus—the most famous being the adobe-clad Cheri Casa—but certainly not enough to house 1,800 students. Aligned to the moral tenets of the day, students were strongly discouraged from renting from coeducational boarding houses, while Horn and Dean of Students Thomas Gaston encouraged local residents near campus to offer their spare bedrooms and back houses to students at fair rates. Homes in the Overton and Tech Terrace districts even today owe their character of backhouse buildings and garage loft apartments to the early absence of housing at Tech. Even when tuition for a semester at Texas Tech in 1925 was only $10.75 (about $144 in present-day value), boarding house rent that ranged between $25 and $37.50 per month became an impossibility for many, making backhouse flats that

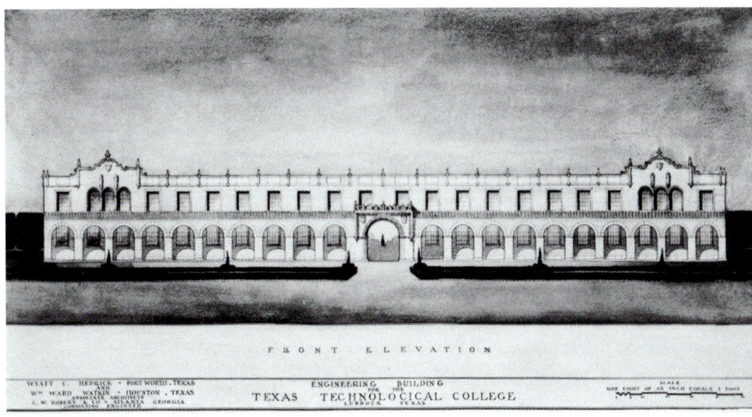

East elevation of the proposed West Engineering Building; William Ward Watkin, design architect, 1927.

much more enticing.[3] If enrollment at Texas Tech were to continue to grow, then the college had a crisis brewing.

In the meantime, the state legislature did approve $465,000 in funding for additional construction of its academic core, beginning first with a new Engineering Building.[4] Known today as West Engineering, Watkin had developed concepts for the facility as early as 1926, but these were put on hold until the outcome of the 1927 biennium was known. As Watkin envisioned in the 1924 master plan, the Engineering Building was to be another cloistered complex, in this case established west of the prado-like mall known today as the Engineering Key. The Engineering cloister would, like the Administration Building, connect to the Engineering Key through an articulated salle-porte. For many, Engineering was a welcome addition to the college physical plant, providing some form of infill to the more than one thousand feet of blank space between Administration and Textile Engineering.

For Engineering, the Board of Control only recommended funding $240,000 of the $282,000 requested by the college, and not the $282,000 that Tech requested for only the eastern half of an Engineering complex.[5] The legislature and Governor Moody concurred

Entry façade of the former Hospital del Estudio, Universidad de Salamanca, maestro mayor unknown.

with the Board of Control instead. A C-shaped plan emerged, tailored to the $240,000 budget—the first of many C-shaped plans to dot the Tech campus, though other design economies would be required. While Watkin had originally proposed the same durable, attractive red clay floor tile used for flooring at the Julia Ideson Library for Texas Tech facilities, budget limitations led to the substitution of terrazzo and green-tinted concrete floors at Engineering.[6] Stone ornament was toned down on the west cloister façades to the new Engineering Building, resulting in a building compositionally similar to Textile Engineering, albeit with a smaller and less ornate salle-porte entry. Yet, Watkin's recent travels to Spain in 1925 introduced to him an ideal source of Spanish inspiration for that salle-porte entry.

Deep within the collection of buildings that comprise the Universidad de Salamanca lies the Patio de Escuelas, today both a popular tourist destination and home to the iconic entry façade—the *fachada estandarte*—of the university. Lesser known along the south side of the plaza—facing a statue of Fray Luis de León, Augustinian friar and seminal theologian of the university—is the entrance to the present-day office of the university rector (or president), and the former home of the Hospital del Estudio. More Gothic than Renaissance in appearance—reflective of its transitional Isabelline style—the Portada del Hospital is often overlooked to other architectural highlights at the university. As with the iconic Escuelo Mayores façade nearby, the exact maestro mayor remains unknown to this day. The façade consists of a pair of flattened-arched doorways—*arcos carpaneles*—with overhead stone surrounds crested by a trio of arched heraldic escutcheons, topped further by an acanthus-detailed stone drip edge that frames the entire entry. Atop the building parapet sits a stone filigree railing divided equally by three slender finials—an irregular geometric subdivision solution from a renaissance standpoint, but such imperfections were in themselves commonplace to the Isabelline and Plateresque eras. Watkin adapted the three-finial rhythm of the Hospital del Estudio façade to a single-arch rhythm that further demonstrated his abilities to skillfully incorporate Spanish departures from renaissance purism into the Texas Tech fabric. In lieu of random filigree over the Engineering salle-porte, Watkin used the spaces dividing the three pilasters to locate an engineering-specific vernacular into the façade. Watkin incorporated sets of cherubs flanking four elongated shields, each representing the four academic departments to be housed there—architecture, electrical engineering, civil engineering, and mechanical engineering.

Looking west through the neo-Gothic salle-porte arch of West Engineering; William Ward Watkin, architect.

Long considered a mystery compared to the engineer or confederate politician considered for the West Engineering façade, the two "Mystery Busts" appear to be inspired by the bust of Saint Paul in Alcalá.

It was during the design of the Engineering Building that a prior conundrum reared its head once again with the college leadership. In the course of selecting individuals whose names were to be either inscribed or carved into busts on the Administration Building, Horn and Watkin had settled on including Abraham Lincoln among the ten busts escutcheoned over the second-floor windows of the north façade. While the choice of Lincoln makes perfect sense today, such was not the case in 1920s Texas, where many Southerners still reviled the Civil War Union leader. Horn, and in particular Amon Carter, endured a flood of vitriol in the form of letters and telegrams over the matter, and though two years had passed since the "Lincoln Controversy," the matter had not been forgotten by many. Whether to state politicians or members of the Daughters of the Confederacy, who continued to write Carter protesting the matter even after his resignation as chairman,[7] the matter was pressing enough for Horn to write Watkin less than a week before bid documents were issued for the Engineering Building inquiring if a suitable location be found for a roundel or bust of confederate president Jefferson Davis somewhere

Bust of Saint Paul holding a sword (located at center of composition); façade of Colegio de San Ildefonso, Universidad de Alcalá, 1543; Claudio de Arciniega, sculptor.

Present-day detail view of the corner tower of the Palacio de Monterrey, Salamanca. Rodrigo Gil de Hontañon, maestro mayor, begun 1539.

Undated, but early photograph of Chemistry Building, showing both the building's telltale Salamanca-inspired building corner, as well as the seven-foot-height elevated Court of Honor berm the building was set upon.

on Engineering.[8] This had arisen after prior discussion in the previous year contemplated construction of a statue of Davis on campus to appease pro-Southern sentiments. Watkin had two potential locations in mind—under either of the two finial-capped gable pediments located at the north and south parapets of the east façade. Watkin's prior recommendation for the gables were to instead display noted engineers such as Ferdinand de Lesseps or James Buchanan Eads.[9] (Ferdinand de Lesseps was a French engineer who designed the Suez Canal in the late 1860s, while James B. Eads was an American engineer who designed the first bridge in Saint Louis across the Mississippi River from 1867 to 1874.) In Watkin's September 2 letter to Horn, he acknowledged that locating Davis's bust for one of the roundels was possible, and perhaps the other could be "someone such as [George] Goethals."[10] (General George Washington Goethals was the Army Corps of Engineers administrator who supervised completion of the Panama Canal between 1907 and 1914. Ironically, one could argue that had Goethals failed in his task, the outcome of California-Panama Exposition in San Diego, and as a result the campus plan for Texas Tech, would have unfolded differently, making him an ideal candidate for being memorialized at Tech.)

For inexplicable reasons, and thankfully, the Jefferson Davis matter disappeared just as quickly as it had appeared. Rather, the pair of roundels Watkin did include became for many decades a mystery as to their meaning and source, as neither de Lesseps or Eads were memorialized instead. In Nolan Barrick's 1985 book *Texas Tech: The Unobserved Heritage*, the resulting bearded figure in both roundels were referred to as "The mysterious busts" by Barrick.[11] A likely source of inspiration may have been Andrew Noble Prentice's drawing of the Colegio Mayor de San Ildefonso at the Universidad Complutense in Alcalá, in his compendium *Renaissance Architecture and Ornament in Spain*.[12] At Alcalá, located over a reja-clad window to the Colegio Mayor de San Ildefonso façade is a strikingly similar bust of the

(*Left and above*) Present-day detail photograph and author's elevation drawing of the TTC shield-ensconced Corinthian capitals incorporated on the laboratory's north colonnade.

apostle Paul, holding a sword much like Tech's "mysterious busts." Interestingly, Spanish historians now know the stone carver responsible for that bust in Alcalá was a young Claudio de Arciniega,[13] who later in his career would make the transatlantic voyage to Mexico and as himself a maestro mayor would design the Metropolitan Cathedral of the Assumption in Mexico City. Bid documents for the Engineering Building were issued in the first week of September 1927 and slated for an August 1928 completion date.[14]

Just as the Engineering Building was proceeding, Watkin and Hedrick had shifted focus toward another arguably more visible academic project at Texas Tech. In the same letter Horn inquired regarding the

Alchemical symbols carved into limestone representing sulfur (above), and vinegar (below on ancon) on the east façade.

Jefferson Davis proposal for the Engineering Building, he authorized Watkin to proceed with design of what was alternately referred to as the Chemistry-Physics or Science Building.[15] A chemistry laboratory was not only important to Tech's curricular needs and legislative charge, but it reflected the growing importance of both instructional and research laboratory space within American higher education. The new laboratory would initially be tasked to house all sciences, but also be able over time to transition back entirely to a chemistry laboratory as other adjacent science facilities came on line. Watkin proposed on the exterior of the new building a similar alchemical vernacular to what he and mentor Ralph Adams Cram had designed in the 1922–23 Chemistry Building at Rice.[16]

While the Administration Building incorporates arguably the most thorough range of Plateresque inspiration into its façades, and the Textile Engineering possesses the most ornate stonework on campus, from a massing and vernacular standpoint, the Chemistry Building is easily the most fascinating of all early Texas Tech buildings. Still relatively ornate and formatively unique, the Chemistry Building also proved to be in many ways even mysterious. Watkin drew from modern chemistry and physics, alchemy, and even the occult in adorning the building that today anchors the southeastern end of the Mathematics and Science Quadrangle.

In an October 10, 1927, letter from College Secretary E. W. Provence to Watkin, Provence announced that the state was reducing the construction budget for the Chemistry Building to $225,000 in lieu of the original $275,000 allocation.[17] Biology, physics, geology, and general science would account for nearly 50 percent of the laboratory space, with the remainder dedicated for chemistry, greatly concerning Watkin whether minimum space needs could be met.[18] Dating back to the original master plan, Watkin intended to frame his Court of Honor with similar tower massing at the northeast corner of the new Chemistry Building based upon case studies he had observed framing the eastern boundary of the Plaza de Panama in Balboa Park.

Situated at the north end of the Plaza de las Agustinas in Salamanca, the Palacio de Monterrey had become an icon of Spanish

The mysterious Rosicrucian-inspired VITRIOL tablet inset overhead (both present-day photograph and line drawing) of the east façade lower entrance.

architecture. From the nineteenth century until World War I, every pavilion built by Spain at a world's fair featured the unmistakable three-arched-opening tower form inspired by the Palacio de Monterrey. Countless neoclassical buildings in Spain and the Western world owed inspiration to the palacio's tower form—it had become a fundamental element of the Spanish architectural lexicon. Begun in 1539 by Rodrigo Gil de Hontañon—the same maestro mayor to the Colegio Mayor de San Ildefonso at Alcalá—the imposing four-story palace had been commissioned by Alonso Fonseca Zúñiga y Acevedo, the third count of Monterrey.[19] The palace's corner tower was not lost on Bertram Goodhue and Carleton Winslow in their 1914 designs for Balboa Park as the Electricity Building featured a near-identical homage of the tower overlooking the Plaza de Panama.

While Goodhue and Winslow's 1914 Electricity Building was a more direct application of the Palacio de Monterrey tower, Watkin's tower at the Chemistry Building was not nearly as literal an interpretation, with slightly different proportions, and windows in lieu of an open belfry. Watkin also opted to integrate more delicate araeostyle-proportioned colonnades along the south façade of the Administration Building, subtly signaling the importance Watkin regarded the Court of Honor over the more pedestrian colonnades that had been built along the Engineering Key. But where Administration's colonnade was a more generic interpretation of engaged pilasters and detailing drawn from the Colegio Mayor Fonseca in Salamanca, Watkin opted to add more distinctive vernacular to the Chemistry colonnade. In the first architectural use of a beloved institutional logo, the engaged Corinthian capitals of the proposed colonnade were interposed with elongated shields bearing a raised Double T, crossed by a tapered C. Though Watkin or Hedrick would not repeat use of the detail on campus, use of the shield was an important architectural precedent in the display of the now-ubiquitous Double T.

Unlike Administration, to remain on budget Hedrick had imposed a $5,000 allowance limit—barely 2 percent of the project—for custom carved stone.[20] Long gone were the elaborate Arabesques of the Administration Building or the custom acanthus-clad columns

Detail drawing of the north gable louver to the Chemistry Building replete with a wrought iron iteration of the service emblem of the US Army Chemical Corps that inspired the inset louver reja.

Present-day photo of the north gable louver and US Army Chemical Corps–inspired reja, likely a warning for maintenance personnel and laborers to keep their distance.

on Textile Engineering. Repetitive egg-and-dart patterns and simple carved reliefs would account for much of the stone detail on the Chemistry Building. Simple vertical bar grilles were incorporated in lieu of the ornate floral transom rejería installed at Administration. Any remaining ornate stonework, like engaged pilasters and springline capitals, were concentrated at the ground floor so they could be visually appreciated. Watkin's strategic application of ornament coupled with the formative nature of the building and colonnade presented a false perception that Chemistry was one of the more ornate early buildings on campus.

During design of the Chemistry Building at Rice five years earlier, Watkin was guided by a helpful letter from Dr. William M. Craig of the Rice Chemistry Department outlining the range of centuries-old symbols used by alchemists for identifying elements and compounds.[21] The ultimate objective of alchemy—the magnum opus act of refining other elements into gold or silver—represented a medieval protoscience that within its practices intermingled elements of the occult. Ralph Adams Cram's suggestion of incorporating alchemical symbols at Rice was a glimpse into his mystical side that may too have influenced his protégé, William Ward Watkin. Cram was many things: a Beaux-Arts master, an eminent medievalist, and a lesser-known Hispanophile. But Ralph Adams Cram also possessed a Bohemian slant whose interests occasionally crossed into both the spiritual realm and the occult. A prolific writer of horror and ghost stories, Cram authored many non-architectural novels, such as his 1895 book *Black Spirits and White—A Book of Ghost Stories.*[22] Pivotal horror and science fiction writer H. P. Lovecraft later admitted that Cram's short story, *The Dead Valley,* was an influential favorite of his.[23] Cram was friends and colleagues with members of the Rosicrucian Order,[24] a secret society with ties to freemasonry and alchemical pursuits, and thanks to a mysterious purple-gray stone tablet on the Chemistry Building façade, evidence suggests that Cram's occultist interests may have influenced Watkin and with that the architecture of Texas Tech.

On the 1922 Rice Chemistry Building, Cram incorporated alchemical symbols suggested in Craig's letter into the building façade, fashioned either in stone or polychrome stucco. Watkin had selected a similar series of symbols at Texas Tech, in this case, carved in vee-relief onto the keystone ancons set over the arches of the laboratory colonnade. Basic elements such as fire and water, metals such as iron, tin, and copper, and acids such as vinegar, hydrosulfuric and hydrochloric acid were all included into the colonnade. Yet, the addition of the mysterious tablet on the east façade, and the profuse use of rose florets on the colonnade pilasters—a common Rosicrucian symbol—are curious detail additions to say the least. No direct ties are known between Watkin and Rosicrucianism, but the purple-gray slate tablet over the east entrance bears a near-exact representation of a seal representative in Rosicrucianism, which first appeared in the fifteenth-century text *L'Azoth des Philosophes* by a supposed alchemist

The Home Economics Practice House, undated. Wyatt C. Hedrick and William Ward Watkin, architects, completed 1928.

Texas Technological College Power House (foreground); later undated, completed 1930.

While most of the Tower's details are both Gothic and Isabelline, it was the later addition of Plateresque entry portal details at the Torreon de los Guzmanes—namely the deep voussoir stonework that adorns many building entries in Ávila.

named Basilius Valentinus, whose very existence has never been verified to this day.[25] Surrounding the seal is the Latin burial motto of Rosicrucianism's presumed founder, Christian Rosenkreuz: "Visita Interiora Terrae Rectificando Invenies Occultum Lapidem," forming the curious acronym "VITRIOL." When translated, the motto reads "Visit the interior of the Earth; and by rectification thou shalt find the hidden stone," a general description of the alchemic goals of the order's magnum opus.[26] Furthermore, the stone's quarry source both in terms of stone type and inspiration is a mystery. The tablet and its meaning would go largely unnoticed for nearly six decades. Neither Hedrick nor the Tech leadership questioned the VITRIOL tablet—certainly not Paul Horn, the Sunday school teacher who might have objected to such pagan ornaments decorating Tech buildings.

If the Chemistry Building bore aesthetic eccentricities that seemed pulled from a Dan Brown novel, its façades also read straight out of a circa-1920s chemistry textbook. With input from Professor Read of the Tech Chemistry Department, a host of other chemical vernacular would be carved into the building, including abbreviations of the first sixteen elements of the periodic table, and illustrations of lab equipment such as retorts, a mortar and pestle, and a weight scale. Additional carvings illustrate the progressive history of the understanding of the benzene ring, first showing early molecular diagrams developed by Karl Ernst Claus and Friedrich August Kekulé, followed by present-day diagrams accepted today.[27] Above one benzene ring diagram, another curious triangular symbol was snuck into the panel—the logo of the American Chemical Society.[28] Other diagrams carved onto the building façades included a monoclinic face-centered cubic crystal, while another presented an early diagram of protons and orbiting electrons to an atom.

Even on the west façade of the building, a round louver responsible for discharging laboratory exhaust fumes was decorated in wrought iron representing the new logo for the US Army's Chemical Corps[29]—another benzene ring flanked by a pair of retorts. The Chemical Corps logo may also have served as a subtle warning to maintenance staff to steer clear of hazardous exhaust from the louver, as public awareness of the horrors of chemical warfare during World War I made the army insignia an apropos decoration.

Despite Watkin's efforts to maximize every opportunity for vernacular detail on the Chemistry Building, the project remained on budget and construction of the Chemistry Building commenced in 1928. Perhaps most strategic to the laboratory's design as well as the overall implementation of the master plan, large quantities of earthen fill were shipped onto the site to form an elevated ground plane seven feet above campus grade for the Court of Honor. This follow-through with Watkin's design intent would ensure a quadrangle constructed at an elevated grade at the western boundary of the college campus. The Chemistry Building was in fact built nearly to campus grade, as the laboratory's partial basement to the building was six feet below court grade.

(*Left*) William Ward Watkin (seated center) in Moorish garb with friends and family while enjoying a prior vacation in Granada, Spain in 1925.

(*Right*) Watkin family photograph dated in the late 1920s. Annie Watkin, who would die in France in early 1929, is seated far right.

WITH ENGINEERING AND CHEMISTRY under construction and the next state legislative biennium nearing, the design team and administrators shifted attention to another academic need—a library. Horn and the board hoped to allay complaints from their highly respected but discontented librarian—Elizabeth Howard West. West, the former state librarian—only the second woman in the nation to hold such a post[30]—did her best to deal with the limitations at hand, but impatience led West to constantly bombard college leadership and legislators with pleas for a new library building. At the time, the library was stuffed into the Administration Building's northwest first floor—home today to the President's Office—a space equivalent to two large offices that had already been filled to capacity with stacks and reading tables since 1925. Books were so crammed into stacks that students were instructed to ask library staff to carefully pull books from shelves lest an avalanche of paper occur.[31]

In March 1928, Watkin forwarded concept drawings of a new Tech library to Horn and West for their review, and with that made his first proposed change to the campus master plan, siting a library more prominently on campus somewhere between where Holden and West Halls reside today.[32] This, along with the Home Economics Practice House, which had been built in 1927 as a Spanish-stylized model training home for home economics majors to perfect their skills, were the farthest constructions east on the still-largely void campus. Sadly, Watkin's elevations of this new library, which West described in correspondence as "beautiful,"[33] are lost to history, and little remains known of the concepts proposed in 1928.

Watkin and Hedrick's office did complete drawings for one other project in 1928, in fact the only building the state would fund in the 1929 biennium. When Texas Tech had first opened, there was no endowment remaining to build a permanent power plant, so initially Tech's dynamos and central boilers resided in a glorified corrugated metal shed. Though the state legislature would not fund the elaborate masonry campanile smokestack Watkin originally envisioned for a permanent power house—a campanile inspired by Rice's Physical Plant—they would in 1929 fund a handsome gabled, cruciform-plan Power House that would be completed in 1930. The building was the first to introduce quoined building corners to Tech architecture, though in the estilo plateresco quoining was employed to ensure clean, dressed stone at building corners, rather than the more decorative use of quoins seen elsewhere in Europe. Watkin's Power House entry design was also unique to Tech; visually dominated by the ponderous south entry arch consisting of deep voussoirs set over the entry door to the building. This arch detail was not unusual to Spanish architecture, seen in case studies such as the Casa de Doña María la Brava in Salamanca, but most common to the renowned medieval-walled city of Ávila, northwest of Madrid. Many such deep-voussoir arches can be found in the old walled districts of the city, most noteworthy of which is the entry to the otherwise-Gothic Torreón de los Guzmanes—built in 1503 as a five-story turreted watchtower and fortified home for hidalguía.[34] In lieu of the balconette and reja often seen built above the traditional arcos de Ávila, Watkin instead incorporated an aediculed window over the entry flanked by two escutcheons.

Watkin hurried drawings of the Power House to Fort Worth in late June 1928 for Hedrick's incorporation, as Watkin and his wife and children sailed in July from New York City for France.[35] Watkin was embarking on a prolonged year-long sabbatical for him and his family to experience the architecture and culture of France, Italy, and Spain. That summer and fall, the Watkins left their daughters Ray and Rosemary and son Billy with a French caretaker in Compiègne, while the elder Watkins toured much of France, with sojourns to Italy and Spain. It was during their travels, what had first appeared as chronic fatigue to Watkin's wife, Annie, progressed first into discomfort, then into pain that left Annie bedridden. First believed to be a gall bladder problem, and later believed to be a "liver attack," by late 1928, Annie Ray Watkin was admitted to the American Hospital in Paris.[36] Her pain and weakness progressed to a point where the US ambassador to France Myron Herrick enlisted the assistance of Charles de Martel, one of France's finest surgeons, who operated on Annie in late February 1929. The surgery confirmed de Martel's fears, as Annie had terminal pancreatic cancer. She died in her Paris hospital bed on March 2, 1929.

William Ward Watkin, devastated, exhausted, and himself sick with pneumonia, returned on the SS *Paris* across a stormy Atlantic with his children later that month. In a final ignominy, Watkin's severe illness left him remanded to a New York City hotel for several weeks as the body of Annie Watkin arrived in Houston for interment and a funeral that William Ward Watkin and his children would not be able to attend.[37] Watkin finally returned to Houston in April to limited duties at Rice, and essentially a suspension of work at his architectural atelier through much of 1929. The death of Annie Ray Watkin led to Watkin's withdrawal from many things, not the least of which was his future design role at Texas Technological College.

9

FRIENDS IN HIGH PLACES

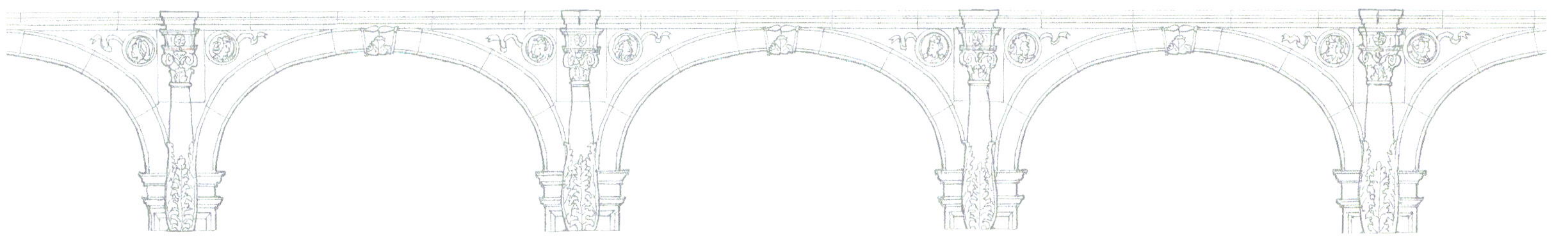

EARLY ON WEDNESDAY, April 13, 1932, Maud Horn awoke to find her husband Paul Whitfield Horn dead of apparent heart failure.[1] For eight years, Horn was the indisputable frontispiece of Texas Technological College, and his death proved a punch in the solar plexus for an institution already gasping for air. Tech teetered on a wobbly precipice in 1932, still rattled by a range of austerity measures imposed by Austin that bleakly reduced staff, funding, and salaries. Texas Tech had not built any new facilities since the Power House in 1930, with no future building funding on the horizon. Enrollment was waning in its second straight year to just over 1,800 students, with still no permanent student housing, and shortcomings in instructional and library space remained acute.

It had taken a final objection from board member John W. Carpenter to quash a proposal to honor Paul Horn by burying him on campus,[2] and the question of whether any replacement could equal Tech's late leader remained. At sixty-two, Bradford Knapp, a bald, bespectacled alumnus of Vanderbilt and Michigan, and son of one of the greatest agricultural scientists of the nineteenth century—Seaman Knapp—left the presidency at Alabama Polytechnic Institute (now known as Auburn University) on July 2 to become the second president of Texas Technological College. Knapp confided prior to his hiring that he was fed up with the lack of funding from the Alabama Legislature at Auburn,[3] but little had prepared him for the fiscal onslaught he would face in Lubbock. In December 1932, a biennial report by the State Board of Education presented an unsatisfactory opinion on operations at Tech,[4] and presented recommendations to the state legislature that if acted upon, would be a suicidal poison pill for the college. The State Board of Education perceived Texas Tech's agricultural education endeavors as duplicate to Texas A&M, prompting a proposal that Tech be stripped of any agricultural curriculum, including associated faculty and facilities. The idea particularly chafed the agriculturalist Knapp, forcing him to employ his formidable experience as a litigator in prior years in Iowa. It took much of the 1933 legislative session to fight off the wolves in Austin, and only with Knapp's begrudging acceptance of severe budget cuts, salary cuts, and of course a continued hold on new facilities.

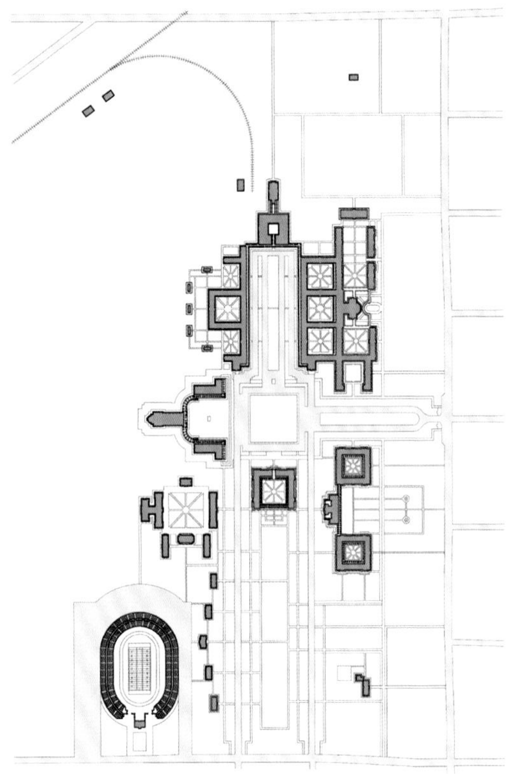

Comparative plan of the Watkin Plan for the Texas Technological College campus, dated 1924.

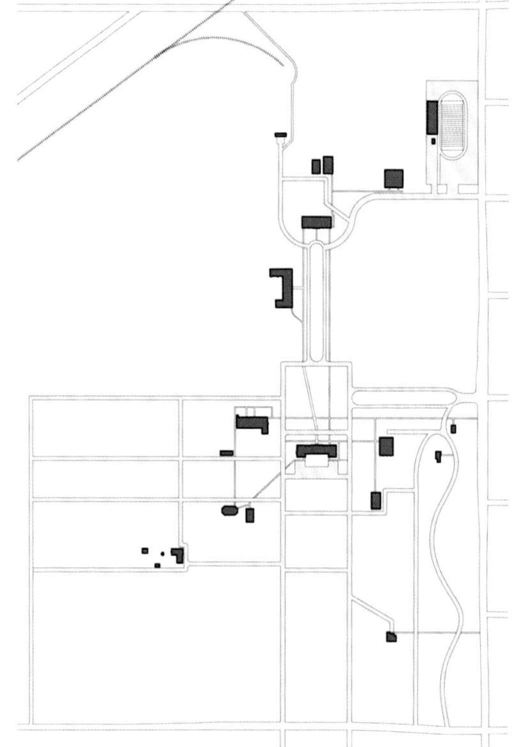

Following the initial construction of buildings at Texas Tech, the above plan represents extents of the campus in 1930 (the Power House was only then beginning construction).

But Knapp had friends in high places, and eight months after his arrival, a letter of thanks arrived in Knapp's office at Tech. President-elect Franklin Delano Roosevelt was writing in thanks for Knapp's role as agricultural advisor to Roosevelt's recent presidential campaign.[5] Roosevelt and John Nance Garner, an Uvalde, Texas, native, won a resounding landslide—four out of five votes in Texas alone went to the Roosevelt-Garner ticket—a victory of great portent to the struggling college in Lubbock. Three years into the Great Depression, Roosevelt's election reflected the national discontent with rampant unemployment, economic stagnation, soup kitchens, strikes, and riots. But beyond that, to the north of Lubbock, one of the greatest ecological disasters in modern history was unfolding across the Great Plains. Years of irresponsible farming spurred by a bullish post-war wheat market had left millions of acres of prairie grasslands fallow across swaths of western Oklahoma, the Texas Panhandle, Kansas, New Mexico, and Colorado. The wheat market collapse of the early 1930s, coinciding with the arrival of a multiyear drought of epic proportions generated what would become the Great American Dust Bowl.

Though the worst of the Dust Bowl struck the Texas and Oklahoma Panhandles, even for Lubbock, it was a time of profound hardship. No Tech building in the early 1930s possessed the expensive luxury of air conditioning, relying on ceiling fans and insect-screened windows to allow breezes into buildings. Piles and even drifts of brown dust accumulated in campus buildings.[6] To this day, it is unknown how many Tech students, faculty, and alumni succumbed to dust pneumonia, but many did. One Tech football letterman, Matt Hitchcock, is known to have succumbed to lung consumption in 1935, prompting the planting of a tree and shrub garden in Hitchcock's memory beyond the south end zone at Tech Field Stadium.[7] The parched earth and blowing dust mirrored the funding drought Tech had to endure in the 1930s.

Bradford Knapp pressed on, determined to turn the corner at Texas Tech and address critical institutional needs, beginning with facilities. In June 1933, Roosevelt signed Executive Order 6174, establishing the Federal Emergency Administration of Public Works within the Department of Interior—later simplified to Public Works Administration or PWA.[8] Often confused with the more frequently mentioned Works Progress Administration (WPA), which focused on smaller-scale civic projects with artistic or cultural value, the PWA was a national economic clearinghouse for billions in infrastructure dollars invested into projects nationwide that would spur economic growth and counter unemployment. At times criticized for its bureaucratic inefficiency, the regional- and district-based implementation system for the PWA did have one particular benefit for Texas Tech—political allies to the White House in turn received lucrative appointments as PWA administrators, most notably Bradford Knapp.

Even if Knapp had to be recused from proposals submitted by Texas Tech, it was an unspoken truth that Tech would benefit from his role as regional PWA administrator. But Tech had one other ace up its sleeve. In another example of Wyatt Hedrick's adroit marketing capabilities, Hedrick had developed a relationship with PWA Deputy National Administrator, Colonel Harold M. Waite.[9] The appointment of General John A. Hulen of Fort Worth as Knapp's superior as regional PWA administrator proved fortuitous, as Hulen was a member of the Tech Board of Directors. These relationships, coupled with Amon Carter's friendship with interior secretary Harold M. Ickes guaranteed PWA grant funding would flow to Tech, while concurrently ensuring Hedrick's firm as architects and engineers for millions of dollars worth of PWA projects both regionally and nationally.

Influence in action; Tech's second president, Bradford Knapp, dresses Vice President John Nance Garner in a Texas Tech–produced suit.

John Hulen was a railroad man who had served in the army with distinction during the Spanish American War, and as second-in-command of the Fort Worth and Denver Railroads, Hulen was in frequent contact with their railroad architect, none other than Wyatt Hedrick.[10] Hedrick's relationships coupled with Horn's death were enough to prevent the retention of William Ward Watkin's role as design consultant, who himself had only begun reconstituting his business since the passing of his wife four years earlier. Interestingly, minutes from the December 9, 1933, Tech Board meeting indicated that Chip Robert's firm had been secured once again as an engineering consultant for any upcoming projects—a decision that made Watkin's exclusion that much more noticed.[11] Hedrick was already in consultation with Hulen as early as September 1933 in the development of a project scope for two dormitories and a student gymnasium on the Tech Campus.[12] In an August 31 letter to Hulen, Hedrick projected

Aerial photograph of West Hall (originally named Men's Dormitory No. 1); undated.

that a 302-bed men's dormitory and 253-bed women's dormitory, plus a gymnasium could be built and equipped with fixtures, furniture, and equipment for $790,000.[13]

It was at the same board meeting that Board Building Committee Chair, Senator Robert A. Stuart, outlined the legal strategy Tech would use in applying for PWA grant funding and also indicated the likely PWA funding limit would be no more than $650,000,[14] a ceiling that would shutter plans for a gymnasium for the time being. (Stuart, a state senator from Fort Worth, reinforced a continuation that had begun in Amon Carter's tenure as board chairman that much of the political power used to lobby Tech's position both in Austin and across the state would reside in Fort Worth.) Students would have to continue to contend with dust, heat, and sparrow excrement on the floor of the Old Barn. Stuart and Hedrick anticipated approval from Washington for the grant request that would result in a construction start date of mid-January 1934.[15] For Hedrick, the sooner the better, as financial hardships of the Great Depression had caught up with him.

It had been a tough time for Wyatt Hedrick, regardless of his political and marketing prowess, but even the smooth Virginian had his limits. One particularly influential relationship for Hedrick was with his father-in-law, Texas Governor Ross Sterling. Hedrick's grandson and Fort Worth architect Ames Fender would once remark: "Hedrick married well. It was good for business."[16] Prior to the Crash of 1929, Sterling as financier and Hedrick as architect and junior financier had partnered to build the twenty-nine-story Sterick Building in Memphis, Tennessee. Completed in 1930, the massive Sterick—a portmanteau of both investor's names—was both aesthetically and fiscally a head-scratcher, and totally unneeded in a time when the bottom was falling out of the commercial office market. The Sterick proved to be an albatross, and by January 1934 had increased the architect's debts to nearly $3 million, reducing his personal account holdings to less than seven dollars. Hedrick would file for bankruptcy that month and begin to rebuild, but the impact for Governor Sterling was far more devastating. Sterling, a co-founder of the Humble Oil Company, chairman of the board of Houston's largest bank, and newspaper owner, was left penniless from the Sterrick disaster and forced to subsist off of his comparatively meager governor's salary for the time being.[17]

The sudden stream of PWA projects proved so lucrative for Hedrick that he, Herman Koeppe, and their respective families temporarily relocated to Washington, DC, to work on PWA projects from there. Drafting tables were set up in rooms in the Mayflower Hotel, as families slept in adjacent rooms.[18] The strategy paid huge dividends, as Hedrick secured commissions for hundreds of PWA-funded projects not only in Texas, but also across the nation. Post offices, high schools, armories, courthouses, and an assortment of other public work projects were first conceptually designed by Koeppe at the Mayflower, then shipped by train to Fort Worth, where the main office would complete working drawings and specifications in a breakneck effort to keep pace. Interestingly enough, many Texas Tech projects of the 1930s would be first conceived from a drafting board in a Washington, DC, hotel room.

Texas Technological College's first two dormitories, ingloriously

Undated photograph looking south toward Doak Hall (originally named Women's Dormitory No. 1); showing the habit of growing ivy on the north walls of Tech buildings—a practice that continued into the 1940s.

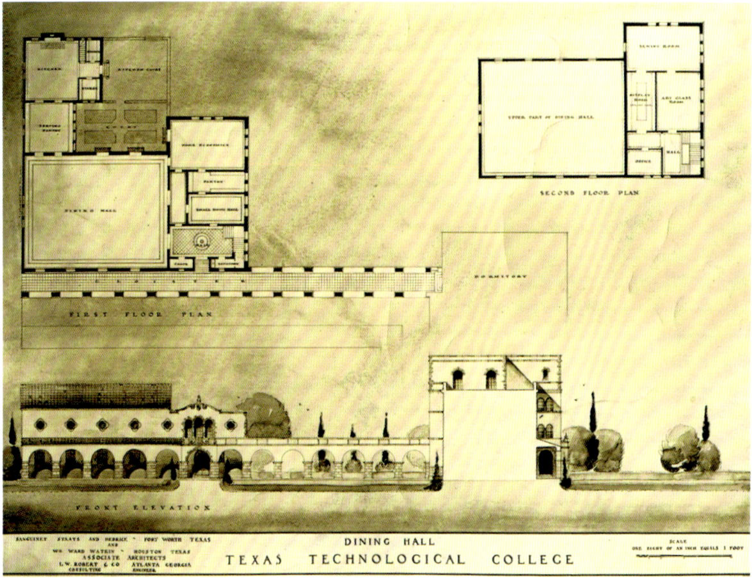

Plan and elevation of proposed Dining Hall and adjacent housing as envisioned by Watkin during planning of the college in the 1920s. Quaint and handsome, Watkin's stucco-clad, cloistered student housing concept would be discarded in 1934 in lieu of centralized residence hall facilities, largely in an effort to achieve PWA grant submission approval.

named as "Men's Dormitory" and "Women's Dormitory," represented a significant departure from the student residential vision originally proposed by Watkin. One of the most novel elements of the 1924 master plan were the residential districts, envisioned as Spanish-stylized monastic cloisters formed with two-story blocks of living units. However quaint and picturesque, Watkin's housing vision was comparably inefficient to the three- and four-story residence halls becoming more typical of contemporary collegiate design. The competitive nature of the PWA grant process inherently required that any Tech residence hall proposal involved maximizing square footage and bed count within a minimal volume, with Koeppe using a C-shaped floor plan often employed in Sanguinet's and Staats's prior hotel work, in lieu of Watkin's Balboa Park–like cloister concept. Hedrick's team did generally situate both dormitories in locations similar to the intended districts in Watkin's plan, with each dormitory located 750 feet apart astride and facing the Broadway mall. Yet, the Women's Dormitory—Doak Hall today—was positioned farther south of the entry mall than the Men's Dormitory—or present-day West Hall, potentially as a symbolic gesture in further sequestering women's residences from male housing.

Designs for the two residence halls were hailed in local newspapers for both their handsome appearance and economical cost. Neither had clay tile roofs, and individual windows had notably less detail at their surrounds but did feature multistory stone entries and elaborate stone finials at corner parapets. A PWA requirement stipulated that Franklin Delano Roosevelt's name was listed largest and first on the cornerstone, a less-than-subtle political reminder that Roosevelt—Bradford Knapp's friend in the White House—and his administration deserved special thanks for the two dormitories. While Koeppe's design demonstrated the ability for Hedrick's office to indigenously produce a Plateresque-revival design, both West and Doak Halls suffered from a growing schizophrenic tradition at Tech of dichotomy between interior and exterior architecture. While Spanish finials, ailerons, and aedicules adorned the exterior, the main stairway to each dormitory featured generic neoclassical iron handrails, while columns in the main dining room were capped with Egyptian capitals with papyrus reed details.

The Men's and Women's Dormitories proved divergent from Tech's initial vision as Watkin had never envisioned Texas Tech to be clad in a uniform fabric of buff-blend brick and Leuders stone. Proposed elevations of the student residential blocks from the previous decade illustrate the use of stucco as a predominant exterior veneer with simplistic stone detail at archways and quoining at building corners. Early secondary buildings at Tech like the President's House, Agriculture Building, and Livestock Judging Pavilion all bear this aesthetic strategy out. Driven largely by the 1934 Board of Directors, who assumed a uniform campus palette was intended, Koeppe's designs for West and Doak Halls inadvertently eliminated this hierarchy by applying a uniform brick and stone veneer to all future buildings, regardless of type, for decades to come. Even Castilian Spanish cities, or post-earthquake Santa Barbara had no such material consistency in their urban environs. Furthermore, using only buff-blend brick would have other unexpected consequences.

The primary highway between Dallas and Lubbock—State Highway 114—is named within the Dallas area for the Dallas judge and one-time Ku Klux Klansmen—John W. Carpenter. From 1931 to 1937, Carpenter set a vociferous precedent for how board members could ramrod pet initiatives into reality. As if Bradford Knapp didn't already have enough headaches to deal with, in early 1934 Carpenter learned that the brick for the two PWA dormitories—the same brick that had been used at Tech for a decade, was not Texas-made.[19] Originally, Watkin had selected a dark sandy-to-olive brown brick blend reminiscent of the color of Lubbock-area soil, but drawn from the Ouachita River Valley at the Acme Brick Perla Plant outside Malvern, in central Arkansas. Carpenter threw a fit, demanding that Texas products only be used for Tech buildings, and in a moment of state pride the remainder of the Board agreed.[20] At first, Bradford Knapp defended the selection, worried that a Texas duplicate for Perla brick was not possible, leading Carpenter's brother Lewis—the legislative author of Texas Technological College eleven years before—to submit a seven-page rebuke and diatribe to Knapp.[21] Knapp relented and ordered Hedrick to find a Texas-made brick equal to the Perla product.

Carpenter's "Brick rant" would have further profound impact on Texas Tech architecture whose ripple effects were still three decades from realization. Following Tech's 1925 opening, a surge in buff-blend-brick use swept the state—particularly in West Texas—and usage had not abated. Hedrick and Acme successfully located a native source of clay that matched existing buildings at Tech, but a source far less abundant than the clay pits at Perla. From school buildings in Friona to downtown Fort Worth skyscrapers—hundreds if not thousands of buildings were being clad with a Texas brick whose popularity would eventually result in the extinction of a particular clay color in the state of Texas.

SUCCESS IN PURSUING the dormitory grants spurred applications for other PWA monies for projects at Texas Tech—a development that uncovered Bradford Knapp's penchant for campus architecture and planning. Not long after his arrival, Knapp had ordered the Architecture Department to produce a scale model of the campus with detachable building models carved of soap.[22] Visitors ushered into Knapp's office for meetings would often find Knapp hovered over his model in the corner of the office engrossed in some wild-hare vision of future projects on campus. Often, such wild-hare visions found their way to Hedrick and the Board as a PWA Grant opportunity. Herman Koeppe, still parked at his drafting board at the Mayflower, was frequently engaged in developing concepts of all sorts at Tech. One proposal never to see fruition was the Dairy Manufacturing Building—also known as PWA Project No. 1064, developed in the summer of 1935.[23] The 10,900 square foot, two-story design reflected Hedrick's and Koeppe's design ethic using more generic Spanish motifs in lieu of Watkin's strategy of finding inspiration in specific Spanish case studies. PWA 1064 also reflected Knapp's curricular shift from growing college enrollment at any cost as Horn had pursued, to developing specific technical curricula for the institution and building

The Dairy Technology Building would have replaced—the Dairy Barn. Seen here (undated) with the Dairy Manager's house that was later removed. The Dairy Barn would eventually become a priceless part of the Tech Physical Plant.

the facilities to support that. Koeppe's design was not overly ornate, as details were concentrated at the building's main entrance. No site plan survives of the Dairy Manufacturing Building today to indicate its proposed campus location, but an elevated berm identical in height to Watkin's proposed Court of Honor is shown in elevation, suggesting that the Dairy Building was to be situated somewhere near the Chemistry Building. However, the project was cancelled as Washington administrators rejected Tech's application for PWA 1064.

Coach Pete Cawthon arrived in 1930 to coach a beleaguered Matador football squad, and in short order helped usher the program into the Border Intercollegiate Athletic Conference, and quickly righted a 3 to 6, 1930 squad into a team that never lost more than two games between 1932 and 1935. Tech's unimpressive single-sided stadium built for a 1927 inaugural matchup against Texas A&M only sat 2,200 spectators on one side of the field only—a venue that most national programs rebuffed when invited to play in Lubbock. Throughout the 1930s, Cawthon eagerly offered for Tech to play away games, prompting the Matadors, clad in flashy scarlet-and-black uniforms, to travel as far as Florida, California, and Michigan for games. An October 26, 1934, victory over West Coast power Loyola Marymount of California led *Morning Avalanche* writer Collier Parish to nickname the squad the Red Raiders—a name that would in short time stick. Regardless of success, athletics fundraising revenue at Tech in the 1930s was meager at best. A godsend $500 donation from Amon Carter in 1925 to the Tech Athletic Fund had been enough to buy uniforms for the football team their first year of play, but even that was an outlier.[24] Major programs could afford large permanent stadium venues, while Texas Tech's home field possessed no press box and no lighting to support the growing popularity of nighttime football matches. Cawthon was happy enough to have quasi-green irrigated grass on the fields, and players liked the irrigation too, as water breaks were in fact forbidden during practice, so players knew exactly where to fall in an open-field tackle so they could steal a gulp of water from one of the hose bibs when no one was looking. Coaches loved using the cross-bracing under the bleachers of the stadium as obstacle drill space for the players,[25] but the value ended there as Tech was overdue for a stadium upgrade to match their growing on-field success.

During this time, Louisiana Governor and later US Senator Huey P. Long defied Works Progress Administration (in this case, not PWA) requirements barring funds for sports venues and "assisted" Louisiana State University to grant-fund a twenty-four thousand-seat expansion to Tiger Stadium by adding hundreds of dormitory living units ringing the façade of the stadium, dubiously arguing the project was a housing project and not intended for recreation. Likewise, the State College of Washington at Pullman (today known as Washington State University) secured PWA funds to rebuild bleachers to Rodgers Field.[26] The precedent existed for PWA funding of stadium projects, prompting Tech to push forward with a grant proposal for PWA Project No. 1044. The Tech Board met in Hedrick's office on December 4, 1935 to approve their submission to Washington for 1044.[27] Bradford Knapp personally approved the drawings, as the Tech Board recommended application for an $83,000 grant from the PWA to complement $67,000 the college had scraped together for the project. Sadly however, 1044 was ultimately rejected.[28]

Hedrick's stadium design was nothing elaborate—an east and west

Concept elevations for a failed PWA proposal for a Texas Tech Dairy Technology Building.

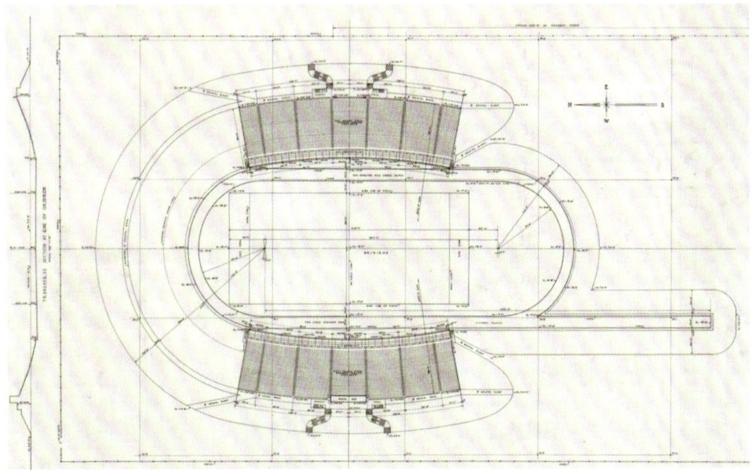
Site plan for Texas Tech PWA Grant Proposal No. 1044—a concrete-and-earthen-bermed football stadium that would predate Jones Stadium by twelve years, but whose application to Washington, DC, failed in late 1935.

arc of concrete bleachers set atop earthen berms with a squat, masonry-clad press box. Interestingly enough, the 1935 Tech Field design bore remarkable similarities to the design developed twelve years later for Jones Stadium, albeit somewhat smaller with only a 14,300 seating capacity.[29] But Hedrick's proposal included a horseshoe embankment enclosing the east, south, and west sides of the stadium that would have eventually proven an Achilles' heel to any future expansion of the stadium. Based on that, the college would have likely faced more expensive expansion solutions in the 1950s to meet Southwest Conference entry requirements, or potentially abandon the site altogether. But with 1044 dead, Tech was forced to undertake a half-measured expansion of Tech Field by focusing their $67,000 in retained funds to add an additional 9,800-seat horseshoe expansion out of wood-framed bleachers.[30]

While construction at Tech Field was underway, a pair of wood crates arrived at Tech from the E. W. Vanduzen Foundry in Cincinnati, Ohio. The Class of 1936 had purchased two bronze bells as class gifts from the same foundry that fabricated the carillon chimes for the pair of Spanish Renaissance–revival towers at the Lewis and Clark Centennial Exposition in Portland three decades earlier.[31] Class gifts

Class gifts to the college would become indispensable additions to the campus that the college could not afford. Predating Tech's now-iconic granite entry seal by thirty-eight years, the Class of 1934 paid for a stuccoed concrete entrance sign on Broadway that was in fact the only art deco-styled work of architecture on campus.

An expanded ten-thousand-seat Tech Field ready for play in the fall of 1936. Essentially a wood-framed expansion of the 1927 steel bleachers built for Tech's first game against Texas A&M, Tech Field would serve as home of the Red Raiders for another eleven years.

had became invaluable sources to grow the college physical plant, as luxuries like street lamps and the now-iconic Double-T bench installed south of the Administration Building salle-porte could not otherwise be afforded either out of the college budget or by state appropriations. By early May, the two bells were ready for ringing at the graduation ceremonies.

By September 1936, Tech Field construction was complete, and the local press did their best to describe the newly painted light gray-and-green facility as the "New" stadium,[32] though the original 1927 steel bleachers remained on the west side of the field, connected by a ten-row horseshoe of bleachers that connected to a new twenty-five row bank of wood-framed bleachers east of the field—now totaling twelve thousand seats in all. Interestingly, the project budget included electric lighting for night games, although with standards situated between the bleachers and the field. On the night of September 29, 1936, in the second-ever game played at the "New" Tech Field, the recently renamed Red Raiders hosted Texas Christian University, led by star quarterback Sammy Baugh. Tech had never bested TCU before, while the defending national champion TCU squad remained ranked in the top ten of the newly created Associated Press polling system. Texas Tech bested the Horned Frogs 7 to 0.[33] Pandemonium ensued as fans stormed the field and Arch Lamb, founder of the newly formed Saddle Tramps organization made good on a pep rally promise earlier that week and locked himself in the East Tower of the Administration Building.[34] Lamb would joyously ring both of the new Cincinnati-made bells until 6 a.m. the next morning—an event that would pass into Tech mythos. But in fact, nine months later, on June 9, 1937, it was Elizabeth Howard West who repeated Lamb's feat,[35] and, regardless of the city of Lubbock's new ordinance passed over the Lamb incident which limited bell ringing to thirty minutes,

West rang the Victory Bells away. After an eight-year fight for funding, the 45th Texas State Legislature had finally appropriated $275,000 for the new College Library Building at Tech.[36] West's and her library's twelve-year purgatory in the Administration Building was finally coming to an end.

ONLY A FEW WEEKS BEFORE Elizabeth West's outburst in the East Carillon, a slim ruddy-haired man arrived at the Scanlan Building in Houston to begin his professional career in architecture. Just weeks before, he had successfully defended his thesis on the future of the gas station in architecture to Architecture Department Chair William Ward Watkin and a committee of graduate faculty committee at the Rice Institute. At twenty-three, Nolan Ellimore Barrick caught Watkin's attention as a capable designer and draftsman, but Barrick had also caught the eye of Watkin's daughter, Rosemary. It took a bold man to work for his former professor, but even a bolder man still to ask for his daughter's hand in marriage, which Barrick would do two years later. Watkin welcomed Barrick, toured him through the atelier, and led Barrick to his drafting station. Throughout the day, Barrick kept looking up at a handsome building elevation framed on the wall above his drafting board.

Late in the day, Watkin came by to check on his young protégé, prompting Barrick to ask Watkin about the building on the wall. Watkin replied, "Oh, that is the Administration Building for a college I designed in Lubbock, called Texas Technological College."[37] Barrick was not familiar with Texas Tech, but little did he know that in sixteen years' time, his office would look out of one of the windows in that elevation.

10

THE X-BUILDINGS

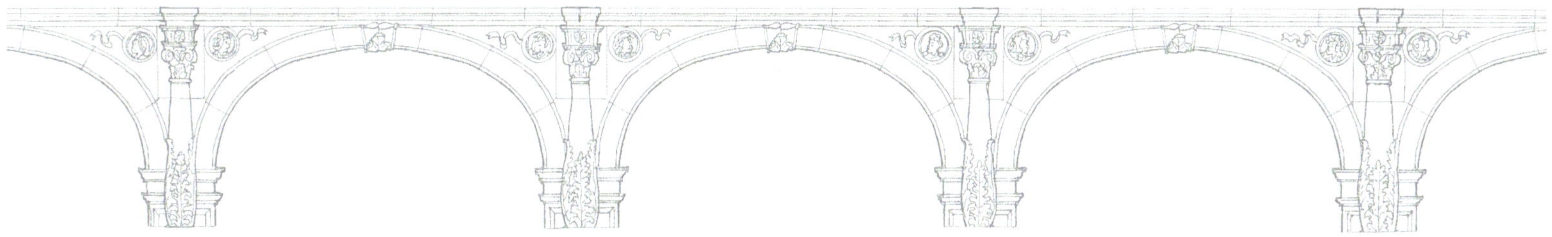

INGLES & SIKES, a Dallas-area contractor, was delayed in completing the new Wyatt C. Hedrick–designed two-story Agriculture Sciences Building—located south of the Chemistry Laboratory—until the summer of 1942. The Japanese attack at Pearl Harbor abruptly altered plans for A. H. Leidigh, Wenzel Stangel, and the Tech agriculture faculty, who had longed for offices and classrooms away from either their rickety stucco-clad building at 15th Street and Boston, or a ditch in a research crop field. In mobilizing for war, the army needed institutions like Texas Tech as bases for training officers and technical specializations. Under the authority of the recently passed War Powers Act, the army ordered the state to appropriate the new building as a command center for ongoing training programs at the college. Three years would pass before Texas Tech faculty would even get to set foot in the new building.[1]

Wartime priorities brought construction at Tech to a halt, but the human war effort had sapped enrollment at Texas Tech to a degree that made the hardships of the Great Depression pale in comparison. Tech had achieved a record 3,800 students in 1939, but by the fall term of 1943, Texas Tech would only enroll 1,622.[2] In the late 1930s, Texas Tech had finally fought its way past the skeptics in Austin, and gained steam in the continued construction of its physical plant, albeit in a manner that under Wyatt Hedrick's firm deviated in a number of aspects from the 1924 Master Plan. But several crucial buildings would sprout up at a crucial time, though the human cost paid for those buildings—the cost of a single man in fact—proved an expensive transaction.

LIKE PAUL HORN BEFORE HIM, Bradford Knapp loved Tech's Spanish Renaissance campus style, and likewise despised anything, whether dust, tumbleweeds, or in particular pigeon excrement, that threatened its appearance. Hard to imagine in the present-day era of campus security, Knapp had organized college-sanctioned pigeon shoots where students were welcome to bring firearms onto campus

Handsome and understated, completion of the Agriculture Building would become lost in America—and Texas Tech's—entry into World War II. Note the elevated berm denoting a continuation of Watkin's elevated Court of Honor.

Bradford Knapp on horseback, supervising Tech's iconic first Arbor Day, not long prior to his passing.

to decimate the feral bird population. Knapp's tireless advocacy, along with continuous nagging from Elizabeth West, also brought funding at long last for a college library.

Governor James Allred had personally attended the cornerstone laying ceremony prior to completion of the two-story-plus-basement, sixty-seven-thousand-square-foot distant relative to the 1928 Chemistry Building that was completed in spring 1938.[3] Though not nearly as ornate as Watkin's Chemistry Building design, Herman Koeppe would distantly imitate Chemistry's Palacio de Monterrey-inspired corner tower with a five-windowed, clay tile roofed tower situated at the southeast corner of the library. From a planning standpoint, the building was seminal in that the Library added a better sense of composition to Watkin's Court of Honor. Leuders stone-crafted details such as finials, framed stone conches over the second-floor windows, and false tower balustrades were simpler and more generic in nature than Watkin's aesthetic flare employed on Chemistry. Much of the budget had been consumed by a steel-framed multistory stack bay set deep within the building—crucial to providing West and the Library the three hundred thousand volume capacity desired.[4] Budgetary limitations would also leave the new Library Building without the fletched stucco vaulting so characteristically unique to the Chemistry Building colonnade. The new Library budget would only allow for exposed painted wood joists.

Bradford Knapp was not content to settle with new construction alone, and he was determined to change the aesthetic image of the dusty, flat Lubbock campus at all costs. Though chronic fatigue hounded Knapp that spring, he nonetheless presided on horseback over the largest conscripted work program in college history—a makeshift early Arbor Day—advanced two-and-a-half months from its usually observed date to March 2, 1938. Classes were ordered cancelled that day, as all who could stand on their two feet were conscripted with picks, shovels, or rakes. What has been estimated at roughly twenty thousand plants—Siberian elms, Russian olives, honey locusts, hackberries—anything that could grow in the tough South Plains climate—were planted.[5] Further thousands of smaller

Conch and finial details flanking and overhead of a second-floor window to the Old Library Building (today Mathematics and Statistics).

The curious interrupted gable design to the west façade of the Old Library Building.

shrubs were planted. Students looking up to see the foreboding sight of Knapp on horseback quickly resumed their work, not realizing that the president did not have a gun. But to students that Arbor Day, now iconic in Tech lore, the event had to feel somewhat like a chain gang at work.

Countless public events, mountains of paperwork, and a taxing meeting schedule continued to take its toll on the president. Having already survived a minor heart attack in 1936, Knapp failed to take heed of warnings from his doctor, wife, and friends to warning signs. At 11:20 a.m. on Saturday, June 11, 1938, Bradford Knapp became the second man killed by the insurmountable weight of the role as president of Texas Technological College when he died of a massive heart attack.[6] Recent positive momentum at Tech almost ground to a halt not because of his death, but due to a subsequent bitter internal political fight within the board of directors over Knapp's replacement. Most on the board, including the student body, supported advancing Board Chairman Clifford Bartlett Jones to the presidency. Jones, whose temperament, political qualities, and institutional memory made him supremely qualified for the role, still faced scrutiny as Jones had never earned a college degree. Only after a contentious voting process and year-long vitriolic battle between Jones and a minority

Present-day detail photograph of the south tower form to the Old Library Building, featuring an arcature of five windows in lieu of Watkin's Palacio de Monterrey-inspired triple-arch form.

of board members was the affable ranch manager and former West Texas Chamber of Commerce president affirmed as the third president of Texas Technological College.[7] Jones's strategy was largely a continuation of Knapp's strategy—hammer Austin for more funding—not as much for new buildings as it was needed for added faculty and increased salaries to offset the severe austerity measures of the early 1930s. Regardless, PWA grants were already funding two more dormitories already under construction at Tech—Men's Dormitory No. 2 and Women's Dormitory No. 2—today known respectively as Sneed and Drane Halls.

Sneed Hall, completed in the summer of 1938, and Drane Hall, completed in 1939, reflected marked improvements in Hedrick's and Koeppe's aesthetic approach to dormitory design at Texas Tech. Koeppe's designs for Sneed and Drane's design sacrificed ornate stone work at entries, building corners, and parapets in lieu of the addition of red clay tile hip roofs in the project scope. The simpler stone entry façades of Sneed and Drane dormitories still retained a Castilian character, and in the case of Men's Dormitory No. 2—now the closest campus building to College Avenue—retained Plateresque details such as arched windows on the third floor to simulate a *piso de la* hidalguía. In addition, Men's Dormitory No. 2 (later Sneed Hall) included stone building corner compositions replete with engaged Corinthian columns and ailerons and corner rows of roof-edge finials set atop parapets that broke the hip edges the clay tile roof. Both buildings, albeit classic Sanguinet, Staats & Hedrick C-plans in form, demonstrated that though nowhere near as ornate as Watkin's compositions, Koeppe and the Hedrick team were in fact adding their own unique aesthetic to the Tech palette, just not necessarily with the direct inspiration of sixteenth-century case studies.

Clifford Jones, third president of Texas Technological College, seated with his wife Audrey, undated.

Clifford Jones convinced the State Legislature in the 1939 Biennium to fund two capital projects at Tech—first, a much-needed Agriculture Sciences Building, and a Press Building for the college's journalism programs.[8] The two-story Press Building would be one of the smallest of the brick-clad buildings from the prewar era at Tech. Less than twenty thousand square feet and with a challenging budget, exterior details for the Press Building were limited to rusticated stone quoins around the entry and a false second-floor balconette and reja. The choice of the Press Building site, a building never identified in Watkin's Master Plan, may literally have been to further visually close the northwestern horizon of what was inadvertently evolving into a circle at the center of the campus, rather than Watkin's original Goodhue-esque square plaza.

The other 1939 capital project—the 43,300-square foot Agriculture Sciences Building—is a building that today remains often overlooked by students, faculty, and observers—though is one of the best designs ever produced by Wyatt C. Hedrick's office at Texas Tech. Though not particularly eye-catching in its form and massing—Herman Koeppe and the Hedrick team had finally broken away from designing generic Spanish-revival detailing, instead seeking to add vernacular details that imparted the Agricultural Sciences Building with a unique identity. The building itself replaced in siting what had been intended originally by Watkin as the site for the College Library in 1924. It's east entrance, designed to axially align to a future walkway south of a future fully built Administration Building, visually reinforced a perception that agricultural education, even after Dr. Knapp's passing, would remain important to the college.

Two stories tall with a partial-height basement, Agricultural Sciences was a handsome facility and an ideal exemplar to the future group of agriculturally focused academic buildings that would be situated over the next two decades along Fifteenth Street. Koeppe also

Sneed Hall (previously named Men's Dormitory No.2); a clay tile roofed dormitory iteration on the Hedrick U-shaped PWA dormitory model, completed shortly before the Second World War.

Agricultural escutcheon set over the Agriculture Building entrance featuring a longhorn skull, ears of corn, and shock of wheat.

opted to continue the same elevated ground floor proposed for the Court of Honor—the same plane envisioned for the failed proposal for the 1936 Dairy Laboratory Building. Agricultural Science's northeast entrance featured a stone filigree parapet, stone quoining, a pair of Castilian-paneled wood entry doors, a handsome range of rejería, and finally, over the entrance, an escutcheon featuring a cow's head, plow, and a shock of wheat. Sadly, Agricultural Sciences would be Koeppe's last design at Texas Tech, as Hedrick's vital lead designer died in 1941 while the Agriculture Building was under construction.[9] In his passing, Hedrick turned to Koeppe's son, Earl Emmet, who would prove similarly adept in design as his father, particularly with neoclassical commissions like work at Tech, and with good reason. Earl Koeppe was a Rice architecture graduate, class of 1929,[10] and too had been mentored by William Ward Watkin in the years prior to Watkin's wife's passing. Ingle-Sikes, whose workforce was likely decimated by the war effort, was barely able to finish their touch-up work to the building by August 1942. Fighting a war effort across two global theaters of operations was kicking into full gear just as planning and construction at Texas Technological College ground to a halt.

It was an utterly frustrating time for Texas Tech. With no money from Washington, DC or Austin, over half of the student body now serving in uniform, and much of the faculty drawn away for technical assignments in the armed forces, there was nearly no point to be in operation in the first place. When Jones submitted with his 1942 Annual Report to the board of directors a roster of students and faculty fighting in the war effort, the list filled seven pages.[11] Even keeping the grass alive on campus remained a huge problem, not because of drought or limited water, but rather due to trampling. The army loved Watkin's broad axial campus plan, as the Engineering Key and Broadway Mall made for excellent drill grounds. Coach Dell Morgan could barely field a full football platoon not only due to budget cuts and wartime travel rationing, but also because most college athletes were now serving in the military. The Red Raiders found themselves playing army airfield intramural squads just as often as real schools.

The diminutive Press (Journalism) Building, completed in 1941.

Even if Texas Tech had funding to construct new buildings, the powerful federal War Production Board would likely not divert precious building metals away from the war effort, and Tech was unlikely to find an architect to design anything. Wyatt Hedrick's firm was buried in a hoard of War Department projects ranging from Consolidated-Vultee's massive new mile-long Fort Worth B-24 Production Plant, to airfields, and a new base in Bermuda designed to stem the U-boat scourge in the Atlantic.[12] Lubbock-area architects—a growing local cadre of professionals like Sylvan Blum Haynes and Myrick Strange—were too snowed under with government work, in their case dozens of wood-framed buildings for US Army Air Force airfields across Texas and New Mexico. With the tide turning with the war, in February 1944, Strange received a letter from his friend—none other than William Ward Watkin. Watkin was inquiring to the possibility of teaming to pursue future work at Texas Tech, whose relationship he hoped to rekindle.[13] Watkin even reached out to President Jones in hope of rekindling interest in the Hall of Texas vision.[14] Alas, Tech still had no funding for new construction, and other than Clifford Jones, few even remembered the tall, slim architect from Houston.

The stress of keeping Texas Tech open on a shoestring wartime budget proved too much for Clifford Jones. Almost perfectly mirroring the events that presaged Bradford Knapp's death six years earlier, Jones would too suffer a minor heart attack in early 1942.[15] He was not going to press his luck and repeat Knapp's mistake, and tendered his resignation to the board of directors that April. The board initially refused it, urging that Jones take a medical leave of absence to recover while remaining at the helm. Jones returned in late May 1942, still tired and weary. On February 12, 1944, he once again tendered his resignation to the Tech Board[16]—this time adamant to break a dark tradition among past Texas Tech presidents. The board could not defer the matter any longer, and in late June grudgingly accepted Jones's resignation with the condition he be named president emeritus, and helm the fledgling new Texas Tech Foundation.[17]

CLIFFORD JONES'S REPLACEMENT, William Marvin Whyburn, still holds the record today as the youngest president in the history of Texas Tech. Opinions vary as to the effectiveness of the forty-two year-old mathematician's short tenure as president, though when measured by enrollment growth, Whyburn did well. Of course, postwar growth was automatic, as from fall 1945 to fall 1946, enrollment skyrocketed by a rate of nearly 120 percent,[18] an annual record that still holds today. His advocacy of much-needed funding referenda like the 1947 College Building Amendment to the Texas State Constitution—a five-cent ad valorem tax—paved the way for much-needed postwar campus academic construction at Tech.[19] When he left office in 1948, Whyburn left Tech a building fund of $2.8 million—an unheard-of balance in the young college's history—enough money in that era to build nearly 140,000 square feet of new construction. On

Hermann Koeppe, Hedrick's talented chief designer who emigrated from Leipzig, Germany, in his youth, survived the 1900 Galveston hurricane, and would go on to design millions of square feet of architectural commissions across the United States, undated.

Army Air Forces trainees parade upon the campus traffic circle Broadway Mall beyond.

paper, William Whyburn had accomplished a bevy of successes in only four short years.

Whyburn has also been roundly criticized for his cold, martinet-like demeanor, and a "check off the box" mindset extending everywhere from submitting an essentially worthless application to the Association of American Universities for membership, to applying slap-dash facility solutions for the rapidly growing college. It was the latter that marks Whyburn as one of the less admirable Texas Tech presidents in terms of enriching the architectural palette of the campus. One particular Whyburn decision introduced a wood-framed pestilence onto the Lubbock campus that proved difficult to eradicate for decades to come.

With the Allies winning in 1945 and large numbers of veterans already returning home, the Tech registrar noticed a sizeable uptick in enrollment that January. Continued wartime training demands prevented the army returning all of Tech's dormitories back to college control, leaving the institution short on beds to address the sudden surge. To provide beds, Whyburn negotiated an agreement with the Federal Housing Administration to house students temporarily in surplus barracks at the Lubbock Army Airfield north of the city.[20] But the surge continued, and with the war over and rapid demobilization of military facilities nationwide underway, Whyburn seized on the "surplus" concept and concluded a purchase agreement with the War Assets Administration for thirty-two disused wood framed barracks and office buildings. Tech would arrange for the structures, mostly US Army single-story buildings built at Camp Bowie in Fort Worth and Camp Barkley in Abilene,[21] to be cut from their foundations and shipped by heavy truck to Lubbock. On April 25, 1947, onlookers watched curiously as the first trucks arrived to deposit the buildings at selected locations across campus.[22]

By September, the contractor J. B. Leftwich & Company had completed foundations, utility connections, and setting of the wood-

Arrival of the X-buildings: two former army barracks assembled side-by-side have been refashioned as the College Faculty Club and are being relocated.

Men's Dormitories Nos. 3 and 4 (today known as Bledsoe-Gordon Hall), as construction nears completion in 1947.

framed turkeys onto their new sites. Whyburn was ecstatic at his genius decision. By the stroke of a pen, over 115,000 square feet of much needed academic, support, and student life space had been added to the college at a fraction of the cost of expensive Plateresque-revival architecture. Tech now had a stand-alone cafeteria for the first time since the furtive attempt to operate a profitable dining establishment in 1925. Students had a clinic and dispensary, a student auditorium, a dance hall, new engineering shops, a band classroom, and an office for the college's ROTC detachment.[23] But Texas Technological College campus now consisted of two distinctive architectural styles—Plateresque Spanish Renaissance and a mass of whitewashed army barracks—buildings that side by side proved a hideous blend. Further, the buildings had the inadvertent effect of presenting Austin with the false sense that Texas Tech now had all the academic space they needed for the time being. Even though ad valorem tax revenue would fund two new larger residence halls, it would not be until the 1949 General Session that Tech would receive funding from Austin for badly needed laboratory and classroom space. The army of new buildings were numbered sequentially and were identified with the ambiguous and uninspiring prefix "X." The era of the X-buildings at Texas Tech had begun.

Even as oversize trailers were delivering old barracks buildings to Lubbock, four new dormitories—essentially two large complexes—were underway on the eastern boundary of the campus. Contracts were awarded on April 4, 1946, by the Tech Board of Directors for Men's Dormitories 3 and 4, and Women's Dormitories 3 and 4—today known respectively as Bledsoe-Gordon and Horn-Knapp Halls. The latest creations from Wyatt C. Hedrick's office introduced a totally new building footprint to the Tech campus—best described as an "H" plan with dining and lobby space at the center of the building, and housing wings flared diagonally from the tip of each "H." The design approach, though cost-effective and still displaying some limited vestiges of Plateresque detail, was the final nail in the coffin to Watkin's more humane monastic concept for grouping housing on campus. From a siting standpoint, the haphazard placement of

Designed by Amarillo atelier Walsh & Hazelwood, the Music Building (1951) was one of many postwar projects that marked the end of Hedrick's monopoly on architectural design at Texas Tech.

Postwar inflation and continued funding limitations took their toll at Tech. Hedrick's Petroleum Engineering Laboratory (1950) was scant in ornament and detail, even around the entry.

Horn-Knapp and Gordon-Bledsoe seemed an anathema to the quadrangles of a Beaux-Arts campus.

Regardless, Horn-Knapp and Bledsoe-Gordon were crucial to Tech given they provided 1,400 beds at the same time enrollment exceeded six thousand students—coincidentally Watkin's original target enrollment for the college Master Plan.[24] With the total cost for both buildings of $4,001,145, the two demonstrated that Tech was already getting less for more. Inflation on the construction dollar had already jumped nearly 28 percent in the two years since the end of the war.[25] Earl Koeppe and the Hedrick team had incorporated every bit of Spanish-revival detail that could be afforded for the budget, but those details were limited to a clay-tile roof, a simple stone covered entry crowned with a set of squat finials, and repetitive third floor masonry pilasters incorporated as a nod to the piso de la hidalguía treatment seen often in the estilo plateresco.

The boon of New Deal-era work and the mobilization needs of World War II had brought great financial dividends for Hedrick personally, as his firm had by the late 1940s grown into the second-largest multidisciplinary design firm in the nation. Long removed from his bankruptcy, Hedrick had accumulated an impressive range of ranch properties throughout Texas, totaling over 375,000 acres and home to more than ten thousand head of cattle by the late 1940s.[26] One property—the Anacacho Ranch west of Uvalde—happened to sit astride John Nance Garner's ranch,[27] which was likely an adroit political move by Hedrick, who always made sure to visit the former vice president when in town. Hedrick and his wife now regularly flew by private plane to Anacacho to enjoy the finer accoutrements of life, as the ranch featured an Italianate villa replete with a very respectable art collection.[28]

DESPITE THE CHALLENGES of running one of the largest design firms in the nation, Hedrick continued to invest a personal level of attention to maintaining a strong relationship with Texas Tech through the 1940s, including personally attending meetings with Whyburn and other college leaders, and dispatching his brother Russell to Lubbock to manage construction administration. Despite his personal wealth, the miserly Hedrick never missed an opportunity to enlist his daughter Mildred to chauffeur him to and from Lubbock in the family sedan. (Hedrick had and regularly used gratis passes for those railroads for which he was the architect.) Cheaper than a rail fare, Hedrick could sprawl out in the back seat, review drawings or correspondence, and on occasion catch five- or ten-minute cat naps. His daughter later remarked about Hedrick's constant energy, noting that, "While people are often measured by their 'Intelligence Quotient,' some people [like Hedrick] also had a very high 'Energy Quotient,' or 'EQ.'"[29]

One pragmatic reason for Hedrick's personal interjection into projects at Tech in the late 1940s was growing competition. Whereas Wyatt Hedrick had to travel from Fort Worth for meetings, Lubbock—now a city of over sixty thousand people—boasted a number of reputable local architectural ateliers whose principals frequently crossed paths with Texas Tech leadership, and were too actively marketing the college for new work. These relationships were bound to eventually penetrate the walls of Hedrick's fortress market as architect at Tech, which finally occurred in 1946 with the selection of Lubbock architects Haynes & Kirby for the design of Tech's new football stadium. The College Building Amendment to the State Constitution and Tech's resulting $4 million building program finally shattered any remaining vestiges of that fortress wall; as between 1949 and 1951 a blend of ad valorem tax revenue and Whyburn's building fund paid for seven different academic and student life projects at Tech. The expansion was by far the largest academic building growth to date—over four hundred thousand square feet would be completed by 1952—and did not even include other projects paid for outside of state funds, namely the Museum of West Texas and new Student Union Building. Only two of those projects—the new Science Building and at long last an expansion of the Administration Building—would be designed by Wyatt C. Hedrick Architects.

II

LORD CALVERT

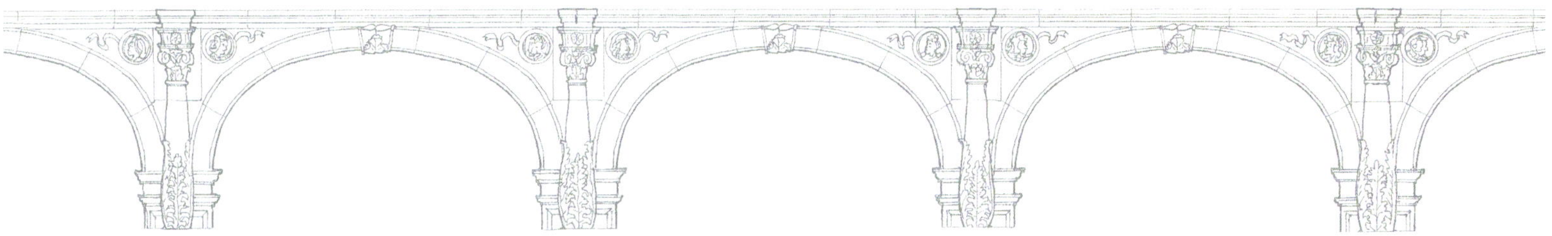

On March 13, 1950, the latest edition of *Life* magazine hit the newsstands nationwide featuring a showcase of spring dress fashion for ladies. Buried in the pages of that issue was an advertisement for the Lord Calvert Distillery—part of a long and successful ad campaign titled "Men of Distinction" that been featured since the late 1930s. The "Men of Distinction" ads featured the likes of artist Robert Ripley, journalist Ernest K. Lindsey, Chilean pianist Claudio Arrau, modernist architect William Lescaze, and actor John Loder, always displaying each at work or leisure, with a glass of Lord Calvert in hand. Even author James Michener—who two decades later would visit Texas Tech and memorably remark about its campus beauty—was featured in a November 1949 Lord Calvert article.[1] But it was none other than Wyatt Cephas Hedrick featured in a Lord Calvert advertisement in that March 1950 edition of *Life* that would inexplicably and forever change the course of campus design and planning at Texas Tech.

In 1946, Hedrick secured a sizeable commission from Houston oilman Glenn H. McCarthy to design an unrivaled "destination" hotel in the southern edge of Houston. Coined in the press as "Diamond Glenn," McCarthy was the epitome of the rags-to-riches oil wildcatter—rough-edged and charismatic—he had worked his way from roughneck in the 1920s to becoming a college-educated wartime oil baron. By the end of World War II, McCarthy had expanded his investment interests outside of petroleum, and the next leap in his entrepreneurial vision was the Shamrock Hotel. Named in salute to his questionable Irish heritage, McCarthy would heavily micromanage the project, forcing upon Hedrick and designer Earl Koeppe a pastiche of dated, eclectic, and unnecessary design decisions that produced the largest, if not the most expensive single hotel in US history at that time. McCarthy favored the art deco architectural style, which was by the late 1940s démodé both with the public and certainly among architectural circles, and made even less sense when combined with McCarthy's universal insistence on the use of the color green in the new building. Stylistic issues aside, Hedrick assembled a team of consultants to meet the high demands of the project, including the Los Angeles interior design firm of Robert D. Harrell,

The infamous March 13, 1950, Lord Calvert advertisement for *Life* magazine featuring Wyatt C. Hedrick. Incredibly, this otherwise tasteful ad would forever alter the architectural history of Texas Tech.

(*Left*) Marketing photograph of the Shamrock Hotel produced by Wyatt C. Hedrick, Architects, undated.

(*Below*) Caricature by Rice alumnus and architect Francis Vesey of William Ward Watkin and Frank Lloyd Wright. Though the two architects had entirely different design preferences, the two would strike up a strong friendship and mutual respect for each other up until Watkin's death.

furnishings and carpets custom manufactured by Ellison Furniture of Fort Worth, and outdoor gardens to be designed by noted landscape architect Ralph Ellis Gunn.[2]

With an owner's program demand of 1,100 rooms, Hedrick and Koeppe had to find a manageable scale and volume to the building as the site was situated in the largely single-story residential area of Houston. Koeppe developed an eighteen-story C-shaped plan—a proven configuration that dated back four decades to the Sanguinet & Staats era. Formatively, the result was an austere, green-tile roofed behemoth, which local and national press attempted to describe in articles without insult. Even if externally austere, features ranging from a massive swimming pool to push-button radios in hotel rooms and plush interior finishes, all of course adorned in some color of

Tech's Home Economics Building, designed by Watkin in 1925, would be expanded in 1951 into an L-shaped form through the design vision of Lubbock; architect Sylvan Blum Haynes.

green—combined to a price tag of $21 million[3]—over three times the cost of land and buildings spent at Texas Technological College since its founding! The Shamrock opened on Saint Patrick's Day 1949 to a fireworks-studded evening gala that is still talked about in Houston lore today.

McCarthy bought a converted Boeing airliner direct from Howard Hughes expressly for flying a bevy of celebrities from Hollywood for the Shamrock's opening night. In addition, a Santa Fe Super Chief was also chartered to bring further hoards of celebrities by train to the opening. Four thousand residents and Tech students alone crowded the station in Lubbock to see the stars when the Super Chief stopped while en route to Houston.[4] The opening gala quickly boiled over into a raucous, drunken bash overflowing with some fifty thousand attendees. Houston mayor Oscar Holcombe and his wife at one point lost their dinner seats to usurping party crashers and spent the evening sitting in a hallway. The party was nationally broadcast via NBC radio, until an expletive accidentally uttered on air sent the on-stage performer, celebrity Dorothy Lamour, fleeing in tears.[5] In the midst of all of this madness, Hedrick, his wife Mildred, Earl Koeppe, his wife and son, E. Paul, the Ellisons and their daughter Nancy, were gathered in the lobby of the Shamrock early that evening, when another architect happened to wander by.

The inestimable Frank Lloyd Wright was not in Houston for the Shamrock's opening, but rather for the first ever convention event scheduled at the Shamrock's spacious twenty-five thousand square foot convention hall, the 1949 American Institute of Architects National Convention. Wright was attending the convention gala to accept the AIA Gold Medal, but had already made it publicly clear his loathsome disdain for the hotel where he had to accept the award. Earlier, local reporters happened upon Wright, asking his opinion of the Shamrock and receiving a classic response: "I see the sham, but I don't see the rock." [6] Later in the day, a young Euine Fay Jones, who had recently transferred from the University of Arkansas to Rice to complete his architectural education, went to the Shamrock to see what was happening, and encountered Wright by accident. Wright, ever eager to take a willing protégé under tow, proceeded to guide Jones on a personal tour of the Shamrock, pointing out every horrific component to the building's design.[7] Humor aside, it was an encounter that would forever change Jones's life, whose relationship with Wright from that day forward and his own Wright-inspired style and approach to design would earn Jones the AIA Gold Medal in 1990.

PRIOR TO THE AIA GALA, Wright arrived in the lobby to find Hedrick and Koeppe, and immediately confronted Hedrick, launching into a tirade about the hotel design, while poking Hedrick in the chest with his cane.[8] Standing nearby in shock was young Nancy Ellison, daughter of the owners of Ellison Furniture. Assuming that some mean old man was accosting the gentlemanly Mr. Hedrick, young Ellison instinctively kicked the eighty-two-year old Wright in the shin with every force she could muster. Everyone froze in shock at what happened, and then Wright quickly stumbled away, angered and humiliated. Frank Lloyd Wright had made many enemies in his

Haynes's detailing on the 1951 Home Economics Building Expansion would mark some of the finest Plateresque detailing during the final years of Tech's Beaux-Arts–design era.

Second floor west façade window surround and finial parapet; Home Economics Building Expansion, 1951.

time—clients, critics, colleagues, employees, and at least one husband enraged at Wright's dalliances with his wife—but a seven-year-old girl had to be a first. Some question if Wright's vitriol toward Hedrick was not as much over design of the Shamrock as it was at Hedrick himself. Considered one of the wealthiest architects of that era and owner of America's third-largest architecture firm, Hedrick was regarded as hardly an equal designer in Wright's eye, and likely represented a target of envious ire for a renowned architect who could never hold onto a buck in his life.

Hedrick's team was performing double duty that evening by attending both McCarthy's raucous grand opening and the AIA gala next door, where Wright both accepted his Gold Medal and perhaps propelled by a lingering pain in his shin, proposed to the audience that the front façade of the Shamrock Hotel receive a giant gray neon sign that spelled "WHY?" [9] Though guffaws filled the ballroom at the

Present-day view of the Agricultural Engineering Building looking northwest.

Present-day view of the west wing addition to the Administration Building, Wyatt C. Hedrick architects, completed 1951. Though the additions "completed" the Administration Building, the omission of the interior courtyard colonnades and second pair of carillon towers left the complex short of Watkin's original vision.

quip, the remark must have been a sour shot to Hedrick and Koeppe. Another Texas architect was present that evening to be invested as a Fellow in the AIA. It was Wright's friend, William Ward Watkin—an unexpected friendship that had emerged in the 1930s as Watkin frequently invited Wright to Houston to lecture to architecture students at Rice.[10] Amazingly, the two architects—whose design backgrounds were as far from each other as imaginable—maintained a mutual healthy respect for one another—and regularly corresponded with each other. It was surely an ironic moment for Watkin to watch Wright unload a pot shot at his former Texas Tech collaborator.

The sheer size and glamor of the Shamrock opening garnered press attention nationwide, exposé articles in newspapers across Texas, and even a multiage spread in *Life* magazine.[11] The gala inspired Edna Ferber to write a bestselling book, *Giant*, in 1952, replete with a massive new hotel named the Conquistador modeled off of the Shamrock hosting a grand opening gala, with Ferber tailoring her fictional wildcatting character of Jett Rink based upon Glenn McCarthy. The bestselling book followed with a 1955 Academy Award–winning movie of the same name, which, in an ultimate bit of irony would become the first major motion picture in history to ever mention Texas Tech.

ALTHOUGH MCCARTHY'S heavy-handedness left Earl Koeppe and Wyatt Hedrick with a portfolio project that was hardly avant-garde, few architects in 1949 could boast a $21 million project on their résumé. The notoriety led representatives from Lord Calvert Distilleries to contact Hedrick in late 1949 and inquire if he would like to appear in a "Men of Distinction" ad in the coming year. Ironically, Hedrick rarely drank, despised smoking, and his guilty pleasure consisted of eating Frito chips and drinking a glass of cold buttermilk.[12] His consent to appear in the advertisement was likely more for marketing value than anything else, though Hedrick would never expect the damage it would ultimately generate.

It was during this same time that Hedrick was successful in securing a project for a client he had been soliciting for decades—Baylor

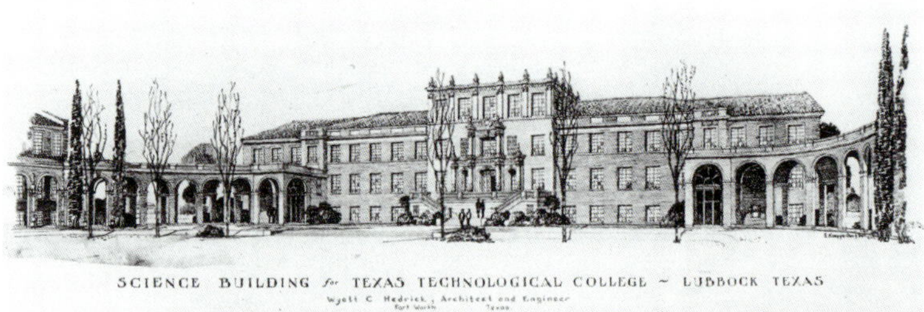

Emmett Earl Koeppe's design and ink rendering of the Science Building, dated 1950. Though not nearly as imposing as Watkin's lost vision for a great Commencement Hall, the connecting colonnade peristyles went far to visually "complete" the Court of Honor.

Present-day photograph of the central palladian stairway entry façade to the Science Building at Texas Tech.

University. Pat Neff—the same former governor who signed Texas Tech into law in 1923, only later to lose a bet to Paul Horn—was Baylor's president at the time after having left the post as commissioner of the Texas Railroad Commission, where he likely maintained a relationship with Hedrick as architect for numerous Texas-based railroads. Baylor needed a new library, and Neff, who himself contributed a $100,000 personal gift for the project, hired Hedrick's firm to design what would become the Armstrong Browning Library. Drawings for the $1,750,000 handsome stone-clad neoclassical structure were completed in the spring 1948,[13] just as Neff retired from his presidency. Neff's replacement, William Richardson White, was not a politician but rather a pastor by profession, and was inaugurated as Baylor's eighth president in early 1948 following his tenure as president at Hardin-Simmons University. Relations between Hedrick and White were cordial, up to and immediately after the cornerstone laying ceremony for the Armstrong Browning Library held on February 25, 1950.[14] Sixteen days later, an edition of *Life* magazine hit the stands with a tasteful, full-page photo of Wyatt C. Hedrick in a well-cut suit leaning astride a table with the model of the behemoth Shamrock Hotel in the background.[15] Hedrick was holding a tall glass of Lord Calvert whiskey on ice.

No public record exists of White's reaction to learning that his university's new library had been designed by a whiskey-drinking architect, however inaccurate that perception was, but it is a fact that Hedrick's firm would never work for Baylor University again. In the two years following the publication of the Lord Calvert ad, church work—once a staple of Hedrick's workload—dwindled significantly. The damage would have stopped there, except for one other unfortunate coincidence of history involving Texas Tech. One church that William R. White had led as pastor prior to his tenure in higher education was First Baptist Church of Lubbock, Texas.

First Baptist Church in Lubbock had recently completed a new worship and activities building located just east of the Texas Tech campus on Broadway. As part of its opening celebration, church leadership suggested to Tech's new president, Dossie M. Wiggins, to invite White to give the commencement speech to the Texas Tech graduating class of 1950 that May. Wiggins thought that was an excellent idea. White arrived in Lubbock on May 20, was feted by Wiggins and representatives of the college and First Baptist Church, and gave his commencement addresses on May 21 and 22 at Jones Stadium.[16] White

The Science Building's aesthetic half-cousin—the Andalusian-inspired Veteran's Administration Hospital in Amarillo, designed by Hedrick and completed in 1949.

toured the campus and learned of the many buildings built and under construction by Wyatt C. Hedrick Architects. Although no public record exists of this, it is clear that William R. White spoke his mind about the "whiskey-drinking architect" from Fort Worth. While the Science Building and Administration Building expansion—both part of Tech's first multimillion building campaign—were underway, they would be for a time Hedrick's last work at Tech. Tech administration did not wish to risk ire from the considerable political influence of the churches on Broadway by continuing to use the services of an architect who may have been perceived by some to be morally questionable. Though other firms like Haynes & Kirby and Atcheson & Atkinson, Davis & Foster were designing projects at Tech during that time as well, and they too could design in the Plateresque-revival aesthetic, the larger strategic impact resulting from Hedrick's banishment was far more catastrophic to Texas Tech. With Hedrick's departure, the last linkages of institutional memory to Watkin's original campus master plan had been cut, as most of the original administration dating from the beginnings of the college were now either gone, retired, or dead. With increasing demands from a rapidly developing city of Lubbock that was beginning to surround the college's perimeter on three if not all four sides, increasing enrollment, and ongoing needs for new facilities, Hedrick's departure could not have come at a more inopportune time.

A FLURRY OF construction was already underway when William R. White made his fateful commencement visit to Lubbock in May 1950. State tax revenue combined with Marvin Whyburn's building fund allowed the college to embark upon a $4 million building campaign early that year. Fresh off their work in the design of Jones Stadium, Haynes & Kirby were designing a pair of academic buildings—a long-needed expansion to the Home Economics Building, and shortly thereafter the Agricultural Engineering Building—located west of Agricultural Sciences Building and facing the old Judging Pavilion on Fifteenth Street. Myrick Strange had left the partnership with Haynes following the war, and Haynes had promoted architect Laverne Kirby to junior partner.[17] In his first iteration of Spanish Renaissance–revival design at Texas Tech, the near-deaf Haynes had developed a fitting two-story expansion north of the original Watkin-era Home Economics Building. Haynes was careful to continue the Flemish bond brick patterning that the original building possessed—a pattern that due to cost efficiency and changes in brick veneer construction had quietly disappeared from new Tech construction beginning in the 1930s. The addition to Home Economics featured numerous stone Plateresque details at window surrounds and roof eave details that, albeit generic in nature, consisted of handsomely composed ailerons, pilasters, ancons, and finials that were equally ornate to any Tech work from the Hedrick era. Curiously, Haynes would introduce the use of flattened arches into the Tech architectural lexicon at entrances at both Home Economics and Agricultural Engineering, while both buildings were the first at Tech to feature the postwar novelty of the aluminum-framed window.

As Haynes & Kirby-designed projects were constructed, Hedrick's two final projects built within the historical core of the campus—the Administration Building expansion and Science Building—were completing their design stages. Both were crucial to establishing some form of cursory realization of key components to the original college Master Plan—both the Administration cloister and the Court of Honor quadrangle, though budgetary limitations and institutional

Present-day photograph of the entry façade of the Colegio Mayor Fonseca, Universidad de Salamanca.

(*Above*) Florian Kleinschmidt (seated right) during a presentation with O. R. Walker and William C. Holden of the Museum of West Texas design in the late 1940s.

(*Left*) Nolan Ellimore Barrick; photographed sometime during the 1950s.

needs resulted in significant differences from Watkin's original vision. The Administration Building had originally been envisioned as an enclosed building cloister so the two 130-foot-long south wings to the building, this time constructed with basements, reflected a half-measure response to the intent of the master plan and lacked the additional two carillons that Watkin had envisioned. Office space demands for the college, coupled with budgetary limitations also eliminated the continuation of the more delicately scaled araeostyle colonnades to along the east and west perimeters of the new Administration wings. While the expansion accomplished the visual effect of "completing" the Administration Building, the expansion unintendedly reinforced an evolutionary mutation in campus planning at Tech, in which C-shaped plans would take the place of enclosed, Spanish-stylized cloistered quadrangles, a reality that remains today.

Northwest of the Administration Building, Hedrick and Koeppe had an even greater challenge in developing a western building enclosure to what is today the Math and Science Quadrangle. For years, little existed beyond the western edge of the Chemistry Laboratory and the old Library other than a water tower and for a time, the famous Double T neon sign that today resides on the southeast façade of Jones AT&T Stadium. Long forgotten was Watkin's basilica-like vision of a Hall of Texas or Alamo Commencement Hall envisioned as a centerpiece to the Court of Honor. Rather, Tech was in desperate need for general science laboratory and classroom space. Thankfully, Hedrick and Earl Koeppe's institutional memory kept the general concept of the Court of Honor alive, and incorporated a pair of flanking peristyle colonnades that connected both the Chemistry Building and Library to the newly proposed Science Building. Regardless of Ruth Horn Andrew's sharp criticism leveled at the design of the Science Building in her book *The First Thirty Years*, today, particularly among the public, the Science Building has become a cherished part of Tech heritage, namely due to the centerpiece role it plays in the annual Carol of Lights Festival.

Emmett Koeppe's design for the Science Building featured a blend of hip- and gable clay tile clad roof forms set atop yet another three-story C-shaped plan, albeit with two asymmetrical west wings. At the center of the building a single four-story form broke the clay tile roofs whose general form may have been inspired by Hedrick's recently completed Veterans Affairs Hospital in Amarillo, which featured the same four-story form detailed in a stuccoed Andalusian Spanish-revival style. The centerpiece of the east façade features pairs of engaged Corinthian columns set atop a dual pair of similar columns with a crown escutcheon set over the composition. Access to this ceremonial entry included the curiosity of a stone-clad Palladian staircase ascending to the building's second floor. The Corinthian column-framed entry bears striking resemblance to the main entry façade to the Colegio Mayor Fonseca in Salamanca, with the only difference being the deletion of two of the four upper-floor columns found on the Salamanca façade. Hedrick also introduced aluminum-framed windows with the Science Building, as well as a pair of misplaced aluminum-clad stile-and-rail doors situated at the upper landing of the Palladian stair best described as bearing similarity to the art deco-stylized ceremonial entry doors to the Gold Depository Building at Fort Knox. When completed in the summer of 1951, the Science Building accomplished much for a neoclassical building built some two decades removed from the end of the Beaux-Arts movement. Once the Science Building was finished in accordance with directives from Tech leadership, Russell Hedrick packed up his office in the Administration Building.[18] Texas Tech leadership was blissfully unaware that a whiskey-drinking architect who did not drink whiskey, his firm, and their invaluable store of institutional memory, were now gone at a time when they would desperately need both.

BY EARLY 1953, Architecture Department chair Florian Kleinschmidt still looked the part of the stocky University of Minnesota lineman that he had once played. Few would have guessed that the thick-accented man with a square jaw and butcher's hands held a Harvard graduate degree, as well as an appointment to the coveted École des Beaux-Arts. Architecture students recalled the presence of the imposing Kleinschmidt in class. Unhappy with a student's progress on a charcoal drawing, Kleinschmidt would liberally apply his butcher thumbs to the student's work in reblending the applied charcoal, and within moments would vastly improve the composition to the student's astonishment.[19] While Kleinschmidt still enjoyed teaching, like so many of the long-serving faculty at Texas Tech—weathered by austere budgets and myriad responsibilities as much as by the unrelenting West Texas wind—Kleinschmidt was ready to settle down. But architectural education in the United States was evolving from the Beaux-Arts method Kleinschmidt and his contemporaries had themselves experienced into the new "studio" method, defined by professor-led courses with students working on individual projects in a more collaborative atmosphere, a method advocated by the recently established National Architectural Accrediting Board (NAAB).[20] Transitioning Texas Tech into the new studio method, and earning the department a NAAB accreditation was a job for a young lion, and with that, Kleinschmidt was in search of his replacement.

In fact, finding a replacement department chair was his ulterior motive when Kleinschmidt attended a regional architectural faculty conference in Austin in June 1953. It was there he struck up a conversation with a thin, middle-aged UT professor sporting a bowtie. It was Nolan Ellimore Barrick. Barrick's road from Watkin's office fifteen years earlier had been a long and global affair. After Pearl Harbor, Barrick found himself in Naval Cartography School at Harvard, where the architect-turned-naval officer learned tactical mapping skills. He was then posted to the South Pacific as a war plans cartographer on the staff of Rear Admiral Daniel E. Barbey—considered the father of modern naval amphibious warfare. Barrick would draft many of the maps that General Douglas MacArthur would use in his island-hopping campaign across New Guinea and the Southwest Pacific Theater.[21]

Barrick returned from the war interested more in architectural education than architectural practice, and found a faculty posting first at Iowa State, followed by a stint in the School of Architecture at the University of Texas at Austin. Florian Kleinschmidt had a plan to attract Barrick to Texas Tech, as he had authorization from Dossie Wiggins to offer him not one, but two roles if he were to come to Lubbock.[22] If he accepted, Nolan Barrick would become chair of the Architecture Department *and* college architect. To the nearly forty-year-old Barrick, the dual titles and extra pay were enticing, though he knew little more about Texas Tech than the elevation of the Administration Building described by his late father-in-law sixteen years before. Kleinschmidt and Barrick were both to attend the AIA National Convention in Seattle in a week's time, so Kleinschmidt recommended Barrick consider the offer and come back to him at the convention with a reply.

A week later, Nolan Barrick opted to drive from Austin to Seattle, in part to talk matters over with Rosemary, but also to see some of the beauty of the American West. Somewhere along that 2,130-mile journey, Nolan Barrick made his decision.

PART III

WORKS OF INSPIRATION
OBRAS DE INSPIRACIÓN

What we like determines what we are, and is the sign of what we are, and to teach taste is inevitably to form character.

—John Ruskin, *The Crown of Wild Olive*, 1866.

Salamanca
Sigüenza
BARCELONA
Ávila
Alcalá de Henares
MADRID
S P A I N
Córdoba
SEVILLE
San Diego
San Antonio

The following section surveys those known façades, structures, or edifices that provided a direct inspiration in the first twenty-five-plus years of architectural development at Texas Technological College. The estilo plateresco has always been regarded from both an aesthetic and formative standpoint as a nuanced and challenging architectural style, so it is not surprising that the Beaux-Arts–era architects turned to what available case study materiel existed on the style for direct inspiration. Thanks in part to initial research completed by Nolan Barrick in the 1970s and early 1980s for his book *Texas Tech: The Unobserved Heritage*, and research associated with this publication, a total of twelve architectural landmarks—ten located in Spain, one at Balboa Park in San Diego, and the Mission San José y San Miguel de Aguayo in San Antonio, Texas—served as direct inspiration for formative building construction at Texas Technological College. Recent research has determined that the last two of the twelve above, and their inspirational impact at Texas Tech, differ in their inspirational value from Barrick postulated in his 1985 book. The San Diego and San Antonio case studies also differ from those Spanish case studies in that they are not Plateresque Spanish Renaissance in nature, but rather are Churrigueresque-style structures.

As William Ward Watkin would not travel to Spain until a year after he had designed three of the first academic buildings at Texas Tech, many of the Spanish case studies were drawn from limited architectural publications available in the United States in the 1920s, most notably *Renaissance Architecture and Ornament in Spain* (1893) by Andrew Noble Prentice and *Spanish Architecture of the Sixteenth Century* (1917) by Arthur Byne and Mildred Stapley.

The following twelve comparative drawing compositions and accompanying photographs review building details and inspirations in chronological order, beginning with the 1924 design for the Administration Building, and concluding with the 1950 design for the Science Building. Though there have since been modern additions to the Texas Tech campus that incorporate direct vernacular influences from other buildings in Spain (which are highlighted elsewhere in this book), this section focuses purely on the historical architecture of Texas Tech as part of the Texas Technological College Historic District.

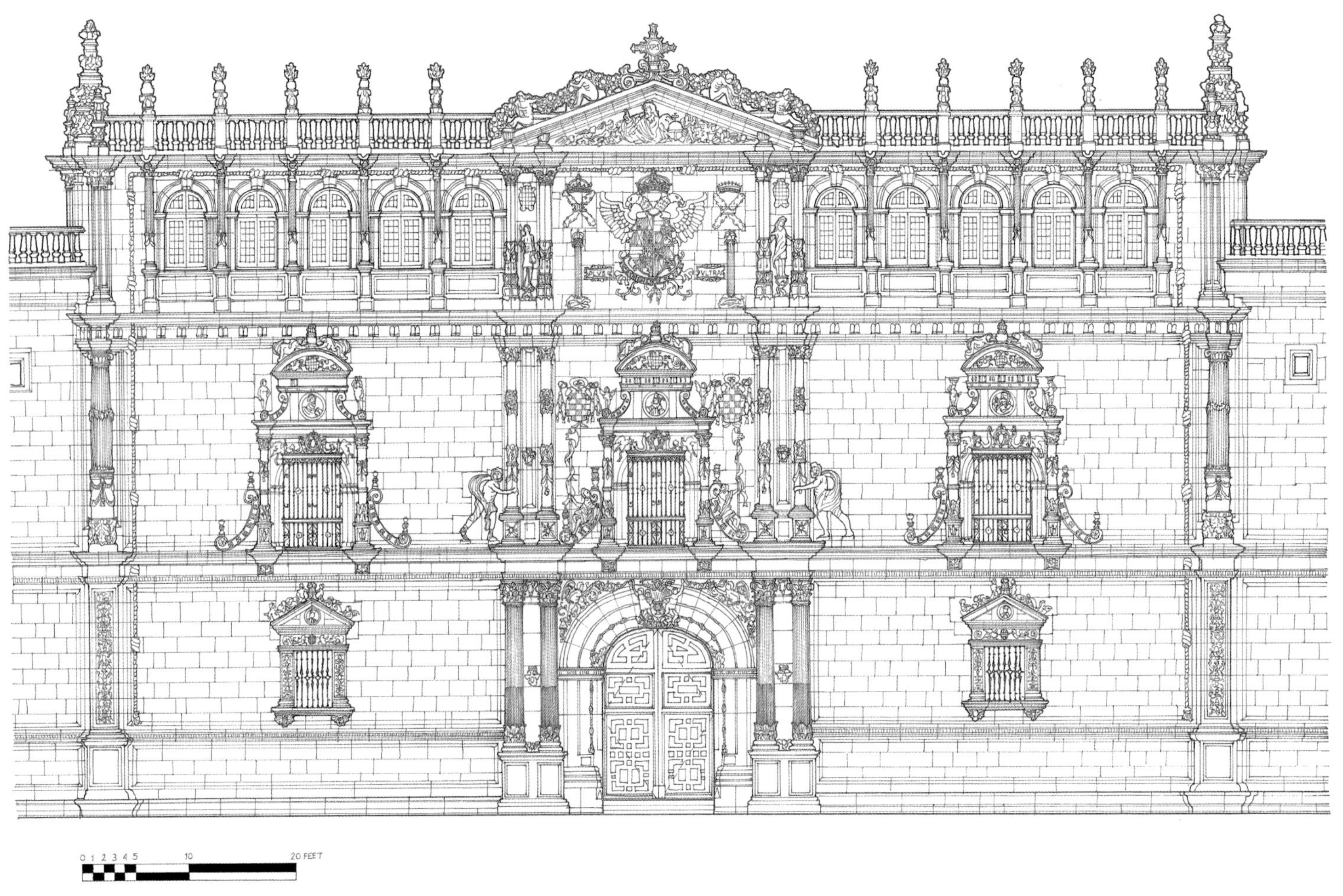

NORTH FAÇADE ELEVATION, COLEGIO DE SAN ILDEFONSO, UNIVERSIDAD DE ALCALÁ (PREVIOUSLY UNIVERSIDAD COMPLUTENSE), RODRIGO GIL DE HONTAÑON, MAESTRO MAYOR, COMPLETED 1543

Completed in 1543 by renowned maestro mayor Rodrigo Gil de Hontañon, the north façade of the Colegio de San Ildefonso at the Universidad de Alcalá has long been regarded as one of the apex examples of Plateresque work constructed in Spain in the sixteenth century. Originally home to the Universidad Complutense—one of the oldest universities in the world, and an institution that was relocated to Madrid in 1836—the building and frontispiece are today the physical symbol of the newer, separate Universidad de Alcalá. Beginning in 1499, thanks to the leadership and patronage of Cardinal Fray Francisco Jiménez de Cisneros, whose signature checkered-shield coat of arms adorns the façade, the Universidad Complutense had in the 1500s rapidly become one of the great and respected institutions of learning throughout Europe.

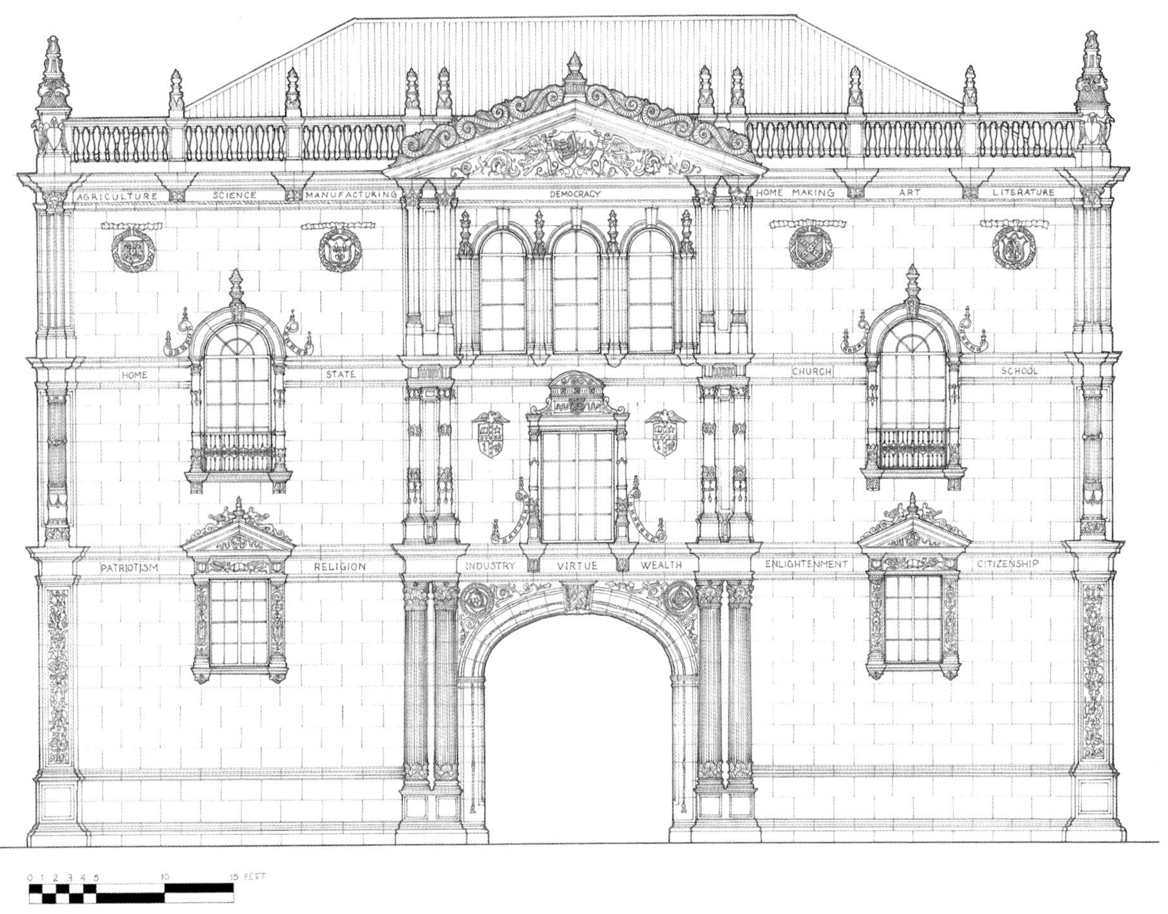

FRONTISPIECE NORTH FAÇADE ELEVATION, ADMINISTRATION BUILDING, TEXAS TECHNOLOGICAL COLLEGE, SANGUINET, STAATS & HEDRICK, WITH WILLIAM WARD WATKIN, ARCHITECTS, COMPLETED 1925

It is very clear that the Colegio de San Ildefonso façade had inspired Ralph Adams Cram more indirectly in his entry façade concept for the Julia Ideson Library in Houston, but the Alcalá masterpiece would be drawn upon in a more direct, literal fashion by William Ward Watkin in the north façade of the Texas Tech Administration Building. As one of the most ornate façades across the Tech campus, the north Administration frontispiece includes a broad range institutional messages and elements of Texas history as adaptations to heraldic details so often found in Plateresque architecture. Both Watkin and Tech President Paul Horn would carefully select and coordinate many of the quotes and words inscribed upon the façade. A number of key elements of the frontispiece are drawn directly from Hontañón's case study—namely pilasters and engaged columns, the lower stair windows, finials and balustrades, and second floor central window surround.

Detail photograph of the central frontispiece to the Colegio de San Ildefonso façade, Universidad de Alcalá, The bilious shield and eagle overhead is the imperial seal of Spanish King and Holy Roman Emperor Charles V. Running below the parapet eave above is a broad continuous cord of rope punctuated by a pattern of three-loop knots—symbolic of the Franciscan Order (the knots represented the three vows of the order. Both Cardinal Cisneros and many university faculty were members of the order when this edifice was built.

Situated on an Arabesque pilaster on the lower western side of the Colegio façade, the date of completion of the landmark Plateresque structure—ANO 1543—is inscribed in stone.

Detail photograph of the central north façade, Texas Tech University Administration Building. Note the federal and state escudos appear twice on shields at skewbacks over the salle-porte arch, and overhead at the parapet pediment. Inset along the carpanel arch and jambs is the Franciscan rope detail which is carried over from the Colegio de San Ildefonso façade in Alcalá

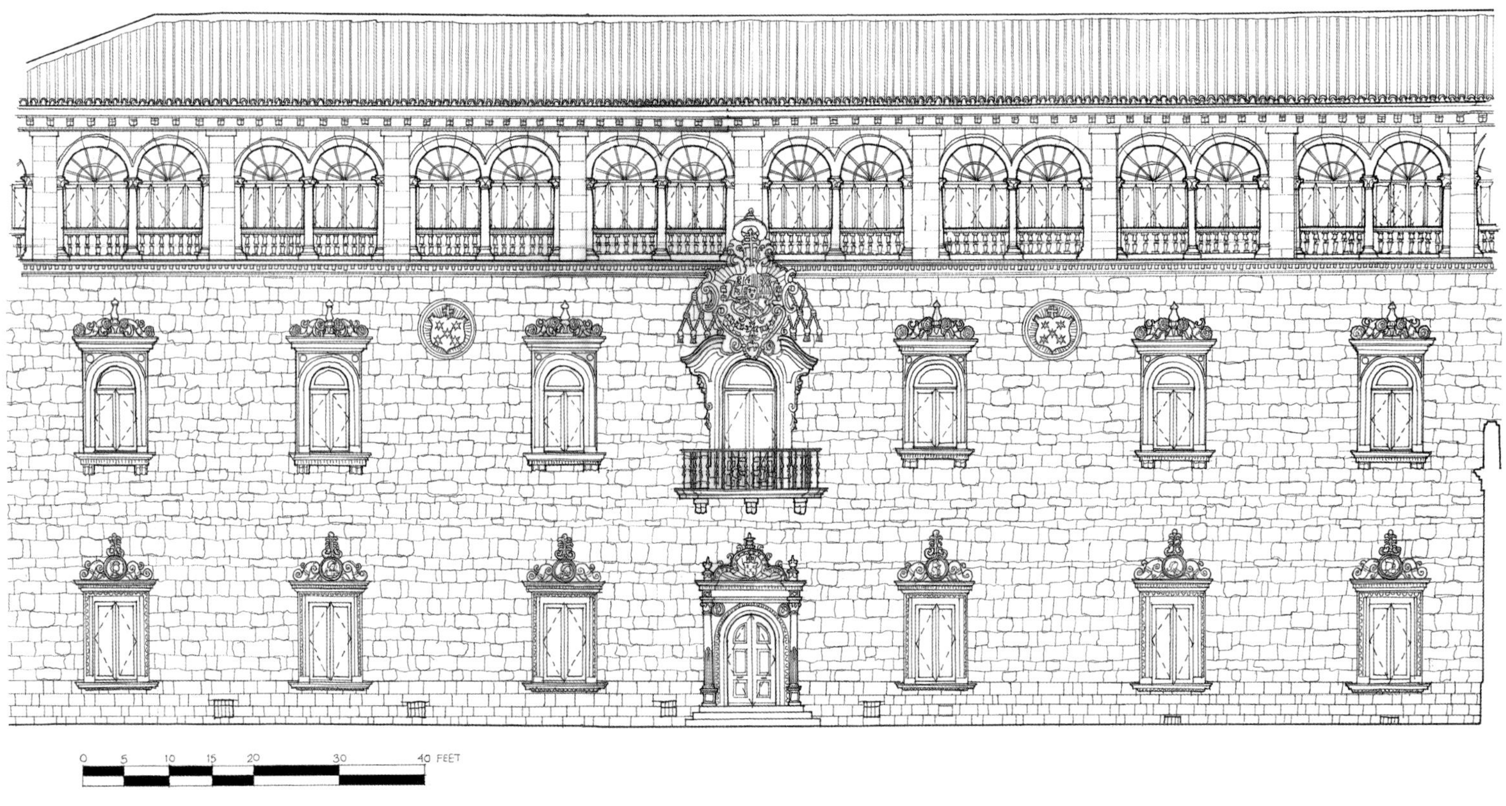

SOUTH FAÇADE ELEVATION, PALACIO ARZOBISPAL, CATHOLIC DIOCESE OF ALCALÁ DE HENARES, ALONSO DE COVARRUBIAS, MAESTRO MAYOR, BUILT 1523–1534

A great deal of Spanish and European history took place in the palace of the Archbishop of Alcalá. It was in this palace that Catherine of Aragon was born, and it was here that Christopher Columbus first suggested to Queen Isabella to finance an expedition in search of a westward sea route to the Indies. A victim of the Spanish civil war, two-thirds of the palace would be destroyed in an August 1939 fire, and while many parts (notably the archbishop's stairway) would not be rebuilt following the fire, this façade would be fully restored in 1996. In his design, Alonso de Covarrubias would continue the tradition of designing a more ornate field of window details on the uppermost floor, in the piso de hidalguía style.

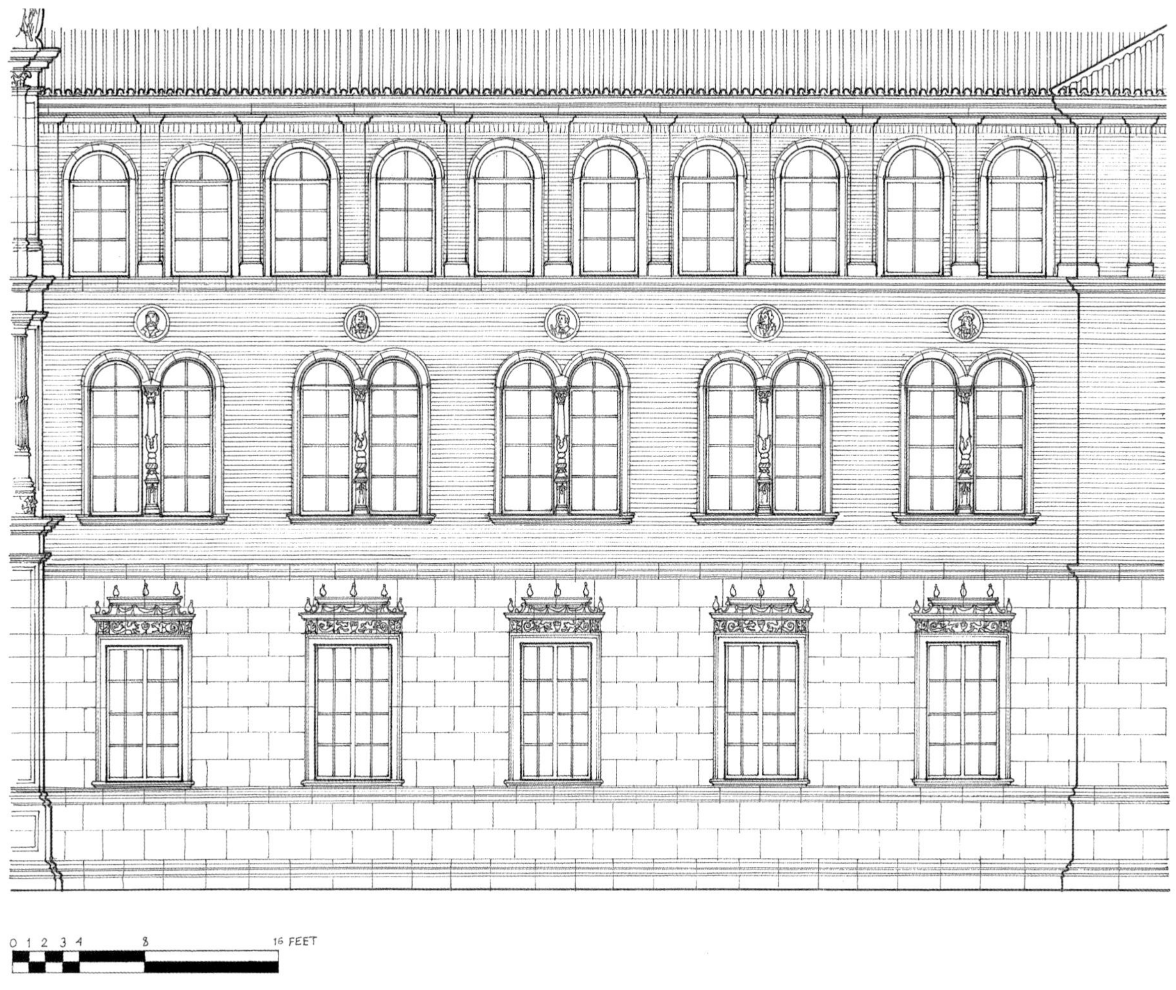

OUTER NORTH FAÇADE ELEVATION, ADMINISTRATION BUILDING, TEXAS TECHNOLOGICAL COLLEGE, SANGUINET, STAATS & HEDRICK, WITH WILLIAM WARD WATKIN, ARCHITECTS, COMPLETED 1925

The Plateresque tendency to design more elaborate window detailing for the residences of nobility on the uppermost floors of Renaissance-era buildings in Spain was not lost on William Ward Watkin. The outboard sections of the north façade of Administration featured arched windows in the same vein as those designed into the Palacio Arzobispal, as well as similar first floor window surrounds as seen on the Palace's façade. Above each pair of second-floor windows resides a bust roundel of ten figures from national and state history, including Christopher Columbus, George Washington, Robert E. Lee, Woodrow Wilson, James Hogg, Albert Sidney Johnston, Davy Crockett, Stephen F. Austin, and Sam Houston. A tenth bust, one of Abraham Lincoln, would prove controversial at the time of Tech's opening by contemporary Southerners who reviled the former leader of the Union.

One can observe the same general patterns—cased rectangular windows on the first floor, arched windows and roundels on second, and an arched-window piso de hidalguía on third on the restored south façade of the Palacio Arzobispal as seen on the outboard façades to Administration.

One of the ground-floor rectangular stone casements to the Palacio's façade crafted in the rich, warm-colored Piedra de Villamayor stone. Note the inscription entablature—"AUDIENCIA DEL VICARIO" carved in the curious interposed Spanish style—announcing the office window of a vicar's receiving room.

Detail photograph of the westernmost edge of the north outboard façades to the Texas Tech Administration Building, highlighting the bust roundels of Davy Crockett, Stephen F. Austin, and Sam Houston.

SOUTHWEST CLOISTER FAÇADE ELEVATION, COLEGIO DEL ARZOBISPO FONSECA, UNIVERSIDAD DE SALAMANCA, PEDRO DE IBARRA, JUAN DE ÁLAVA, AND JUAN MARTIN, MAESTROS MAYORES, BUILT 1525–1534

Don Alonso de Fonseca y Ulloa III, archbishop of Toledo, would found a college in 1519 in Salamanca on land donated to the archbishop by the Franciscan Order. Himself a wealthy hidalgo of the Fonseca family, for the next fifteen years, Alonso III would personally fund the construction of a college built by at least four known maestros mayores. Originally built as a college of higher learning dedicated to the apostle James, son of Zebedee (Santiago el Zebedeo), the stunningly beautiful courtyard would become one of the first truly Italianate colonnaded cloisters in Spain.

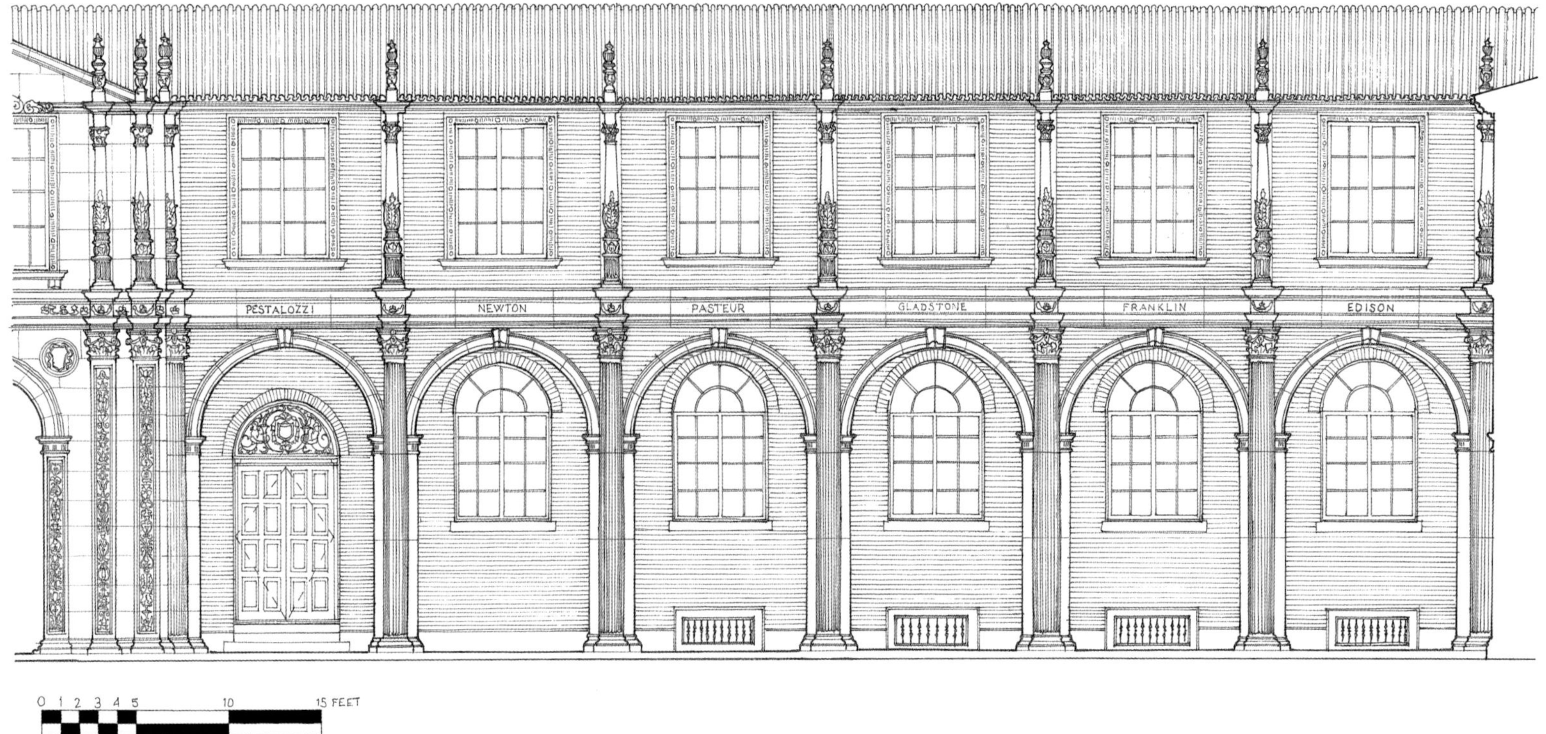

SOUTH COLONNADE FAÇADE ELEVATION, ADMINISTRATION BUILDING, TEXAS TECHNOLOGICAL COLLEGE, SANGUINET, STAATS & HEDRICK, WITH WILLIAM WARD WATKIN, ARCHITECTS, COMPLETED 1925

The south façade of the Administration Building provided students and the West Texas public a glimpse of ornate neoclassical architecture the likes of which did not exist west of the Brazos in 1925. Watkin's south colonnade design for Administration matched both proportions and detailing from the first floor of the Colegio Del Arzobispo Fonseca colonnade, while incorporating offices above in lieu of an arco carpanel-lined second floor colonnade. Sadly, when Wyatt Hedrick's firm added wings to Administration a quarter century later, either due to spatial needs, budgetary limitations, or both, the araeostyle colonnade and fletched stucco vaulting was not continued.

View of the southeast corner of the Colegio Del Arzobispo Fonseca cloistered courtyard in Salamanca.

The team of maestros mayores constructing the Colegio Del Arzobispo Fonseca courtyard designed individuality into every corner, including a different second-floor railing baluster at each of the four colonnades, and 128 different ornate bust roundels, each depicting a biblical character, two unidentified examples of which are shown here.

View looking northeast into the south courtyard of the Texas Tech Administration Building.

Detailed photograph of one of the highly ornate twin pairs of Arabesque pilasters flanking the south salle-porte arch to the south colonnade arch at Administration.

CHAPEL ENTRY PORTAL ELEVATION, CAPILLA DE SANTIAGO EL ZEBEDEO, CATEDRAL DE SANTA MARÍA DE SIGÜENZA, MARTÍN GARCÍA, MAESTRO MAYOR DE REJA, BUILT 1512–1532 (FAÇADE BUILT 1522)

Funded by Don Antonio de Mora, a hidalgo of the region, to become a chapel and resting place for members of the Mora family, the Capilla de Santiago el Zebedeo was, as its name suggests, dedicated to the apostle James, son of Zebedee, a figure of great importance in Spanish Catholicism, and at that time, the patron saint of Spain. This façade is unique as it was not constructed of carved stone, but was rather built of finished plaster formed over a stucco and stone substrate and was originally painted in lavish colors, including gold, silver, black, and sable brown. The façade bears two coats of arms, the smaller pair of skewback shields representing the Mora family and the larger overhead seal representing the then-bishop of Sigüenza, Don Fadrique de Portugal.

CARILLON TOWER ENTRY ELEVATION, ADMINISTRATION BUILDING, TEXAS TECHNOLOGICAL COLLEGE, SANGUINET, STAATS & HEDRICK, WITH WILLIAM WARD WATKIN, ARCHITECTS, COMPLETED 1925

It is not known why Scottish architect Andrew Noble Prentice was led to drawing the obscure and little-known Capilla de Santiago el Zebedeo entry portal in the early 1890s, but it is clear that Prentice's drawing of the entry inspired William Ward Watkin and his drafting staff in details not only on the Texas Tech Administration Building, but elements of the same entry surround crown also appear on the Julia Ideson Library in Houston. Aside from the conch feature to the crown, and trio set of eternal flame finials, the defining similarity between the Tech entry surround and chapel portal in Sigüenza is the shield of Don Fadrique de Portugal. Though Lueders stone carvers likely did not know what they were carving, they carved remarkably accurate representations of the late bishop's coat of arms.

SACRISTY WINDOW ELEVATION, MISSION SAN JOSÉ Y SAN MIGUEL DE AGUAYO, SAN ANTONIO MISSIONS NATIONAL HISTORICAL PARK, MAESTRO MAYOR UNKNOWN, BUILT 1768–1780

Practically nothing is known about the maestro mayor who crafted the beautifully ornate Churrigueresque stone surround and reja to the window of the sacristy that had been added to the eastern end of the south nave wall of Mission San José. It is this detail and that of the mission's memorable entry façade that make it the most ornate of the four San Antonio missions that today make up the San Antonio Missions National Historical Park and UNESCO World Heritage Site. Today, the church remains an active Catholic parish to the San Antonio community.

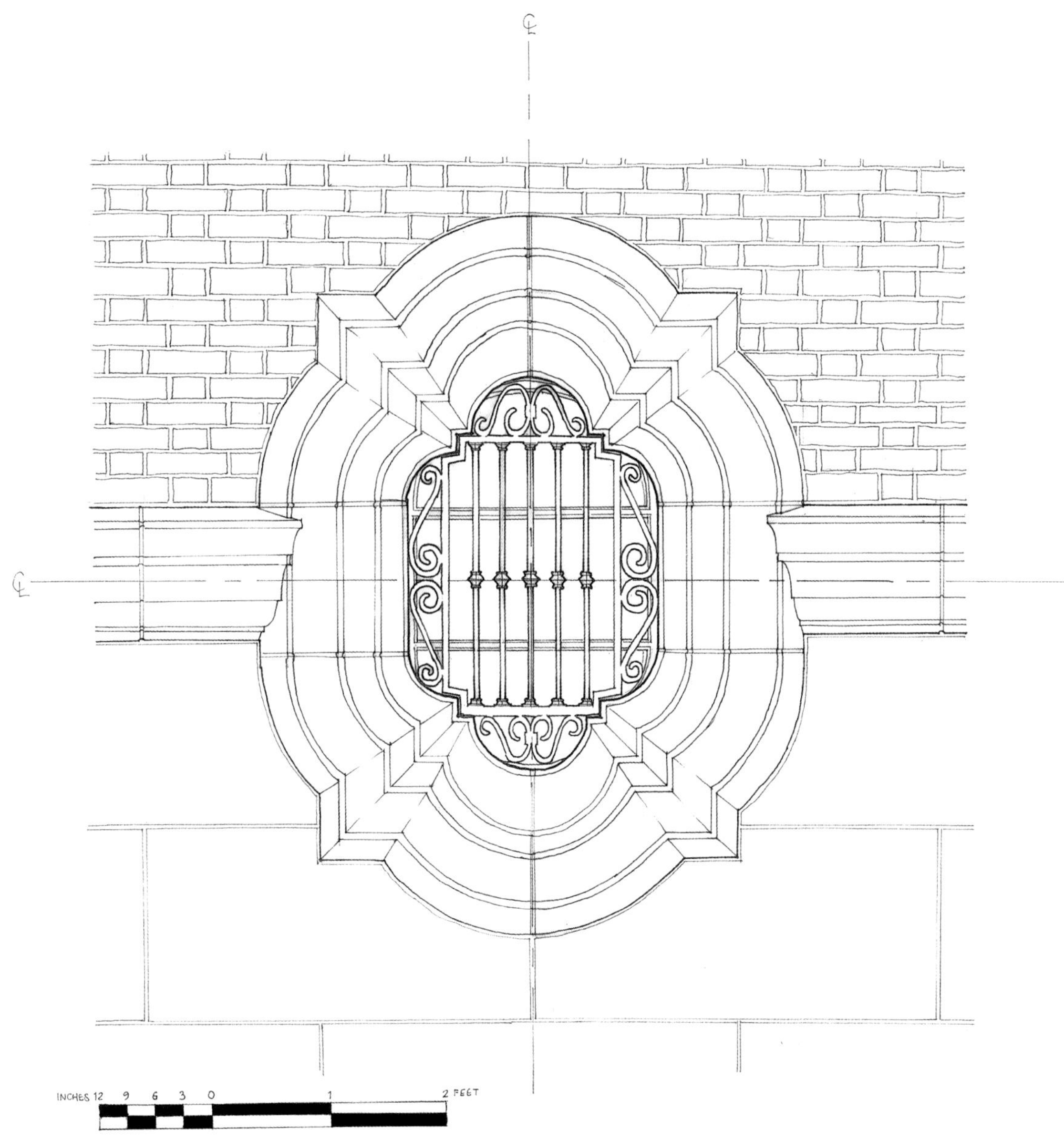

CARILLON ROSETTE WINDOW ELEVATION, ADMINISTRATION BUILDING, TEXAS TECHNOLOGICAL COLLEGE, SANGUINET, STAATS & HEDRICK, WITH WILLIAM WARD WATKIN, ARCHITECTS, COMPLETED 1925

William Ward Watkin had likely visited Mission San José at some point prior to undertaking the design of the Texas Tech commission (published drawings of the sacristy windows would not become available until the late 1930s), as the outer stone surround proportions and reja grill pattern are nearly identical to the eighteenth-century San Antonio case study, with the exception of the Churrigueresque detail. Interestingly, Sanguinet, Staats & Hedrick's working drawings for this window show a different ovular shape that was likely modified in shop drawings submitted by Watkin's office to the Bedford-Carthage fabricators in Lueders.

Hidden behind the austere Gothic and Romanesque exterior of the Sigüenza Cathedral complex is a Gothic-styled garden cloister of indescribable beauty. It was here amidst an idyllic example of Gothic tracery and groin vault work that a collection of Plateresque-detailed chapels and tombs reside, one of which would later inspire the architecture of Texas Tech University. Chapel entry is located at the distant right.

Oblique overview photograph of the imposing entry portal to the Capilla de Santiago el Zebedeo at Sigüenza Cathedral.

Though Watkin's team designed a notably less ornate entry at the base of both carillon towers to the Texas Tech Administration Building, the ornate transom reja to the Capilla de Santiago el Zebedeo entry portal may have inspired transom rejería over south colonnade entry doorways, including the doorway into the present-day President's Office.

(*Above*) Photograph of the ground-floor sacristy window to the Mission San José y San Miguel de Aguayo, illustrating the ornate Churrigueresque detail of the window surround.

(*Right*) Overview photograph of the entry door and overhead rosette window composition, east carillon tower, Texas Tech Administration Building.

SOUTH TOWER ELEVATION, TORRE DEL ALMINAR (TORRE CAMPANARIO), MEZQUITA-CATEDRAL DE CÓRDOBA, HERNÁN RUIZ III, JUAN SEQUERO DE LA MATILLA, AND GASPAR DE LA PEÑA, MAESTROS MAYORES, BEGUN 1593, COMPLETED 1664

In 1589, an earthquake damaged the octagonal spire to the one-time minaret of the former Mosque of Córdoba, so the Diocese of Córdoba proceeded with designs by maestro mayor Hernan Ruiz III to entomb the former minaret in a new, Renaissance-era belfry edifice. It would require four separate phases of work over seventy-plus years to complete the Torre del Alminar, also known as the Torre Campanario. Though not built during the Plateresque era, and regarded by most historians as a baroque-era structure, it would nonetheless inspire William Ward Watkin three centuries later in the carillon tower designs for the new Administration Building at Texas Tech.

EAST CARILLON TOWER EAST ELEVATION, ADMINISTRATION BUILDING, TEXAS TECHNOLOGICAL COLLEGE, SANGUINET, STAATS & HEDRICK, WITH WILLIAM WARD WATKIN, ARCHITECTS, COMPLETED 1925

In a design vision reminiscent of the massive palace and monastery of El Escorial, William Ward Watkin had in the General Plan for Texas Technological College proposed an eventual cloister complex to the Administration Building bounded by four Córdoba-inspired carillon towers. Sadly, Watkin's imperial vision for Administration would never be realized. Even though six stories in the air, Watkin's team included hints of regional vernacular in the towers, capping each finial with a cotton boll. In lieu of the Gaspar de la Peña–designed promontory lantern and statue of the archangel Saint Raphael seen on the Torre del Alminar, Watkin designed a more simplified, stately lantern capped by an artichoke crown.

(*Left*) View looking northward from the famed Patio de los Naranjos, the irrigated garden plaza of orange trees that reside in the north portion of the cathedral complex, toward the south façade of the Torre del Alminar.

(*Above*) Not only is the Torre del Alminar an iconic inspirational symbol to Texas Tech aficionados, it remains today the centerpiece to the bishopric seal of the Diocese of Córdoba, as seen in this carved relief symbol of the seal found on a Cathedral pew.

(*Left*) Though the East Carillon Tower retains the beloved Victory Bells, lesser known is the Baird Memorial Carillon which was first installed in the West Carillon Tower in 1973 and expanded in 2005.

(*Center*) The signature red-and-cream voussoir arches and hypostyle columns of the Mezquita-Catedral de Córdoba, which though being an accomplished work of Moorish architecture, underwent centuries of transformative reconstruction as a Catholic cathedral.

(*Right*) An *escudo* over the Puerta de Santa Catalina at the Mezquita-Catedral de Córdoba provides a glimpse into the earlier appearance of the mosque's minaret prior to the tower expansion begun by Hernan Ruiz III in 1593.

SECTION THROUGH STAIRWAY, PALACIO ARZOBISPAL, CATHOLIC DIOCESE OF ALCALÁ DE HENARES, ALONSO DE COVARRUBIAS, MAESTRO MAYOR, BUILT 1535

A handful of Plateresque-era grand stairways had been designed and built by maestros mayores, but none equaled the handsome appearance and ornate detail of the archbishop's stairway designed and built by Alonso de Covarrubias at the complex of the Palacio Arzobispal in Alcalá de Henares. No one of the numerous intricately detailed stone-rusticated panels that adorned the spandrel beneath the stairs were alike. Even more majestic was the overhead wood artesonado ceiling, of which little historical record remains today as to its design and detailing. A belated victim of the Spanish civil war, most of the stair would be destroyed in an August 1939 fire, as the one-time palace had since been converted into an archival building, only then to be remanded as an ammunition storage building for the Spanish Nationalist Army during and after the war. The grand stairway would never be rebuilt.

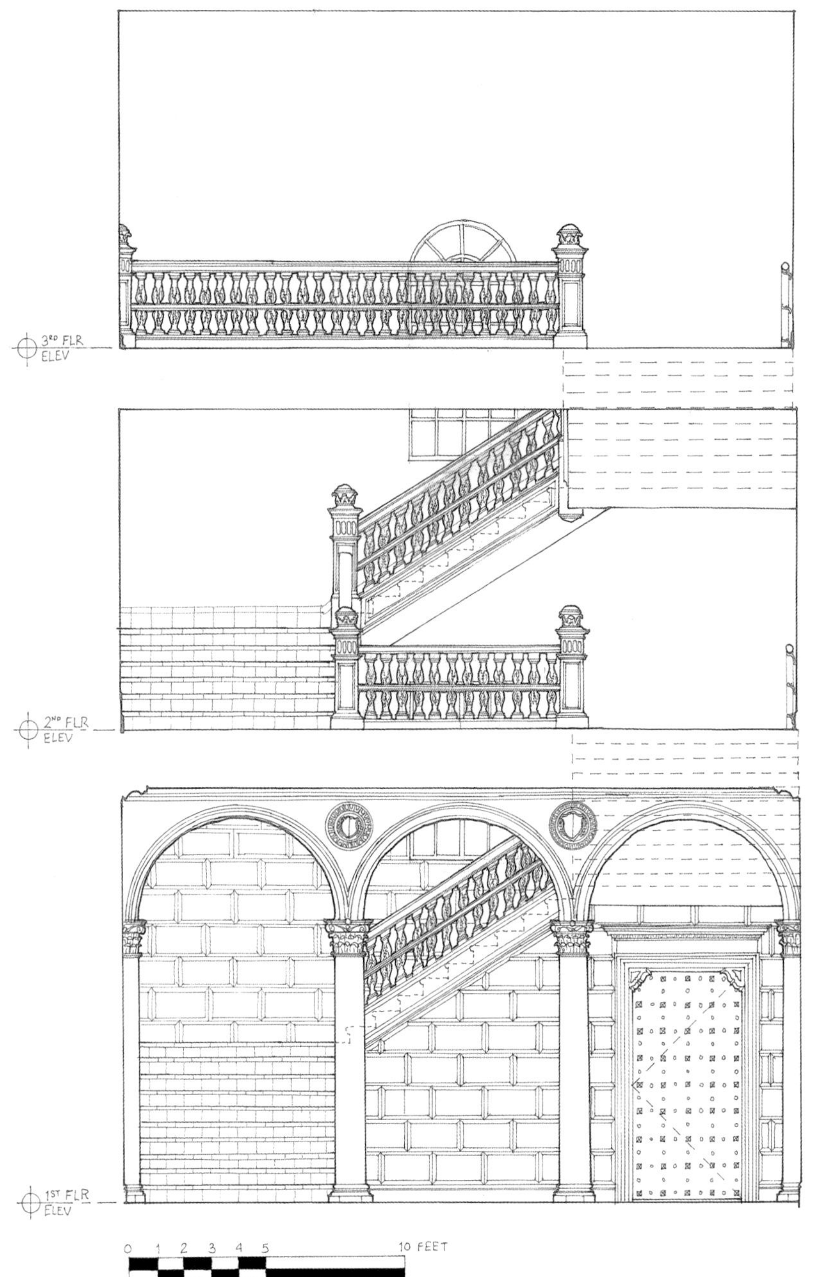

SECTION THROUGH EAST STAIRWAY, ADMINISTRATION BUILDING, TEXAS TECHNOLOGICAL COLLEGE, SANGUINET, STAATS & HEDRICK, WITH WILLIAM WARD WATKIN, ARCHITECTS, COMPLETED 1925

With less than a million dollars of state endowment funding available for initial construction at Texas Tech, a great deal—both practically and symbolically—was still expected of the built product of Tech's new Administration Building. Though William Ward Watkin and his mentor Ralph Adams Cram were designing more elaborate stairs along with a stunning artesonado-capped atrium at the separate Julia Ideson Library commission in Houston, the Texas Tech Administration Building would face greater austerity in scope. Though never crowned with an artesonado ceiling, Watkin's twin central stairs at Administration would be built of Lueders-limestone balustrades, newel posts, and rusticated spandrel panels inspired by Covarrubias's Alcalá masterpiece.

In the aftermath of the 1939 fire, this doorway and spandrel panel of ornate rusticated stone was the only component of Alonso de Covarrubias's magnificent stairway that survived, and today resides in the Museum of the Cathedral of Alcalá de Henares.

View looking upward from the east central stairwell to the Administration Building, showing both the stone rustication and balustrade design—both modeled from the Palacio Arzobispal.

SOUTH ENTRY FAÇADE ELEVATION, CALIFORNIA STATE BUILDING, PANAMA-CALIFORNIA EXPOSITION, BERTRAM GROSVENOR GOODHUE, ARCHITECT, BUILT 1914–1915

Rarely did the neoclassical works of the nineteenth and twentieth centuries equal the level of intricate ornament incorporated by maestros mayores in Spain and the New World in their original works of centuries prior. The one exception is the California State Building at Balboa Park. Designed in the frenetic Churrigueresque style—a favorite of architect Bertram Grosvenor Goodhue's thanks to his journeys to Mexico early in his career—it is doubtful that any other edifice in Spain or Central America has ever equaled the sheer volume of ornament that exists on the California State Building's entry façade. Built between 1913 and 1915 as the flagship building of the daring Panama-California Exposition, the highly ornate façade, along with its adjacent telescoping tower and polychrome-clad domed roof, form what remains one of the most iconic buildings in San Diego today.

SOUTH ENTRY FAÇADE ELEVATION, TEXTILE ENGINEERING BUILDING, TEXAS TECHNOLOGICAL COLLEGE, SANGUINET, STAATS & HEDRICK, WITH WILLIAM WARD WATKIN, ARCHITECTS, COMPLETED 1925

Watkin, Hedrick, and Chip Robert had a far more limited budget available in the design and construction of the Textile Engineering Building than with Administration. This led Watkin to adapt the broader design ethos of the Churrigueresque style of architecture adapted to the colonial environment of New Spain where otherwise simply detailed façades were accented with concentrated ornate features at entries and centerpieces. At Textile Engineering, the building built at the northern apex of the prado-like mall now known as the Engineering Key, Watkin adapted this aesthetic strategy by substituting Churrigueresque with Plateresque. While colonnades and general façades had simple brick and openings, ornate engaged columns and scrollwork adorned the central salle-porte entry to the façade, whose features were clearly drawn from Goodhue's 1915 San Diego masterpiece.

Upward detail photograph of a portion of the south façade and telescoping tower of the former California State Building, now the San Diego Museum of Man.

Detail photograph of the paired engaged columns flanking the central salle-porte of the Textile Engineering Building at Texas Tech, now home to the Mechanical Engineering Program.

ENTRY FAÇADE ELEVATION, HOSPITAL DEL ESTUDIO, UNIVERSIDAD DE SALAMANCA, MAESTRO MAYOR UNKNOWN, COMPLETED 1492

In 1413, King Juan II of Castile donated property to the Universidad de Salamanca for use as a hospital. Seventy years later, work would commence on expanding that hospital—the Hospital del Estudio—to bound the southwestern edge to what is today the iconic Patio de Escuelas of the university. Nine years later in 1492, the hospital addition, including its curiously detailed entry façade would be completed. The entry façade of the Hospital del Estudio is not Plateresque in style, but rather a blend of the earlier Gothic and Isabelline styles, and is easily recognizable due to its two-arch/three-pier ordering that served as one of many different examples of Spanish straying from the strict adherence to more classical ordering principles in architecture. The Hospital del Estudio today serves as the rectory (equivalent to the office of the president) of the Universidad de Salamanca.

EAST SALLE-PORTE ENTRY ELEVATION, WEST ENGINEERING BUILDING, TEXAS TECHNOLOGICAL COLLEGE, WYATT C. HEDRICK ARCHITECTS, WITH WILLIAM WARD WATKIN, ARCHITECTS, COMPLETED 1928

William Ward Watkin continued the same massing concepts, simple field façade work, and ornament concentrated at entries on the 1927–1928 West Engineering Building as used on Textile Engineering two years earlier. Watkin turned to the hospital entry in Salamanca (perhaps a building he visited in his 1925 travels to Spain) for inspiration in the salle-porte entry façade to West Engineering. In lieu of filigree, Watkin incorporated a set of four French-styled shields, each bearing one of the four departments (three engineering and one architecture) that were to be based in West Engineering. This similar form, archway, and ordering would be adapted and repeated by Atcheson, Atkinson, Davis and Foster a quarter century later on the entry façade to the flanking East Engineering Building opposite the Engineering Key.

Overview of the Hospital del Estudio façade—the oldest case study drawn upon in the inspiration for the architecture of Texas Tech. The escudos over the entry façade represent the combined kingdoms of Ferdinand and Isabella, while the façade features a heavily weathered dividing column between the two entry doors that historians suspect may have been salvaged from an earlier building. The seated figure carved in stone over that column represents Saint Thomas Aquinas, who among others is the patron saint of colleges, academies, and universities.

View looking northwest toward West Engineering, illustrating that the salle-porte entry to West Engineering was a comparably smaller entry feature in size to other early buildings at Tech.

SOUTH FAÇADE ELEVATION, PALACIO DE MONTERREY, RODRIGO GIL DE HONTAÑON AND PEDRO DE IBARRA, MAESTROS MAYORES, BEGUN 1539

It is arguable that no other Renaissance-era building in Spain has had the inspirational impact upon neoclassical architecture in the Spanish-inspired world than the Palacio de Monterrey. The Palace's iconic three-arched corner tower can be found in countless works of neoclassical architecture in Spain and the Americas—the Spanish Military Officers Academy at Valladolid, the Palacio Nacional of Guatemala, the City Hall buildings bounding the Zócalo in Mexico City, and the University of Puerto Rico Medical School in San Juan are just a few examples. Aside from the corner and mid-façade towers, the palace features a prominent piso de hidalguía and is decorated with the coats of arms of no less than seven different noble families of Spain—representatives from each having held at one time the title of duke of Monterrey. Today, the palace remains one of several residences maintained by the duke of Alba, one of the highest-ranking grandees, or noblemen of Spanish aristocracy.

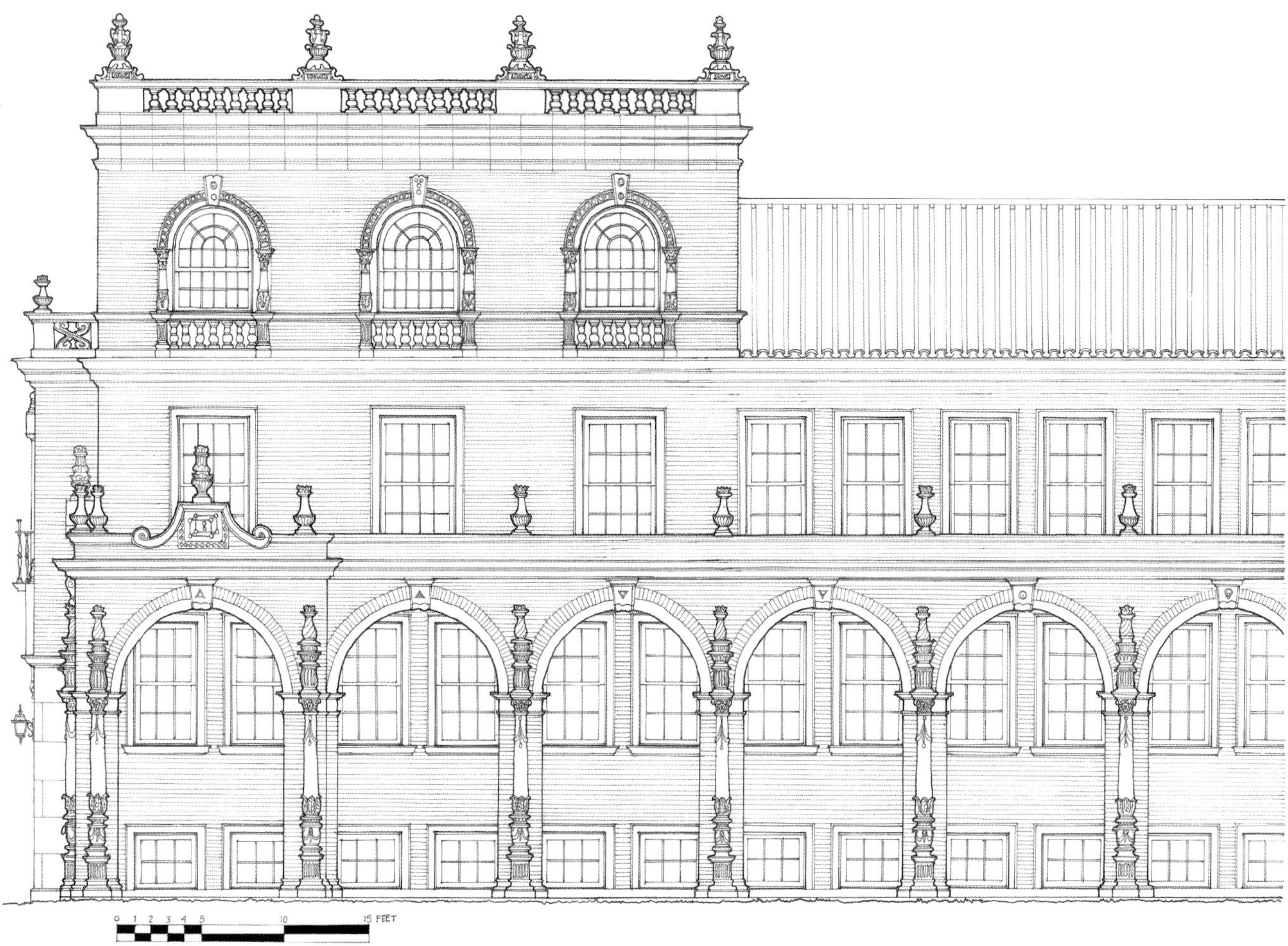

NORTH FAÇADE ELEVATION, CHEMISTRY BUILDING, TEXAS TECHNOLOGICAL COLLEGE, WYATT C. HEDRICK ARCHITECTS, WITH WILLIAM WARD WATKIN, ARCHITECTS, COMPLETED 1929

In his design for the Chemistry Building, William Ward Watkin would repeat the use of the more slender, engaged-pilaster colonnade style that had been used three years earlier in the south colonnade of the Administration Building along Chemistry's north façade. That colonnade was combined with a corner tower that loosely mimicked the three-arched-opening rhythm found on Hontañon's iconic Palacio de Monterrey tower form, albeit with windowed openings. The Chemistry Building would set many standards in the establishment of Watkin's envisioned Court of Honor, including its higher-grade elevation and continuation of a more araeostyle colonnade along the court perimeter, which Wyatt Hedrick and Hermann and Emmett Koeppe would continue in their subsequent designs for a Library (1938) and Science Building peristyles (1951).

View looking north toward the iconic corner tower form of the Palacio de Monterrey. Note that at the time of visit and photography, much of the western side of the south façade remained shrouded in scaffolding as restoration of the palace's façade was underway in 2017.

Photograph highlighting the east corner tower form of the Chemistry Building and foreground colonnade.

Watkin curiously did not repeat the three-window rhythm of the Palacio de Monterrey façade on the east face of the Chemistry corner tower, as seen here in this photograph looking southwest. Note the mysterious VITRIOL tablet overhead of the east stairwell entrance.

View looking east along the north colonnade to the Chemistry Building, highlighting similar detailing and fletched stucco vaulting finish as seen on the south colonnade to the Administration Building.

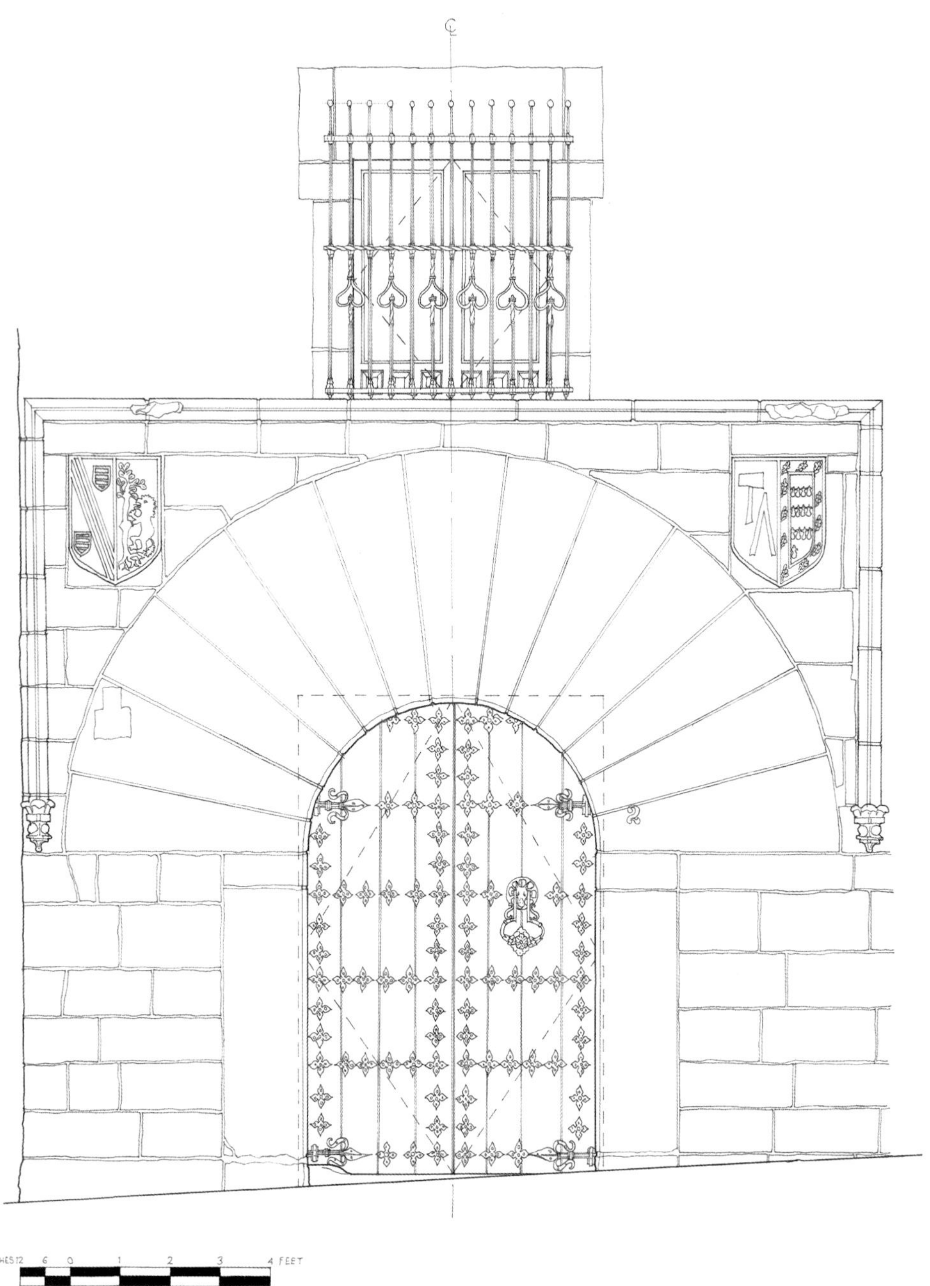

SOUTHEAST ENTRY FAÇADE ELEVATION, TORREÓN DE LOS GUZMANES, MAESTRO MAYOR AND DATE COMPLETED UNKNOWN

Little is known regarding the architectural history of the Torreón de los Guzmanes, other than it and other characteristically deep voussoir-arched frontispieces found in the historic walled city of Ávila were documented by elevation drawings in Andrew Noble Prentice's seminal book *Renaissance Architecture and Ornament in Spain*. This is likely how the unique detail came to the attention of William Ward Watkin and his staff for Watkin's final building design at Texas Tech, the Power Plant of 1930. Visual evidence indicates that the more Plateresque detailing and drip edge to the Torreón entry was added later to the tower. Today, the building and grounds are home to the Diputación Provincial de Ávila, the Spanish equivalent to a county government administration over the province of Ávila.

SOUTH ENTRY FAÇADE ELEVATION, POWER HOUSE BUILDING†, TEXAS TECHNOLOGICAL COLLEGE, WYATT C. HEDRICK ARCHITECTS, WITH WILLIAM WARD WATKIN, ARCHITECTS COMPLETED 1930

In his General Plan for the Texas Technological College Campus, Watkin had called for a more formally devised power plant complex that served as a northern terminus to the pedestrian axis through Textile Administration, and visually noted by a formal masonry campanile stack to exhaust from the plant's boilers. This proposal almost certainly emerged from Rice's similar Physical Plant Campanile, designed by Cram & Ferguson, which provided a far more architecturally pleasing solution to a concrete or steel smokestack. Unfortunately, though the Texas State Legislature did fund the Power Plant Building, no masonry campanile was ever funded. Sadly the Power Plant was one of the few original Tech buildings to be razed, as central plant operations had by the 1960s moved to the northwest campus. Tech's original Power Plant Building would be bulldozed in 1998 to make room for an expanding College of Engineering. Stone details from the demolished Power House facade were salvaged and installed over the entrance of the present-day Frazier Alumni Pavilion.

SOUTH ENTRY FAÇADE ELEVATION, COLEGIO DEL ARZOBISPO FONSECA, DIEGO DE SILOÉ, AND FERNÁN PÉREZ DE OLIVA, MAESTROS MAYORES, COMPLETED 1529–1534

Like its nearby cloistered courtyard, the entry façade to the Colegio del Arzobispo Fonseca had long been a handsome and proud frontispiece to the institution. The building has in its life served an eclectic range of roles: as a general higher education institution, a school to train Irish priests, the inglorious role as German Embassy to Nationalist Spain from 1937 to 1939, and its role today as hospitality housing for visiting faculty and dignitaries to the Universidad de Salamanca. Diego de Siloé's design for the entry façade included the pronounced use of scallop shells, a seminal symbol of the apostle James, and a large circular crowning escutcheon, depicting a fictional scene of Saint James from the mythical Battle of Clavijo—a legend heavily purported in Spanish lore.

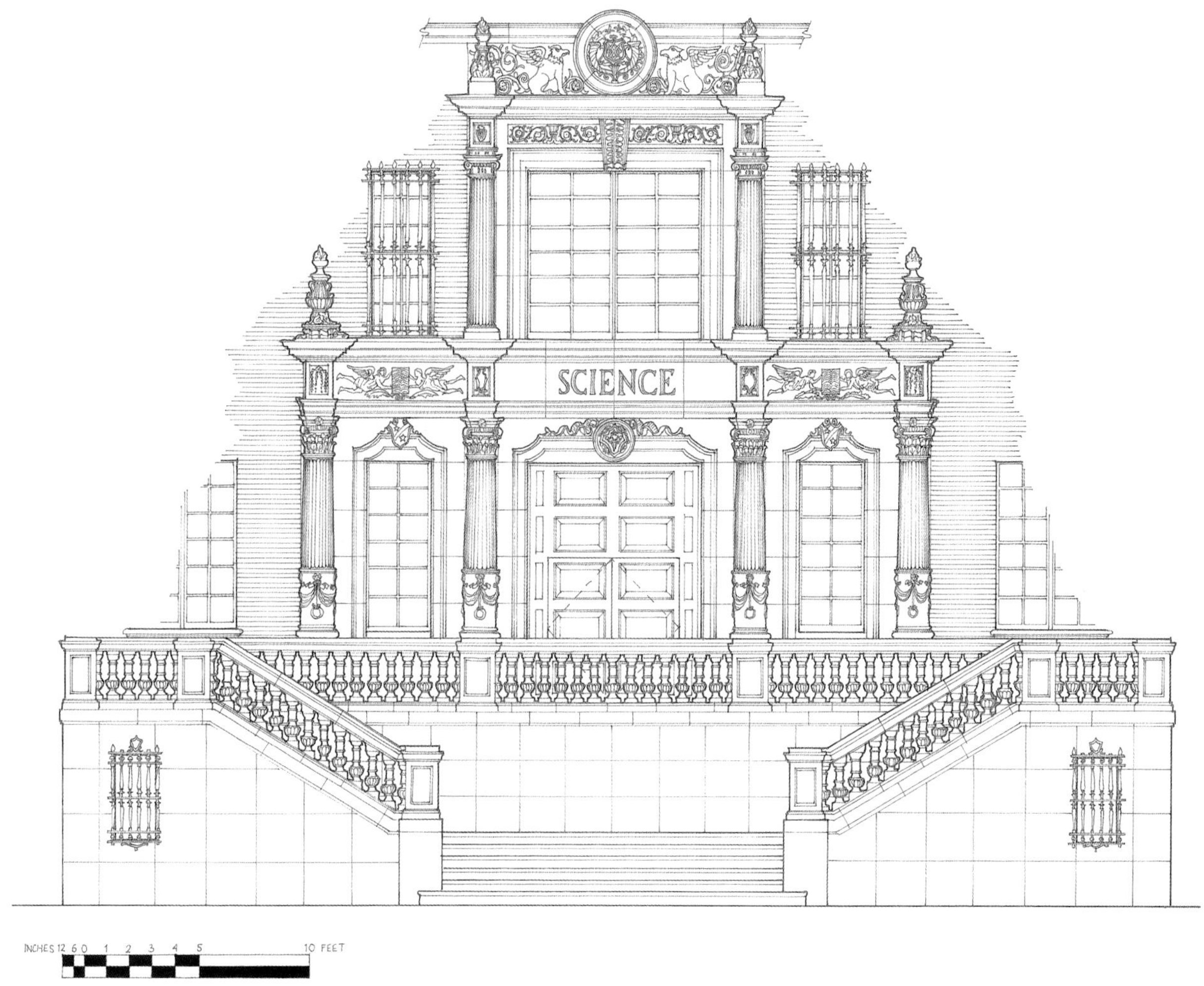

EAST ENTRY FAÇADE ELEVATION, SCIENCE BUILDING, TEXAS TECHNOLOGICAL COLLEGE, WYATT C. HEDRICK ARCHITECTS, COMPLETED 1951

In what would be Wyatt Hedrick's final contribution in the design of the Texas Tech campus core, the Science Building in effect completed the Court of Honor, albeit to a lesser degree than what William Ward Watkin had envisioned in his proposed Alamo Commencement Hall. Centerpiece to the Science Building façade was a two-story gradated edifice of engaged Corinthian columns capped with a smaller and nondescript crowning escutcheon to its entablature, all set atop a Palladian stairway that is best known today as an idyllic stand for the Texas Tech Choir every fall during the university's "Carol of Lights" lighting ceremony. The incorporation of aluminum-framed windows and a pair of aluminum-clad ceremonial doors at the piano nobile entry makes for an odd differentiator to other traditional openings found on historic buildings at Tech.

Overview photograph of the main entry façade, Colegio del Arzobispo Fonseca, Universidad de Salamanca. Note that to help façade features stand out from the surround piedra de Villamayor stone, columns, finials, and cornices were carved from a gray granite.

A detail photograph of the entablature and escutcheon overhead of the Science Building ceremonial façade. Note the similar horn and gryphon details carved into the stone to details found on its Salamanca source counterpart.

(*Above*) Even today, the towering form of the Torre Campanario remains the tallest structure in the City of Córdoba, as seen here looking north toward the Mosque-Cathedral Complex from south of the Guadalquivir River.

PART IV

GROWTH

Every attempt to bind [colleges] to a pattern laid out in advance has failed—and ought to have failed. . . .
We must set [colleges] free to develop their environment in whatever way may best suit their existing needs.
—Joseph Hudnut, dean, Harvard Graduate School of Design, "On Form in Universities,"
Architectural Forum, December 1947, p. 91.

12

SHEER MADNESS

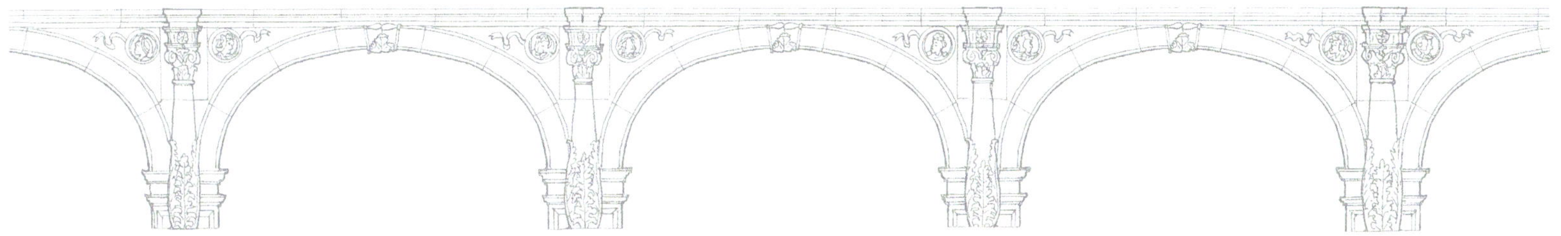

NOLAN BARRICK AND HIS WIFE Rosemary arrived at Tech ahead of the fall semester 1953, and the college they observed upon their arrival was at a unique crossroads in its short life. Korean War conscription had resulted in a slight decline in enrollment, but cohorts were soon growing once again. Texas Tech had grown just as Barrick's late father-in-law William Ward Watkin had remarkably predicted exactly twenty-five years earlier in an article for *American School and University*, envisioning a college of five thousand students by 1950,[1] in fact beating Watkin's projection by 475 students that year. But Texas Tech now faced an entirely new set of dilemmas no one could have imagined. Barrick had been assigned an office in the third floor of the Administration Building, formerly occupied by Russell Hedrick, looking out of one of the windows Barrick had once observed in the rendered elevation above his drafting desk in Watkin's office some fifteen years earlier.

Barrick walked out of the glass-enclosed salle-porte of the Administration Building. The glass storefront had unfortunately been installed under orders from Bradford Knapp in 1935 in an effort to abate high winds, along with Florian Kleinschmidt and Tech's recently appointed president, Dr. Edward Newlon Jones.[2] At first, nothing seemed amiss to Barrick, only then to notice how hundreds of cars were parked everywhere in front of buildings. Many college students now possessed their own automobiles, and Texas Tech had few if any parking restrictions on campus. Buicks, Chevys, Nashs, Hudsons, Fords, Studebakers, and Oldsmobiles—coupes, sedans, trucks, and cars of all kinds, sat in crude rows in front of the library, in front of the engineering buildings, and in front of Administration itself. Grass and finished pavement were still a rarity at Texas Tech, and the hoards of parked cars left dirt ruts everywhere. The Victory Bells suddenly rang, as they did those days to mark class change. Within less than a minute, students came streaming out of buildings—moving like angry ants charging out of a kicked-over anthill. While many students still walked to class, it was the cars that caught Barrick's horrified fascination. The ten-minute class change descended into a sea of maddening traffic and honking horns, much of which bottle necked at one of the five—*yes, five* traffic lights surrounding Memorial Circle,[3]

Circa-1948 photograph of the recently renamed Memorial Circle at Texas Technological College. Traffic jams had become an everyday occurrence, requiring the installation of multiple traffic lights (one seen in the center foreground).

Undated photograph of the new University Center shortly after opening, noting its more Romanesque-detailed, mission-revival forms; Atcheson & Atkinson, architects.

renamed five years earlier in honor of Tech student veterans who died during World War II. Hundreds of students drove from classes in Engineering to another class in Administration, or Music, or Chemistry, and vice-versa—an unheard-of idea today. Making matters worse, the once-independent campus plan envisioned by Watkin had since been chopped into a checkerboard grid by Lubbock streets that now ran everywhere through campus. Akron, Boston, and Canton Avenues, along with 8th and 15th Streets cut through campus and added everyday community vehicular traffic into the already frenetic melee of student traffic. It was sheer madness. Much of Barrick's visit thus far had focused on his role as head of the Architecture Department, but Barrick caught but a glimpse of what challenges lay ahead in his other role as college architect.

Barrick quickly realized any proposed efforts to counteract the devolution of Tech's master plan required both support from college leadership and the establishment of a governance structure to enforce planning and design measures. Hedrick's departure from Tech two years prior had left the college devoid of any knowledgeable personnel to champion strategy for the future physical development of the campus. Barrick, in the meantime, did his best to acquaint himself with the campus plan by having a plot model of the campus built for planning purposes, while contacting anyone still alive who could shed light on Tech's original master plan.[4] With Hedrick exiled and Watkin dead, Barrick went so far as to reach out to Chip Robert in Atlanta, who was soon to retire from his firm and who relayed what information he could by letter to Barrick in October 1953.[5] Beyond that, Nolan Barrick was starting from scratch.

By spring 1954, with authorization from President Jones, Barrick convened an organizational body with the purpose to propose, enact, and enforce planning and design decisions for the college. The Campus Planning Committee (CPC) would for the next fifteen years wield a critical role in shaping the Texas Tech campus from an embryonic rural institution to a much larger and complex physical plant equipped to support twenty thousand students or more. Barrick was joined on the committee by two other individuals: Marshall L. Pennington,

Present-day view of University Center (Student Union) former main entrance, aligned with Administration Building salle-porte to the north. Photograph by Author.

Tech's vice president for Business Affairs and later executive vice president for the college, and landscape architect Elo Joe "Prof" Urbanovsky.[5] Pennington was a pragmatic bean counter who in his mundane role of comptroller had established a clear, simple fiscal plan for future construction at Tech. Urbanovsky was a Texas A&M alumnus and former project administrator for the Department of Veterans Affairs who had arrived in Lubbock four years ahead of Barrick and was tasked with transitioning the Departments of Horticulture and Park Administration—a forerunner to landscape architecture—into the Division of Agriculture. Urbanovsky was notoriously outspoken in his opinions on design matters—even matters of architecture or engineering—which led to occasional friction with Barrick and

The Len & Harriet McClellan Memorial Infirmary. Not long after his arrival, Barrick had become disillusioned by the lack of detail and quality on new Tech projects, while construction costs continued to rise.

Rendering of the Mechanical and Civil Engineering Building (East Engineering), 1952; Atcheson & Atkinson, Davis & Foster, architects and engineers. With Watkin's men's residential plan for the campus having since been forgotten, constructing a near-symmetrical complement to West Engineering on the Engineering Key seemed an ideal response.

others. The CPC wanted free reign in their role, excepting Board of Directors input, but it would take President Jones until October 1958 to receive official sanction from the board for the CPC's existence.

Following postwar housing construction on campus, popularity with Texas Tech's on-campus housing and dining programs were such that the college was in fact accruing a profit. In an era before the strict business silos of Housing and Dining, Traffic and Parking, and other departments, Texas Tech was able to amass aggregate retained earnings to a degree that regardless of whether appropriations from Austin arrived, a new building could be constructed approximately every two years.[6] This method, which Barrick later jokingly nicknamed the "Pennington Plan," worked well for the time being for a smaller institution with limited growth. But from 1954 on, Texas Tech was growing at a rate of one thousand new students every two years—a rate that would soon render Pennington's plan obsolete. Thankfully, Tech continued to have some success in securing additional ad valorem tax revenue from Austin to fund other larger projects. And many larger-scale projects were emerging as needs at Tech in 1954, including a new library, an indoor athletics venue to replace the decrepit practice barn northeast of the Engineering Key, and additional housing as student enrollment increased. Agriculture, engineering, and a once unknown body—the Division of Commerce, soon to be renamed Business Administration—were all rapidly growing and were in need of new academic space.

A number of campus projects were already underway or opening upon Barrick's arrival—the one project generating greatest interest being the Student Union Building. Designed by Atcheson and Atkinson, Davis and Foster, the Student Union was unique in that it matched the material palette of the Tech campus, but the broad circular entry arch with ground-set springlines and ponderous filigree designed into balcony railings gave the building almost a Romanesque appearance. But stylistic details did not matter, for if the building had been painted with pink polka-dots, the student body would still have

Present-day detail photograph of East Engineering main entry arch, revealing a simpler, almost neo-Gothic/neo-Romanesque portal to Watkin's flanking salle-porte of twenty-five years earlier.

preferred it over the hot, dusty, leaky patchwork of X-buildings that had served as an earlier temporary student union building nearby.

One other smaller project set to be located east of the new Student Union across Akron Avenue was the Len and Harriett McClellan Memorial Infirmary—a two-story, eighteen-bed clinic designed to provide on-campus medical care for students if needed. Roy McClellan, a Waco-based contractor had offered Texas Tech a land-swap donation to pay for the $295,000 clinic's price tag.[8] Designed by the Butler-Brasher Company of Lubbock, McClellan Hall became the college's fiftieth permanent building upon completion in spring 1956. But McClellan was, from both a budgetary and design standpoint, symbolic of the growing endemic problem Tech faced with both the Pennington Plan, the continuation of neoclassical design at Tech, and the broader issue of rising construction costs nationwide. Himself a Watkin-trained neoclassicist, Barrick had no qualms about advocating Beaux-Arts design for a college regardless if the architectural world now resided in the age of modernism, but it was becoming exceedingly expensive and difficult to expand Tech's physical plant with traditional Spanish Renaissance architecture. First was the simple matter of cost. The postwar economic boom in the United States had resulted in significant inflation on the construction dollar. Perhaps more influential to the architectural image of Texas Tech was the massive postwar decline of craftsman-centric, often-patriarchal construction trades—particularly among trades like decorative

Weeks Hall, completed in 1957, fulfilled a formative role in finally forming a complementary frame to the Broadway campus entrance opposite Sneed Hall, though the undersized, one-off residence hall proved ultimately a disappointment.

ironworking, stone carving, and woodworking. The Len and Harriett McClellan Memorial Infirmary cost nearly 80 percent of the cost of the original Administration Building for a clinic not even one-fifth its size and with very little architectural detail whatsoever. Barrick lamented the lack of craftsmanship and detailing at McClellan Hall, and later projects of the day. One such project—Weeks Hall Dormitory—located to the northeast near the Broadway entry was limited in Plateresque stone detailing to a drip edge over entrances crested with the checkered *escudo* of the Cisneros family, which architects Atcheson, Atkinson, and Cartwright likely never realized represented the one-time archbishop of Alcalá de Henares. Unless the prevailing architectural style at Texas Tech changed, or funding dramatically increased, Texas Tech would soon be unable to keep facilities growth on pace with enrollment growth.

The other challenging dynamic was quite simply modernism in architecture. No neoclassically styled American college or university was immune from modernism from the 1950s on. Architectural critics viewed Beaux-Arts–era campuses like Texas Tech as anachronistic relics—institutions that were slow to embrace avant-garde design in the atomic age. But from a pragmatic standpoint, modernism offered architects and institutions alike an easy answer to the ongoing dilemmas of rising construction costs, as simpler forms and details, and the predominance of cheaper materials like concrete, steel, and glass resulted in a lower cost per square foot. Modernism had not yet emerged at Texas Tech, but conversely new buildings at Tech in the mid- and late-1950s could hardly be described as Plateresque revival. Three new campus facilities—two Texas Tech student dormitories and one city of Lubbock–owned facility—were the largest building projects ever built at Tech at that time, and marked the onset of a transition from neoclassical designs possessing detail and ornament toward simpler structures with a greater focus on simple forms and composition.

The first of the three projects was the Lubbock Municipal Coliseum and Auditorium, designed in another partnership between Haynes & Kirby and Parkhill, Smith, & Cooper, and completed in March 1956. Lubbockites had backed city plans for a new, large, indoor venue by approving a $1.75 mllion bond referendum as early as late 1945, but bond funding remained untapped into the 1950s until Lubbock Mayor Murrell Tripp established a commission in 1953 to determine its site and scope.[9] Lubbock experienced something akin to the state's land acquisition perils with Texas Tech three decades earlier, as most sites of public convenience throughout Lubbock were ruled out due to suddenly exorbitant land costs. Tripp came to the novel solution of partnering with Tech, as President Jones and Nolan Barrick saw little need for lands bordering Brownfield Highway west of Jones Stadium. Given that the state owned the parcel, it would take a solution from State Representative and future Texas Tech Board of Directors Vice Chairman Waggoner Carr when he proposed House Bill 478 in March 1953 to set aside 7.5 acres of land as leased to the city of Lubbock for the proposed coliseum and auditorium.[10]

The Municipal Coliseum and Auditorium was hailed in the press and by the public when it opened, though it was not a particularly

A line of X-buildings situated east of the Engineering Key. The absence of a completed Museum of West Texas in the background and East Engineering in the foreground dates this photograph sometime between 1946 and 1949. While fulfilling a needed stopgap role, X-buildings would soon become an unwanted nuisance at Tech.

With state authorization for a land lease, construction of a city-owned Coliseum and Auditorium proved an ideal partnership opportunity for Texas Tech.

Undated interior photograph taken during a college fair.

ambitious building design. Combined, the complex featured a 9,500-seat capacity indoor arena venue enclosed under a steel-truss compression-framed roof, set astride an adjacent 2,800-seat auditorium.[11] The east entrances of both facilities were designed to align with an arced walkway to the west entrance of Jones Stadium, which navigated through a new large asphalt parking lot designed to support both facilities. The Coliseum/Auditorium had the ugly mark of being one of the last public facilities in Lubbock ever designed with separate white and colored toilet facilities. In striking a balance between the need to distinguish the Coliseum/Auditorium from the architecture of nearby Texas Tech while retaining some distant aesthetic harmony, Haynes & Kirby selected a more golden-tan color brick reminiscent of that seen on W. L. Bradshaw's Lubbock High School, a selection that may have been in part due to the growing scarcity of Tech's buff-blend brick. With the new $2.2 million venue complete, both the Lubbock community and Texas Tech got what they wanted. As the official home for the Red Raiders Basketball Team, Tech no longer had to worry about dust, heat, and sparrow droppings falling on spectators at basketball games.

NOLAN BARRICK was at times a contradiction-in-terms. Barrick's introduction of thin bowties to the otherwise staid wardrobe of the engineering faculty and later into the 1960s his penchant of zipping around in an MGB Roadster countered the otherwise reserved outward demeanor of Tech's ranking architect. Barrick also sported a highly cultivated sense of humor and a diplomatic ability to speak his mind. While walking with President Jones along the Engineering Key one day in the late 1950s, Jones asked, "Mr. Barrick, what are we going to do about these X-buildings? These whitewashed barracks just don't mix with the rest of the campus." Barrick, who secretly hoped a bulldozer would send all of the hated X-buildings to a violent demise, replied sarcasticly: "Well, we could clad them in buff brick and install clay tile roofs on them." [12] Barrick's wit backfired as Jones turned and shot back, "Nolan, that's a great idea! Look into what it might cost to do something like that." Jones had to hurry off, while an ashen-faced Barrick hoped the president would soon forget the idea. But there were other occasions when Barrick's wit found some practical usefulness.

Barrick was determined to return the Texas Tech campus to some semblance of the 1924 master plan, and in doing so wrest the campus from the clutches of the automobile. He and the CPC had one key opponent to that objective—the city of Lubbock. By the 1950s, residential growth west of Texas Tech was well underway, while proponents, namely city managers Steve Matthews and later H. P. Clifton, and highly vocal partisans like the *Avalanche-Journal*'s Editor-in-Chief Charles A. Guy pushed a traffic and planning editorial agenda that stressed unfettered rights-of-way through the Texas Tech campus.[13] But in 1955, eleven different city streets or avenues crossed onto or through the boundaries of the campus. Lubbock's policies only added

Following completion of the Coliseum and Auditorium, the Old Barn—now relegated to intramural athletics needs—would soldier on for another two decades.

fuel to the fire of uncontrolled student vehicular traffic on campus, as the college grew anywhere from five hundred to nine hundred students per year, with anywhere from 30 to 50 percent of those students bringing their cars to campus with them. Barrick was determined to block the flow of cars and realized that buildings made excellent dams. His first target was 8th Street.

With support from his CPC colleagues, namely Urbanovsky, Barrick executed an act of architectural sleight of hand by conducting a "thorough planning exercise" for new buildings at Tech,[14] only then to determine a best site for a new facility happened to reside over an existing street, and use the project as pretense to street closure. With the Coliseum now open and the Old Barn decommissioned, Barrick convinced leadership to move on building an indoor intramural recreation facility—a space Tech had needed as far back as 1926. Barrick commissioned Herbert Brasher & Associates to design the Men's Gymnasium Building near the site of the Old Barn, but sited south of the former gym on grounds that it would be more student-accessible there. This siting required closure of 8th Street west of

South façade of the Men's Gymnasium, designed by Butler-Brasher; completed 1957. Unassuming in appearance and often overlooked by the public, the new Gymnasium proved a vital element in Barrick's strategy to reducing automobile traffic on campus. Note the new terrazzo Southwest Conference bonfire circle in the foreground, which dates this image sometime after 1960.

Akron Avenue, then one of the busiest entry points for students onto campus. The city balked, but was helpless at the decision, as Tech was state property, and Jones and the Board of Directors supported the plan. Brasher and his team had a bare-bones budget to work with, and so the resulting Men's Gymnasium was little more than an unadorned collection of three masonry-clad blocks arranged in a stair-step plan, but its value to Barrick and Texas Tech was far greater than anyone realized. After its completion in early 1958, the Men's Gymnasium emboldened Barrick to propose a similar solution with a new Women's Gymnasium Annex to be located southwest of women's housing at Horn-Knapp Hall in the southern quadrant of campus. The city of Lubbock threw up their hands in frustration again as the CPC proposed that the gymnasium be located over Akron Avenue—then the busiest north-south street at Texas Tech. Herbert Brasher, whose firm had been reorganized into Brasher Spencer & Goyette, was commissioned to design the single-story, 3,473 square foot modernist-styled women's gymnasium that opened in 1961.[15] Concurrent with these new projects, the college instituted CPC-recommended policies

Undated aerial photograph, likely sometime between 1959 and the early 1960s showing the Thompson-Gaston and Carpenter-Wells Complexes as completed. Inefficiently configured, the spidery plan of both would become a hallmark symbol of what went wrong during the modernist era at Tech.

heavily restricting student-owned vehicles from parking in the campus core, and concurrently built a series of commuter-service parking lots around the campus periphery. Other unloved vestiges of the era of the automobile were removed, namely the five traffic lights on Memorial Circle. Barrick's strategy worked, as vehicular traffic on campus fell precipitously.

Tech administration continued to see significant increases in enrollment in the final years of the 1950s, with annual growth rates of 10 percent or more annually to the student body. Larger-scale housing complexes would be needed with capacities of a thousand-plus beds, and some Tech leadership, including the CPC, were unconvinced that Lubbock-area design firms could handle projects of that scale. At a CPC meeting on October 15, 1958, minutes recorded the following:

"The committee was of the opinion that it might be necessary to recommend architects other than Lubbock [firms] for some of the projects." [16]

But the Lubbock regional architectural marketplace of the 1950s was booming, while also dramatically changing as older architects such as O. R. Walker, W. L. Bradshaw, and Sylvan Blum Haynes were retiring or had passed away, with new firms emerging in their place. Despite a highly competitive market that existed in Lubbock, many local architects in fact were close friends, drinking buddies, regular card-playing counterparts, and some rivals even vacationed together with their families. Such relationships offered the unique opportunity for joint ventures. Three firms—Stiles, Roberts, Gee & Messersmith, McMurtry & Craig, and Schmidt & Stuart—resentful of the perception that local firms could not handle larger projects emerging at Tech, consolidated to form the joint venture Associated Architects and Engineers of Lubbock. The partnership proved ideal, as each firm possessed unique resources they could bring to bear on a project. Architects Robert Messersmith, a Fort Worth native, Tech alumnus and former army paratrooper, and Howard Schmidt, a tall, handsome, and gregarious marketer, emerged in time as leaders of the partnership.[17] Messersmith's expertise in management, operations, and contracts, and Schmidt's marketing qualities gave AA&E a strong position against larger firms marketing from eastern half of the state. In early 1956, AA&E won the commission to design two five-hundred-bed dormitories—one for male and one for female students—later to be known as Carpenter-Wells and Thompson-Gaston Halls.

Placement and orientation of the two new residence halls has long been a point of controversy as far as the campus plan was concerned. CPC records and board minutes indicate the predominant factors in dormitory siting was that the northwestern corner of campus was the only available site relatively close to the Old Central Plant, but clear of the Division of Agriculture range and crop lands, or athletics fields.[18] The spidery wing configuration of the two twin complexes was a radical departure from the rectilinear and axial dynamics that had long dominated the Tech campus. Long dormitory wings protruding outward in unusual angles left large swaths of land surrounding them virtually unusable from a future planning standpoint. To finance the two residence halls, Pennington turned to the Federal Housing Home and Finance Agency (HHFA, a forerunner to the US Department of Housing and Urban Development) for loans to finance the expansion. Drawings first for Thompson-Gaston, followed by Carpenter-Wells, were released for bid in November 1956 and construction was completed in early 1958 on two projects that, albeit were greatly needed for the college, marked one of a notable range of architectural and planning departures for Texas Tech.

13

RADIATORS AND REACTORS

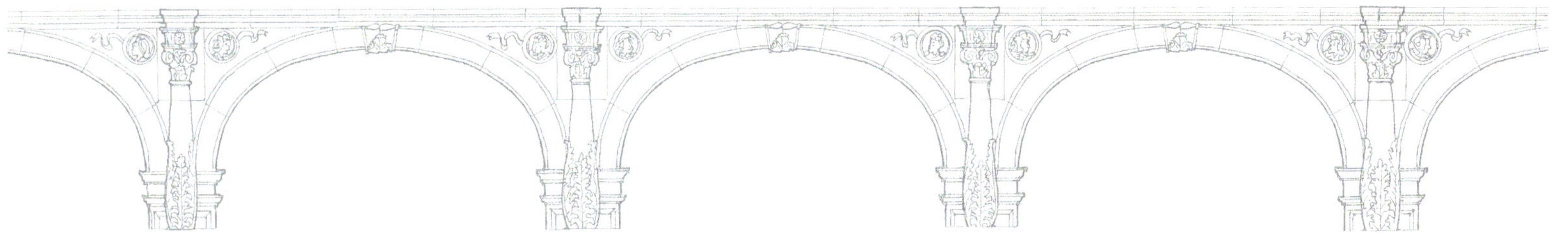

IN REMARKS AT THE GRAND OPENING of the new Rawls College of Business on the evening of January 17, 2012, Chancellor Kent Hance, with characteristic grin, wit, and drawl, sent the crowd into laughter when he declared, "Folks, this building is fantastic! It is so far from. . . the old Classroom and Office Building. That was the ugliest building in the history of Texas Tech!"[1] The infamous Classroom and Office Building, or COB—later renamed the English and Philosophy Building to note the building's later tenants—became a hated and premiere symbol of what was perceived as Tech's wayward era of modernism. Buildings at Texas Tech beginning in the late 1950s strayed entirely away from the Plateresque-revival roots of the original campus. Lueders limestone was replaced by painted cast-in-place concrete. Clay barrel-tile roofs would all but disappear, substituted with an experimental range of differing terra-cotta colored materials—wall-mounted quarry tile, porcelain mosaic tile, and clay hollow solar tile. The COB was an obvious scapegoat—its austere angular forms, pale mosaic tile walls, odd undulating concrete entry awning, and later in life a history of incessant roof leaks and complaints from tenants ranging from sick building syndrome to ghost hauntings only fueled public belief in the failure of modernism at Texas Tech.

Much of the decisions that led to Tech's modernist era were inevitable given the popular design fashions at the time not only at Tech, but also nationwide. But it was also the inherent programmatic demands of these new buildings that drove the prevailing style. In the science-and-technology furor in American higher education that paralleled both the Cold War and the Space Race, so much new construction in American higher education consisted of computer centers, laboratories, or newer, larger libraries whose functions did not easily mesh with classically decorated buildings. So was the case at Texas Tech. Continued construction cost inflation, a decline in more artisan-heavy construction trades such as stone masonry that were vital to neoclassical construction, and the meteoric rise in nationwide enrollment caused by the baby boomer generation all made modernism an unavoidable course at Texas Tech.

Butler & Kimmel, so named following Herbert Brasher's departure,

Circa-1960s photograph of the entry façade of the Classroom and Office Building. The building would become an albatross symbol of modernism's failure at Texas Tech.

Partial view of the south façade and single-story wing to the Computer and Architecture Building, Haynes and Kirby's final design commission at Texas Tech. The introduction of red clay solar tile would become a commonplace staple in modernist projects completed at Tech over the next decade.

designed the 68,100 square foot, two-story Classroom and Office Building in spring 1958. Intended as a polyglot academic building intended for multiple college divisions, shortly after completion in 1960,[2] the COB had been transferred to the rapidly expanding Division of Commerce for their exclusive use. Formatively, the COB accomplished one goal in providing a permanent building backdrop to the long-bare northwestern corner of Memorial Circle in lieu of the banal backdrop of tall grasses and a handful of X-buildings. Butler & Kimmel incorporated the traditional Texas Tech blend brick on its façade, but the building was otherwise totally different. Covered walkways consisted of dark bronze-painted steel columns supporting a rhythm of undulating concrete awnings. Entrances were prominent not due to ornate stone entries or rejería, but rather from the use of large swaths of curtain wall glazing framed with clear aluminum mullions. Bioclimatically, the building was forward thinking, thanks to a saw-tooth exterior plan where no window faced directly to the south or west. Classrooms and offices were undersized and cramped, and the building suffered from poor acoustics generated by the thin borrowed-lite partitions separating corridors and classrooms. Not long after their arrival, the Division of Commerce—soon renamed Business Administration—wanted out, and proceeded with efforts to build themselves a new home.

By 1959, Edward Jones was, much like his predecessors, tired and ready to retire. His tenure had been an outwardly prosperous one in terms of enrollment and facility growth, and Tech recently became a full member of the Southwest Conference. But constant antics from a politically charged Board of Directors, and meddlesome pressure from boosters, faculty, and the community had left Jones feeling adrift, to a point that he offered his resignation at the August 22, 1959 board meeting.[3] Accepting the resignation, the Board of Directors opted

Aerial view looking north down the Engineering Key, estimated during the 1962 College Engineering Fair (given the presence of army Nike missile displays and a Minuteman ICBM mockup located around the Engineering Key). The addition of two modernist-era buildings along the Key, along with the continued nuisance presence of X-buildings conspired to visually destroy much of the prado-like vision Watkin desired for the Key.

The United States Embassy at New Delhi, India, designed in 1956 and completed in 1959; Edward Durrell Stone, architect. Stone's regionally sensitive use of solar tile to diffuse solar heating on the glass façade behind would influence a generation of southern and southwestern architects in the United States.

to advance Robert Cabaniss Goodwin from his post as dean of the Arts and Sciences Division to president later that year. Goodwin was a safe hire, given his West Texas pedigree, scientific background, and Harvard credentials. Six months following Goodwin's appointment, he is handed a report by his academic vice president, Dr. W. M. Pearce that left him speechless.

Texas Tech—the onetime West Texas rural college one governor was certain would never enroll one thousand students—was anticipated to more than double to an eventual enrollment of twenty thousand by 1970.[4] Deans were already sounding alarms, insisting the college embark on an institution-wide analysis to establish goals and direction of the school, which the Board of Directors authorized in February 1960 followed shortly thereafter by a two-year self-study imposed by Texas Tech's accrediting body—the Southern Association of Colleges and Schools (SACS). The findings of the self-study, completed in September 1962, were manifold.[5] Texas Tech still suffered from a chronic shortage of funds, remained chronically understaffed, and deficient in facility needs (namely the library, graduate division, and research spaces). But fundamentally, SACS discovered a larger strategic problem plaguing the college, with everyone at Tech rhetorically asking themselves, "Who are we?" Tech had been running at a breakneck pace of expansion since the Second World War, but in the process had evolved, and perhaps had even mutated, beyond its founding academic and cultural identity. Even former President Jones was aware of Tech's identity crisis, pleading with the board in his 1959 departure that the college should be structurally reorganized and renamed to reflect a university. One telling statement in the SACS self-study explained it best: "The name Texas Technological College does not adequately and accurately describe the nature of this institution. A suitable name, recognizing its potential as a multipurpose state university of the first class, should be adopted immediately."[6]

ONE EVENING IN JANUARY 1960, architecture students were hard at work in a second floor studio in West Engineering when a deafening boom rattled the whole building. Barely had heads shot up from their drafting boards when a second and third thud hammered through the building.[7] Students ran outside to see a cloud of dust where the ferroconcrete superstructure for the new Architecture and Computer Building once stood. Inexplicably, the roof deck of the new building's structural frame collapsed, pancaking onto the third floor deck and triggering a domino effect of collapses. Architects Haynes & Kirby and their engineers had turned to a recent, but short-lived innovation in structural framing known as lift-slab construction. Lift-slab technology—later outlawed in many US jurisdictions, was a process where slabs were poured while resting on the slab or deck below them, and once cured hoisted up and secured to steel framing above. Though cost- and time-efficient, a series of spectacular collapses nationwide led to the process being discredited. Thankfully, the Tech collapse took place when the job site was vacant, but completion of the Architecture and Computer Building would be delayed until spring 1961.[8]

The Architecture and Computer Building—Haynes & Kirby's final Tech commission—was a bold, modernist departure, particularly given its prominent location along the otherwise Spanish Renaissance–stylized Engineering Key. Location notwithstanding, the building was an aesthetic compromise in which Blum Haynes attempted to reconcile the simple aesthetic language of the modernist building with the formality of building massing and colonnades of nearby older buildings. Its cruciform three-story plan was faced on its Engineering Key façade with an austere buff-blend brick façade

(*Top*) The New Library Building at Texas Technological College, as seen looking northwest from across Boston Avenue, shortly after opening in 1962.

(*Bottom*) SRM's Agricultural Plant Sciences Building, as completed in 1961, prior to construction of a later south wing that would expand it into an L-shape.

broken by a random-pattern screen wall of solid and open-cell clay solar tile, which visually softened the abrupt mass of a three-story east-west-oriented classroom and studio block.

Solar tile had become hugely popular as a solar heat diffusion solution to glass façades in the United States in the 1950s, particularly in warmer southern climes, spurred by New York architect Edward Durrell Stone's use of a cream-color concrete solar tile as a sunscreen cladding to his design for the 1954 US Embassy Building in New Delhi.[9] In fact, Haynes & Kirby's design was well received, particularly by architecture students and faculty delighted to finally be in their own building, though Barrick himself had two reservations about the project. For one, the Architecture Department shared the new building with Tech's Computer Engineering Department and their new set of massive IBM mainframes— enormous machines that despite being able to compute little more than a modern-day scientific calculator—generated copious amounts of heat. The 1,600 square-foot computer room alone required sixty tons of refrigerated air—enough air conditioning to cool *fifteen* single-family homes.[10] Barrick's other concern was more strategic to Texas Tech's aesthetic future. In late 1959, the Acme Brick Company wrote Barrick notifying him that this project would be the last building *anywhere* to receive the Texas Tech blend of brick produced in Texas.[11] John Carpenter's ridiculous insistence on using a Texas-extracted clay had resulted in Acme rendering any known veins of clay in Texas for the buff-blend brick virtually extinct. Thanks in part to publicity generated from Tech's founding, and the frequent specifying of Acme buff-blend brick by Wyatt Hedrick's firm and others across the Southwest in decades since, countless projects built over three decades used the popular buff blend. Acme was having difficulty retooling kilns in their Perla Plant in Arkansas to achieve the original blend color at Tech in the 1920s, and due to a loss of institutional memory, not even Barrick was initially aware of the Arkansas option. For the next decade, achieving the correct brick blend color at Tech would be a hit-or-miss affair.

ONE KEY SPACE deficiency identified at Tech in the SACS self-study was an undersized library. While library stack shortages in the late 1950s were not nearly as severe as in the Elizabeth West era, it was still a problem. The old Library had been designed for no more than three hundred thousand volumes, but now possessed well over a half million, and many college divisions had created their own departmental satellite libraries within academic buildings across campus, against the recommendations of the CPC. In September 1958, Tech librarian R. C. Janeway reported to President Jones a need for storing an extra three hundred thousand volumes that the existing building could not support.[12] Planning for a new library began in 1959, and Barrick had curiously recommended a respected Beaumont design firm for the commission—Pitts, Mebane, and Phelps.

Skeet Pitts had come full circle since first reviewing textile equipment shop drawings for a brand new Texas Technological College at Chip Robert's office in Atlanta over three decades earlier. Pitts had moved to Beaumont on the eve of the Great Depression to become a partner with a new firm. Pitts's firm steadily grew in the 1950s thanks to a myriad of work including office buildings, banks, warehouses, and federal projects. Respected as a business leader in Southeast Texas and soon to become president of the Texas Society of Architects, higher education work was not a major focus of Pitts's firm. Pitts, Mebane and Phelps had completed work at Centenary College in Louisiana and largely planned and designed the Lamar Institute of Technology in Beaumont from the ground up,[13] but had completed little other college or university work.

The rising tide of modernism at Texas Tech brought the question of the future of aesthetics direction for the new library to the forefront. Here, the Hotel Cortez paradox emerged. Plateresque architecture in Spain taller than four stories in height simply did not exist and revivalist, taller Plateresque-revival buildings built in the last century had a mixed reputation of success. But more practically speaking, few if any architects were designing in neoclassical styles anymore. Pitts's team projected that a one-million-volume library would require at least 180,000 gross square feet,[14] making the new Library one of the largest buildings at Texas Tech. Budgetary limitations demanded that building surface area be kept to an efficient minimum, and the most efficient stack floor plan meant a building five or six stories in height. Such a tall, almost cubic structure could not in all practicality be Spanish Renaissance in style.

The more hotly contested challenge to the Library project was location. Two site options emerged among stakeholders for debate—one site west of the Student Union Building, and the second deep within the core of the campus. The "core" option initially considered was at the northwestern corner of Memorial Circle, the future site of the Mass Communications Building built fifteen years later (now known as the College of Media and Communications following its relocation to the former Business Administration Building in 2012). When the CPC learned of the required height of the library, and the visual imbalance such a tall building would create astride the Court of Honor, a faculty-suggested alternative site was proposed—the middle of Memorial Circle itself. The alternative proposal was a disastrous threat to Watkin's original master plan, Barrick immediately opposed the idea, but unhelpful political maneuvers by Goodwin in forming a broader library exploratory task force led by *Avalanche-Journal* editor Charles A. Guy nearly brought the proposal to reality. Watkin's overly broad system of axial malls inadvertently worked in favor of the faculty Library plan. Faculty proponents argued that if the Library was built in Memorial Circle, the college still retained handsome open malls to the east, the north, and the Science Quadrangle to the west. Their fundamental argument was that central learning resources center for the college needed to be close to all academic buildings, which in 1959 still largely resided north of the Administration Building. They pointed out many major US universities—Michigan, Columbia, Virginia, and one in particular, the Love Library at the University of Nebraska at Lincoln—had libraries situated at the core of the campus and often in locations that interrupted major axial malls. Even Watkin had been unable to persuade Rice from ignoring Ralph Adams Cram's master plan and break Rice's main east-west axial mall with the construction of their Fondren Library in the late 1940s.[15]

Barrick, Pitts, and the CPC did their best as Guy held court over task force meetings in late 1959, culminating in a particularly heated meeting that November. In it, Guy publicly expressed dislike of either option, but a growing angst between Guy and Barrick gave the faculty proposal a slight edge in deliberations. After one pontification by Guy, the usually reserved Barrick, thoroughly fed up, blurted out, "Where would you like the library to go, Mr. Guy?" [16] Barrick's final plea argued that locating the new library on Memorial Circle would drastically upset Tech's system of utility tunnels, thus imposing additional physical plant costs upon the project, while claiming that siting the Library near the Student Union would foster synergy between two buildings with heavy student use. Guy relented, and the task force recommended the site west of the Student Union. Barrick's victory proved somewhat pyrrhic, as the episode permanently soured Guy's relationship with Barrick, a prickly issue that would rear its head again in coming years on a future controversy over Indiana Avenue.

Contrary to popular belief, Pitts's library design was neither inspired by a stack of books set on their side, or a radiator, though both have remained popular urban legends to this day. Inspiration for the Library façade was nothing more than the colonnades of the Tech campus. A continuous row of slender arches formed in precast concrete were situated at the crown of the stacks tower, with columns extending down to the concrete deck of a cantilever-edged second floor. Octagonal terra-cotta solar tile filled the voids between each column, which like Stone's New Delhi Embassy abated the solar heat load on perimeter windows into stack spaces. But Physical Plant personnel, students, and faculty alike would lament for decades to come that the Library would become a massive pigeon sanctuary. Single-story brick-clad wings north and south of the main block were designed for logistics and publishing workspaces for the Library, each clad with an anemically pale brick blend to the north and south wings, which punctuated Acme Brick's continued difficulties in finding an equivalent color blend for the Texas Tech blend. In fact, Pitts, Mebane and Phelps would have problems on a number of Texas Tech commissions, and never quite got the brick color right.

Many were taken aback at the combination of such an aesthetic departure and massive size of the new repository. Barrick had to parse his words carefully in a description of the Library in the July 1960 edition of *Tex Talks*, exaggerating the modernist behemoth as "Spanish Mediterranean style" in design.[17] Nonetheless, when the Library opened in October 1962, it was hailed as a flagship addition to the college. National campus planning guru Richard Dober showcased the design in his 1964 book *Campus Planning*.[18] Faculty previously concerned with the placement of the Library were content as well, having shifted their attention onto the heated battle over what Texas Tech's new name should be.

SUCCESS WITH the Thompson-Gaston and Carpenter-Wells projects led to additional project wins by Associated Architects & Engineers, and beginning in 1959, AA&E became inundated with Tech work, designing over seven hundred thousand gross square feet of new housing, academic, and student life space at the college in a five-year period. The first AA&E project was the Plant Sciences Building. Texas Tech's Horticulture Department, for long the red-headed stepchild of the Agricultural Division, was determined to grow into a respectable program, and department head Elo Urbanovsky was determined to leverage his position in the CPC to accomplish that. AA&E completed design of the two-story, 26,500 square-foot building in summer 1959, with construction commencing on October 10.[19] Plant Sciences was yet another divergent modernist iteration at Tech, straying from adjacent building aesthetics with the use of slender cast-in-place concrete columns and shallow arches, and like the Computer-Architecture Building continued the use of square red clay solar tiles. AA&E's design bore some distant similarity to the yet-to-be unveiled Library design, confirming that contemporary designers were attempting to reconcile a modernist iteration on neoclassical elements of the Tech campus with similar deconstructive methods.

Perhaps most fascinating of all of AA&E's modernist works was the Chemical Engineering and Nuclear Reactor Building—located west of the new Architecture and Computer Building. Engineering Division Dean John Bradford was keen on introducing nuclear engineering into the curriculum at Tech, with administration and politicians alike supporting such a move that would turn more heads toward Lubbock. Barrick had to scramble and contact Wyatt Hedrick of all people for advice on what was initially perceived as a complex project.[20] When Hedrick referred Barrick to Convair's nuclear engineering division in Fort Worth, the college architect was shocked to learn that design and construction of a fissile training reactor was far simpler than anyone at Tech had anticipated.

The Argonne National Laboratory had been tasked in the mid-1950s to develop a simple, low-power nuclear reactor suitable for university training and research. By early 1957, Argonne had developed ArgoNAUT (Argonne Nuclear Assembly for University Training)—a small ten-kilowatt prototype so compact and straightforward in fact that the Argonne researchers secretly shipped its parts from Illinois to an international conference in Geneva in September 1958,[21] assembling and bringing the reactor online much to the shock of attendees. Dozens of universities now expressed interest in Argonaut reactors on their campus. Excluding the cost of nuclear fuel, AA&E determined the cost of an Argonaut reactor at Texas Tech would be only $250,000.[22] The balance of the proposed building was a two-story classroom and laboratory addition to the small Hedrick-designed Petroleum Engineering Laboratory built a decade earlier and bearing a resemblance to Haynes's & Kirby's nearby project for Architecture and Computer Sciences. But inexplicably, the reactor component of the project was cancelled with little explanation in early summer 1960,[23] just as AA&E was issuing bid documents, leaving the project limited only to the Chemical Engineering addition component.

Southeast of the Plant Sciences Building, AA&E would in 1962 design a duo of projects that would for the time being sound the swansong of Spanish Renaissance neoclassicism at Texas Tech. The thirty-three thousand square-foot Charles E. Maedgen Jr. Theater, and the three-story Psychology Building would be the last academic buildings completed as generally traditional additions to Tech's physical

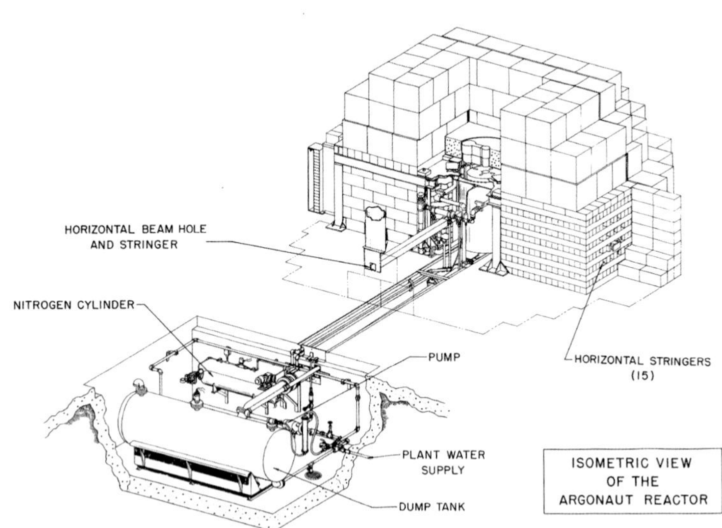

An isometric diagram displaying the relative simplicity of an ARGONaut-class nuclear reactor; a type nearly constructed on the Texas Tech campus in the early 1960s.

plant for some time. Both buildings were sited north of the recently completed Wall-Gates Hall Complex, forming a curious open-ended courtyard along 18th Street. Budget limitations once again forced spartan detailing on both buildings—more so on the Psychology Building—a trend that had been irritating Barrick for the last decade. Why AA&E reverted to traditional aesthetics for these two projects, shortly following completion of Computer and Architecture and Plant Sciences Buildings, remains unknown. In time, the Psychology Building would suffer the butt of many student jokes following the later 1973 addition of an ill-advised windowless fourth floor, spawning an urban legend that Tech students were being subjected to sleep deprivation experiments in the Psychology Building's uppermost floor.

The year 1961 was pivotal in that Tech surpassed ten thousand students that fall, or an increase of 1,034 students in a single year.[24] With a capacity of 4,489 beds, 1961 also marked when Tech could house fewer than 50 percent of students in dormitories—the first year since the completion of West and Doak Halls in 1934. In fall 1962, enrollment grew by 1,601 students, and three years later would set a single-year growth record that still stands today at 2,478 additional students. Housing expansion now would require thousands of additional beds built annually simply to keep pace. Goodwin ordered Barrick and the CPC to evaluate how many additional beds could be built if the college reallocated the majority of retained earnings purely to new dormitories. Barrick's 1962 report indicated that if institutional-retained funding were reallocated only to housing construction, Texas Tech could by 1972 add 8,700 beds to their housing portfolio.[25] But there were too many other facility demands that made such a plan infeasible. Marshall Pennington sought out alternative solutions from any peer institution he could find, including the University of Texas at Austin, Texas Western College (today the University of Texas at El Paso), and North Texas State University (today the University of North Texas). Barrick dispatched architects Hoyse McMurtry and Calvin Craig of the AA&E partnership to California to survey student housing recently built at rapidly growing institutions there. To everyone's surprise, the survey revealed that even the oldest of Tech's residence halls provided better amenities than any of the California state institutions, including flagships UC Berkeley and UCLA.[26]

Realizing their conundrum, Tech administration first considered alternative strategies, such as partnerships with private housing developers on land adjacent to Tech, or executing land leases with housing firms to provide on-campus housing—forerunner concepts to present-day industry models of private-public partnerships—or "P3s." Pennington's office was bombarded with queries from contractors, developers, and financiers, as Tech negotiated or discussed terms with nine different companies about potential housing projects, but all of whom by 1965 had gone nowhere.[27] Only one private dormitory, built west of campus, would emerge from the P3 housing brouhaha.

P3s aside, Texas Tech continued to build housing as quickly as possible. The AA&E consortium completed designs for the next two housing complexes—the twin Wall-Gates Hall and Hulen-Clement Hall Complexes—situated at Barrick's recommendation immediately

East courtyard to the Wall-Gates Complex, Associated Architects and Engineers of Lubbock, completed 1963. The restrained wing plan and addition of cloistering arcades gave the Wall-Gates and Hulen-Clement Complexes much more Spanish-revival feel.

Stiles, Roberts, & Messersmith's design for Maedgen Theater, regarded as one of the last neoclassical projects at Tech until the 1970s, undated.

The east façades of the taller, more broad-winged Stangel-Murdough Hall, Tech's last HHFA-grant-funded residence hall, completed in 1964.

north of 19th Street between Boston and Flint Avenues. The projects marked the beginnings of a massive southwesterly shift in campus expansion beginning in the early 1960s. Limited distance between 18th and 19th Streets meant that both dormitories required a more compact footprint as compared to Carpenter-Wells or Thompson-Gaston, with outer wings folded inward in an L-shape. Wall-Gates begun in October 1961, and Hulen-Clement begun in November 1962, were perhaps the most Spanish Renaissance–revivalist Tech buildings of their day, thanks to colonnaded arcades that connected each dormitory's pairs of wings to each other along their south façades, and the interplay of each complexes' four- and six-story residential housing blocks. Five decades since completion, and with the benefit of mature landscape surroundings, today both dormitory complexes provide a handsome perimeter to the southern boundary of campus. Oddly enough, Stangel-Murdough Hall—a third AA&E-designed residential complex bid at the same time as Hulen-Clement, but was not completed until 1964—combined the aesthetic innovations developed in the 1960s-era residence halls with the long-wing plan layout of the earlier circa-1950s dormitories. Located north of its two half-sisters near 15th Street, Stangel-Murdough was also taller, with seven-story residential blocks on each wing group in lieu of the six-story units built to the south. Within three years, Tech labored frenetically to add 1,500 beds to campus, but with little solace given enrollment grew by more than 3,600 students in the same time. Breakneck design and construction, and additional HHFA financing resources still only equated to constructing new housing for four-out-of-every-ten new students arriving each year. Unless alternative housing methods or additional revenue was found, Texas Technological College would culturally and functionally devolve into the hated and emerging moniker in 1960s higher education of a *commuter campus.*

14

GOING VERTICAL

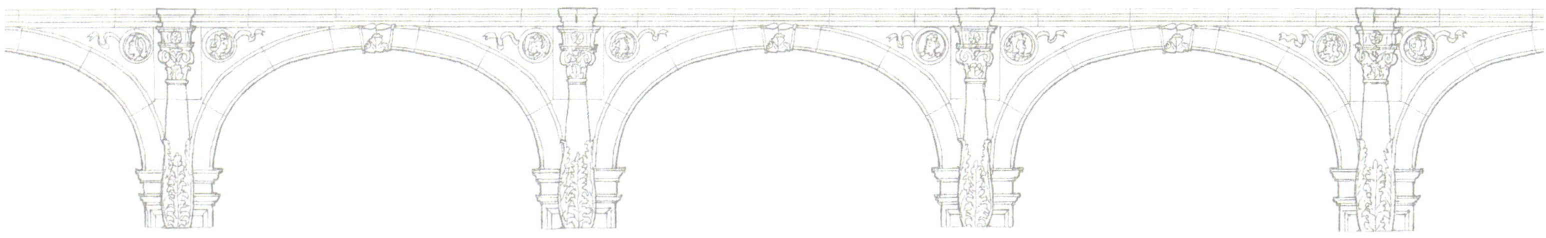

On November 8, 1965, hundreds of spectators and news media descended upon San Marcos, Texas, on the campus of Southwest Texas State College (today known as Texas State University) to witness President Lyndon B. Johnson sign House Resolution 9567—An Amendment to the National Education Defense Act.[1] Johnson, himself a Southwest Texas State alumnus, found it fitting to return to his alma mater for what became a pivotal moment in the history of American higher education. As a lesser-known piece within the gamut of Great Society legislation, it is best known today as the Higher Education Act (HEA) of 1965.

The HEA had many aims—expand the ranks of a national corps of trained faculty, provide financial aid for students, as well as massively increase federal funding in the form of grants, rather than the low-interest HHFA loans offered during the Eisenhower and Kennedy administrations—to colleges and universities nationwide. It would prove to be a transformative mechanism in the history of American higher education architecture and campus planning, as countless institutions could barely handle the same baby boomer-generation enrollment spikes that Texas Tech was facing. But, unlike the New Deal–era PWA grant system three decades earlier, Department of Health, Education, and Welfare (DHEW) HEA grants would not be regionally administrated, but rather centrally administered from Washington, DC. Invariably, grant reviewers were predominantly urban-oriented, East Coast–born personnel whose background was rooted in the glut of postwar DHEW-backed urban housing projects, and so reviewers naturally favored higher-density, high-rise, urban-oriented building design, even at near-rural institutions like Texas Tech.

The effects upon the built landscape of the American university were profound. In the 1960s and into the 1970s, countless institutions across the country proceeded with constructing massive, and sometimes hideously out-of-scale, skyscrapers as additions to their physical plant. Minnesota State University in Mankato built a pair of high-rise dormitories on a campus that had never seen anything taller than three stories before. East Texas State University in Commerce (today known as Texas A&M University–Commerce) would

President Lyndon B. Johnson signs the Higher Education Act into law in a gymnasium at Southwest Texas State College on November 8, 1965. Not since the Morrill Land Grant Act a century earlier had any piece of legislation in US history so profoundly impacted American collegiate architecture and planning.

build the new twelve-story Samuel A. Whitley Hall—a monster that remains to this day the only skyscraper in a rural town of barely eight thousand people. Louisiana Tech, Ohio State, University of Cincinnati, Washington State, and countless other schools commissioned high-rise projects—residential and academic alike paid for by DHEW grants—in which many have since been demolished in lieu of more appropriately scaled campus planning. At Texas Tech, administrators already knew of the coming massive shifts in facility dynamics. Seventeen months before Johnson had signed the HEA into law, President R. C. Goodwin confided in an *Avalanche-Journal* interview, "Do not be surprised if some day you see high-rise buildings on the campus." [2]

Between 1966 and 1975, Texas Tech completed five projects consisting of seven high-rise buildings across campus—most of which were DHEW-funded buildings that provided Tech with the much-needed infusion of square footage needed to survive its enrollment boom. For Tech, the HEA was a godsend, but it was only a third of the story, as the HEA required states to provide matching funds to DHEW grant appropriations for new higher education facilities. The next third of the pie came from Texas voters, who six days before LBJ's visit to San Marcos had voted to approve Amendment One—a state constitutional amendment allowing an increase in ad valorem taxation specifically to match DHEW disbursements.[3] Combined, the two sources unleashed $100 million for new facilities at the sixteen public colleges and universities statewide. The final and perhaps most influential piece came from Lubbock Representative and US House Appropriations Committee Chair George Mahon, who ensured Texas Tech would receive a disproportionate value of just over $13 million of that pot.[4]

The HEA and Amendment One infusion was pivotal to Texas Tech funding a range of future vital building projects—Business Administration, Biology, Art and Architecture, the Wiggins Residential Complex, and expansion of Chemistry—all of which helped the college survive the ongoing enrollment onslaught. While these buildings provided more than 1.1 million square feet of crucial housing and academic space at Tech, they also had a distinctive and arguably detrimental impact on the campus plan and college culture. From the 1970s even until today, much of the western campus is visually dominated by mid- and high-rise construction that suffered into the 2000s from a lack of pedestrian friendly site improvements, cohesive campus planning, and sustainable campus density. Even with Mahon's clout, DHEW projects were often overloaded and underfunded, leaving the CPC and design firms scrambling to pare down project scopes, leaving out value-added features like quality interior finishes and landscape enhancements, while sometimes deleting entire buildings out of the project.

The arrival of DHEW funding came at a crossroads for Nolan Barrick in his Texas Tech career. In twelve frenetic years, Barrick had not caught a break, as his role as supervising architect transformed from that of overseeing design, development, and construction at a five-thousand-student rural college to the same role over

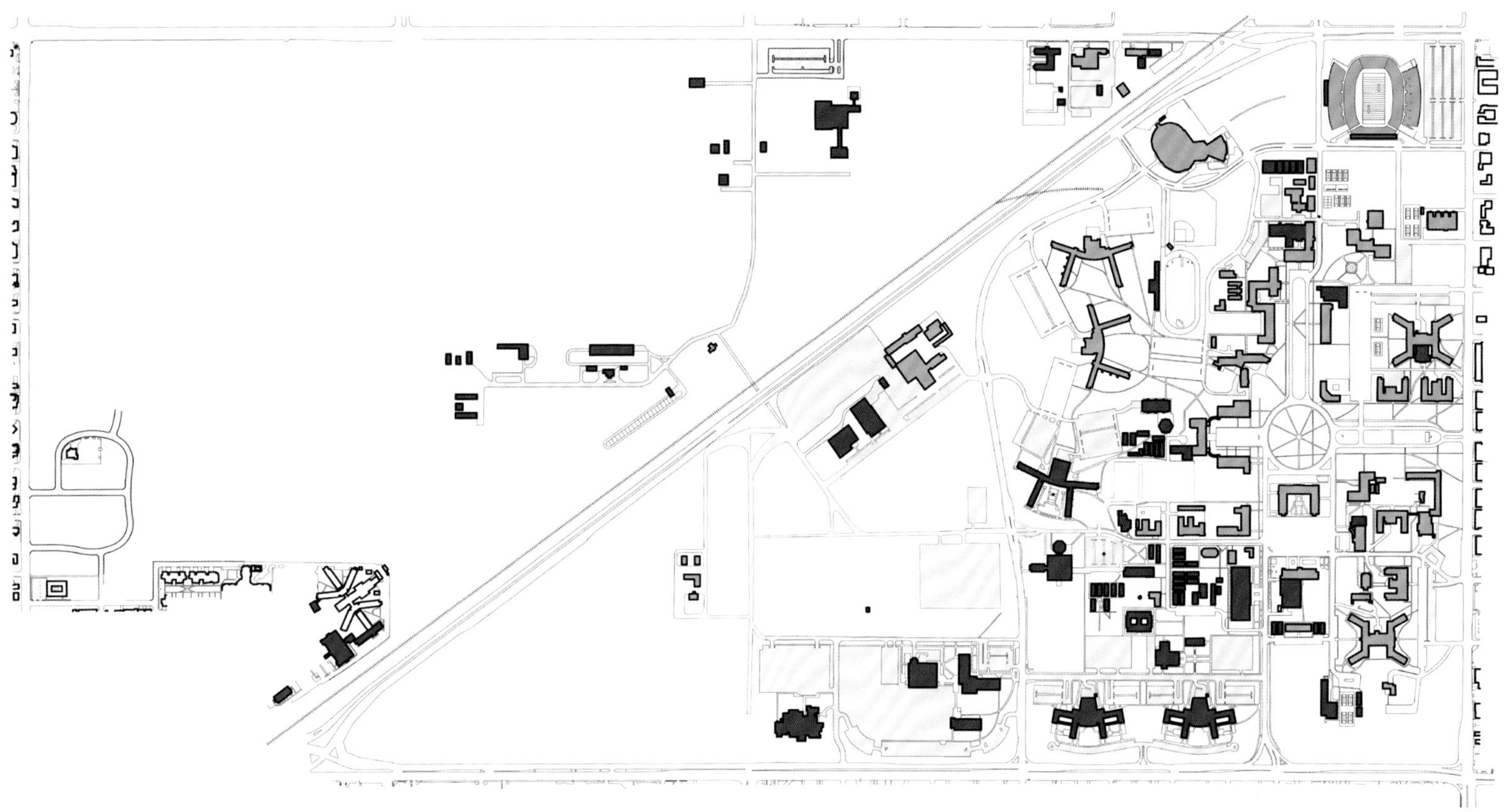

Circa-1970 campus plan of Texas Tech, illustrating the massive exodus of building construction, ranging from high-rises to new X-buildings that expanded the campus first to the south and then to the southwest.

a thirteen-thousand-student university in everything but name. A decade earlier, Barrick could count on his hired architects and engineers to manage smaller projects of the Pennington Plan era, but the scale and complexity of recent projects had proven to be something else altogether. The CPC now maintained their own project management staff, including Barrick's assistant Bill Felty, architect Jerry Kirkwood, and field supervisor Norman Igo.[5] Even with the help, both Barrick and the CPC felt adrift in the sea of project minutia; totally unable to focus on strategic matters of campus planning. To complicate matters, new departments had since formed whose responsibilities often overlapped with Barrick's and that of the CPC, such as the Physical Plant Office, which opened in their new facility in 1961. Physical Plant operations would expand over the next decade adding additional resources such as a Central Foods Warehouse in 1964, followed by a new $3.2 million Central Heating and Cooling Plant (or CHACP—pronounced "CHAP"), which would open in 1968 farther

Undated view looking north from 19th Street at the southwestern area of campus after 1971 demonstrates the profound visual impact of the high-density-favored HEA upon the architectural fabric of Texas Tech.

Rendering of the proposed Central Heating and Cooling Plant (or CHACP), designed to replace the thirty-five-year-old undersized Power House north of the Engineering Key.

northwest along Main from the Physical Plant Office.[6] Tech had long since outgrown Watkin's little Ávila-inspired Power House north of the Engineering Key.

Even the CPC itself was changing. Pennington stepped down in early 1966, replaced within the CPC by a tandem pair, Haskell G. Taylor, a former accounting professor who now served as Tech's vice president for Financial Affairs and Dr. Glenn Barnett, Pennington's official replacement, Taylor's boss, and the new executive vice president of the college.[6] While both maintained amicable relationships with veteran members Barrick and Urbanovsky, correspondence belied the two new leaders' disinterests in strategic campus planning in lieu of their first priority of paper pushing the existing projects at hand. Suggestions at CPC meetings made by Urbanovsky and Barrick regarding larger-scale improvements to the campus went mostly unheeded. At one 1965 meeting, Barrick prophetically suggested that parking needs in some areas of the campus warranted consideration of a parking garage as a solution.[7] Barrick was practically laughed out of the room, as his colleagues thought it ridiculous that a two thousand-acre campus would ever warrant so ridiculous and expensive a structure.

Looking to simplify, in summer 1965, Barrick tendered his resignation from the role of college architect, requesting to retain his role as chair of the Architecture Department and focus on matters there.[8] Barnett accepted Barrick's resignation, but requested he stay on in the meantime as a member of the CPC—a request Barrick reluctantly agreed to. The decision left Texas Tech in a vulnerable position, with no architect serving in a leadership role championing a cohesive plan for the college, as Kirkwood and Igo now reported directly to Barnett. Barrick, further disillusioned with the CPC having devolved into a body constantly "putting out project fires" stepped down from his role on the Campus Planning Committee in 1968;[9] an act that in reality marked the death knell for the CPC for good. For the time being, architects and engineers engaged at Tech would largely be the

Aerial rendering of the Wiggins Complex, Stiles, Roberts & Messersmith, architects, illustrating the initial massive six-tower development plan that seemed more akin to the high-rise design visions of Le Corbusier than of Tech's Plateresque roots. Ultimately the HEW Department would grant fund only three of the six towers.

Tech CPC architect Jerry Kirkwood (left) and architect Howard Schmidt (right) review construction progress at the Wiggins site, as the massive new P. C. Colean Tower looms in the distance.

only checkpoint in ensuring quality design work was being added to the campus fabric for the next fifteen years. Some projects were quality additions to the campus. Others were not.

TEXAS TECH'S FIRST high-rise addition to the campus remains its tallest, even today. The 1966–1969 Business Administration Building—today home to the College of Media and Communications—at over two hundred thousand gross square feet was the largest single academic building added to the Tech campus to date and was a radical aesthetic departure from anything seen on campus before—even those modernist buildings recently completed. Business Administration leadership was impressed with Page Southerland Page of Austin and their new Business School design at the University of Texas at Austin. Upon that recommendation, the college eagerly hired Page to design a home that moved the division out of the hated COB. Regardless of the division's move into the COB in 1963, Business Administration leadership had been internally planning for a new building for their division as early as 1955 and had a particular case study in mind.

In February 1949, the University of Michigan became the first in the nation to build a high-rise school of business. The 180,000-square foot complex featured an elongated three-story academic building that was in turn connected to a nine-story office tower.[10] This organizational model resonated with then-Commerce Division leadership and became a fundamental case study for the resulting Business Administration Building. The new Tech business school would consist of three components—with Page Southerland Page proposing an office tower for faculty and staff, a classroom block consisting of smaller tiered- and flat lecture classrooms, and a hexagonal-plan rotunda containing a 460-seat lecture space and ground-floor business library. In yet another architectural urban legend, students would later perpetuate rumors that the Business Administration tower was inspired by console of a pocket calculator, failing to realize that Sanyo, Sharp, and Texas Instruments would not unveil pocket calculators to the US market until 1970.

Curiously, each of Business Administration's three activity blocks had their own distinctive aesthetic with the two-story rotunda capped by a flat clay tile hip roof (a modernist play based upon Tech's traditional barrel-tile roofing), an austere three-story mushroom-like classroom block whose exterior was dominated by an exoskeleton of white-painted cast-in-place concrete, and a largely buff-brick-clad twelve-story tower punctuated by a grid of dark anodized bronze-clad protruding bay windows. Unable to afford the wood-paneled corridor treatments desired by BA leadership, halls were instead clad in dark walnut-patterned plastic laminate, while conversely, panels of polished starry night black granite—a new material to the Tech palette—would clad segments of the exterior façade. Completed with a $4.5 million turnkey budget, Business Administration provided the BA Division with the head-turning facility they wanted, but to Barnett and the CPC the project was a nightmare. The contractor, J. J. Fritch Construction of Dallas, ran four months behind in completing the facility and consistently ran afoul with the college and CPC, ensuring they would never work at Tech again. But more towers would soon be joining Tech's dramatically changing skyline.

Running shortly behind the BA project schedule was an even larger project—the largest urban-scaled project of any kind in Texas Tech history. The CPC continued hiring AA&E, though by 1965 the departure of McMurtry & Craig from the joint venture had simplified the partnership into Stiles, Messersmith, Schmidt, and Stuart (SMSS). Within two years' time, even Messersmith and Schmidt would split their firms back onto separate courses, each with an independent role at Texas Tech.[11] In the meantime, SMSS had received their largest Tech commission yet—a complex of six twelve-story, 572-bed student residential towers, divided into clusters of three, with each cluster oriented around a central dining complex. If fully built out, the new complex would allow Tech to boast an overall total of more than ten thousand beds for its student population.

Only one of the two three-tower residential clusters of what would be named the Dossie M. Wiggins Residential Complex—named for the college's fifth president—would be built. Two towers—R. C. Chitwood and Chanslor E. Weymouth Halls—were adjoined with common support spaces configured in an L-shaped ground floor plan, and a third tower—P. C. Coleman Hall—sited alone farther to the south. The three towers, along with a fourth 78,875-square-foot single-story-and-basement central food services facility anchored the 480,000-square foot complex.[12] Many of the aesthetic features incorporated into the Wiggins complex design reflected SMSS's prior experience at Tech, most notably the Plant Sciences Complex. Messersmith and Schmidt's team continued the use of precast concrete flattened-arch iterations of Tech's Spanish colonnades that ringed the ground floors of all four buildings at Wiggins. Clear anodized aluminum glazing remained, but SMSS used a single color of buff brick in a stacked coursing as a distinguishing masonry detail under window sills on the three Wiggins Towers in lieu of the mosaic tile prior incorporated at Plant Sciences. SMSS also incorporated another simplified strategy to maintain a hint of Tech's longtime use of red clay tile roofing, where all buildings within the Wiggins Complex featured a thin parapet line of red clay quarry tile to cap each building's roof profile. The $6 million first phase of the complex began construction in the summer of 1967 and was completed just over two years later.[13] Though the 1,716 additional beds were an invaluable addition to the college's housing fleet, additional efforts to secure the final $5 million in DHEW grant funding for the Phase II Cluster were unsuccessful. Even farther west of the new Wiggins Complex, another element of Texas Tech's south-westerly campus migration was emerging.

In further efforts to develop a unique breadth of curriculum for Texas Tech, and in response to the unmet regional educational needs

The Business Administration Building (now Media and Communications) at Texas Tech; Page Southerland Page, Architects, completed 1969.

Rendering of the proposed Biology Complex, Pierce & Pierce, architects, 1968

A minimalist building with an almost Pueblo-like approach to massing, present-day image of the southeastern side of Harrell+Hamilton's Law School building, undated.

of West Texas, on July 15, 1963, the Texas Technological College Board of Directors approved the creation of a law school.[14] The early architectural history for the Texas Tech School of Law had, like so many organs of the college, been a proud body born in the most humble of architectural surroundings. Despite vehement protests from Barrick and Urbanovsky, prior to his departure, Marshall L. Pennington proceeded with the $163,500 purchase of an additional nineteen wood-framed temporary barracks from the air force, shipped from Sheppard Air Force Base in Wichita Falls onto campus in 1966.[15] The purchase essentially replaced those Camp Bowie–era X-buildings that the college had already razed, thus returning the college back to a starting point in efforts to rid the wood-framed pestilence. These new additional barracks made convenient temporary quarters for Tech's newest academic body. Disgruntled law professors had to make do with ramshackle offices and classrooms in temporary barracks sited south of the Coliseum, while administration feverishly worked to build a new permanent home for the school.

Even with hundreds of thousands of square feet of DHEW-funded projects risisng at Tech, additional space was needed to handle the enrollment onslaught of the 1960s. Regrettably, Tech would purchase additional X-buildings from Sheppard AFB in Wichita Falls to add to the physical plant in 1966.

Present-day detail photograph of the austere façade of the Biology Tower.

Harrell & Hamilton of Dallas (today known as OMNIPLAN), had turned heads in 1965 with their design of the posh new North Dallas retail enclave—NorthPark Mall. Critics praised NorthPark's elegant marriage between a simple palette of materials—beige-color vertical brick surfaces combined with clean, simple building forms and stately landscaping. Harrell & Hamilton's 1968 Texas Tech School of Law design reflected many of the same design strategies. Partnered with Howard Schmidt as local architect, Harrell & Hamilton opted to propose the Law School Building at the far southwestern-most bounds of the campus, northeast of 19th Street and Indiana Avenue intersection. The distant site, however ill advised in terms of synergy with the balance of the college, was purposely chosen in establishing a perception that the School of Law was separate and unique from other Tech academic divisions. The building siting also accentuated Indiana Avenue itself, a thoroughfare that had become a vitriolic topic between a college that had come to embrace Barrick's and Urbanovsky's pleas to keep the campus undivided, and a city whose leadership not only demanded that Indiana Avenue bifurcate the campus, but some insisted Tech pay for and maintain it.[16]

From the exterior, the School of Law was a play of simple rectilinear block forms—interrupted by a grid of simplified flattened-arch windows. Programmatically, the new facility consisted of classrooms, offices, and spacious new moot court that were accompanied with a stand-alone student canteen and commons space. Inside and out, the brick was so prevalent a material in the walls and floors that in a rare moment by the Tech Board of Directors—who had rarely interceded in architectural matters since the time of John Carpenter—demanded some minimal reference to a red clay tile roof—even if limited to a band of quarry tile such that used atop buildings at the Wiggins Complex. The CPC joined in the meddling, as Urbanovsky, a landscape architect, demanded the building's glazed brick-and-tile floor be softened with red and gold carpeting.[17] Harrell & Hamilton weathered

The south façade of the Chemistry Building Expansion; Pitts, Phelps, Saxe & White, architects, 1970. Massive and imposing, the Chemistry Addition failed to tastefully integrate with Watkin's circa-1928 adjacent laboratory.

the creative intrusions to see construction commence following a July 20, 1968, ground breaking,[18] and the new facility was completed in the spring of 1970.

Nolan Barrick likely had a hand in selecting Pierce & Pierce Architects of Houston—a longtime design staple for facilities at Rice and the firm that had recently planned Houston Intercontinental Airport—for the design of Tech's new Biology Building. Unlike Pierce & Pierce's prior efforts to adhere to the Cram-inspired Mediterranean aesthetic of the Rice Campus, the six-story laboratory tower and hexagonal-plan lecture hall reflected yet another unpredictable modernist mutation that attempted to embody the material palette of Texas Tech, but little else. On the Biology Tower, fenestration was left to a series of vertical ribbon windows, punctuating vast panels of buff-blend brick framed in concrete on the tower's façades. To fit within the project's limited $5.4 million DHEW-stipulated budget,[19] the facility's 320-seat tiered lecture hall had to become a disconnected annex southeast of the Biology Tower connected by an open plaza.

Texas Tech had also retained Pitts, Mebane & Phelps—now Pitts, Phelps, Saxe & White—to design a massive new multistory classroom and laboratory addition south of William Ward Watkin's beloved 1928 Chemistry Building. Pitts and his firm remained in Tech's good graces following completion of the Library despite having designed an unremarkable two-story classroom and office building for the Foreign Languages and Mathematics Departments located west of the new Library, completed in early 1966. But if the Foreign Languages and Mathematics Building was blandly forgettable in nature, Pitts's 1968–1970 Chemistry Building expansion was unmistakable, a massive monolith of inappropriate scale when compared to the nearby delicately Plateresque original Chemistry Building. The $4.5 million DHEW grant-supported addition failed first and foremost due to its dark drab, monotone brick color, which in a final attempt by Pitts's team, still failed to match the traditional Texas Tech buff blend. Perhaps most frustrating about the Chemistry Building expansion was the unfortunate combination of its austere appearance and prominent visibility. Given its proximity to Memorial Circle, the massive 125,000-square foot, three-story expansion visually overpowers every nearby building even today, including the Agricultural Sciences and the Administration Building. Pitts's team, led by firm principal Robert White,[20] continued the use of full arches and solar tile at façade corners as in prior Tech commissions, as well as at the building's central multistory glass lobby.

In the midst of his role as senior designer at Stiles, Roberts, Messersmith, and now Johnson—or SRMJ—Walt Calvert happened to also be a popular studio and design professor in the Architecture Department at Texas Tech. Tall, lanky, and outwardly unassuming, Calvert had been responsible for many Texas Tech facility designs built over the past decade, but he and SRMJ had just garnered their most fascinating Tech commission to date.

In September 1966, Grover E. Murray became the eighth president

Undated aerial view of the Museum of Texas Tech University, highlighting the moated and iconic Moody Planetarium located in the left foreground.

Ground-level view of the new Museum, denoting Calvert's Elgin-Butler glazed brick-clad minimalist design that departed entirely from the material palette and shape grammars of the rest of the Texas Tech campus.

of Texas Technological College. Murray, a geologist by discipline was unique from his predecessors in being an outside hire for the college who ironically proceeded to champion West Texas regionalism as a distinguishing element to Texas Tech's identity more than any president before him. It was little surprise that when the Museum of West Texas had outgrown their $180,000 building along Memorial Circle in the 1960s, a vision would emerge for a new museum that too would be rooted in West Texas regionalism. Murray was instrumental in establishing ICASALS—the International Center for Arid and Semi-Arid Land Studies—in hopes that Texas Tech would become the penultimate research institution in the Southwestern US on arid land and climate issues.[21] These priorities would transcend institutional policy into a design ethos when Walt Calvert and the SRMJ design team were selected in late 1967 to design the new $2.5 million Museum for Texas Tech.

Calvert was, like Murray, fascinated with the landforms of the region—canyons like the Yellowhouse, Ransom, and Blanco—and sought to capture the canyon form in the formative language and massing of the Museum building. Calvert and SRMJ developed a structure for a convex cyclorama façade, hoping initially to clad it in a sandstone veneer indicative of local canyon walls. The soft, porous sandstone proved difficult to work with and cost prohibitive, so a cream-color, glazed brick manufactured by the Elgin-Butler Company was eventually decided upon as the exterior veneer. [22] The museum was located to the far northwest of the existing campus, and even then was set back noticeably from nearby 4th Street so that the approach to the building would accentuate the prairie conditions of the South Plains. Conversely, a water feature set north of the Museum surrounding what would become the iconic rising form of the Museum's Moody Planetarium accentuated a sense of precious scarcity of water to the region.

The Museum was above all else a notable departure from the styles commonly seen at Tech, and with that reception toward the design was mixed. Urbanovsky hated it and did not hide his contempt of the design from the administration. Bob Messersmith, Nolan Barrick, and even President Murray himself had to intercede to tamper Urbanovsky's verbal troublemaking.[23] Perhaps most gratifying for the SRMJ team came in the fall of 1970 following the Museum's completion when the project garnered a Texas Society of Architects Design Award, validating what remains today one of the most aesthetically unique facilities at Texas Tech.

15

THE FORGOTTEN MASTER PLAN

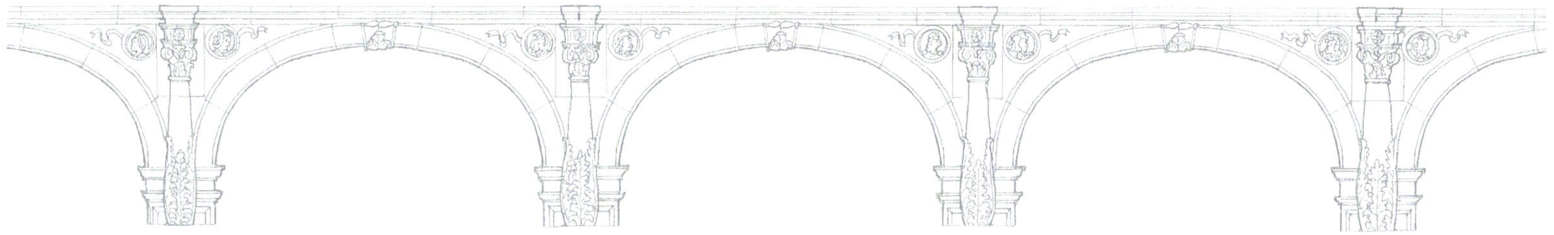

Tetsuya Fujita was a lucky man. A physicist by training, Fujita's expertise had spared him from conscription in the Imperial Japanese armed forces during World War II. If that were not luck enough, on one rainy morning in early August 1945, Fujita was working in his University of Kokura laboratory when air raid sirens sounded announcing the presence of a lone American bomber over the city. Fujita rushed to a nearby shelter unaware that the B-29—unable to sight its target through rain clouds, gave up and proceeded to an alternate target—Nagasaki. The intended target within Kokura for Fat Man—the first plutonium-fueled nuclear weapon ever exploded in anger—was a scant mile from the university. Tetsuya Fujita, the man destined to become one of the greatest meteorologists of the twentieth century, had the ironic luck of having his life spared by a rain storm.[1]

Twenty-five years later, Fujita—known as Ted by his American colleagues, found himself trusting his luck once again as he hung precipitously out of a helicopter, camera in hand, over Lubbock, Texas. It was May 1970 and Fujita, now a University of Chicago researcher, was photographing acre upon acre of devastation from one of the worst tornado strikes on a major American urban area in decades. His damage assessment of the Lubbock tornado was crucial to completing his new technical scale of measurement that could classify the severity of that most frightening of American meteorological phenomena—the tornado. It was within the carnage of the 1970 Lubbock tornado that Fujita had struck—from a research perspective—pay dirt.

Mid-evening on May 11, radar displays in Lubbock began to detect large vertical cloud formations forming south of the city. Two hours later, warnings were issued and sirens sounded, as radars detected the telltale hook echo associated with tornado-producing storm boundaries over East Lubbock. The East Lubbock event proved to be a tornado that thankfully struck only a sparsely populated area, leading the public to a false impression of an all clear. At 9:35 p.m., a second, far more violent tornado touched down near the southeast corner of the Texas Tech campus and proceeded to march northeast toward downtown. Once over downtown, the funnel cloud, now over a thousand feet in diameter, stripped façades of brick and glass, and so violently struck the Great Plains Life Building—Lubbock's tallest building—that the high-rise remains in a permanent state of torsion today. The twister suddenly veered west toward the North Overton neighborhood, and beyond that, Texas Tech. Just as the tornado passed onto the northeastern boundary of the campus, snapping the light standards of Jones Stadium like twigs, the twister just as suddenly reversed course to the northeast. For Texas Tech at least, the course shift had been merciful. Exactly seventeen years before to the day, a similar tornado had smashed through downtown Waco, ripping swaths of brick and roofing off the neoclassical-styled old Dr Pepper Bottling Plant, demonstrating that ornate, masonry-clad structures like those at Tech did not stand a chance against a high-velocity tornado. The twister continued east, practically flattening the nearby Guadalupe neighborhood, then marched toward the Lubbock Airport before disappearing.

The Lubbock tornado of 1970 forever changed the city, killing twenty-six people, injuring more than a thousand others, and destroying scores of homes, apartments and businesses. Adjusted to present-day dollars, over $1.5 billion of Lubbock property and infrastructure had been destroyed[2]—which makes it still today one of the ten costliest tornadoes in American history. Comparatively, the damage to Tech was light, and no students were injured as the spring semester had ended a week earlier. Dozens of trees, many original to Bradford Knapp's 1938 Arbor Day blitz, were uprooted or torn apart. For Lubbock, the vast destruction of residential property displaced thousands of residents—a diaspora that would have tremendous effects on the geopolitical development of Lubbock itself, as South and Southwest Lubbock experienced a mass exodus of new residential and commercial construction. For the next three decades however, North Overton would never really recover from the events of May 11. The neighborhood was already a hodgepodge of Victorian-era houses, efficiency apartments, and small commercial buildings, many of which were now flattened.

Based on historic structural damage data he had already been gathering, Fujita estimated tornado winds on the night of May 11 were in excess of 250 miles per hour. Following gathering the data from the Lubbock disaster and other tornadic events, Fujita introduced a measurement scale system named in his honor to this day. While the first tornado that struck East Lubbock earlier on May 11 was an F1[3]—comparably the weakest tornado on Fujita's scale, the second tornado was something else entirely. Lubbock had been hit by a one-in-one-thousand tornadic event, a monster known as an F5.[4]

Tetsuya "Ted" Fujita; one of the seminal meteorological researchers of the twentieth century, undated.

THE CAMPUS PLANNING COMMITTEE, at the urging of Grover Murray, was urged to redirect energies toward more strategic matters of campus planning,[5] in an attempt to steer CPC focus from construction minutia back toward campus planning policy, just as Nolan Barrick had once urged. Though Barrick had issued a Master Plan for

Texas Tech in 1957,[6] it consisted of nothing more than a glossy project overview of capital work on the horizon for the growing college. Past presidents such as Jones, Goodwin, and now Murray had turned to the CPC for guidance in developing a true master plan for the institution, but efforts up to 1971 had been executed without any outside planning firm input, and often consisted of nothing more than departmental surveys to identify "wants and needs" lists. Beginning in 1967 and culminating with its completion in 1971, a Long-Range Development Plan (LRDP) had been developed by the CPC with the commissioned assistance of local staple Howard Schmidt. It was the first true master plan undertaken by Texas Tech in nearly a half-century, and sadly had since been lost until Facilities Planning and Construction discovered a copy in the early 2000s. Murray instructed the CPC to base their planning on an ultimate enrollment goal of twenty-five to thirty thousand students.[7] The long-range planning team, consisting of Schmidt, Murray, Glenn Barnett, Haskell Taylor, Elo Urbanovsky, director of new construction Norman Igo, and Jerry Kirkwood had a simple list of objectives:

- Eliminate parking and vehicular traffic from the center of campus.
- Maintain academic development within the core of the campus. Stop academic development at Flint [Avenue].
- Transition intramurals and recreation away from [Physical Education (i.e., the northeast campus)]. Develop recreation [facilities] west of Flint [Avenue].[8]

Beyond those objectives, there were other "Areas of Study" within the plan, including development of additional pedestrian malls into

"FIRST In Lubbock—FIRST On The South Plains"

LUBBOCK AVALANCHE-JOURNAL

MORNING

48th Year, No. 166 46 Pages Lubbock, Texas, Wednesday Morning, May 13, 1970 Price 10 Cents Full Leased Wires: (AP), (UPI)

20 DEAD, MORE THAN 500 HURT

Stunned City Digging Out

DETAILS, PHOTOS, PAGE 2

(*Right top*) Front Page of the *Lubbock Avalanche-Journal* on May 13, 1970, following the tornado.

(*Right bottom*) East light standards to Jones Stadium snapped due to tornado damage sustained during the May 1970 Lubbock tornado that would have lasting impacts upon the city, and in time, Texas Tech.

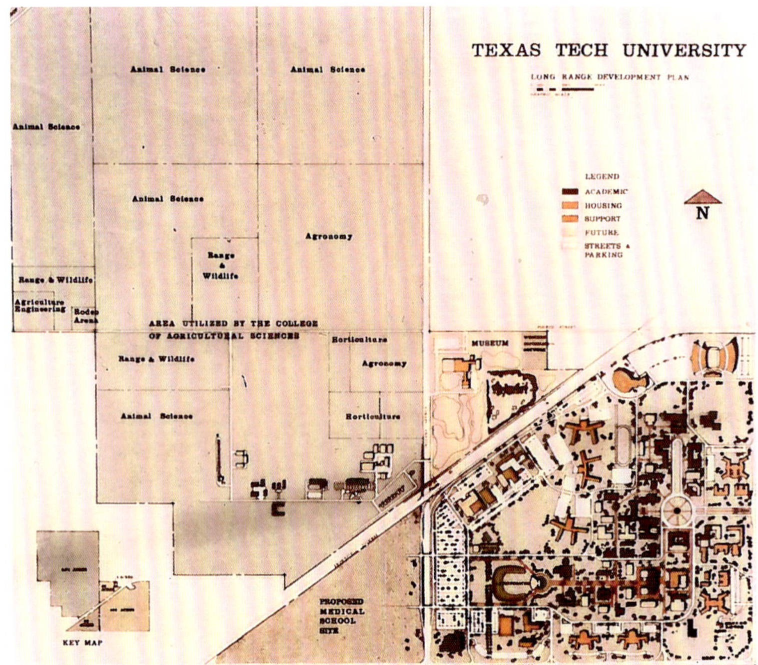

Long Range Development Plan, dated 1972, as created in concert between the CPC and architect Howard Schmidt.

While they had designed notable design additions to other Texas institutions, Ford Powell & Carson's Art and Architecture Complex—namely the Architecture Building—only served to hasten Board of Regents and public interests to disengage Texas Tech from its modernist era.

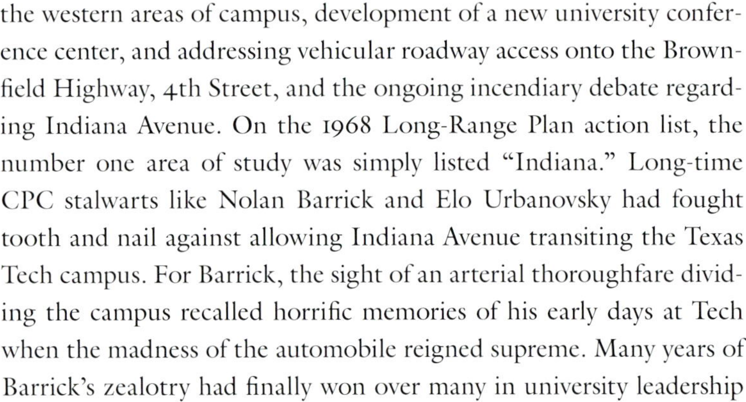

the western areas of campus, development of a new university conference center, and addressing vehicular roadway access onto the Brownfield Highway, 4th Street, and the ongoing incendiary debate regarding Indiana Avenue. On the 1968 Long-Range Plan action list, the number one area of study was simply listed "Indiana." Long-time CPC stalwarts like Nolan Barrick and Elo Urbanovsky had fought tooth and nail against allowing Indiana Avenue transiting the Texas Tech campus. For Barrick, the sight of an arterial thoroughfare dividing the campus recalled horrific memories of his early days at Tech when the madness of the automobile reigned supreme. Many years of Barrick's zealotry had finally won over many in university leadership and within the Board of Directors. The city of Lubbock, the chamber of commerce, and vocal proponents like Charles Guy however, regarded an Indiana Avenue transiting across the Tech campus as vital to a growing Lubbock.

Shortly after Marshall Pennington stepped down from his longtime post as executive vice president, Haskell Taylor wrote to Pennington's interim replacement, Gerald Thomas, in April 1968, on the city's 1967 proposal to extend Indiana through the Tech campus. In it, Taylor wrote: "May I call to your attention that the Campus Planning Committee is not in agreement with any of the proposals made by the City and wishes to avoid any controversy in regard to Indiana Avenue at the

Undated photograph looking east into the Art and Architecture subcourtyard. While the building and courtyard placement provided fair summer shading, the subcourtyard never proved hugely popular in large part due to the powerful wind vortexes produced due to the Architecture tower's placement and aerodynamics.

The basement and elevated first floor plate to the Museum of West Texas sat as an incomplete storehouse for more than a decade before sufficient funding was raised to complete the facility.

upcoming Board Meeting."[9] The Texas Tech Board of Directors—soon to be renamed the Board of Regents—were now siding with the advice of the CPC on a continual basis as the "Indiana Question" became just as much of a heated question into the early 1970s as the controversy had been over Texas Tech's name change from Texas Technological College to Texas Tech University.

FORMER PRESIDENT R. C. Goodwin's planning team had proven amazingly accurate at foretelling enrollment ten years earlier, as 20,008 undergraduate and graduate students now attended Texas Tech, off by only eight students from the 1960 prediction.[10] Enrollment was now more than double its 1960 levels, and more than three times what Watkin had ever envisioned his original master plan

The Museum of West Texas, designed by Lubbock architect O. R. Walker, and completed in 1949 would be vacated in 1970 to make its home in the new Museum of Texas Tech University.

Rendering depicting the proposed renovation and addition design for what would become the Social Sciences Complex; Harper & Kemp, architects, 1972.

could accommodate. To achieve such growth, Tech had to make great compromises with its own aesthetic identity to have a physical plant in 1970 anywhere near the capacity to support enrollment. To have built the same square footage in Plateresque-revival construction would have been an insanely expensive endeavor. Buildings along the Broadway Mall, Memorial Circle, and Engineering Key had largely remained true in plan and motif to the original Spanish-revival Beaux-Arts heritage of the institution, but beyond that, the campus had devolved to a low-density collection of street grids and often spartan-detailed modernist-era buildings. Simple present-day principles in campus planning, such as the half-mile maximum distance a student can comfortably walk in a ten-minute class change cycle, was a practicality lost on university leadership.

It was immediately following Texas Tech's great southwesterly campus expansion that the Art and Architecture Complex was built. It represented one of the last divergent attempts to reconcile modernism with the palette of building materials used at Texas Tech, in this case with little if any reference to Spanish motifs. Known to Tech administrators as Housing and Urban Development Project

Texas Tech opted to rename the repurposed and expanded Social Sciences Complex in honor of the individual vitally responsible for the former Museum's founding—William Curry Holden.

No. 4-7-00079-0, on December 2, 1968, the Tech Board of Directors approved bids and alternates for the grant-funded project with a construction value of $4,968,228.[11] The Art and Architecture Complex was a totally different departure into what could arguably be described as brutalist modernism. Designed by Chris Carson and Andrew Perez of noted San Antonio atelier Ford, Powell & Carson, the design mated the simple forms and modernist lines that were signature to Ford, Powell & Carson's work of the period with the building material palettes—mainly Acme Perla-blend brick, cast-in-place

Nearly fifty years after William Ward Watkin's master plan envisioned as many as ten cloistered courtyards on the Texas Tech campus, Harper & Kemp's design introduced only the first of those courtyards, replete with a fountained pool and public artwork.

Rendering of the two-story Mass Communications Building (now Maddox Engineering Research Building) designed in 1974, reflected a heightened interest by University Regents to at least establish an aesthetic compromise between the latter period of modernist design and Tech's Spanish Renaissance roots; Calhoun, Tungate, & Jackson, architects.

concrete, and red clay pavers commonplace to Tech. Defined greatly by the work of senior designer O'Neil Ford, in the 1960s Ford, Powell & Carson developed a reputation for thoughtful, modernist additions at Texas institutions such as the University of Dallas and Trinity University. Some of that same character can be observed in the design and detailing of the Art and Architecture Complex, though budgetary limitations combined with the resulting mélange of Texas Tech materials and brutalist forms yielded what today remains the butt of jokes among architecture students and alumni alike.

For Nolan Barrick, now serving only as Architecture Department chair, despite being pleased to soon have a new stand-alone facility, he was irked by colleagues at Faculty Senate meetings, where the going joke was, "Faculty are encouraged to apply for the position of campus architect. Once you serve your term, the University extends you their appreciation with a new building!" [12] Site selection for the complex reflected the college's recent unfortunate habit of locating new buildings near street intersections rather than integrated within a homogenous campus plan. With nearly two hundred thousand square feet in overall spatial needs, the Art and Architecture Building was crippled from the outset with design compromises and scope reduction mandates to meet its federally stipulated budget. Barrick had initially lobbied for teak flooring through the building, notably in the studio spaces, but the budget allowed only for vinyl asbestos tile.[13] Carson had selected a custom pebble aggregate–faced glazed concrete flooring in the lobby and basement gallery that too had to be cut from the project due to cost in lieu of glazed brick pavers. Perhaps most novel was a proposal by Perez to address Barrick's concerns that the Architecture

Tower would be one of the first instances at Tech where people in the Architecture Tower could look out onto unsightly flat rooftops below. Perez proposed using different colors of roofing ballast—the pebbled aggregate used to weigh down sheet roofing—on the two-story Art Building below, but installed in unique rectilinear patterns. CPC director of new construction Norman Igo was quick to dash that idea.[14] One feature did remain—the CPC had insisted that the Architecture Tower retain the structural capacity for an additional four floors to be added at a later date, resulting in a telescoping stair and elevator penthouse that prominently sits atop the Architecture Building to this day.

Undated 1970s or early 1980s image of Memorial Circle with Mass Communications in the background. Completion of the transitional modernist building completed the "framing" of buildings surrounding Memorial Circle.

When completed in early 1971—delayed for several months by a trade union strike during construction—the Art and Architecture Complex was like so many buildings of Tech's modernist era both hailed and derided by many. For architecture students in particular, the combination of broad, uninterrupted studio bays and the omnipresence of hard, acoustically reflective surfaces made studio life noisy and lacking in privacy. The landscaped subgrade courtyard that divided the complex never attracted much use, as the subcourtyard was often subject to the brutal aerodynamic wind vortexes generated by the Architecture Tower, particularly in winter and spring months. The cantilevered roof eaves to the Architecture Tower appeared in many ways an afterthought, like a saucer left hanging over a teacup. Igo and CPC representatives instructed Ford, Powell & Carson to carefully match the exterior brick blend to that recently used on the new Law School Building to the west, in large part due to recent difficulty with achieving accurate brick blends from the Acme Brick's Perla Plant.[15] But the brick veneer proved to be a larger problem when in 1985, a massive 500-square-foot swath of face brick fell away from the upper-floor façades of the tower crashing down onto the west entrance to the Architecture Building.[16] Professor John White was sitting at his desk turned away from the window behind him when he suddenly heard a low rumble outside. He turned to witness a wisp of sandy-colored dust blowing in the air outside his window, not realizing that over eight tons of masonry had peeled from the building

Present-day view of the north façade of the University Library. SRMJ executed a seamless expansion in doubling the depth of the stacks tower of the Library to the west.

substrate and had fallen below.[17] Had the failure occurred during a class change, anyone standing in the entry plaza below would have likely been killed. Even today, the steel nosings of many Nelson studs can be seen from below protruding from the brick façade—telltale signs of remediation to the brick veneer of the tower.

THE MASSIVE SURGE of enrollment in the 1960s resulted in the continued use of every remaining old wood-framed X-building left in inventory. Universally despised by everyone, the CPC did their best to hide the old barracks structures from major viewpoints on campus. By 1970, the majority of the old eyesores had been clustered into three separate areas—a group of fifteen sat west of the University Library, another seven were situated farther west between Foreign Languages and Business Administration Buildings, and yet another dozen sat just south of the new Biology Tower and Conservatory. Executive Vice President Glenn Barnett had given express orders that any X-building deficiencies were to be reported to the CPC immediately in hope that the deficiency was sufficient reason to tear it down.[18] In 1969 alone, CPC Planning Coordinator Jerry Kirkwood had reported to CPC Chair and Comptroller Haskell Taylor the recommendation to demolish X-40, X-41 and X-42.[19] Most of the X-buildings were becoming dangerous fire-traps—some in fact more than others. By 1973, another twelve were planned by the University Space Committee—the successor to the CPC—for razing.[20] X-34 was leaking badly due to an old roof that needed replacement, but had to be demolished in 1975 given that its framing was overloaded and buckling.[21] Adding a new roof alone would have likely caused its collapse. Tech leadership was trying as quickly as they could to construct new academic spaces on campus as catalysts to ensure that all of the old wood-framed barracks could be thoroughly removed for good.

One expansion project that leadership hoped would improve the availability of instructional space on campus, was the future of the Old Museum of West Texas Building on Memorial Circle. Tech had moved quickly after the Museum's vacancy in 1970 to relocate offices for both the College of Arts and Sciences and Murray's International Center for Arid and Semiarid Land Studies (ICASALS) into the vacant structure, but that was only a stopgap maneuver. In 1972, Tech commissioned Dallas firm Harper & Kemp—the same firm then working as local architects-of-record with I. M. Pei on the revolutionary new Dallas City Hall—to expand and renovate the Old Museum Building into an academic classroom and office building. The tolerance for the Museum renovation and addition project among Tech leadership modernist architecture was wearing thin, and conversely appreciation of Tech's older Plateresque-revival architecture was back on the rise. For architect Terrell Harper and his team, retaining the O. R. Walker-designed Plateresque-revival entry on the southwest façade of the Old Museum was an easy decision, while the new northeastern addition to the former museum would not be nearly as out of place as Pitts, Phelps, Saxe & White's austere Chemisty Building addition that sat opposite of Memorial Circle. The fact that the Old Museum was even reused is worth noting. Tech leadership contemplated having Harper & Kemp design a new building and raze the Museum, until William Curry Holden reminded them that Peter Hurd's rotunda-set Pioneer Mural was worth $2 million.[22] Harper's 1973 addition was a mirrored L-shape multistory block of classrooms, situated and connected to the wings of the existing former Museum Building so as to form an enclosed courtyard—which despite William Ward Watkin's intentions otherwise was the first of its kind built at Texas Tech in nearly a half-century. The courtyard, surrounded by shade tree terraces, featured a simple circular reflecting pool with the bronze of a child titled *Freedom of Youth,* executed by Texas Tech alumnus Rosie Sandifer. The original Museum rotunda and fresco murals by Peter Hurd were retained, while Harper carefully blended the simple forms and trim of the more modernist classroom addition by replacing the unit windows of the museum wings with more vertically oriented stone-framed ribbon windows. Completed in 1974, the renovated Old Museum Building and Classroom addition was fittingly named in honor of the man who had championed for the Old Museum in the first place—William Curry Holden. Holden Hall remains, even today, a ubiquitous stop for hundreds of thousands of Tech students attending College of Arts and Sciences courses.

It was also during this time in the early 1970s that a host of other projects were completed across the campus, and though enrollment growth was waning, those completed projects reflected a response to the remaining space needs at Tech due to the massive student influx of the 1960s. Sizeable additions to the Civil Engineering Building (1970–71) and an even larger expansion to the University Center would occur. In the case of the UC, Tech already had enlarged the original 1953 UC Building in 1962 from thirty-three thousand to more than fifty-five thousand square feet, but even that expansion—sized to support twelve thousand students—proved obsolete before it even opened.[23] In 1972, work commenced on a $5.2 million, 110,000-square- foot expansion to the UC and Music Building to the south—a project which essentially integrated the two buildings into one.[24] Designed by Atcheson, Atkinson & Cartwright (AA&C), the objective of the expansion was to provide more commons space for students to congregate, as well as a range of new theater-sized, tiered and conference room spaces for the myriad university events. A major component of this expansion included construction of the Allen Theater, designed originally with continental seating for one thousand attendees. At the urging of the Board of Regents to reinstitute neoclassical Spanish-Renaissance detailing in new capital projects, the UC expansion—from an exterior detail standpoint at least—remained relatively uniform in its Spanish-revival styling. Even so, given AA&C's design role, like the original building, several façades to the UC expansion too appeared more Romanesque-revival than Plateresque.

The last of the modernist-era mid-rise/high-rise buildings at Texas Tech—the Food Sciences Tower (today part of the Human Sciences Complex); designed by Tisdel & Adling and completed in 1977.

Along Memorial Circle, one corner of the campus hub had remained bare throughout Texas Tech's history, except for the unsightly time when a group of X-buildings once resided there. The Mass Communications Department of the College of Arts and Sciences had long outgrown Hedrick's diminutive Journalism and Press Building, prompting funding in 1973 for a new 60,480-square-foot, $2.5 million Mass Communications Building,[25] connected by basement and open-air plaza to the 1939 facility. Like Holden Hall and the UC expansion, the Board of Regents gave little modernist slack to architects Calhoun, Tungate & Jackson of Houston in their expectation to make Mass Communications an appropriate addition to the Spanish Renaissance–revival surroundings to Memorial Circle. The Houston firm responded by incorporating a red clay tile mansard roof across the building, while the ground floor façade was inset with a simply detailed, but visually dominant colonnade whose proportions mimicked the araeostyle colonnades of nearby Mathematics and Statistics (the Old Library).

Downtown, another byproduct of the Lubbock tornado had been the city's determination to construct a new Lubbock Memorial Civic Center built atop the former facility flattened by the 1970 twister. Once again, Bob Messersmith, himself a member of the Mayor's Disaster Recovery Commission,[26] was prudently concerned that a larger out-of-town firm would win the commission for the massive new facility, prompting him to turn to Lubbock colleagues once again to form a new joint venture—this time named Architects III. Messersmith and his SRMJ colleagues partnered with AA&C, as well as longtime collaborator Howard Schmidt, whose firm recently grew to include architect C. Berwyn Tisdel as a partner. Architects III formed in late 1971, and shortly thereafter won the Civic Center commission—an expansive project that would not be complete until 1977.[27] In the meantime, the three collaborating firms continued the awkward process of completing individual projects for Texas Tech while concurrently securing further Texas Tech work combined as Architects III. Walt Calvert was underway designing an SRMJ-commissioned $4.2 million expansion to the University Library scheduled for completion in 1975 that essentially doubled its massive stacks bay to the west, while the AA&C-designed expansion to the University Center across the street was underway. While all of this was happening, separate Architects III–designed expansions to the Psychology Building and Home Economics Complex were being designed. In time, Berwyn Tisdel and Howard Schmidt's partnership transitioned to a new firm Tisdel & Adling, with the addition of architect and former Tech assistant to Norman Igo, Bill Adling. Tisdel & Adling, on the heels of the Home Economics addition, issued drawings in November 1975 for a Food Sciences classroom, laboratory, and office tower located as an addition southeast of Home Economics.[28] The Food Sciences Tower paralleled SRMJ's and Calhoun, Tungate & Jackson's strategy of incorporating less experimental, but still simplified modernist iterations of Tech's Spanish-revival aesthetic grammars, such as clay tile roofed mansards and flattened arches, as compared to the total departures of previous Tech high-rise buildings. The Food Sciences Building was completed in 1977, only two years following the marking of the university's fiftieth anniversary when Texas Tech both celebrated and reflected upon many insane, frenetic decades of recent growth. But the completion of Food Sciences marked the beginning of a malaise period for construction at Texas Tech, as stagnant enrollment, an energy crisis, and other factors ended thirty years of unrelenting, breakneck growth.

16

PLENTY OF COTTON BALE STORAGE

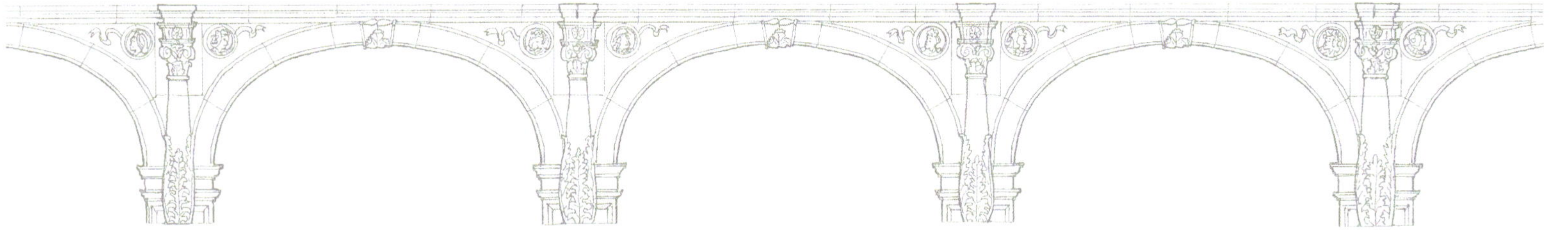

On January 21, 1969, Preston E. Smith was inaugurated as the fortieth governor of Texas. Born a central Texan into a very large family of twelve brothers and sisters, Smith's parents opted to follow Horace Greeley's advice, only to stop short while heading west and stake their claim in Lamesa, Texas. Preston Smith personally experienced both the Great Depression and Dust Bowl when he attended Tech, and though the 1960s had brought his alma mater the blessings of over three million square feet of college expansion, there was hope from Tech administrators that Smith's clout might spur further appropriations Lubbock's way. Smith's intervention as lieutenant governor had prevented Governor John Connally's horrific 1965 plan to roll Texas Tech into the Texas A&M University System from seeing the light of day. But one other controversy—a decade-long heated debate that pitted the Board of Directors, students, the public, and a fanatical hoard of English professors who distributed bumper stickers reading "TECH IS NOT A WORD" over the future institutional name of Texas Tech also crossed Smith's desk. In the end, it was Tech's beloved logo—the Double T—that likely was the last vestige that prevented a drastic name change to the institution. Exasperated in determining what proper name change bill to file, state representative Delwin Jones filed no less than six bills in the House in March 1969, each with different proposed names for the college.[1] As "Texas Tech University" finally emerged as a last-minute leading candidate, Preston Smith signed House Bill 923 into law with great satisfaction, placing Tech's name change into effect on September 1, 1969. The college had finally become a university.

Aside from the practicalities of having to rename College Avenue to properly reflect Texas Tech's new status, the new university charged ahead with myriad endeavors as if the contentious name change ordeal were an imperceptible speed bump. The name change did afford Tech an excuse to proceed with an albeit scaled-down version of a 1966 plan to replace a diminutive art deco-stylized Texas Technological College Broadway entry sign with a new entry feature commensurate of the renamed and rapidly growing institution. Completed in spring 1972, the Amon G. Carter Memorial Fountain and Plaza would be the only vestige of the Tech campus dedicated to the late publisher whose impact upon Texas Tech was supreme, while ahead of the plaza, a near-nineteen-ton red granite disc bearing William Ward Watkin's seal design and the new institutional name was installed.[2]

Renaming his alma mater was not the only effort Preston Smith was engaged in at Texas Tech. Smith spearheaded legislative action to reorganize Tech's governance body—the Board of Directors—into the Board of Regents recognized today. But most memorable during his tenure would be the establishment of a medical school for the new university. By the end of the 1960s, West Texas suffered from a severe lack of trained medical professionals, and though the concept of equipping Texas Tech with a medical school had been bandied about for nearly two decades, all prior attempts had failed to see fruition. With continued help from Delwin Jones, Smith also enlisted another Tech ally from within the House Appropriations Committee. As a former Red Raider running back, Elmer Tarbox had nearly won Tech the 1939 Cotton Bowl, later served as a *Flying Tigers* pilot in the China-Burma-India Theater during World War II, and so fighting off political opposition to secure legislation for a new Tech Medical School was a comparably easy proposition for the Lubbock representative. The medical school bill in fact beat House Bill 923 to the governor's desk, though it lacked any facility funding to support the new school. To mark the occasion, Smith ordered Pat Neff's old Spanish-styled desk out of storage to sign the Texas Tech Medical School bill into law.[3]

The operational structure to what would one day become the Texas Tech University Health Sciences Center involved combining health sciences academic and support space with the resources of a separate-but-adjacent teaching hospital operated by the local government. Lubbock County had already mobilized support for the teaching hospital by passing a bond referendum in 1971 establishing the Lubbock County Hospital District,[4] the forerunner to today's University Medical Center. President Murray selected John A. Buesseler—a doctor, administrator, and former US Army Medical Corps officer as Tech's first Vice President for Medical Affairs. Buesseler moved immediately

Preston Smith—first Texas Tech alumnus governor, signs legislation into law on May 27, 1969, establishing the Texas Tech School of Medicine.

Following passage of the Medical School legislation, Tech's initial space solution was to decommission and repurpose one Hedrick-era dormitory—the former Drane Hall Women's Dormitory—into health sciences office and classroom space.

In an effort to immerse himself with the TTU Medical School project, CRS architect Jack DeBartolo went so far as to sketch the campus and site environment as he flew over Lubbock in 1972, providing a unique, if abstract glimpse of Tech at that time.

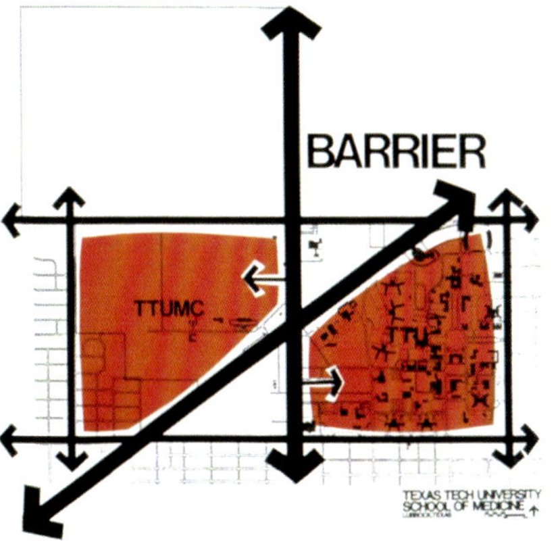

BUILDING COMPONENTS

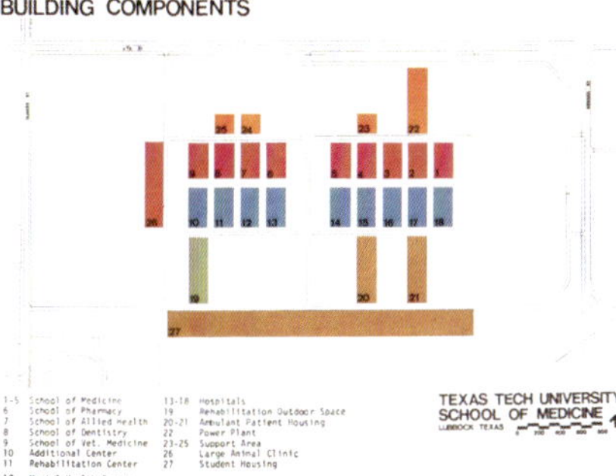

TYPICAL CLINIC FLOOR

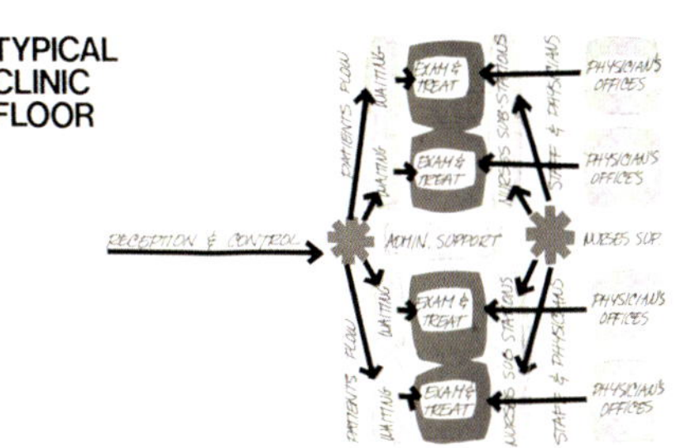

Facility programming was still a new and emerging architectural science when CRS was hired by Tech in 1972 to plan and program the new school. The insistence to thoroughly diagram site, space, and function factors was a new and novel concept to Tech leadership.

to form a faculty and administrative body for the new School of Medicine, as the university scratched its collective head figuring out how and where their medical school would be housed. With enrollment growth beginning to stagnate after 1970, and with decreasing on-campus housing demand, Haskell Taylor's immediate solution was to decommission one of Tech's older New Deal-era dormitories, Drane Hall, and reconfigure it for office and classroom space for the new school. But Drane Hall proved to be only a temporary solution, as SRMJ was hired in 1971 to convert yet another dormitory—the fifteen-year-old Thompson-Gaston Hall Complex—into further office, classroom, and clinical space for the medical school. All the while, Murray and Buesseler searched for funding and siting solutions for a permanent complex that could grow the program for decades beyond.

Initial concepts for a permanent home for the School of Medicine were included in Howard Schmidt's long-range development plan, where he envisioned the large triangular tract of land remaining south of Brownfield Highway and west of Indiana Avenue would be ideal for the new medical campus. That scheme assumed that nearby Methodist Hospital would serve as the teaching hospital in lieu of a county hospital that did not yet exist. Schmidt incorporated updated land use recommendations for the new medical school within the western

Dr. John Buesseler (left) and Jack DeBartolo (center) during a planning charrette for the new Medical School, 1973.

triangle of the campus just as his plan and the LRDP were issued to Grover Murray and the Tech Board for approval in late 1971.

But no one at Tech, even healthcare management experts like Buesseler, yet had an accurate impression of the magnitude of facilities required to operate a medical school. Even more spatially conservative peer institutions of the day maintained physical plants of a half-million square feet or more, in addition to copious amounts of laboratory spaces and support facilities like vivaria and biomedical storage. Texas Tech's programmatic challenge for a new medical school was manifold—establish a modern, accredited medical school with research and clinical capabilities while remaining tailored to their primary and legislatively mandated directive to meet the rural healthcare needs of West Texas. For so many previous Texas Tech projects of any scale, administrators would simply seek out case studies elsewhere, visit them, and emulate them. This problem was different, and Texas Tech needed a customized space program to fully understand their needs.

By 1970, the Houston-based firm Caudill, Rowlett & Scott—CRS—had become a global leader with 1,200 employees specializing in many markets, particularly healthcare. Much of their success came from the emerging predesign science of architectural programming, which under the guidance of CRS programming guru William Peña, had become a proven methodology to determining what spaces and functions were needed in a facility before any plan was produced—

Photograph of the progress design model developed by CRS for Phase I Medical School facility. While the final design would adopt DeBartolo's proposed piano nobile concept, other features such as sun-shaded terraces and a skybridge walkway between the complex and parking lots would be eventually discarded.

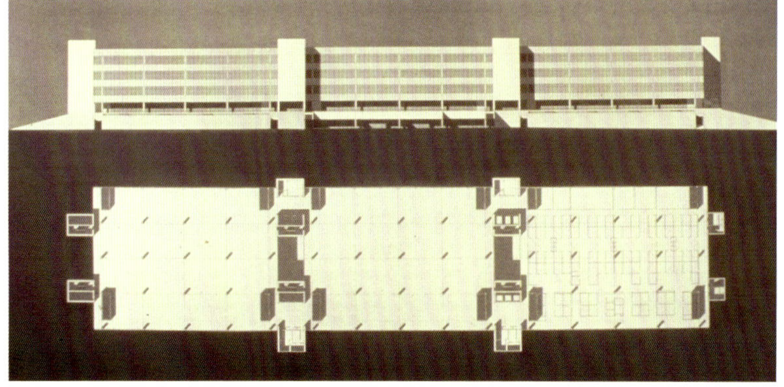

Upon transfer of design roles from CRS to HKS, the simple building mass and materiality of the three Phase I Pods began to take shape. No one in administration or Board of Regents expected a Spanish Renaissance–revival facility design.

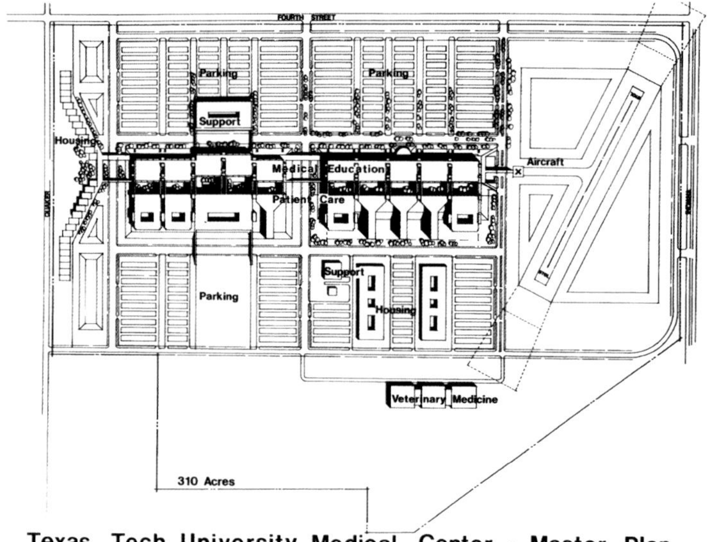

CRS's and HKS's final master plan for the TTU Medical Center—a modular westward expanding plan with linkages to a future County Teaching Hospital to the south. Few people realize today that the reason for the setback distance between the Medical School and Indiana Avenue was for an elevated STOL runway that would never be realized.

a process later codified by Peña in his much-lauded programming treatise *Problem Seeking*. In early 1970, Texas Tech selected CRS, teamed along with growing Dallas-based firm Harwood K. Smith, Inc.—HKS, mechanical and electrical engineers Zumwalt & Vintner, and Carter Burgess as civil engineers to program and design the new medical school. The project team featured a constellation of emerging stars in architecture, including six future AIA Fellows, two future chancellors of the AIA College of Fellows, and a future AIA national president.

Jack DeBartolo was one of the those young lions tapped by CRS principal Wallie Scott to travel to Lubbock that summer to launch into a Schematic Design Program for the new School of Medicine. DeBartolo immersed himself in the project from the outset, sketching montages of the Tech campus from the air when he first arrived in Lubbock to best associate himself with this flat, dry place so foreign from his office in Houston.[5] The programming team quickly ruled out the western triangle site proposed by Howard Schmidt in the LRDP as too small, while they began to focus on the farm and range land north of Brownfield Highway and south of 4th Street as a leading site candidate suitable enough to handle both academic buildings, the teaching hospital, and support facilities. But, selecting that site effectively ensured that the city of Lubbock would get their way with Indiana Avenue, as hospital ambulatory access demanded a direct north-south arterial road, with Indiana Avenue as the only appreciable option available. Even as the programming team began to gravitate toward this vehicular access approach, President Murray, Haskell Taylor, and forces within the Board of Regents remained dead set against the Indiana Avenue corridor.

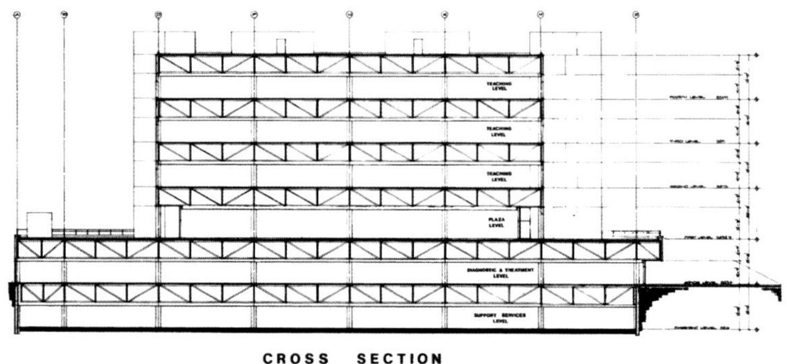

Typical cross-section through one of the Phase I Pods, illustrating the near full-floor-height interstitial spaces between floors—a design feature met with editorial ridicule in Lubbock at the time. Today, practically all of those Warren truss interstitial spaces are packed to the gills with medical and research-support systems.

At the same time—CRS coordinated their programming efforts with Lubbock architectural firm Brasher, Goyette & Rapier—BGR—selected by the Lubbock County Hospital District to design the Teaching Hospital that would connect with the CRS/HKS-designed medical school. A modular organization scheme began to emerge from CRS, where multistory modules to the medical school would over time be constructed, and then connected to corresponding patient care bays of the Teaching Hospital built south of the medical school. In time, these modules would become known as "pods." While the Teaching Hospital would house some three hundred inpatient beds, surgical suites, a birthing center, and support spaces, much of the specialized spaces—laboratories, radiology services, inhalation therapy, and a triage bay would all be housed in the School of Medicine's Ambulatory Care Unit, in addition to academic, research, and office spaces of the medical school.[6] By March 1971, DeBartolo and his team completed their program, reporting to Buesseler that the Phase I medical school module alone—a minimum module that could function self-sufficiently as a medical school—would cost Texas Tech $35 million in 1971 dollars,[7] or $217 million in present-day dollars. Adjusted for inflation, construction of a new medical school would cost over $325 million, making it still today the largest single project in Tech history.

It would require the considerable political resources of Smith, Tarbox, Jones, and even powerful US House Appropriations Committee Chair George H. Mahon to assemble a such a mammoth source of funding as required for the medical school. When a funding plan was finally established by spring 1973, Tech's $35 million pot of gold was more akin to a patchwork quilt of funding measures, as Tech was able to secure additional state appropriations, buttressed by yet another sizeable Mahon-endorsed federal DHEW grant. $16.1 million of that funding came from a novel form of financing known as a Tuition Revenue Bonds (TRBs)—financing in which bonds were issued and pledged from a revenue stream provided by income from tuition charges levied against students or the institutions itself.[8] One anonymous Texas university president later described TRBs, which have since become a commonplace staple to capital project funding in Texas public higher education as "the State of Texas writing itself an IOU."

Jack DeBartolo and the CRS team—now supported by Jack Nottingham's HKS design team who now included Ron Skaggs—a former CRS architect who had jumped over to HKS to focus on healthcare design[9]—were underway developing the master plan for what now would be a massive medical school complex. Given it was a new state-of-the-art campus with an academic charge separate from the university, no one expected to implement Spanish Renaissance motifs at the new campus. The new complex would be a totally modernist iteration—clean, sleek, and a symbol of modern medicine. DeBartolo proposed key functions for the school be situated on a sprawling *piano nobile*—a European concept for a public second story—equipped with a medical library, cafeteria, and administration offices.[10] CRS's initial concepts for parking access involved sky bridges that connected the piano nobile to public parking lots arrayed north of the new school. Ground floor functions included heavily used activities like diagnostic and outpatient treatment spaces, while floors above the piano nobile were intended for specialty clinics and research spaces with more limited public access. The CRS/HKS Master Plan evoked a Louis Kahn–like nature in its elemental simplicity and repetitive nature that was over time, intended to expand from east to west to well over a million gross square feet of space—far more building than the initial $35 million funding package could pay for. Included in the Master Plan was land for medical student housing, and even a site for a future Veterinary School—a provision that was state-approved over four decades before nose-bent Aggies would grouse over encroachment into their rarified academic domain.

It was during this time that the controversy over Indiana Avenue boiled over, as the location of a new medical school added ammunition in favor of the city's argument for the Indiana Avenue corridor. Beginning in mid-1972, the Tech Board of Regents had promised a thorough review of the "Indiana Question," so that a compromise would result that was palatable to Tech; but for a year, no action had been taken prior to the August 17, 1973, board meeting. Instead, at that meeting, Tech commissioned a civil engineering professor—Dr. Ernest Kiesling—to analyze potential vehicular options in lieu of Indiana Avenue. Kiesling presented an elegant, but fiscally impossible

Circa-1974 rendering of the Phase I construction scope to the Medical School.

plan of removing Brownfield Highway in lieu of a continuous roadway loop around the Texas Tech campus and the future Health Sciences Center. Mayor Morris Turner remarked to reporters after the meeting that Kiesling's idea was a "Pipe dream," and leveled an ultimatum at the university.[11] If Tech was going to have a School of Medicine, then the city of Lubbock was going to have an Indiana Avenue thoroughfare transiting the Tech campus. Murray and Taylor could no longer resist an Indiana Avenue corridor through campus, and the Board of Regents was forced to accept that reality. Howard Schmidt proceeded with updating the LRDP to incorporate an uninterrupted Indiana Avenue through campus.

PLANNING AND DESIGN to the Texas Tech School of Medicine involved a multitude of cutting-edge technologies for their day—methods and systems that had never been seen in a West Texas building project before. Automated conveyor systems fabricated by TRW—the same corporation that helped design the Atlas rocket and practically invented digital signal processing—would carry sterile medical supplies from basement receiving up to each building floor in the new complex. HKS was a pioneer in the design of interstitial support spaces in healthcare—the concept of "floors between floors"—following having first implemented that strategy for mechanical space in the design of a Texas Instruments semiconductor plant in Dallas during the 1960s. Though a commonplace design strategy today,

Rendering of the Central Heating and Cooling Plant II (or CHACP II). HKS architect Jack Nottingham would propose the novel idea of "greenhousing" the Medical School's central plant, and highlighting piping and machinery inside with bright colors to appear analogous to a human circulatory system.

the concept of doubling the number of floors to the medical school flabbergasted many. Between each occupied floor at the new Tech Medical School was a duplicated volume hiding the webs of the massive floor framing Warren trusses spanning across each pod of the building, and interspersed with catwalks providing access to pumps, medical gas supply, filtration systems, and a bevy of other equipment situated to serve the spaces above or below. Though critics would not have believed it at the time, those interstitial spaces today are packed full of equipment with little or no space to spare.

Few realize today that the broad distance between the Health Sciences Center Complex and Indiana Avenue was borne out of an attempt to incorporate an advent in modern military medical technology in Lubbock. John Buesseler's experience in the Army Medical Corps exposed him to revolutionary changes in ambulatory transport of wounded patients that emerged following the Second World War. Single-engine liaison aircraft, followed shortly thereafter with the advent of more reliable helicopters, could ferry wounded personnel to field hospitals much like popular media depictions in the movie and subsequent television show *M*A*S*H*. The air ambulance concept was finally introduced into civilian circles in the late 1960s as medical evacuation, or medevac. Buesseler had convinced Grover Murray of the importance of both fixed-wing and helicopter air ambulances, though Buesseler at the time believed that light aircraft were a more practical answer to connect to the dozens of small county and city airports of West Texas. DeBartolo's early concepts already included a piano nobile–elevation helipad situated near the proposed Emergency Triage Bay. In their site planning, Nottingham and Skaggs simply extended a taxiway from that helipad east to a diagonal thousand-foot runway oriented northeast toward the intersection of 4th Street and Indiana Avenue. The runway and taxiway—essentially a STOLPort, or short takeoff-and-landing airport—was also elevated at piano nobile elevation, lest the landing gear of approaching aircraft strike traffic lights and vehicles of the nearby 4th Street/Indiana Avenue intersection on takeoff or approach.

Buesseler's STOLPort vision never saw reality, as the Phase I budget was going to be difficult to meet, even with over $35 million in funding at play. Already, two full pods of the Medical School Complex were only to be built as shell spaces for later finish-out and occupancy. Buesseler himself would leave in late 1973, replaced by Richard Lockwood as a new vice president, leaving the STOLPort concept without a champion for it. In addition, DeBartolo's initially proposed scheme of terraces and skylighted lobbies, as well as the parking skywalks were all gone, and while HKS's combination of precast concrete paneling, glass, and anodized bronze panels evoked a truly modern facility, budgetary limitations nonetheless left the new complex with a note of austerity from the outset. But as steel and concrete began emerging from the site of the former college farm, the public realized the awesome scale of the 13.6 million cubic foot complex. The *Avalanche-Journal* only fueled public furor, running front-page diagrams demonstrating how six of downtown Lubbock's largest buildings would fit within the new medical school volume with room to spare.[12] One letter to the editor posted by the *Avalanche-Journal* lamented that the new medical school was nothing more than the "world's largest cotton bale storage building." [13] Even if only 380,000 square feet were to be finished out in Phase 1A, a central plant building was needed that could support the eventual full 810,000-square-foot complex, and the HKS team had some innovative ideas of how to accomplish that.

The sheer scale of the Texas Tech Medical School construction project warranted a dedicated project manager, so the university opted to hire local contractor Hap Padgett for that role. Padgett was experienced and capable, but was also a jokester who loved a good laugh at the expense of architects and engineers. Some local architects used Padgett's expertise in specification writing experience for projects—a dangerous proposition if the architect failed to thoroughly review Padgett's specification drafts before they issued for bid. In one finish-out project at TTUHSC in the 1980s, Padgett telephoned the architect, inquiring where his case of bourbon was. The architect was confused, prompting Padgett to remind him that per specifications, one hundred days into construction, the architect was required to submit to the construction manager a case of bourbon. The architect quietly complied, not knowing what was worse—if Tech found out about the transaction or what they would think if they knew the architect had missed the "whiskey clause" in the specifications.[14] Humor aside, Padgett had his hands full managing the 1970s-era version of a "fast-track" project, and as he supervised trades constructing the steel and concrete that were rising out of the ground for Phase 1A, several other HKS-produced bid packages remained in design.

With a plant demand of over six thousand tons of refrigerated air, the medical school required its own Central Heating and Cooling Plant (CHACP) separate from the university's plant situated across Brownfield Highway. Jack Nottingham had a fascinating idea analogous to human anatomy and physiology diagrams he had seen and consulted engineers at Zumwalt & Vintner in developing a greenhouse-style central plant surrounded with curtain wall glazing and capped in the same anodized bronze paneling used on the new campus. Piping and ductwork would be color-coded by the Zumwalt & Vintner engineers in bold colors of red, white, blue, and yellow to mimic the arteries, veins, and capillaries found in the human vascular system.[15] The concept was an immediate hit with Lockwood and the medical school leadership.

With Phase 1A ready for operation in the fall of 1975, Texas Tech University, now entering its fiftieth anniversary of operation, was the only public university in the state of Texas that could boast a law school and medical school, and all on the same campus. Though the new medical school had no more in common with the rest of the Texas Tech campus than Boston's sleek glass John Hancock Tower with the nearby Romanesque-revival Trinity Church, the new complex would have a profound impact upon the Tech Campus plan, while penultimately marking the swan song to modernism at Texas Tech. To the south, BGR was at work designing the other crucial clinical component to the new medical school—the Lubbock County Hospital District Teaching Hospital. HKS would remain at work on the new campus for the next four years as the remaining Pods B and C would be systematically finished out floor by floor. Based upon plans developed by Ron Skaggs and his HKS team, myriad functions ranging from laboratories, teaching classrooms, and a vivarium would soon be finished out within the sizeable, but well-programmed shell spaces of Pods B and C. By the time HKS was complete with their work in 1979, Governor Bill Clements signed Senate Bill 371 into law on June 6—affecting a name change that was warranted as the School was expanding to respond to the growing range of healthcare needs across West Texas.[16] The Texas Tech University School of Medicine was now the *Texas Tech University Health Sciences Center.*

17

MALAISE

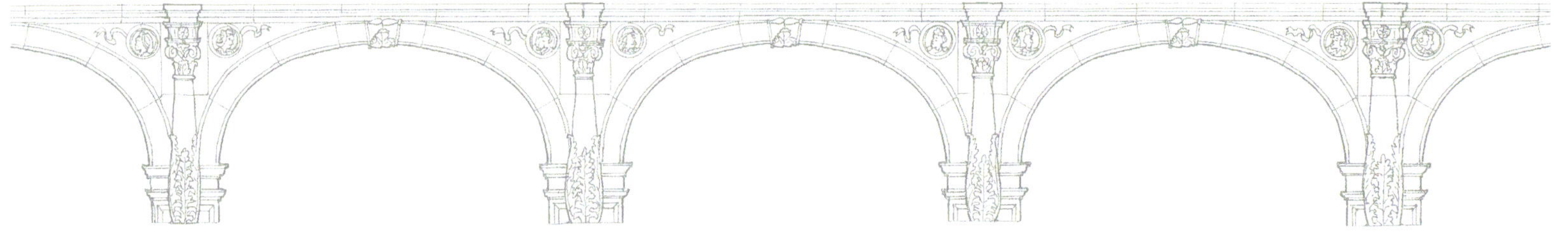

ALTHOUGH TENS OF THOUSANDS of students called Texas Tech home during the 1970s through 1980s and beyond, it could be best described as a sleepy period for enrollment, campus growth, and even arguably for Red Raider athletics. Between 1976 and 1995, Texas Tech University had conferred some 82,567 degrees of all types, but only marking about a 5 percent annual increase in the number conferred in 1975 as compared to 1995.[1] General enrollment had increased by a paltry 9 percent in two decades—a far cry from the frightening 146 percent increase that the student body absorbed between 1960 and the university's silver anniversary in 1975.[2] Following completion of certain key projects in the late 1970s and early 1980s—most notably the expansion to Holden Hall and the Ewalt Recreation Center—little would change at Tech for well over a decade.

What had happened? While Tech now boasted millions of square feet in modern, recently built facilities, that volume of space had been built for twenty thousand or more students—the "more" simply never arrived. By 1960, the American birth rate had begun to fall off from an annual rate of twenty-four births per thousand to only eighteen a decade later.[3] The baby boomer era had run its course. While this rate shift would not have explained everything, the demographic was that much more important given that the growth rate to the percentage of the population participating in college was slowing between 1969 and 1979, and even more so in the 1980s as students opted for more part-time education opportunities.[4] College tuition was still relatively cheap, but in an era before the abundance of financial aid resources, the economic climate of the nation during the Carter administration into the first term of the Reagan presidency coupled with a smaller demographic pool were not going to aid growing enrollment at Texas Tech, let alone practically any public US university. Furthermore, student options in higher education across Texas were, in the 1970s and 1980s, becoming more plentiful, and Texas Tech was no longer the state's second-largest public university. Texas A&M had instituted a policy shift of becoming coeducational beginning in the early 1960s, and as a result would triple in size over the next three decades. Both College Station and the University of Texas System had begun to expand their academic reach even further through the establishment of satellite institutions across the state. North Texas semiconductor magnate Texas Instruments (TI) had in 1961 created a research and training institute—the Southwest Center for Advanced Studies (SCAS). Growing tired of running their own college, TI opted in 1969 to bequeath SCAS to the University of Texas System, thus creating what we now know as the University of Texas at Dallas. The UT System even opted to place a satellite campus in Odessa in 1973—the University of Texas of the Permian Basin. The effect was obvious. Beginning in 1979, Texas Tech enrollment declined for a four-year period and remained relatively stagnant to within a 1 percent delta until 1988.[5]

Demand for on-campus housing fell notably, and even if several academic departments still had worthwhile facility needs, the Texas Higher Education Coordinating Board (THECB) would not readily recommend to the state legislature to fund projects that expanded square footage at an institution whose enrollment was not likewise expanding. It was a malaise of numbers as much as anything else. Not being a land-grant institution, Tech still relied upon a blend of funding sources—ad valorem tax revenue, which was now disappearing for good, state appropriations, and what little in maintenance funds that could be carved away from tuition and fee revenue. Federal funding sources were unlikely, and even George Mahon was gone, as the hugely influential congressman retired in 1979 as outgoing dean of the US House of Representatives.

Interestingly enough, the School of Medicine itself was a cloud that cast a huge shadow over Tech's ability to secure further funding from the state from the late 1970s on. It proved exceedingly difficult to convince state legislators who had only five years earlier approved $35 million dollars in funding (plus over $16 million through 1979 for the finish-out of shell space) for a medical school at Tech to appropriate additional funding for other university needs. Construction work on the massive new medical complex was nearing completion in late 1975 when Glenn Barnett received a memo and report from TTU vice president for Research and Graduate Studies J. Knox Jones outlining the facility needs, priorities, and funds available to the university. Tech had at the close of 1975 only $3.7 million available for use across the entire main campus,[6] and nearly a million of that had already been earmarked to equip the new Mass Communications Building with fixtures, furnishings, and equipment that Austin had failed to properly fund in the first place. The university was now overdue in renovating a number of older historic buildings, such as the former Library and Journalism and Press Buildings—each of which had new roles as original occupants had since relocated to newer buildings constructed in the building maelstrom a decade earlier. The available funds could barely perform that job. Later when President Lauro Cavazos had approved the Texas Tech University Five-Year Campus Development Plan for action in 1985, Objective Four in the plan sent a clear message as to the continued problem: "Continued efforts should be made by administration and faculty to secure additional funding for building facilities, and especially for repair and renovation of those facilities."[7]

NEEDS FROM NON–LANDGRANT-FUNDED institutions like Tech had prompted action in the form of an amendment to the state constitution in 1984 to create a funding source for nonland-grant institutions in the state to draw upon for needs such as these. The Higher Education Fund (HEF),[8] which became operational and began disbursing Higher Education Assistance Funding (or HEAF) to institutions such as Texas Tech beginning in 1986, was a welcome but limited resource. Legislators had initially set aside $100 million per year to disburse, but with nearly twenty eligible colleges and universities requesting funding from this pool, the effects did not immediately satisfy statewide demands. As for Tech, funding was needed just to keep its now massive physical plant in a state of status quo, but even that would be difficult.

The Speech Building (originally Agriculture) would become the first historic building at Tech to face demolition in the 1980s.

DURING THIS MALAISE, Texas Tech administrators were forced to work amid challenges of organizational confusion and lack of a clear leadership. Though the Campus Planning Committee had been dissolved for nearly a decade, its successor, the Space Committee, still faced the same fundamental problems as its predecessor. Space Committee members—administrators such as Glenn Barnett and Vice President for Student Affairs Robert Ewalt, plus a rotating pool of faculty members—found themselves spending more time on managing minor renovation projects rather than establishing strategic planning and design priorities for the university. University politics and turf battles remained an issue. Officially, planning matters into the 1980s were not within the purview of the Space Committee, but rather fell to the responsibility of Robert L. Bray and the university's Planning Office, who did not always appreciate the Space Committee's intrusions into their business. Space Committee members did not want to deal with the minutiae of contractor's pay applications or deal with the hated task of determining which unlucky department would have to relocate to one of the last godforsaken X-buildings. But at least if there was one thing everyone could agree on, it was the hated X-buildings had to go.

Even the X-buildings themselves were proving to be a drain on precious facilities funding, as the Space Committee was forced to allocate precious funds to repair those few left on campus. Despite their loathed status, oddly enough, any time a department was ordered to vacate one, occupants would throw a fit and demand to stay. The Tech ROTC detachment had built a prone rifle range under one of them.[9] Petroleum Engineering faculty infuriated Glenn Barnett by repeatedly conducting experiments in one X-building—X-30—that resulted in the building's interior framing becoming soaked in linseed oil.[10] Not surprisingly, the fire marshal ordered X-30 vacated and razed, lest fifty college students get killed should a flash fire ensue. In April 1977, Barnett ordered the Space Committee to initiate a plan for the final retirement of the last of the old wooden hulks.[11] By September of that year, four buildings—X-45, X-77, X-78, and X-79—were demolished.[12] By March 1978, the ROTC detachment was relocated to the Business Administration Building and their three old former barracks huts—X-31, X-32, and X-33—met the bulldozer.[13] Eight more would be dismantled by late 1978, and after over thirty years, students realized that whitewashed wood siding was not in fact part of the intended architectural vernacular at Texas Tech. In the spring of 1987, X-17, the last of the X-buildings, would be razed—ending Tech's forty-year relationship with a bevy of wood-framed army surplus buildings.[14]

The Space Committee wanted a permanent office to take on the more tactical role of campus planning and architectural and engineering coordination, and a new office had begun to emerge in the summer of 1983 to address that role. Known as Facilities Planning and Construction (FP&C)—the new office would at least allow the Space Committee to focus on more strategic matters, rather than day-to-day meetings and construction coordination. Tech had in August of 1984 selected Jack Fenwick—an architect formerly with the University of

The Pontiac Silverdome, built in 1975, became the novel inspiration for a low-cost, low-height roofing solution for Tech's Athletics Training Center. It likewise nearly spelled doom for the project design when its own roof collapsed on March 4, 1985—days before Tech Regents were to approve on the ATC's design.

Florida's Division of Planning—to helm FP&C[15] and forge a liaison role with the university's Planning Office and the Space Committee. Even with FP&C, the division of responsibility at the university in the 1980s was a mess. Beyond offices such as the Office of Planning, the Space Committee, and FP&C, there were other key personnel who did not clearly fall under any of these organizational chains. Campus landscape architect Art Glick reported to both President Cavazos and to the Office of Grounds Maintenance. No clear line existed between projects led by the new FP&C Office, or lesser renovation projects undertaken by the Physical Plant Office. Even while FP&C was in its organizational infancy, Tech's first major master planning exercise since the Long Range Development Plan of twelve years' prior was underway under the dual direction of Glick and the Space Committee.

3D/International of Houston (today a part of Parsons Corporation) had been selected by Texas Tech to complete a Central Campus Preliminary Master Landscape Plan for the university. Completed in February 1984, the plan was a noble first step in identifying many of the strategic campus planning issues that Tech now faced in the 1980s, and even forecasted many of the sweeping campus plan changes at Tech proposed in the 1990s and 2000s.[16] Two decades of frenetic campus growth to the west and southwest had generated just as much vehicular and pedestrian traffic in the western periphery of the campus as in the historic core. But it was the zone in between the historic core and that more recent western campus growth that 3DI asserted in their plan was underdeveloped, disorganized, and often unsightly. Institutional growth in the 1960s had left much of the campus west of the Library to Flint Avenue a dirt-ridden area dotted by an uncoordinated mélange of modernist buildings and those handful of X-buildings still remaining.

In truth, Texas Tech still faced many of the same basic planning problems Nolan Barrick had encountered when arriving in Lubbock for the first time three decades earlier. In 1983, the campus was still very much a checkerboard plan—an irregular interplay of grid-form city streets forcibly laid over a classical Beaux-Arts core plan of malls and vistas, while interspersed with parking lots. Barrick's quiet twelve-year war against the city of Lubbock had yielded marked improvements, but since the university lost the battle over expanding Indiana Avenue, nothing else in terms of curbing vehicular traffic on campus had changed. One example—Boston Avenue—was an asphalt scythe that cut the southeastern quadrant of the university beginning at Memorial Circle, dividing key academic, student life, and residential nodes from one another. 3DI's planning team took particular note of the unsightly large parking lot south of the Administration Building. The Central Campus Preliminary Master Landscape Plan proposed solutions drawing upon Watkin's original plan through the introduction of new and existing axial malls through the successive interconnection of more organic collection of plazas between Memorial Circle west to Flint Avenue.

The 1984 Master Landscape Plan was an important first step in documenting fundamental campus planning problems that had been building for three decades at Texas Tech. With President Cavazos's and the Board of Regents' approval of the plan, Texas Tech had officially declared that the condition of the campus must change. Sadly, it was a master plan with no teeth. 3DI's plan did not even include a cost estimate[17]—signaling the likelihood that the plan would not likely see implementation anytime soon in the midst of Tech's funding limitations. Additional planting beds and brick-paver walkways commensurate with more of the tactical recommendations of the plan would continue to be implemented piecemeal in decades to come by TTU Grounds Maintenance, but nearly two decades would pass before sweeping changes would appear.

Within the Master Landscape Plan, 3DI proposed the development of a new landscaped pedestrian mall west from the Library toward Flint Avenue, but only one building stood in the way of that realization that 3DI had indelicately proposed to remove—the Dairy Barn. Though the Dairy Barn was never officially part of William Ward Watkin's master plan, its quaint appearance and unique history ensured a special place in the heart of Red Raiders. Watkin in fact had no hand in the design of the Dairy Barn, as correspondence indicates that Tech Agriculture chair A. H. Leidigh ordered Professor W. L. Stangel to coordinate with Wyatt Hedrick on the design of a straightforward Practice Barn for dairy instruction, and Stangel produced a brochure from the Portland Cement Company that included a plan for a prototype cast-in-place concrete barn that Herman Koeppe adapted with a wood-framed structure and stucco cladding.[18]

In the nearly six decades since its construction, Tech had done little more than repaint the old Portland Cement Company prototype barn and silo, but with students no longer bartering livestock for tuition, the building had long since stood neglected and vacant. Despite growing awareness of the Dairy Barn's unique history, regional historic preservation efforts were limited. The Dairy Barn was not the only potential casualty to the 3DI plan, as to the northeast the demolition of the one-story stucco-clad Speech Building had been proposed as well. Originally built as the Agriculture Building in 1925, the old Watkin and Hedrick–designed building had been little more than a stucco version of an X-building—home to at least three different departments since Agriculture had left it for their permanent home in 1945. Although it had been designed with simple Spanish features on its north entry façade, it was wood-framed and simply not the equal of more permanent university buildings, and so it was not surprising when the Space Committee considered razing it starting in the late 1970s.[19] A last-minute effort by Tech architecture professor Glenn Hill in April 1983 to save the building, or at the least the north façade, in a letter directly to President Cavazos, was not heeded.[20] The Speech Building was demolished later that year. Demise of the Speech Building may have very well been the clarion call among local preservation interests, as subsequent public outcry to preserve the Dairy Barn was enough to persuade the university to set aside funds to stabilize the barn and silo's building envelope from the elements. In 1990, the university hired AC Associates to design the renovation work, which was completed in 1992.

Yet, amid the malaise, there were a few bright spots. The Robert H. Ewalt Recreation Center—named for the former vice president for Student Affairs and Space Committee chairman —opened its doors in the spring of 1980 to great student acclaim. Designed by Jarvis Putty Jarvis of Dallas in early 1978, it was arguably the last pure modernist building to be designed at Texas Tech. Any reference to the traditional architecture of the campus had been reduced solely to the material palette of traditional Perla brick and clay barrel tile roofing. Both the building orientation and the clerestory-lit volumes of interior space resulted in an excellent facility in terms of bioclimatic design. The austere exterior forms belied an anthill of interior spaces, where activity-heavy functions such as basketball courts and workout spaces were situated in the basement level with concourse and spectator seating situated above—allowing the facility to remain manageable in height and scale to the adjacent intramural recreation fields. Students accustomed to playing handball in ragged chicken wire-clad outdoor courts south of Jones Stadium loved the quantum shift in intramural facility quality. The newly relocated adjacent intramural recreation field complex, designed as part of a larger park spanning north of 18th Street and west of Flint Avenue, would later be renamed in 1993 in honor of the late professor and founding CPC member Elo J. Urbanovsky.[21]

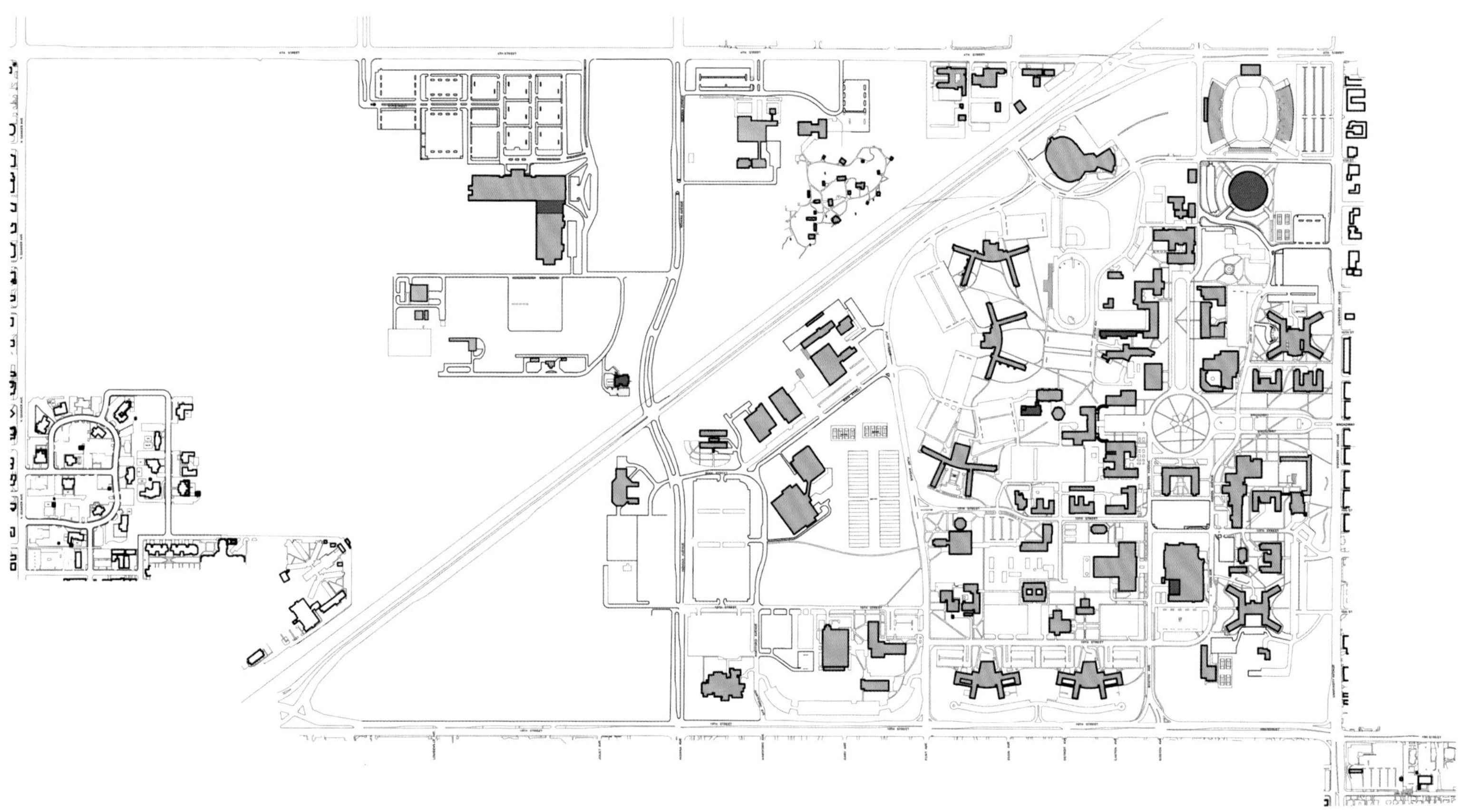

Circa-1990 campus master plan, with what little work had completed since 1980 noted in darkest gray, illustrating the significant downturn in facility growth over the previous thirty years of frenetic expansion at Texas Tech.

While a handful of minor projects were constructed across campus in the 1980s—engineering lab additions, HSC pod finish-out projects, and a new electrical co-generation facility at the Physical Plant—one project that did have a profound visual impact upon the northern zone of the campus was the Athletics Training Center. Built in 1985 for a budget of $4.5 million, the aptly nicknamed "Bubble" was instantly noticeable to the public thanks to its three-hundred-foot diameter pressurized and cable-stayed tensile fabric dome that covered it. Lubbock's notoriously flaky weather resulted in a push by Athletics Director John Conley for an indoor facility to support the practice needs of football, track, tennis, and other programs in winter or inclement conditions. Designed in partnership between local firm Joe D. McKay Architects (JDMA) and architect Ralph O. Spencer of Austin-based Spencer Associates in 1986, the Bubble was the first major new Texas Tech athletics project in over two decades. Regents had ordered Spencer and JDMA to design a building that would not

Circa-2014 aerial view of the Athletics Training Center shortly before its ultimate collapse and subsequent demolition; Spencer Associates, with JDMA Architects, 1985.

compromise the line-of-sight between spectators seated at Jones Stadium and the historic core of the Tech campus to the south. That order had proven particularly ironic given the considerable height and scale of the Gensler-designed Sports Performance Center that resides at that site today.

To meet regents' demands and a daunting project budget, Spencer and McKay turned to siting programmatic components of the facility below grade surrounded by a visual low-profile earthen berm system. The tensile fabric roof system—an Owens-Corning-designed panelized fabric system of Teflon-coated fiberglass that did not require a heavy long-span steel superstructure—proved to be the only option that could practically fit within the project budget. In particular, the design team referenced the success of the Pontiac Silverdome, the popular venue built in 1975 for the Detroit Lions and Detroit Pistons franchises, which used the same roofing system in a pill-shaped configuration, unlike the shallow concentric dome configuration Spencer and McKay had proposed at Tech. The proposed design seemed brilliant until a blizzard struck Detroit on Monday, March 4, 1985, causing a buildup of unusually wet snow on the Silverdome's roof, resulting first in a deflation, followed by a collapse of the entire roof structure.[22] Though no fatalities or injuries ensued, news of the collapse received great national publicity only three days before McKay and Spencer were to present the final design for the Indoor Practice Facility to the Texas Tech Board of Regents. To make matters worse, Spencer was taken ill with a severe case of influenza, leaving McKay solo to endure the scrutiny of the Regents.[23] In the March 7 presentation, Regent Chairman J. Fred Bucy left no question of his skepticism of the tensile dome system, pointing a finger at McKay and bluntly demanding, "Tell me how the same thing that happened at the Silverdome can't happen here?" [24] Having already been in consultation earlier that week with Owens-Corning representatives, McKay adroitly assured the Regents that the snow buildup had occurred at the flat barrel vault portion of the Silverdome's roof—a vulnerability the Tech dome would not have. More practically speaking however, designers believed that Lubbock could never expect to receive the volume of snow and ice events that fell on Detroit. Realizing that a $4.5 million budget could not support any other system—the Board of Regents ultimately approved the design, unaware that just such a high-moisture snowstorm three decades later would indeed collapse the Bubble's roof.

BY THE LATE 1980S, the Space Committee disbanded, while the Office of Planning would ultimately divest its facility planning responsibilities to focus on strategic planning. Even without a bevy of major new capital projects, the ongoing work of lesser renovation and additions projects was tackled by Tech's growing Facilities Planning and Construction Office. Design professionals such as Bill Droll, Jack Barr, and a young architect named Theresa Bartos Drewell helmed this team during a time when the university still lacked clear strategic direction in terms of its architecture and facilities.[25] This team was complemented by a similar team at the Health Sciences Center led by architect Eric Williams and interior designer Jamie McCann, who found themselves constantly busy infilling the once-criticized Cotton Storage Warehouse at the HSC with office, clinical, support, and research suites. Now no longer a hodgepodge of uncoordinated, conflicted departments, both the university and HSC were at least equipped with the basic cogs of project management and campus planning. FP&C staff felt reassured that they were capable of handling any surge of campus facility growth should it ever come.

No one realized it, but the surge was coming.

PART V

COMING OF AGE

According to the grace of God which was given to me, as a wise master builder I have laid the foundation, and another builds on it. But let each one take heed how he builds on it.

—1 Corinthians 3: 10

(*Opposite*) Sweeping changes in leadership, governance, athletics, and the arrival of a new generational population boom would incite a second maelstrom era of expansion at Texas Tech, aligned with the rise of nostalgic popularity in Tech's Spanish Renaissance roots. Here, a circa-1998 rendering for the English and Philosophy Building by HOK highlights Tech's return to neoclassicism.

18

SYZYGY

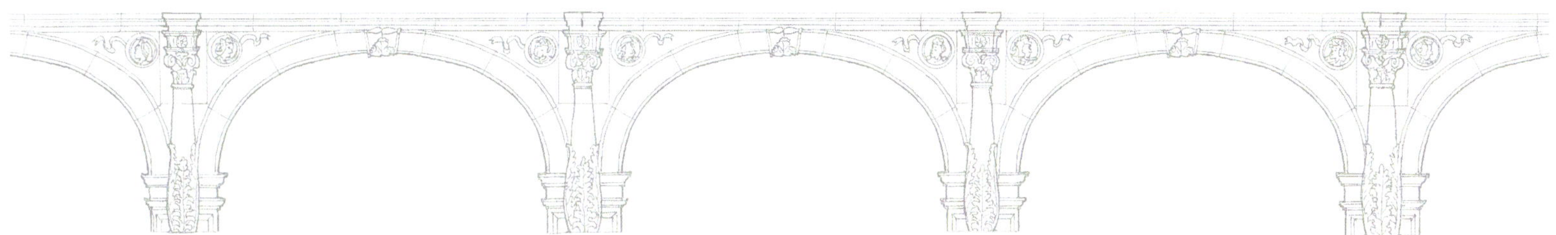

On Sunday, April 4, 1993, in the Omni Coliseum in Atlanta, Georgia, the underdog Texas Tech Lady Raiders and the Ohio State University Buckeyes battled for the NCAA Women's Basketball Championship. Despite two Buckeye three-pointers in the final minutes that erased a Lady Raider lead, Ohio State could never overtake Sheryl Swoopes's sheer firepower, as the Brownfield native would score more points in a title game than any college player since UCLA's Bill Walton two decades earlier.[1] Texas Tech won its first NCAA national championship with a score of 84–82.

Back in Lubbock, all hell broke loose. Hundreds of screaming students came aimlessly running out of their dorms. Kids were seen swimming in the Amon Carter Memorial Fountain, while Lubbockites unaware of the victory were befuddled by the sounds of hundreds of car horns honking throughout town.[2] Thousands celebrated on Memorial Circle to the sounds of ringing Victory Bells, albeit still limited to thirty minutes in accordance with Lubbock's fifty-seven-year old ordinance. The next evening the Lady Raiders returned home and were driven with police escort from Lubbock International Airport to Jones Stadium, where over forty thousand welcomed the national champions.

The Jones Stadium welcome for the Lady Raiders was as much a necessity due to massive turnout as it was because of the problems of the aging Lubbock Municipal Coliseum. Approaching its fortieth anniversary, the Coliseum's roof had long lost its weathertight status, prompting a common joke in the 1990s that the Tech basketball programs were the only teams in the nation trained to play in the rain. Texas Tech needed a new indoor venue but faced fiscal hurdles in the cost of a new arena, as well as political hurdles from the city of Lubbock, which had already attempted their own citywide tax referendum to fund a downtown arena replacement for the old Coliseum. Although that vote failed by less than six hundred votes, the Lubbock City Council lacked the political will to pursue a replacement any further.[3] But one other challenge was imminently more concerning to Texas Tech. The Southwest Conference was dying.

In the previous ten years, all but two SWC members were meted

The transitionally Spanish Renaissance–revival Southwest Special Collections Library, whose design weaved between the Library and the former Livestock Judging Pavilion; Komatsu-Rangel Associates, with AC Associates, architects, 1995.

either probation or sanctions by the NCAA for various violations, with the sharpest falling on SMU, whose programs were shuttered in 1987 and 1988 by the NCAA for flagrant pay-to-play violations while already under probation. SMU's "death penalty" and the lack of television coverage revenue from other SWC schools on probation had by 1990 crippled the conference. Furthermore, poor gate revenue from small private institutions like Rice and TCU further weakened the financial value of the conference. Seeing the writing on the wall, Arkansas departed in 1991 to join the Southeastern Conference, leaving the now all-Texas conference even more weakened and parochial. Remaining powers were preparing to abandon ship, with UT leadership enamored with joining the Pac-10 Conference, and failing that, the Big Ten. The Aggies courted interest from the SEC.[4] Both schools were on the brink of leaving the Southwest Conference.

A *syzygy* is a rare astronomical phenomenon where multiple celestial bodies are aligned with one another. Rarer still in the world of Texas

Designed by JDMA Architects and completed in 1997, the International Cultural Center reflected leadership interests in returning Tech to its Spanish-revival roots.

higher education—often dominated by the hegemony of UT and Texas A&M—is a political syzygy for Texas Tech University where the stars would for once align in the sky for Tech to outmaneuver College Station and Austin. One such moment occurred in early 1994.

Aware of the pending SWC mutiny, Lieutenant Governor Bob Bullock summoned system chancellors and university presidents of UT and A&M to his office on Sunday morning, February 20, 1994.[5] The quartet of administrators—unaccustomed to weekend summons by the head of the state senate—arrived to find Bullock, a Baylor and Tech alumnus, joined by Senator David Sibley, a Baylor graduate, Senate Finance Committee Chairman John T. Montford of Lubbock, and House Appropriations Committee Chairman Robert T. Junell, a former Texas Tech linebacker. Montford, albeit a UT alumnus, would have faced a tar-and-feathering back in Lubbock had he not supported Tech in lockstep. It was a singular moment in Texas political history where not one key lawmaker from the legislature or governor's mansion were either Longhorns or Aggies. Bullock demanded that each school state its intentions in terms of conference alignment, and after a brief interrogation, UT and A&M leadership confirmed Bullock's suspicions.

Built over the site of the demolished Old Carpenter-Wells Hall, a new Carpenter-Wells Complex would be designed and integrated into HOK's ongoing master planning effort and be completed in 1998.

Bullock's next statement was clear. Any conference realignment plans that did not involve Texas Tech and Baylor in tow would result in severe consequences to UT and A&M. As far as Bullock was concerned, if the Red Raiders and Bears were left behind, he would ensure that neither UT nor A&M would see another penny from the legislature for the foreseeable future. The UT and A&M leaders at first recoiled, leading Bullock to double down, threatening to tamper with both system's sacred land-grant resource—the prized Permanent University Fund. Bullock finally had their attention, and an alternate realignment plan was proposed where UT, A&M, Baylor, and Tech would join the members of the Big Eight Conference to form a new conference with favorable national position and revenue opportunities.

Five days later, University of Colorado Chancellor Jim Corbridge extended an invitation for Texas Tech University to join a new conference, with play to commence in the fall of 1996.[6] Although a committee was at work to establish a name for the new conference, the national press had already labeled it "The Big XII"—a moniker that stuck. As for the Southwest Conference—the league Texas Tech had once fought mightily for three decades to join, the next year marked the swan song of an eighty-year era that had profound impact upon collegiate athletics in the Southwestern United States. If 1995 marked the end of the old era, then 1996 marked the beginning of a new era for Texas Tech in more ways than one.

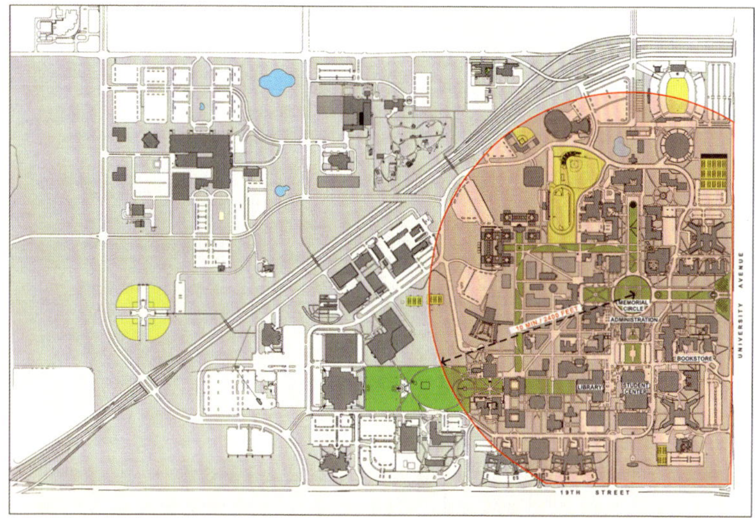

HOK exhaustively analyzed vehicular, utility access, building age, facility need, and pedestrian issues in the 1997 Master Plan. One particular factor—the "Ten-Minute Walk" radius is overlaid to the master plan for analysis, denoting the distance a student can comfortably walk in the ten minutes between class changes.

AT A MEETING IN EARLY 1995, President Robert Lawless was at work with other administrators playing a game of "Pin the tail on the donkey." [7] The "donkey" consisted of an aerial photograph of the Tech Campus, while the "tail" happened to be a proposed new Architecture Building. Several administrators perceived Tech's Architecture Tower as too large and a poor spatial fit for the new college, now independent from the College of Engineering, so they were considering converting the behemoth into another general classroom building much like Holden Hall. The exercise was enjoyable for everyone present, except for senior FP&C architect Theresa Bartos Drewell, frowning in disgust in the back of the room. Into her eighth year at FP&C, Drewell had developed a reputation for cooperation with leadership and regents alike, but also her sweet demeanor hid a pugnacious and plain-spoken side. Irked with the proceedings, Drewell finally blurted out, "This isn't how we should plan for a new facility! First, we need a master plan!" Lawless shot Drewell an annoyed glance, then dismissively returned to his dartboard analysis.

The last fifteen years had been a fleeting time for new building schemes at Tech, and Lawless's Architecture Building planning escapade was no different. But other administrators, and more important a handful of regents, agreed with Drewell realizing that save for 3DI's 1985 landscape plan, Texas Tech had gone decades without a master plan of any kind, and the physical state of the campus still reflected that. Given the lack of institutional memory following CPC disbandment in the 1970s, FP&C staff knew nothing of Howard Schmidt's Long Range Development Plan of twenty-five years earlier, as Schmidt's plan would not be discovered until a routine archive search in the 2000s. Most assumed that no master plan had been contemplated since Watkin's 1924 original vision for the campus.

FP&C did finally receive tepid support in March 1995 to launch a master planning initiative for the Texas Tech University and TTU Health Sciences Center Lubbock Campus—selecting national firm Hellmuth, Obata + Kassabaum (HOK) for the commission. At first, the project lacked a major champion outside of FP&C, in part given a sudden leadership vacuum within the university. Robert Lawless—considered by some a quirky pick as Tech president given his former stint as comptroller at Southwest Airlines—resigned in February 1996 to become president of the University of Tulsa. Sans president or not, HOK commenced their information gathering efforts that spring, as all involved were unsure of the future of the project. Thankfully, the

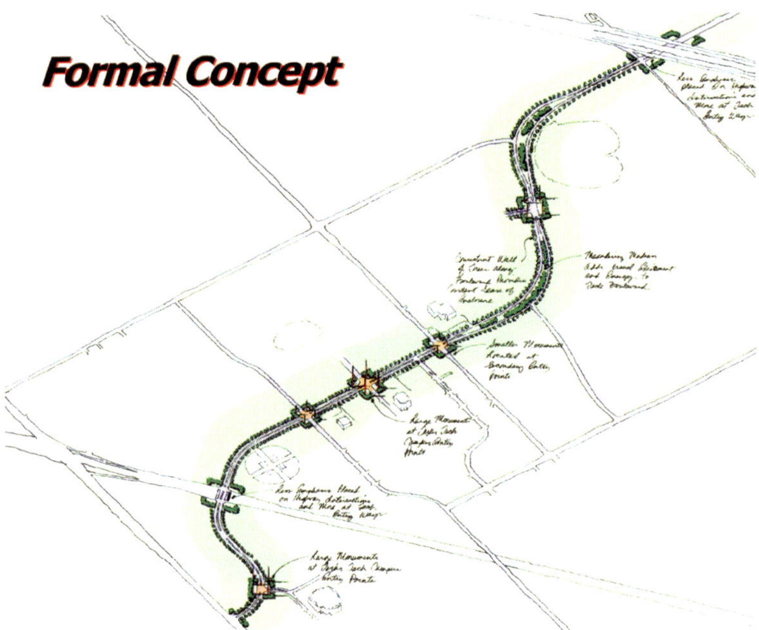

Planning concept developed for Texas Tech Parkway, a new western campus arterial roadway that would replace Indiana Avenue in the early 2000s.

In a precursor to the eventual Rawls Course development, the Master Planning team developed a mixed-use suburban residential golf community development in the late 1990s in response to Governor Bush's charge.

master plan did have one vital proponent—the chairman of the Texas Tech University Board of Regents.

One colleague once described Edward E. Whitacre Jr. as "a smart engineer and an even better businessman who simply knew how to make money."[8] An Ennis native and Tech alumnus, Whitacre was serving as board chairman of Southwestern Bell when Governor Ann Richards appointed him a Tech Regent in 1993. Only two years later, Whitaker advanced to chairman of the Board of Regents, which fortuitously aligned with myriad events that would profoundly transform Texas Tech. It has been suggested that Lawless's departure was a tacit response to his disfavor toward establishing the Texas Tech University System, a proposal that Whitacre and other regents wholeheartedly supported. An organizational structure was proposed that divested functions such as government relations and institutional advancement from the university and president's role and placed them under a chancellor-led umbrella system that, at the behest of the Board of Regents would oversee the university and the Health Sciences Center as separate institutions. On August 20, 1996, the University System plan was adopted by the Board of Regents.[9] The Texas Tech University System now needed a chancellor and Whitacre had an ideal candidate in mind.

Though he was the first to propose the concept of a Texas Tech University System in a failed senate resolution in 1985,[10] John T. Montford was enjoying the chairmanship of the powerful Senate Finance Committee too much to contemplate something as mundane as becoming chancellor of a university system. But Montford, a Democrat, also

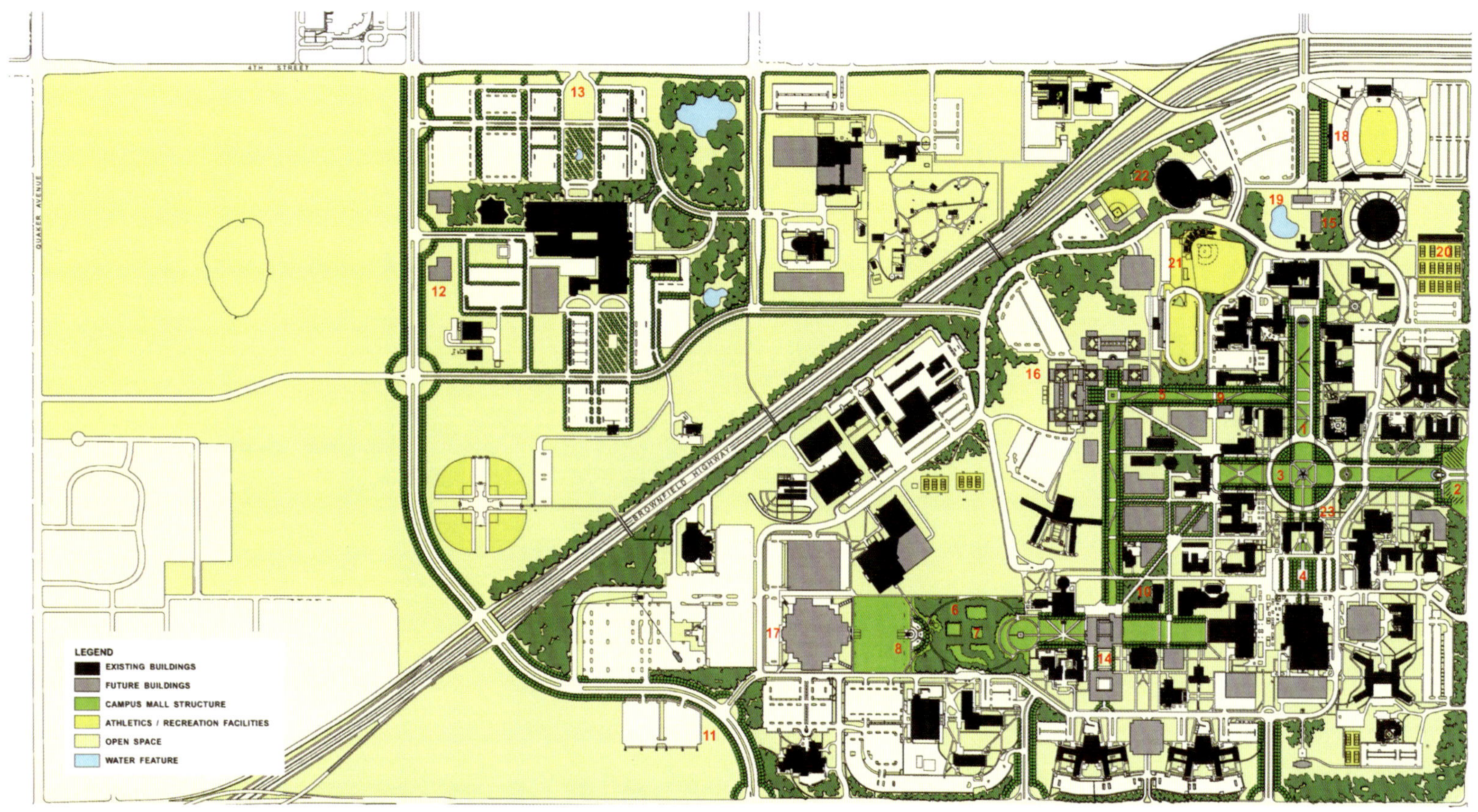

The 1997 Master Plan "2007 Vision" for the Texas Tech University and TTU Health Sciences Center campus; Hellmuth Obata Kassabaum, Inc., architects, et. al.

read the tea leaves as to his political future in a state that was rapidly turning from blue to red, and so after the fifth or sixth time Ed Whitacre had asked, Montford started to listen. Montford was inaugurated chancellor of the Texas Tech University System that same August, followed a month later with the selection of Donald Haragan as president at Texas Tech. Less than a decade removed from football coach David McWilliams's treacherous defection to UT, Tech leadership was careful to keep knowledge of Montford's burnt orange pedigree as discreet as possible. Whenever introduced at luncheons and speaking engagements, MCs conveniently omitted any of his education history following high school, leaving Montford amused and perhaps a little worried that everyone thought Tech had hired a chancellor with only a high school degree.[11]

For the first time in seven decades, all-consuming roles that had previously been vested in one person—roles so burdensome that they essentially killed Tech's first two presidents—were finally divested

Following completion of the master plan, HOK proceeded forward with concepts specific to the implementation of that plan, including entry features like ornamental gateways flanking the Broadway entrance, first developed in 1998.

One Horizon Campaign concept developed was for an on-campus hotel and conference center that would unfortunately never be realized.

between the academic roles of a university president and the political and advancement roles of a chancellor. Tech's endowment lagged measurably behind other comparable national institutions, but for Montford, the task of asking others for money proved a comparably easy task. Three days before his official start as chancellor in September 1996, Montford received a request for a meeting from United Supermarkets CEO Bob Snell, which Montford hastily arranged at Jim Douglass's Alumni Association Office at the Merket Alumni Center.[12] Montford, Haragan, and Douglass were caught off guard when Snell arrived still wearing his striped United apron with company-issue plastic name badge stamped "Bob," just as if he worked in the produce department. Snell, a Duke University graduate, lamented Lubbock's lack of a quality basketball venue similar to Duke's venerated Cameron Field House. Given Tech's recent admittance into the Big XII, Snell felt the time had come for that venue and was prepared to write a $10 million check toward a new arena. Montford and Haragan were speechless as Texas Tech had never received a donation of that size. Having never executed an advancement agreement of that magnitude, the two sent Jim Douglass hunting for a typewriter so that

HOK's Broadway Entrance Gatehouse vision would be realized in 2002 as more traditionally detailed features; designed by PSC.

Pierce's design for the Merket Alumni Center expansion included a very handsome outdoor event courtyard, punctuated by a central fountain.

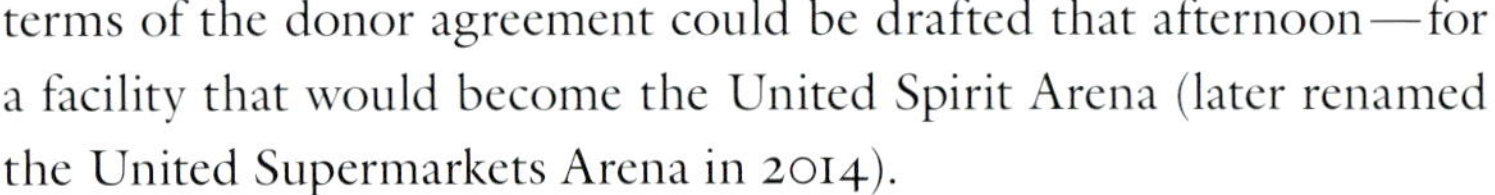

terms of the donor agreement could be drafted that afternoon—for a facility that would become the United Spirit Arena (later renamed the United Supermarkets Arena in 2014).

Even in 1996 dollars, $10 million would not come close to fully funding a new arena. In late 1996, Montford and Athletics Department representatives toured the University of Arkansas's new $40 million Walton Indoor Arena,[13] but following the visit, the Tech delegation agreed that they wanted better. With a sizeable remaining price tag for the United Spirit Arena, plus a host of other facility needs, academic endowments, and additional faculty hiring needs, it became clear that a broader strategic fundraising effort was needed in building a war chest for the fledgling University System. Christened the "Horizon" Campaign, Montford's goal was simple and ambitious—Texas Tech would grow their endowment to $250 million—an unheard-of sum for the West Texas institution. Public reaction toward the "Horizon" Campaign ranged between shock, jest, and incredulity.

Back at FP&C, Drewell was fighting frustration. It should have been a buoyant time for FP&C with more work underway at once than in the past fifteen years combined, but even with new projects, old habits were slow to die. The same month the University System was established, the new Southwest Special Collections Library opened—the first new campus facility in a decade. The seventy-nine thousand-square-foot, $8.8 million annex was built adjacent to the north of the University Library and designed by Fort Worth firm Komatsu/Rangel with AC Associates as local consultants.[14] As a positive step in increasing campus core density, the building's serpentine plan wedged between the blank space spanning from the Library to the iconic former Livestock Judging Pavilion to the north. Clad in a transitional brick-and-stone envelope with clay-tile hip roofs and a prominent south octagonal lantern, the Southwest Special Collections Library signaled the return of neoclassical expectations in future projects by Tech leadership. While the Special Collections Library improved campus core density, it was the exception to the rule.

Before departing for the chancellorship, then-Senator Montford

Rendering looking northeast toward the proposed Frazier Alumni Pavilion; H. Deane Pierce, architect, 1997.

had successfully secured appropriations in the 1995 biennium for a new International Cultural Center at Texas Tech, with nearly $3.3 million funded between the 1993, 1995, and 1997 legislative budgets.[15] As a project heavily advocated by *Avalanche-Journal* editor Jay Harris, a site south of the Museum was eventually selected on the premise that programmatic activities of the ICC would synergize well with the nearby Museum and NRHC. Drewell and the HOK team bit their tongue at the site selected, given that the ICC—an attractive modern iteration of Tech's Spanish Renaissance style designed by Joe McKay and his JDMA team—was nonetheless another building whose siting by leadership at the periphery of the Tech campus continued the low-density policies of the past four decades. Across the Brownfield Highway, Tech's first residence hall complex in nearly thirty years—a cluster of apartment-style blocks slated to replace the "spider plan" SRMG-designed Carpenter-Wells Hall—had little connective relationship to the existing campus around it. Designed by Lotti Krishnan Short and slated for completion in fall 1998, the sixteen-building Carpenter-Wells Complex may very well have been inherently more Beaux-Arts in plan, but last-minute coordination was necessary between Lotti Krishnan Short and the HOK planning team to integrate

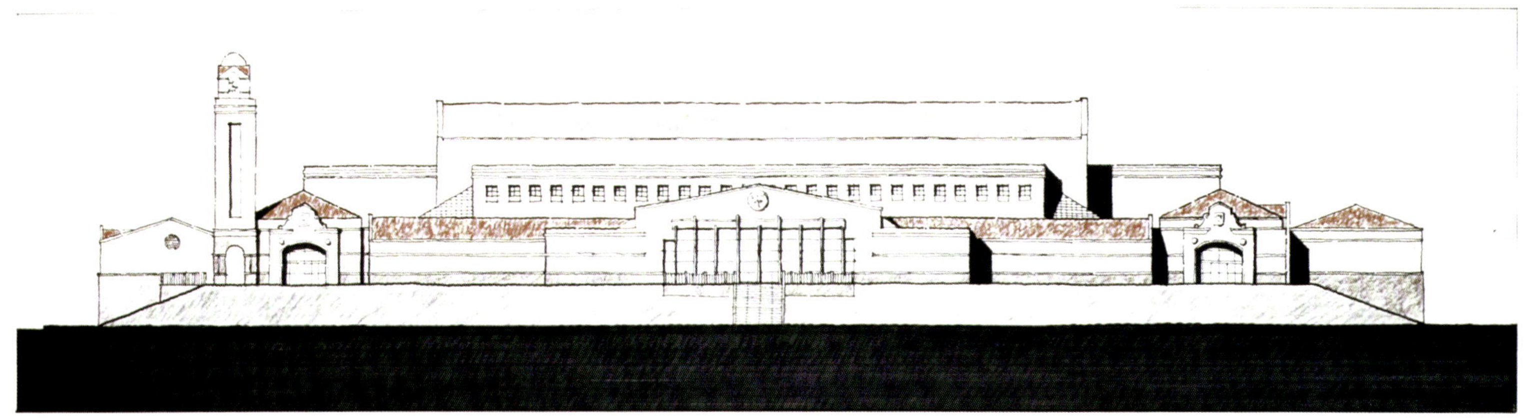

EAST ELEVATION

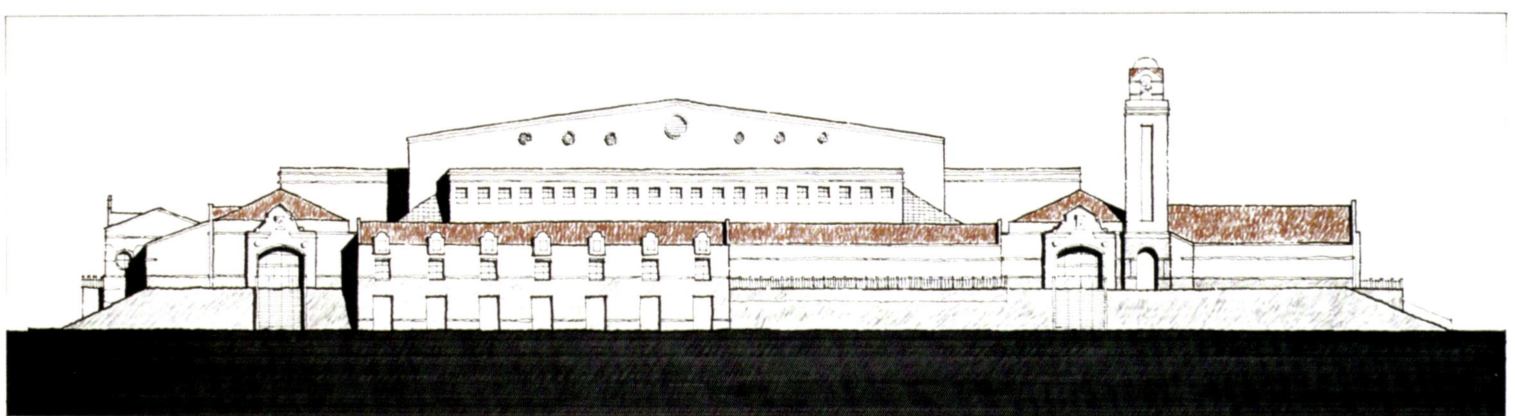

SOUTH ELEVATION

Elevation development studies by Rosser International, 1996, showing a number of formative elements that would be incorporated in the final design—notably the Victory Tower and central gable roof.

complex layout and siting with HOK's broader planning vision. Even more concerning were early sites under consideration by Tech Athletics and the design team of Atlanta-based Rosser International and JDMA, who had been selected to design the United Spirit Arena. By late 1996, the site initially favored by the Athletics Department for the arena was northwest of the intersection at Indiana Avenue and 4th Street[16]—a site that no student living on-campus could easily walk to. Three decades later, Texas Tech had still not learned from the decades of planning sins that had brought them to this juncture.

A Kansas State alumnus and landscape architect by trade, Doug Mann led HOK's campus planning team working on the Texas Tech Master Plan. Mann realized that to gain consensus from all

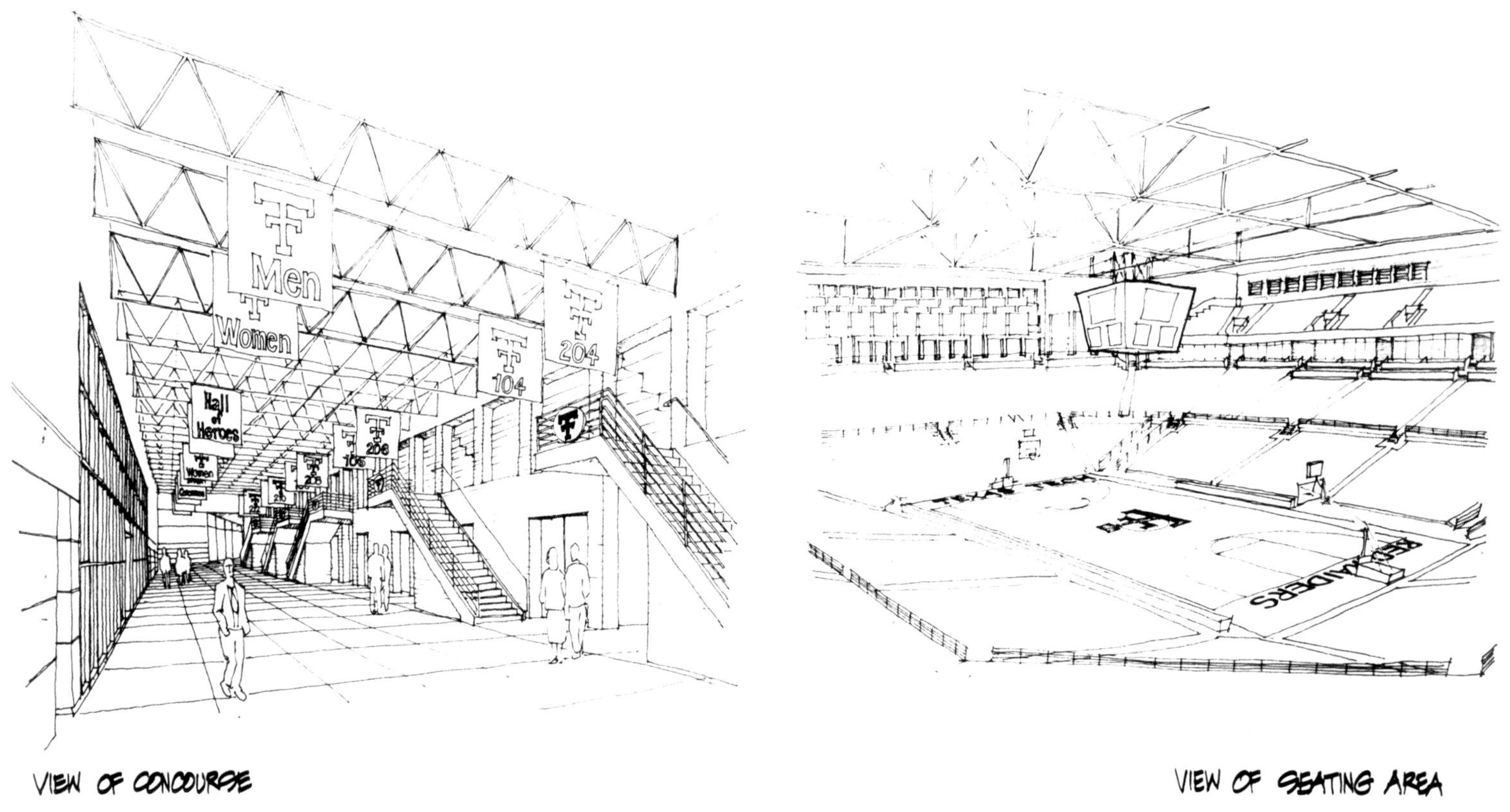

Development sketch renderings of the interior spaces illustrating the anticipated quality and volume of space in the resulting United Spirit Arena.

stakeholders was an impossible goal for a process of such magnitude. Rather, he believed in the concept of establishing "informed consent" from stakeholders. With very little direction from Tech leadership early on in the project beyond a Board of Regents interest in returning Tech to its Spanish Renaissance roots, Mann, his team led by HOK Planning Director Rick Leisner, and FP&C representatives soldiered into 1996 making worthwhile headway nonetheless. Following his arrival, John Montford began joining in stakeholder meetings, sat back and quietly observed HOK's stakeholder engagement effort. After a few meetings, Montford approached Mann, put his hand on his shoulder, and offered, "I like what you're doing. What can I do to help?" [17] Mann, Leisner, and FP&C were relieved to have the chancellor's political support, but little did they know that others, namely Whitacre and another Regent—Jim Sowell—quietly, but eagerly followed development of the planning effort with expectations that great things would emerge.

Political support provided the HOK team the maneuvering room needed to incorporate bolder planning measures into the Tech plan that may have otherwise been ignored. FP&C representatives became justifiably alarmed when HOK displayed a 2,600-foot-diameter

Rendering of the United Spirit Arena (now United Supermarkets Arena), Rosser International, with JDMA Architects, 1997.

walking circle centered over Memorial Circle, representing the reasonable distance a backpack-laden student could walk during a ten-minute class change. Upon receiving feedback from the Provost's Office, and a decade before Tech had comprehensive Citibus commuter transit service throughout campus, the planning team realized that a sizeable percentage of the student body had class schedules that precluded them arriving on time for class even if they ran across campus. HOK championed parking garages as a solution to eliminate acres of asphalt from the campus, which was conveniently decried by critics as a crime risk to people parking in the garage, irrespective of modern developments in garage design, lighting, and security. Proposed new pedestrian malls of green space north and west of the campus core—modeled after Watkin's prado-inspired malls of seventy years' prior—would frame future building development, but would likewise require the demolition of many hundreds of parking spaces. While meeting with TxDOT (Texas Department of Transportation) officials regarding the future of Brownfield Highway as a high-speed freeway transiting through campus, Mann argued for an entirely below-grade freeway punctuated with at-grade pedestrian crossings designed with Plateresque detailing—a more expensive undertaking than TxDOT had ever envisioned. TxDOT District Engineer Steve Warren quietly listened through Mann's proposal, then sardonically rebutted, "Why don't you just cut the corner [of this new freeway] at Jones Stadium and run Brownfield Highway under the north fifty? Because we all know Tech won't be able to score there." [18] Warren, himself an A&M alumnus, may not have been fond of Mann's freeway vision, but his pot shot may have inadvertently instigated a curse on his beloved Aggies. Following his prognostication, twelve years would pass before A&M would ever win again at Jones Stadium.

One controversial master plan proposal involved development of a new northerly arterial vehicular route onto campus in lieu of Indiana Avenue—a proposal that risked resurrecting Barrick and Murray's long battle with the city. Theresa Drewell was quick to advise, "don't touch this issue with a ten-foot pole," but even Montford was unhappy with the concept that a visitor arriving from Lubbock International Airport having to navigate three miles of University Avenue before arriving at the edge of campus, and visitors arriving from I-27 had almost the same distance to travel. Montford wanted a simple and straightforward entrance accessible directly from North Loop 289, a concept that did not sit well with some city stakeholders. Initially, Lubbock City Councilman Victor Hernandez was one of a number of leaders who objected to the such concepts, prompting the direct intervention of Montford's political charm to convince Hernandez of its merits and support the master plan.[19]

Despite a 40 percent increase in the university budget since 1990, Governor Bush had warned Tech along with all public universities in a 1996 letter to prepare for declines in state and federal funding. Montford directed FP&C and HOK to develop alternative land use strategies for Tech's dormant land parcels as a potential alternative revenue generator to replace declining funding. Nearly half of Tech's property in 1997—856 acres in fact—sat empty, with less than three hundred acres of that used for rangeland or crop research.[20] Another fifty acres were dedicated for a new USDA Plant Stress Research Laboratory—the US government's first-ever Spanish Renaissance–

revival laboratory—slated to be completed in 1998, but the vast swath of the northwestern campus remained an unrealized void. In response, HOK proposed 470 acres to be used for a golf course and greenbelt park space, as well as another one hundred acres defined for a future research park, and eighty-seven acres defined for land lease parcels intended for retail or mixed-use development.

On November 7, 1997, Doug Mann, Theresa Drewell, and the planning team presented the Campus Master Plan to the Board of Regents who eagerly voted to adopt it for implementation.[21] Beyond traffic and land planning measures, the plan codified Plateresque-revival architecture as the official livery for future construction at the university. But however elegant and sweeping in breadth it was, the Master Plan's implementation would require hundreds of millions of dollars to execute, ensuring that the silver-tongued Montford would truly have to earn his paycheck over coming years in fundraising. Montford and University System leadership were prepared to launch the "Horizon" Campaign in February 1998, while the success of the Master Plan process had proven the value of the Facilities Planning and Construction Office to Montford and the Board of Regents, who now contemplated elevating FP&C as a department of the University System and not just the university. The master planning process itself demonstrated in a microcosm what departmental and political hurdles FP&C faced on a daily basis, so advancing the office within the system's organizational chart aided in providing the office the political teeth necessary to enforce its new Master Plan and campus design standards. But to accomplish this transition into becoming a system-level office, FP&C would need a vice chancellor to lead it.

Montford had left Doug Mann slightly nervous after one meeting where the chancellor asked him, "Have you ever considered a future in politics?" [22] Only later did Mann realize that Montford was recruiting him to become the inaugural vice chancellor for the Facilities Planning and Construction Office. Following Mann's appointment, Drewell would remain on board as associate vice chancellor, while architect Liz Lonngren—a future leader at Lee Lewis Construction—relocated from HSC Facilities Office as part of the reorganizational effort that centralized FP&C operations, while smaller renovation and maintenance projects became the provenance of the University Physical Plant Office. The revamped FP&C team now charged ahead with a bevy of new projects.

Public interest in ongoing architectural endeavors at Tech was reaching a fever pitch. Thanks to efforts led by local architect Willard Robinson and others, the historic core of the Texas Tech campus had been recognized in 1996 by the US National Register of Historic Places as the Texas Technological College Historic District. Programming phase for a $17 million sweeping interior renovation to the old "Radiator," the University Library, was underway. A new multistory Preston Smith Library of the Health Sciences was under construction west of HSC Pod C. In 1997, local architect and Butler-Brasher protégé H. Deane Pierce designed a ten-thousand-square-foot new alumni pavilion, named for Tech alumnus David P. Frazier and his father George. Located southwest of Jones Stadium, Pierce's design continued the neoclassical trend of adapting Spanish Renaissance motifs onto more specialized building forms at Texas Tech, in this case a large, open-span multipurpose pavilion. Pierce had already won praise for his prior elegantly executed 11,650-square-foot expansion to the former President's House, which since 1969 had housed the university's Ex-Students (now Alumni) Association. Now renamed the Merket Alumni Center and completed in 1995, "The Merket" was equipped to better support the expanded Texas Tech Alumni Association. Pierce's design included an enclosed courtyard, situated between the renovated house and conference spaces to the west, replete with a handsome Spanish fountain. At the Frazier Alunmi Pavilion however, Pierce was reticent to incorporate the salvaged stone escutcheons and decorations of a balconette that previously resided on the Hedrick/Watkin-designed former Power House situated between the Engineering Key and Frazier site. In the recent building flurry, outcry over the loss of the old Power Plant Building was fleeting as the historic building was quietly but sadly razed in 1998 to meet the expansion needs of a northward-surging College of Engineering. Thousands of students and game-day fans who pass by the Frazier Alumni Pavilion

Rendering looking east in commons between Business Administration and Architecture toward English and Philosophy Building; English, Philospohy and Education Complex; Hellmuth, Obata & Kassabaum, architects, 1999.

are likely unaware that the stone escutcheons over the pavilion's entrance in fact represents a cross-section of a nineteenth-century flue boiler.

NO ONE HAD EVER DESIGNED a Spanish Renaissance–revival indoor sports arena before, but Fred Krenson believed he and his Atlanta team at Rosser International were equal to the task. A Rice graduate and a consummate sketchbook traveler, Krenson followed the Watkin playbook himself and traveled to Spain in 1996 to experience Plateresque architecture firsthand.[23] His travel sketches went far in inspiring the design of a United Spirit Arena whose scope continued to expand at the request of athletics and university leadership. Working with Lubbock architect Joe McKay, Krenson and the Rosser team incorporated Plateresque balconettes and carved stone roundels signifying each of the uiversity's academic colleges over each of the quadrant entries to the complex. An eight-story campanile christened the "Victory Tower" was designed to anchor the arena's southeast corner. Spectator seating—originally programmed for 12,600—expanded at the Athletics Department request to more than fifteen thousand seats as the Arena's budget ballooned from $47 to an eventual $62.7 million.[24] Construction of the arena in 1998 was a sight to behold on the otherwise quiet western edge of campus, as the superstructure box-girders—each of which were two-stories tall alone—and surrounding berms gave the arena site the appearance of a massive rocket launching pad. Budget overage aside, the project signaled that Tech was no longer playing second fiddle in terms of athletics facilities, as the United Spirit Arena upon its opening on October 1, 1999, became the second-largest indoor collegiate arena in Texas, and third-largest arena in the already basketball-rich Big XII Conference.

HOK was again selected to design a 211,000-square-foot complex situated between Art and Architecture and the Foreign Languages Building as home to the English and Philosophy Departments of the College of Arts & Sciences, as well as the College of Education. Constructed with a $46.2 million budget, the EP&E as it became known, proved a neoclassical polar shift from the old hated modernist English Building.[25] The EP&E was not unabashed in terms of ornate detail, as a design replete with Arabesque-detailed pilasters, carved stone acanthus detailing, and a prominent blue polychrome-tiled campanile situated within the south courtyard of the English and Philosophy Block. Unfortunately, the complex did perpetuate the continued use of two C-shape buildings—an evolutionary mutation from Watkin's cloistered vision that continues today at Tech. The EP&E was the first new academic building in twenty-six years to open on the Tech campus, while at the same time—save for the Honors College—College of Education was the last academic body to vacate the Administration Building, paving the way for the building to finally function as William Ward Watkin had intended in 1924.

19

MAELSTROM

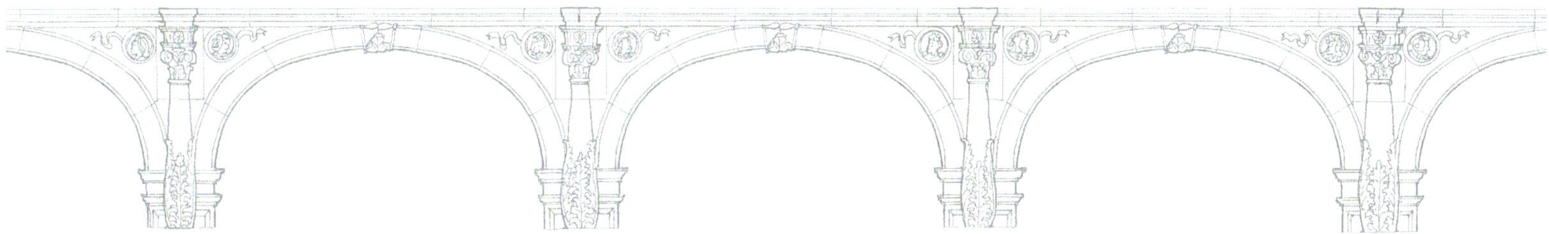

TRAVERSE CITY, MICHIGAN, was in more ways than one no closer to Lubbock than the far side of the moon. And yet for much of 2001, a team at the small firm of Renaissance Golf Design in little Traverse City was intently focused upon a 368-acre patch of former cotton fields located on the north end of the Texas Tech campus. Nervous to uncover any unforeseen site issues as soon as possible, Renaissance Golf Design's chief landscape architect, Tom Doak, could not wait any longer for the site survey. Doak placed a call to FP&C, specifically to the new vice chancellor of FP&C—Mike Ellicott. After Ellicott updated Doak that the survey was not yet ready, he sensed Doak's concern and asked a question.

"Tom, is there a table near where you're sitting?" Ellicott asked.

"Uh," Doak answered, puzzled, "yeah, there's a table here."

Ellicott then asked, "Is it flat? I mean, it's not a drafting table or wobbly or anything?"

"Uh . . . no," Doak responded.

"Great! There's your site survey!"[1] Ellicott was right, for when Renaissance Golf Design did receive the site survey a week later, Doak scratched his head at the flattest piece of land he had ever worked with in his life. In a parcel of land over 4,400 feet in length, there was no more than eighteen inches of elevation change anywhere across the site. For comparison, unless Doak's office table was level to a precision of .03 millimeters or less, the site for what would become the Rawls Course at Texas Tech University was indeed flatter.

Such was an example of Colonel Michael A. Ellicott, US Army, retired, in action. He was direct and considered abrupt by some, but highly cerebral and thorough as one would expect from a mechanical engineer. Ellicott served as facilities director at Wayne State University prior to becoming the second vice chancellor of Facilities Planning and Construction for the Texas Tech University System in late 1999. Ellicott immediately embraced the master plan and would in the near decade in which he helmed FP&C staunchly defend that plan against complaints or whims from anyone at any rank inside or outside the

The No. 12 Fairway, Pacific Dunes Course at Bandon Dunes Golf Resort, Oregon. Here in 2001, Tom Doak sold Jerry Rawls on the Rawls Course commission.

The Rawls Course at Texas Tech; the largest earth-moving project in Texas Tech University history, and today a perennial top-ten nationally ranked collegiate golf course.

University System. Theresa Drewell remained aboard as associate vice chancellor for Planning, given her invaluable depth of experience during her fifteen years at Tech. A former field engineer, Ellicott's former experience included staring across a border at the North Korean Army and preparing for a potential Soviet invasion of West Germany,[2] so little did he fear deans or administrators whose proposed machinations might skirt campus standards or the master plan. Tech needed such a stalwart, as Chancellor Montford's "Horizon" Campaign was still underway, though the public amazement abounded at Montford and Tech's successes in fundraising. "Horizon" had shot well past its initial $250 million goal and even the most wildly successful of public expectations, finally attaining a System Endowment of $511 million at the program's conclusion in the summer of 2001.

The Rawls Course was the first of two major projects to bear the name of Texas Tech alumnus and founder and CEO of global communications firm Finisar—Jerry S. Rawls. Rawls already had a building named for him at the Krannert School of Management at Purdue University, where he pursued graduate studies following his undergraduate stint at Tech. Purdue was also where Rawls learned to appreciate golf as not just a sport, but as an environment ideal for recruiting and networking. Rawls approached Montford and President David Schmidly in early 2001 with his vision of a nationally premiere on-campus golf course at Tech. While Rawls's vision differed from HOK's land lease development plan of four years' earlier, Montford and Schmidly were sold, and turned to CASNR (Texas Tech University College of Agricultural Sciences and Natural Resources) leadership for their assent in relocating existing crop research fields from the 320-acre land parcel south of Erskine Street. Meanwhile, Rawls interjected himself into selecting a golf course architect. In a somewhat unorthodox solicitation process, Rawls personally made the decision to select Tom Doak and Renaissance Golf Design on a windy fairway along the Oregon Coast in April 2001. Rawls was personally invited by Doak to walk the newest addition to the Bandon Dunes Golf Resort—Pacific Dunes—near Coos Bay.[3] Surrounded by the sublime white sandy dunes of the Oregon seashore, but at the same

Cutaway rendering illustrating the court, jogging track, and activity space expansion to the Robert Ewalt Recreation Center, Brown Reynolds Watford, architects, 1999.

time struck by a biting coastal wind oddly reminiscent of winters on the South Plains, the experience sold Rawls on Doak's poignant and experiential approach to course design.

Alas, Lubbock had no dunes, rocky cliffs, or the Douglas firs or madrones of coastal Oregon, though the craggy ridges of the Caprock Escarpment and South Plains vistas provided Doak much inspiration in what would become the Rawls Course. With no latent topography to use, Doak and his field shaper Jim Urbina had to direct the relocation of over a million cubic yards of earth for the pronounced sculpted contours of fairways, greens, and myriad troublesome sand traps that make the Rawls Course such a formidable course today. A decade following its initial completion, Texas Tech built a $3.7 million JDMA-designed clubhouse that complemented what consistently ranks among the top five collegiate courses in the nation today.[4] Visitors arriving at the Rawls Course entered via a newly completed parkway that many doubted would come to fruition, despite John Montford's fervent advocacy for it. Few projects signified the massive scale of change underway throughout Texas Tech quite like construction of the Texas Tech Parkway and the Marsha Sharp Freeway.

Tech leadership assented to adamant recommendations from the HOK team to close Indiana Avenue through the campus, as ironically the city's traffic development plan for Indiana Avenue at the time could not effectively connect with North Loop 289. It proved a late, ineffectual victory for Nolan Barrick and Grover Murray in their long battle with the city over the thoroughfare. Completed in 2002, the Texas Tech Parkway transformed the long-quiet northwestern half of the Tech campus, maintaining a higher-speed vehicular corridor through the campus that was far more efficient than Indiana Avenue had ever been, without slicing through higher-density areas of the institution. The Texas Department of Transportation (TxDOT) had an even more sweeping project underway with the expansion of the Brownfield Highway into what would be eventually named the Marsha Sharp Freeway. Planned since the 1980s and initially funded in 1998, conversion of US Highways 62 and 82 from an at-grade thoroughfare into a course of above- and below-grade freeways made the earthwork scope of the Rawls Course pale in comparison. TxDOT heeded Doug Mann's recommendations that the freeway transit the university below grade, though the three cast-in-place concrete pedestrian bridges designed by TxDOT to cross the freeway proved a milquetoast attempt at mimicking Tech's proud architectural vernacular. It was nonetheless an immense and handsome improvement over the dated, clumsy traffic design of the old Brownfield Highway. By 2009, the university section of Marsha Sharp was completed and operational—a segment of the $131 million second phase of an ultimate five-phase project,[5] lending an entirely different aire to the vehicular perimeter of the campus. Elsewhere on campus, a maelstrom of other changes were underway.

A western expansion to Jones Stadium was under design. Scores of university buildings were overdue for upgrades to install fire alarms, fire sprinklers, and accessible and modern egress routes. HOK's massive new English, Philosophy and Education Complex broke ground in spring 2000, while the construction of a pair of clay tile roofed entry gatehouses flanking the grand eastern Broadway entry to campus began to unfold. Dallas-based Brown, Reynolds & Watford

South courtyard to the Academic Classroom Building at TTUHSC, completed 2002; Parkhill, Smith & Cooper, architects.

(BRW) had designed a sweeping sixty-five-thousand-square-foot multistory addition to the Robert Ewalt Student Recreation Center,[6] including an elevated jogging track, new racquetball courts, and a host of other activity spaces. West Hall—one of Tech's first residence halls—was renovated and expanded to become the new University Welcome Center. Even HKS's sprawling Medical School Complex had long since busted at the seams. Parkhill, Smith & Cooper (PSC) was commissioned in 2000 for a sixty thousand-square-foot Academic Classroom Building expansion to Pod C, equipped with lecture, conference, and seminar rooms.

A growing desire within the Board of Regents had expanded beyond to university leadership to ensure projects firmly remained within the Spanish Renaissance heritage of the university. Even PSC's initial design for the more contemporary HSC Academic Classroom Building was at one point to have a free-standing curved Plateresque colonnade in front of the building's otherwise contemporary precast-concrete

The Pfluger Memorial Fountain at Memorial Circle, completed 2002.

façade. In only three years' time, construction of the United Spirit Arena, Carpenter-Wells Residential Complex, and the English, Philosophy and Education Complex grew the number of Spanish campaniles across campus by 150 percent. Regents and donors clamored for Spanish Renaissance features integrated into every project. When the Pfluger family bequeathed a gift for a grand new fountain intended for the center of Memorial Circle in 2001, it went without question that the walls and copings would be buff-blend brick and stone. The massive arena of seven cascading pools seemed as much an act of sheer determination to make a large-scale water fountain—long regarded as a folly venture in the harsh climate and poor water chemistry of Lubbock—even work. When completed in 2002, students were fascinated by the stereophonic silence created inside Memorial Circle while the sound of cascading water roared outside. Nearby the control station of the fountain situated within an underground vault resembled the massive valve control board of a submarine.

Construction of the English, Philosophy, and Education Complex wiped out hundreds of faculty and visitor parking spaces necessary

Detail photograph, undated, of one of the cascading pools to the Pfluger Memorial Fountain.

Watercolor rendered west elevation of the Flint Avenue Parking Facility, 2001; Walker Parking Consultants with Adling Associates architects.

for other existing facilities in that area of campus. Three decades of growth in the southwestern zone of campus was finally generating sufficient building density that required parking solutions other than surface parking. As with the 1997 master planning process, faculty and administration publicly praised new campus construction, while behind closed doors grousing to FP&C and university administration that they were being deprived of their nearby existing parking stall. During a 2008 planning charrette for the North Campus Gateway Master Plan, noted San Francisco planner and landscape architect Robert Sabbatini turned to Dr. Michael Shonrock—then vice president for Student Affairs, and wryly summed Tech's dilemma best, stating: "You know, Michael, what the most influential college is at Texas Tech? It's the College of Parking." [7] Thirty-six years after Nolan Barrick was nearly laughed out of the room in predicting the need for structured parking, Texas Tech finally built a parking garage.

Walker Parking Consultants of Houston in association with Adling Associates designed what may have been the world's first Spanish Renaissance–evival parking garage at the northeast corner of Flint Avenue and 19th Street. The four-story, eight-hundred-vehicle garage was sited in parallel with the west wing of nearby Clement Hall, resulting in the telltale crook to Flint Avenue that exists between 18th and 19th Streets today. Application of Perla brick and cast stone onto the garage's concrete substrate proved the latest demonstration of commitment by Tech toward continuing Spanish Renaissance architecture on campus.

Even as more literal interpretations of Spanish Renaissance design were being constructed at Tech, nationally recognized architectural design firms unused to the unique style were winning Tech commissions and developing their own iterative response to incorporating the Plateresque aesthetic. Los Angeles–based Anshen+Allen Architects—later renamed CO Architects in 2005—were selected in 2003 to design a three-story Experimental Sciences Building (ESB) as the next generation of bioscience laboratory space on campus. From a planning standpoint, the ESB was, along with BOKA-Powell's nearby four-story Grover E. Murray Residence Hall, next steps in formally framing the first of the two new western axial pedestrian malls proposed in the 1997 Master Plan. FP&C had followed through with constructing a new connecting pedestrian mall from the Engineering Key west to the new Carpenter-Wells Housing Complex. One obstacle to that mall—the old English and Philosophy Building—met

Anshen+Allen's design team adapted traditional Plateresque detailing such as busts and escutcheons set in the flanks between arches (as at the Casa de Salina in Salamanca shown), and incorporated red granite escutcheons of scientific research topics—in the case at right illustrating a cluster of neurons raised in relief on the red granite disc.

its fate by demolition in 2002. The former Classroom and Office Building—a hated symbol of Tech's modernist era—was finally gone.

For Anshen+Allen, unfamiliar with Tech's architectural heritage and preferring not to draw the aesthetic ire of FP&C and the Board of Regents, their solution was simple. Much like Fred Krenson at Rosser International, their team traveled to Spain to visit Plateresque architecture in Salamanca and elsewhere, which proved an eye-opening experience.[8] So much of Spanish Renaissance design at Tech had inherently focused on detail and ornament, but Anshen+Allen instead focused on an elegant, cost-effective organization of deconstructed formative elements like arcades and building masses integrated into an L-shaped plan modeled to the pedestrian dynamics of the master plan. Door and window openings manifested the simple Gothic-originated drip edges exhibited in Plateresque façades, but simplified only to elegant stone casements so as to meet the building's $37 million budget. Ornate stone roundels were substituted with red granite discs engraved with patterns of bacilli, lichen, neurons, and protozoa. Opened in March 2006, the ESB proved that twenty-first century iterations of Spanish Renaissance architecture could exist.

Hardy Holzman Pfeiffer Associates', or HHPA, had gained national acclaim for cultural projects including theaters and museums, having garnered an AIA Architecture Firm Award in 1981. Despite being based in New York City, HHPA had retained a number of Texas Tech graduates—namely architect principal Douglas Moss and then-field representative Darwin Harrison, so having design personnel familiar with Tech aided in HHPA's selection as architect in 2001 for the much-needed expansion to the soon-to-be-renamed Student Union Building, or SUB. HHPA readily embraced Tech's architectural palette, as well as any regional material as vernacular inspiration that they could reinvent uses for, no matter how absurd. In Tech's new era of rigid Plateresque orthodoxy, it was amazing that HHPA's playful and resulting deconstructivist design for the SUB was able to survive scrutiny from FP&C and the Board of Regents. Much like Atcheson & Atkinson's original University Center design of five decades earlier, HHPA simplified entries to a simple radial stone arches with springlines originating at finish grade at the north and west façades to the addition. Otherwise ornate elements seen in the Plateresque vocabulary were too simplified or eliminated in HHPA's design. Straightforward ancons, window frames, and buttresses contributed to a fascinating composition of the 95,000-square-foot expansion to the SUB. In addition, over half of the existing 153,000 square feet of the Student Union was also renovated as part of the project. Inside, a playful menagerie of spaces was created throughout the building for dining, study, breakout meetings, and general circulation routes richly finished with Double T–inset terrazzo floors. The now-iconic northwest pentagonal two-story rotunda-like pavilion included clerestory glazing and curtain wall glass that provided spatial qualities for students seated within the rotunda's common spaces that were both monumental and sublime.

The use of unique regional materials was a signature quality to HHPA's design oeuvre. In 2000, HHPA principal Malcolm Holzman traveled to the Webb Quarry in Lueders, Texas, and while reviewing dressed stone for the SUB's façades, a curious cull of stone on the ground caught Holzman's attention.[9] Leuders stonecutters called it "turkey track"—a fascinating layer of striated calcium crystals encountered just prior to striking sought-after layers of high-grade Oolitic limestone for quarrying. For years, stonecutters discarded turkey track, as it lacked any load-bearing quality and they assumed architects had no interest in it. Holzman was enthralled by the stone's almost alien appearance. Turkey track proved a godsend to HHPA—a naturally occurring equivalent to the hand-carved Arabesques that adorned the nearby Administration Building that could handsomely mimic the historic ornate detail seen elsewhere on the Tech campus. Other eccentric uses of regional materials adorned the building, as cut panels of expanded metal lath—traditionally used as an application backer for stucco—were used as a checkerboard ceiling tile pattern over commons spaces, while walls were broken by backlit panels of

Experimental Sciences Building maintained a significant amount of colonnaded arcade on both the north and south façades, reminiscent of a similar colonnade found on Textile Engineering.

View looking into south courtyard, Grover Murray Residence Hall; BOKA Powell Architects, completed 2005.

stainless steel cattle trough panel. While some faculty and administrators grumbled at the SUB's nonclassical eccentricities, when completed in the summer of 2005, the SUB was an unqualified success with students, and remains so today.

THE YEAR 1999 WAS a bellwether year for Tech. On June 20—thirty years to the day after Preston Smith signed the law renaming Texas Tech University, Governor George W. Bush signed Senate Bill 1088 into law, affirming the establishment of the Texas Tech University System as part of the Texas Education Code.[10] Earlier that year, the Athletics Department enlisted New York–based SME Branding to undertake a twenty-first-century modernization to Tech's long-venerated Double T, which Athletics Director Gerald Myers unveiled emblazoned across the fifty-yard line at Jones Stadium that August.[11] More important, 1999 would also mark the year in which Tech would never look back—in terms of student enrollment. Between 1999 and 2017, total enrollment at Tech would grow by nearly 53 percent[12]—a

2001 exterior rendering of the west expansion to the Student Union Building; HHPA Architects.

product of the combined factors of the children of American baby boomers maturing to college age, the arrival of a larger cadre of second- and third-generation Texas Tech fans, and the growing national sentiment of attending college as a necessary career advancement aspiration. Into the early 2000s, Student Housing at Texas Tech still maintained a surplus, as students could with an additional fee easily reserve a dorm room all to themselves—an unheard-of luxury at Tech today. But with only a 27 percent housing capacity of on-campus housing in 2004, much like the fears of the early 1960s, the sudden influx of students threatened to tip the housing balance and relegate Tech to the dreaded perception of a commuter school. But Tech's housing fortunes would be saved in part by the unintended impacts of none other than the 1970 Lubbock tornado, resulting in what was then the largest privately funded urban redevelopment project in US history.

North Overton had never recovered from the May 11, 1970, tornado. Despite some reinvestment into student-centric low-rent apartments after the disaster, the neighborhood limped into the 1990s when students and the public alike knew not to travel east of Buffalo Beano's—the former bric-a-brac shop at 8th and University Streets—as illegal drug use, theft, and violent crime plagued the area. By the early 2000s, The McDougal Companies—led by Delbert

Detail photograph of Lueders "Sea Trace" stone, also known as "Turkey Track."

Interior watercolor rendering of the northwest commons addition to the Student Union Building, dated 2001 (completed 2003). The unique pentagonal rotunda space became an outstanding and celebrated interior space across campus.

McDougal, and sons (Lubbock mayor) Marc McDougal and Mike McDougal, noted Tech's enrollment trend and saw an opportunity in North Overton's depressed property values. By 2004, over 35 percent of the property in the half-square mile of North Overton had been purchased by McDougal,[13] as the city of Lubbock established a tax increment financing—or TIF—district to focus tax revenue specifically toward street, utility, and beautification improvements destined for the redevelopment. Renamed Overton Park, McDougal established expectations with a two-story Spanish Renaissance–revival bank and office building for City Bank at the corner of University and Glenna Goodacre Boulevard—recently renamed from 8th Street in honor of the award-winning Lubbock artist.

Master planning the Overton Park development began in fall 2004 by PSC and would include a four-star hotel and conference center, mixed-use retail development, garden offices and bungalows, a Walmart, but most important for nearby Texas Tech—over three thousand Class A apartment units—all in short walking distance of campus. Largely completed between 2005 and 2014, students could now choose between such urbanely named venues as the Centre at Overton Park, University Pointe, the Scarlet, and the Village at Overton Park. Street lighting, cedar elm–lined boulevards, and ground-floor shops and restaurants, many clad in the same Perla-blend brick as the rest of Texas Tech, diminished the sense that students were living off campus. Despite developments at Overton Park, enrollment growth required that Housing and Dining match pace with off-campus housing growth, as the BOKA-Powell-designed Grover Murray Hall would come on line in August 2005 as Tech's first traditional residence hall in over thirty-five years.

New additions or buildings such as the Marsha Sharp Center for Student Athletes (2004), the Animal and Food Sciences expansion (2006), the Larry Combest Health and Wellness Center (2006), or the Lanier Professional Development Center expansion to the School

Both the original and redesigned Double T unveiled and incorporated during the 1999-2000 school year.

Looking south toward the Marsha Sharp Center for Student Athletes, completed 2004; MWM Architects.

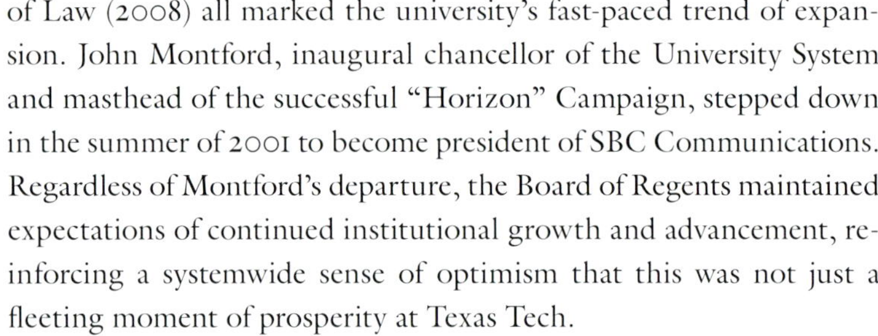

of Law (2008) all marked the university's fast-paced trend of expansion. John Montford, inaugural chancellor of the University System and masthead of the successful "Horizon" Campaign, stepped down in the summer of 2001 to become president of SBC Communications. Regardless of Montford's departure, the Board of Regents maintained expectations of continued institutional growth and advancement, reinforcing a systemwide sense of optimism that this was not just a fleeting moment of prosperity at Texas Tech.

On July 7, 2005, a committee formed by President George W. Bush sought proposals from institutions seeking to become home for the George W. Bush Presidential Library. Despite the Bush family's West Texas ties, little interest had been initially expressed from Montford's replacement—former TTUHSC President David Smith, or Tech President Jon Whitmore—to submit a proposal. Most assumed that Baylor—near the Bush's vacation ranch in Crawford, or SMU—Laura Bush's alma mater—were most favored to win the bid. In March 2005, the *Avalanche-Journal* ran an editorial lamenting the library as a lost opportunity for Tech,[14] but despite Smith and Whitmore committing that Tech would happily donate land for a

South entry façade of the Student Wellness Center, completed 2006; F&S Partners.

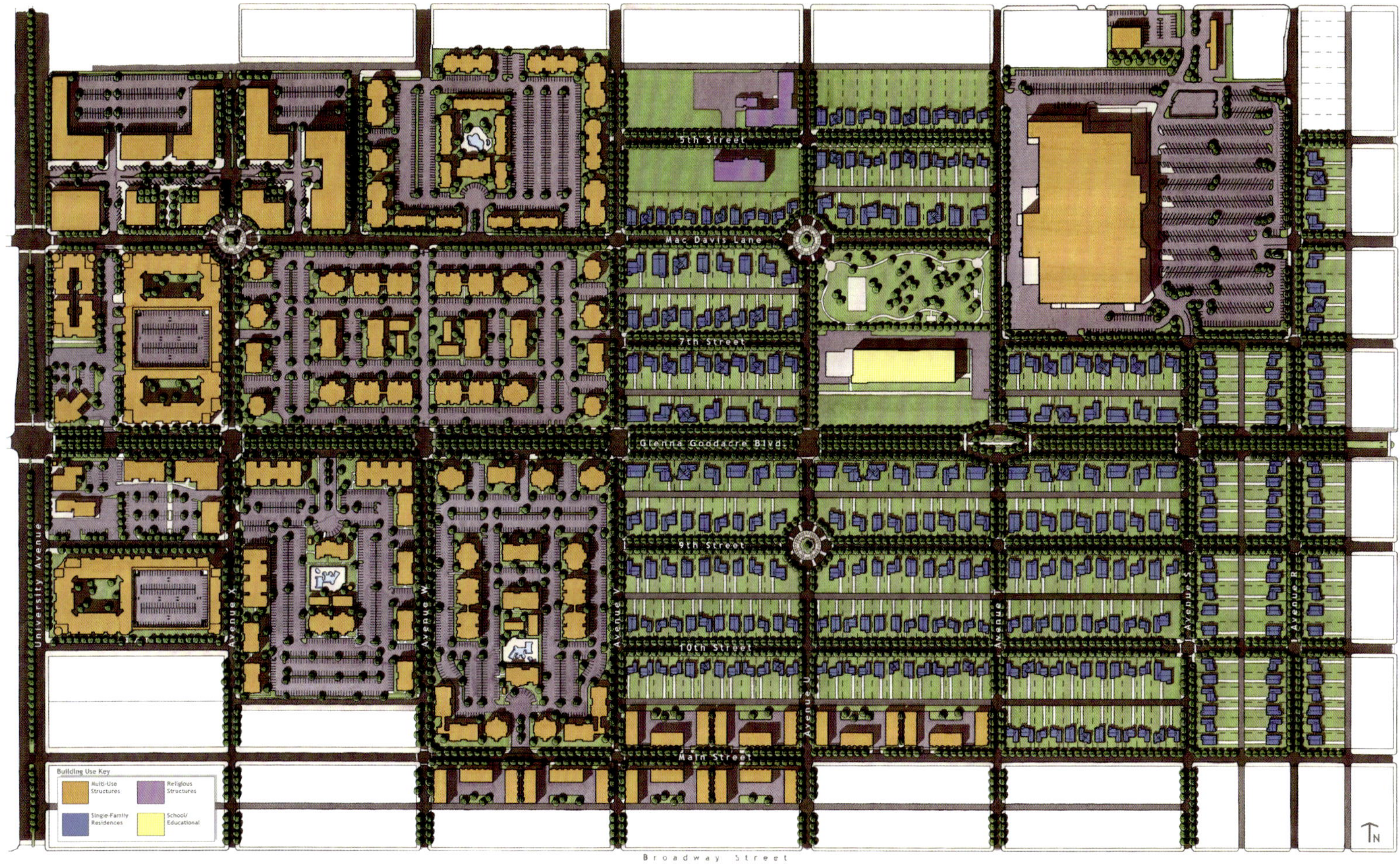

Master Development Plan for the North Overton District of Lubbock, completed early 2005. At the time, redevelopment of Overton Park was the largest privately funded redevelopment project in the United States and would provide thousands of much-needed beds for Tech students located only a short walk from campus.

Library, they remained otherwise apoplectic. Rather, initial interest in pursuing a Bush Library project at Texas Tech emerged from within the Lubbock business community, first championed by Tech Regent Michael Weiss, who later recruited future Lubbock Mayor David Miller and former U.S. Congressman Kent Hance as mastheads championing for the bid.[15] When the city of Midland—hometown of the Bush family—cast their lot into the Tech proposal, pledging a satellite literacy center to be housed at Midland College, a formidable proposal strategy for Tech began to emerge, thus finally dragging Smith and Whitmore into the effort. Mike Ellicott and his team at

East entry façade facing Indiana Avenue, Animal and Food Sciences, completed 2006; Parkhill, Smith & Cooper, architects.

Aerial rendering of the Spanish Renaissance museum option for the unsuccessful Texas Tech University proposal for the George W. Bush Presidential Library, August 2005.

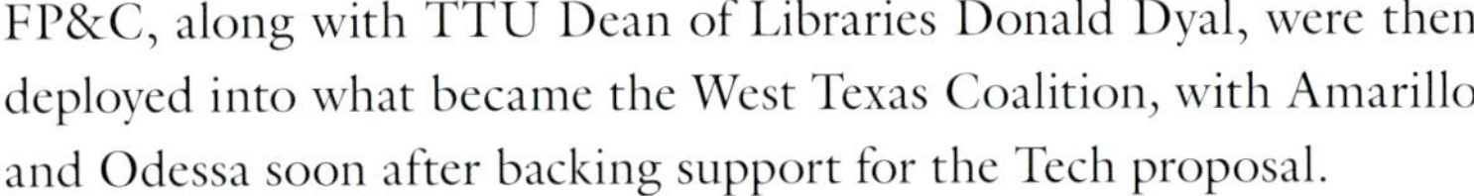

FP&C, along with TTU Dean of Libraries Donald Dyal, were then deployed into what became the West Texas Coalition, with Amarillo and Odessa soon after backing support for the Tech proposal.

It was learned that SMU and Baylor had been working since 2000 and 2001 respectively for their proposals,[16] so for Mike Ellicott, Theresa Drewell, and the FP&C staff, having one month to develop a design for a $300 million presidential library seemed incredulous. FP&C enlisted PSC to support the internal FP&C team in the design and visualization of the proposal. FP&C recommended lands west of the Health Sciences Center, replete with parking, a well water–fed lake, and wildflower gardens in honor of the First Lady's love of Texas native plants. On August 23, Miller and Hance formally unveiled a Spanish Renaissance–revival presidential library proposal at a Lubbock City Council meeting, and the council promptly pledged $50 million in city commitments to the Library.[17] Three weeks later when the Coalition submitted their full proposal, another $50 million had been pledged by other donors, a presage of Hance's fundraising talents. In a last-minute panic, someone suggested that perhaps the Bush Family did not favor Tech's Plateresque style, prompting Ellicott to quickly recruit BOKA-Powell to develop an alternative contemporary design option for the proposal, which accompanied the primary design, along with over seven thousand letters of support from Lubbock-area school children in the leather-bound proposal package shipped to Washington.

The potential of a Bush Library at Tech became more palpable when Miller received a call from Secretary of Commerce Don Evans on October 13 indicating that the Coalition proposal was one of four finalists, along with Baylor, SMU, and the University of Dallas.[18] In November, the Coalition team presented their pitch to the Selection Committee in a short-list interview in Washington ironically led by Kent Hance—the only politician to ever defeat George W. Bush in an election—pressing for the President to select Texas Tech. The team flew back to Lubbock with fingers crossed. In February 2006, as the SMU proposal was at risk of being mired in a lawsuit related to the university's land acquisition plans for the Library, public criticism voiced from Lubbock over the perception of SMU's tight, landlocked site led the Selection Committee to eliminate Tech from the final short list. The action raised speculation in Tech circles that the Library had been SMU's all along, but a public procurement process was required nonetheless. Later in 2006, SMU formally entered negotiation as the sole finalist for the library site.[19] Designed by the Driehaus Award–winning neoclassicist architect Robert A. M. Stern, the George W. Bush Presidential Library and Museum would open at SMU in April 2013.

In a final act of irony, four months after the Bush Library opening, on August 30, SMU welcomed Texas Tech to Gerald R. Ford Stadium in Dallas to open the football season with former President Bush present to make the opening coin toss. Accompanying Bush onto the field that day was the third chancellor of the Texas Tech University System. Tech would win the game 41–23, and while SMU had won a Presidential Library, Tech now had Kent Hance as their system chancellor, who had his own victories to smile about. Hance was close to growing the System Endowment to one billion dollars.

20

ELECTRA

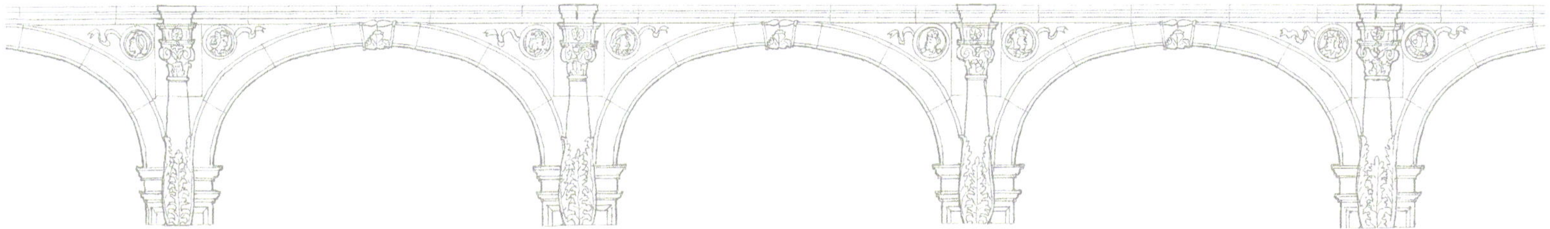

IN GREEK MYTHOLOGY, Electra was the avenging daughter of King Agamemnon, the Argosy patriarch who had fought and won the Trojan War only to return home and be murdered.[1] It was she who inspired renowned Texas rancher W. T. "Pappy" Waggoner and his wife Ella to name their new daughter Electra upon her birth in 1882. Electra was so beautiful that twenty years following her birth, the townsfolk of Waggoner, Texas, opted to rename their town to Electra in her honor—a name that remains today.[2] And though Electra I and her husband were not blessed with a daughter themselves, Electra's brother E. Paul Waggoner and his wife Helen would in 1913 welcome a daughter into the family dynasty who would continue her aunt's proud given name.

If Electra I was beautiful, then her niece Electra II was simply stunning. Legends still persist today that the news of Electra II's dazzling looks spread by her socialite status led Lockheed to name their sleek new twin-engine Model 10 aircraft—the plane Amelia Earhart would disappear in—after her. In the days prior to her wedding to John Biggs, an army officer and son of a well-placed New York family, Electra II was captured for posterity in her wedding dress by noted photographer Edward Steichen for *Vogue* magazine.[3] Between Electra's beauty and Steichen's craft, that portrait remains iconic among the voluminous archives of that magazine's photography even today. The same year that Texas Technological College opened, Electra Waggoner was shipped off to a finishing school in Pennsylvania, followed by a stint at Columbia University. College life only confirmed Electra's disdain for mathematics, and banal business management classes gave her migraines, leading the young Texas socialite to seek some hobby as a release. One friend recommended to Electra: "Take a class in sculpturing, it's divine."[4] In short time, Electra's skills graduated from plastoline to clay, and then to more challenging media such as stone, bronze, and even gold—Electra Waggoner Biggs had finally found her place in the world.

Electra was a prodigy at her craft. One 1934 black marble bust of a woman Waggoner crafted while studying abroad garnered third prize at the Parisian Salon d'Automne, a tremendous accomplishment for a rancher's daughter.[5] Though talented as a sculptress, Electra found

(*Right*) Electra Waggoner Biggs and husband visiting Texas Tech with President Lauro Cavazos sometime in the 1980s.

(*Below*) Tech President Dossie Wiggins speaks to the crowd during the 1950 dedication of the *Will Rogers and Soapsuds* statue at the western end of the Broadway Mall on the Texas Tech campus.

the physical demands of shaping stone and the breathing hazards of fine stone particulates unappealing, leading her to bronze as an alternative. Little did she know her talents would find a unique purpose when on August 15, 1935, an experimental seaplane took off from a lagoon in the hinterlands of Alaska en route to mapping out an air mail route between Alaska and Siberia. At the controls was the adventurous Oklahoman aviator Wiley Post and fellow Oklahoman and friend, the beloved satirist, actor, and writer Will Rogers. Shortly after takeoff, the engine failed, sending the aircraft nose-diving into the shoreline killing Post and Rogers instantly.

Among Rogers's legion of friends, one in particular was left emotionally shell-shocked from the tragedy—Amon Carter. Carter and Rogers were close friends, as Rogers would visit Fort Worth frequently in the 1920s and 1930s. One such 1926 visit involved Rogers and Carter attending Texas Tech's first-ever game against TCU on October 30. Though Tech lost 16–28, the event passed into Red Raider mythos when Rogers personally chipped in $200 for band uniforms remarking he wanted the people of Fort Worth to hear a "real band." [6] The heartbroken Carter went so far as to personally accompany Rogers's body from Seattle to Oklahoma for burial.

Following Rogers's funeral, Carter charged headlong into myriad tributes and memorial projects for his late friend. For the rest of his life, at least three different portraits of Rogers sat or hung prominently in Carter's *Star-Telegram* office. Carter found one ideal project to honor Rogers's memory—a project allowing him to simultaneously continue his favorite hobby of snubbing his hometown's biggest rival—Dallas. Carter would establish a rival Texas Centennial Exposition Fairgrounds in Fort Worth that would eclipse the official state centennial exposition planned in Dallas at present-day Fair Park. Built around the proposed Will Rogers Memorial Center and Coliseum, the unsurprisingly Wyatt Hedrick–designed art deco complex would be built with PWA funding, but not without Franklin D. Roosevelt first extracting some comedic expense from Amon Carter. Lobbying for PWA funds in a 1935 meeting at the White House, Carter, asked to wait outside the Oval Office, overheard Roosevelt asking

Postmaster General James Farley, "Amon wants to build some cowsheds?" a reference to the livestock exhibition component of the fair. A fuming Carter stormed into the Oval Office shouting "It's not a cowshed!"—only to find Roosevelt and Farley laughing over the facetious display at Carter's expense.[7] With an exposition funded with Roosevelt's approval, Carter had another brilliant idea for a lasting monument sited at the entrance to the exposition that would further immortalize Rogers—an idea that led Amon to call his friend, Pappy Waggoner.

Perhaps most remarkable is that the sculpture *Will Rogers and Soapsuds Rides Into The Sunset* would be the first commissions Biggs would ever receive, and at nearly ten feet in height, it was certainly the largest she ever executed. It would require over four years to complete a total of three original castings, which today reside overlooking the tomb of Will Rogers at the National Cowboy Hall of Fame in Claremore, Oklahoma, another at the Will Rogers Coliseum in Fort Worth, and of course the edition that resides at Texas Tech. Biggs later admitted the daunting commission was a "teaching moment," as her initial success in New York and Paris had left her a bit overconfident, as her first test model of *Will Rogers on Soapsuds Rides Into The Sunset* suffered from a range of problems. The horse in her four-foot test model featured misproportioned torso and legs, as well as disparities in scale between Rogers's body and the horse.[8] Biggs even traveled to California and met Soapsuds, still alive and living out his twilight years at a stud farm. But Biggs realized a real-life model was needed to execute her investment casting.

The emboldened New York socialite leveraged some of her status and strolled up to the front door of Gracie Mansion to personally ask Mayor Fiorello La Guardia if she could borrow a police horse. Between Electra's beauty and charm and La Guardia's respect for the late Rogers, La Guardia was only too happy to oblige. So over several weeks in 1938, a New York Police Department Mounted Unit officer reported to the Biggs house on horseback, left the horse to pose, while the officer retreated to a local tavern to enjoy a beer.[9] Having a life-size horse was the solution Biggs needed. By 1939, the bronzes were ready, and in good time with war looming, as it would have been impossible to secure large quantities of bronze from the War Assets Administration for any civilian project. Despite being complete, eight years would pass before Amon was ready to unveil the bronzes, and another three years before the Texas Tech edition was to be unveiled. With a world war raging and Amon's own son being held as a prisoner of war following his capture in North Africa, Carter's attention was obviously elsewhere. It was not until over a decade later, on February 16, 1950, when the Lubbock edition of *Will Rogers and Soapsuds Rides Into the Sunset* was dedicated by Tech President Dossie M. Wiggins before a throng of local residents and Tech students. Carter justified his decision in having the third edition placed at Tech not just because of the 1926 TCU game, but also given that one of Will's favorite ranches to visit in Texas was the Mashed O Ranch west of Lubbock.[10] Unknown to those attending the unveiling that day, the heritage of public art at Texas Tech was born.

One of the lasting legacies of the *Will Rogers and Soapsuds Rides Into the Sunset* bronze has been the long-mentioned siting angle of the sculpture, as the original intent of positioning the bronze riding westward pointed the horse's rear toward downtown Lubbock—perceived as an obvious snub to the city. The popular legend of positioning the statue so that horse's rear geographically points toward Texas A&M University was not the immediate reason, as the bronze was never repositioned after the 1950 dedication, and Tech would not start consistently playing A&M in football for another six years. The legend only became that much more popular following public anger over an act of spray-painting vandalism by an Aggie partisan on Soapsud's rump in the 1960s.

Public art seemed to be the last concern on the Tech administration radar for decades to come. But shortly after the unveiling of the Will Rogers sculpture, another opportunity for public art emerged at Tech. In October 1950, the newly completed West Texas Museum, established since 1929, but having been relegated to an unfinished $30,000 basement revetment built by Bill McMillan northeast of Memorial Circle, finally opened their doors.[11] Museum leadership had intended

Park Place, a bronze collection by Glenna Goodacre, completed and installed 1997.

for a frescoed mural to adorn the new facility's rotunda walls. The idea of a mural originated from William Curry Holden as early as 1936, though it did not quickly gain traction. When finally agreed upon, a selection committee chose New Mexico native Peter Hurd as the muralist for the project.[12]

Hurd was talented, but also a member of an American artistic aristocracy thanks to his father-in-law and mentor N. C. Wyeth. In fact, Hurd's wife—Henriette Wyeth Hurd—assisted her husband in painting would become known as *The Pioneer Mural*—a depiction of fifteen pioneers of various trades and professions at work and life in the Staked Plains. Hurd was eccentric, and an antisocial hermit while at work, as artists were perhaps expected to be, but also devoutly religious and sporting a witty sense of humor. A consummate craftsman who concocted his own pigments from scratch, Hurd assigned them hilariously accurate names, like a tone of cerulean he called "Baboon's Ass Blue." In another bit of humor, Hurd depicted William Curry Holden and himself as historian "Chroniclers" positioned about a campfire in one rotunda fresco, replete with Hurd holding a sketchbook. Assisting Hurd were two other protégés from his New

Headwaters by Larry Kirkland, a granite sculptural fountain situated in the English, Philosophy and Education Courtyard, 2002.

Mexico La Rinconcada studio—John Meigs and Manuel Acosta, who later in life would become well known for his well-recognized portrait of Cesar Chavez. Beginning in late 1953, Hurd and his team set up operations in the museum rotunda, banishing visitors while they completed each character fresco at the rate of one per week.[13] Nolan Barrick recounted how at the end of work each day, he would stroll over to the Museum, often finding Hurd on a chair or scaffold working on a section of wet plaster, jokingly comparing the visits to Pope Julius II entering the Sistine Chapel at night to check on Michelangelo's progress on the ceiling frescoes.[14] Completed in 1954, regrettably, public awareness of *The Pioneer Mural* was diminished somewhat by the departure of the West Texas Museum in 1970 to the new Museum site, while the frescoes themselves became lost in daily transit of students in the rotunda, which had been converted into a glorified corridor to the repurposed Holden Hall.

Square Spiral Arch, a red granite installation by Jesus Moroles, located on the mall between the Math and Science Quadrangle and Carpenter-Wells Clock Tower, 2006.

Artist Peter Hurd adds Tech President Emeritus Clifford Jones by portraiture into one of the Pioneer Mural panels in the rotunda of the Museum of West Texas, sometime in 1953.

DNA, an architectural art glass fabrication by Chinese artist Shan Shan Sheng, situated in the TTUHSC Physicians Medical Pavilion and completed in 2007.

Wind River, a bronze sculpture by Deborah Butterfield, installed outside the west entrance to Grover E. Murray Hall, executed 2004 and installed 2005.

FORTY-THREE YEARS after the unveiling of *The Pioneer Mural,* Regent Jim Sowell and the new First Lady of the new University System—Debbie Montford—found themselves walking along the Engineering Key on an impromptu walk of the campus made at Sowell's invitation. As they walked, Sowell lamented as he pointed out areas that, despite the beautiful architecture of Texas Tech, lacked quality outdoor spaces for students to enjoy.[15] Inspired by a one-time stint as a Tech architecture major and a lasting love for classical architecture, Sowell was convinced that creating a campus environment par excellence—architecture, landscape, and all—was a prerequisite to establishing Texas Tech as a world-class academic institution. At first, Montford was befuddled at why Sowell had invited her for the walk and was telling her all this. But, likewise in the months since her husband's appointment as chancellor, she found herself regularly asking "What does the wife of a University System chancellor do?" [16] Debbie Montford was unaware at that moment that Sowell had just a role in mind for her.

FP&C had already been complaining that recent Tech projects consistently suffered from chronically tight budgets that invariably left low-priority, high-value components like landscaping out of the completed scope. As a result, the physical plant as a whole in the 1990s lacked in landscaping, almost as if Tech possessed scores of "campus bald spots," where many buildings lacked landscaping of any kind. Sowell and Montford observed that public art had proven successful elsewhere as a nodal mechanism in focusing exactly the types of smaller, more intimate outdoor spaces that Sowell was longing for—spaces that were sure to be of value as commons space for students. Only a handful of works of public art had been added to Tech in the thirty-plus years since completion of the Hurd murals. In 1967, a fourteen-foot bronze *Prometheus,* executed by Charles Umlauf, was installed atop a granite plinth in front of the main east façade of the University Library,[17] with Rosie Sandifer's *Freedom of Youth* bronze installed at the Holden Hall courtyard fountain eight years later. In concert with the removal of Bradford Knapp's ill-advised storefront enclosures to the Administration Building salle-porte, a granite-platformed

Four Faces, a bronze collection located in the west courtyard of the J. T. and Margaret Talkington Hall, completed and installed 2013.

bronze of Tech alumnus and former Governor Preston Smith was dedicated south of the Administration Building colonnade in 1985.

Landscaping itself was not inherently expensive—as part of her First Lady duties, Debbie Montford agreed to steward a new "Trees for Tech" program where donors could contribute $1,000 to install an irrigated shade tree somewhere on campus. Tech even reestablished the Arbor Day program in earnest, with John Montford appearing once on horseback as a public relations nod to Bradford Knapp's stunt sixty years earlier. FP&C and the Board of Regents began to distill a clear concept of how to structure future capital projects to ensure that landscaping enhancement did not fall to the wayside, while at the same time including some element of cultural enrichment in the form of public art. Already, Debbie Montford and FP&C were underway coordinating a new stand-alone public art installation to be located north of Human Sciences Building along the Broadway Mall. Titled *Park Place,* the installation consisted of a series of life-size bronze

Stainless steel component of *Texas Rising*, located in the north commons space of West Village Residence Hall Complex, 2014.

figures executed by the nationally renowned artist Glenna Goodacre, depicting a variety of everyday people in a variety of activities. Goodacre, herself a Lubbock native and daughter of Lubbock civic leader Homer Maxey, [18] had designed and executed the Vietnam Women's Memorial in Washington, DC, and would later design the obverse face of the Sacagawea dollar for the US Treasury. *Park Place* changed public preconceptions about public art being unapproachable monumental objects by interspersing her bronzes amidst an undulating brick screen wall, beckoning visitors to sit down or interact with the artwork. Completed in 1997, *Park Place* was instantly hailed a success, and for the Board of Regents, validated the need to codify public art as a prerequisite component of future capital construction within the Texas Tech University System.

Founded in 1998, the Public Art Program established a mandated one percent of FP&C-managed new construction and renovation project budgets be allocated to public artwork,[19] which like architectural commissions would too be separately solicited to artists nationwide and worldwide. Debbie Montford would remain a vital steward and support of the program even beyond the conclusion of her tenure as a regent of the University System in January 2017. Artwork proposals would be evaluated and selected by an appointed University Public Art Committee (UPAC), while the University System likewise selected Cecilia Carter Browne in 2002 as public art manager for FP&C.[20] Whereas the program was dependent upon new capital projects to grow the volume of public art on campus, the massive surge in construction at Tech beginning in the late 1990s proved serendipitous toward a massive and rapid expansion of the Public Art Collection.

Concurrently, the Board of Regents approved a mandated 1 percent budget allocation for landscape enhancement beyond the perfunctory range of turf, site work, and shade trees traditionally included in capital projects. It was also during this same time when the Physical Plant Grounds Maintenance Office finally exorcised decades of taboo opinions from the minds of Tech leadership on the use of groundwater for campus-wide irrigation. Many assumed that Tech's poor groundwater chemistry made well water–served irrigation an ill-advised course of action. But the use of domestic water irrigation had made large-scale landscape enhancement at Texas Tech prohibitively expensive, vexing leadership as high as Chancellor Montford.[21] Using treated well water proved crucial, and when combined with significant outdoor spaces improvements resulting from 1 percent landscape enhancements, drastically changed the face of the Tech campus. More regionally appropriate and drought-tolerant plantings and trees were introduced into xeric landscape designs on new Tech projects that simultaneously reduced strain on both irrigation needs and Tech's limited storm water control system. These strategies worked, as by 2008 Texas Tech had won their first Grand Award by the Professional Grounds Maintenance Society, as well as five Green Star Honor Awards before or since then.[22] Campus beautification today is a quantum distance away from the dusty beginnings of Texas Technological College—as ceremonial planting beds today require the planting of more than twenty-six thousand annuals alone,[23] let alone the hundreds of thousands of perennials that grow in the green spaces of the Lubbock campus.

Public art too swelled rapidly in quantity, value, and national prominence at Texas Tech, as a result of UPAC and the 1-percent mandate. Even the range of artwork across campus varied in fascinating forms, from traditional media like bronze, stone, and finished steel, to stained art glass, ceramics, LED-lit polymers, and even recycled plastic. At times, thought-provoking artwork baffled or even annoyed college deans, donors, and even senior administration, resulting in occasional attempts to thwart or replace selected art commissions on major projects. Likewise, project opportunities suggested for public art by architects, clients, or end users, however well intentioned, often received pushback from the committee given the idea could restrain an artist's exploratory vision for a potential work of art. Both University System and institutional leadership have stalwartly defended this progressive process as crucial to ensuring artistic diversity of works, generating healthy public dialogue, and maintaining the highest quality of each work added. It is undeniable that UPAC's strategy, however stubborn and independently executed it may be, has proven successful. In less than two decades, Tech's Public Art Collection had been named one of the ten finest in the nation by *Public Art Review*,[24] and today, across all University System campuses, the collection consists of over 250 works with an aggregate value of over $12 million. That reputation alone makes public art commissions for the the Texas Tech University System highly sought-after by artists worldwide today. If Lubbock campus expansion proceeds as currently master planned, the value of the Public Art Collection will increase by over 60 percent from its current value by 2025.[25]

21

SAINT CLIFFORD'S CATHEDRAL

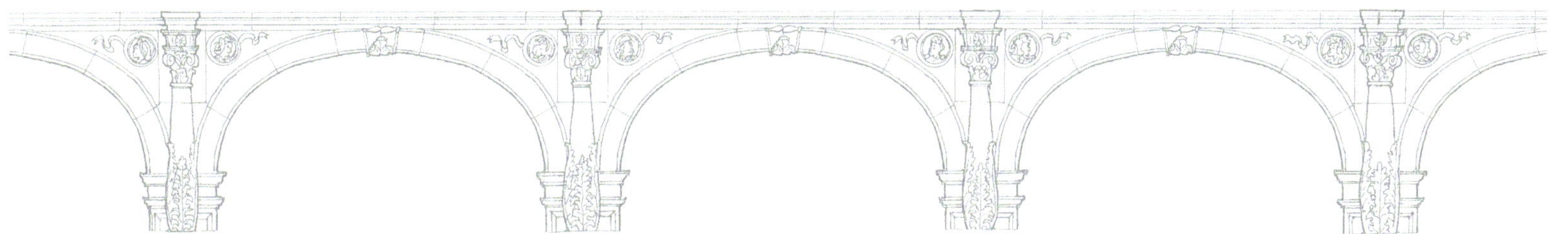

IN THE BLUE ROOM of the Old Arkansas Union in Fayetteville, representatives from six Texas universities and the University of Arkansas took a vote, and just after 10:30 a.m. on May 12, 1956, Southwest Conference Commissioner Howard Grubbs appeared to the press and made a brief statement: "By unanimous vote, Texas Technological College has been invited to appoint a committee to work with a committee of the Southwest Athletic Conference for the express purpose of working out details under which Texas Tech may become a member of the Southwest Conference."[1] Almost instantly in Lubbock, pandemonium erupted on a scale not seen since the ending of the famed 1936 TCU football match. Caught up in the frenzy, President Edward Jones, while lunching at the Pioneer Hotel, was hurried onto the promenade deck to make an announcement to thousands of happy Lubbockites who massed outside the hotel and blocked traffic on Broadway. Texas Tech would be a full member of the conference by 1960, with transitions into conference play for some sports to happen even sooner.

Tech was finally in, and it was not as if Tech had not already tried—six times in fact. In one application in 1937, Tech's acting athletic secretary Wenzel L. "Runt" Stangel ironically submitted the application to the rotating post of the SWC secretary—who at the time was the Rice golf coach—none other than William Ward Watkin. Watkin, who personally knew Stangel in his role as an agriculture professor, had the awkward task of denying acceptance to the college he had recently designed.[2] In 1956, Tech's entry into the SWC was not without sizeable hurdles for the still small West Texas school to overcome. Only a month before the Fayetteville announcement, the city of Lubbock had completed the Lubbock Municipal Coliseum and Auditorium[3]—a definite upgrade in basketball facilities that the SWC likely took note of. But athletics luxuries ended there. Dewitt Weaver—Tech's dual football coach and athletics director could not even make a long-distance phone call without first getting permission from Marshall Pennington at the Administration Building.[4] The Red Raiders were joining a conference where even the smaller institutions

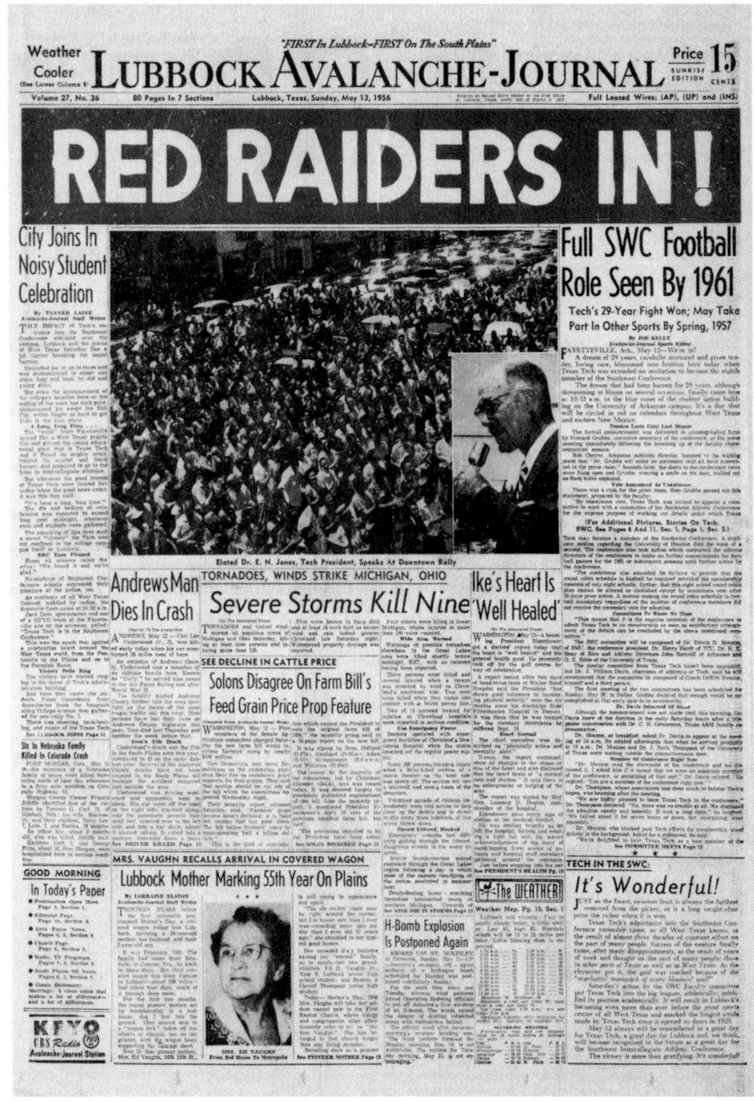

Weather Cooler (See Lower Column 8)

"FIRST In Lubbock—FIRST On The South Plains"

LUBBOCK AVALANCHE-JOURNAL

Price 15 CENTS SUNRISE EDITION

Volume 27, No. 36 | 80 Pages In 7 Sections | Lubbock, Texas, Sunday, May 13, 1956 | Full Leased Wires: (AP), (UP) and (INS)

RED RAIDERS IN!

City Joins In Noisy Student Celebration

Full SWC Football Role Seen By 1961

Tech's 29-Year Fight Won; May Take Part In Other Sports By Spring, 1957

Elated Dr. E. N. Jones, Tech President, Speaks At Downtown Rally

Andrews Man Dies In Crash

TORNADOES, WINDS STRIKE MICHIGAN, OHIO

Severe Storms Kill Nine

Ike's Heart Is 'Well Healed'

SEE DECLINE IN CATTLE PRICE

Solons Disagree On Farm Bill's Feed Grain Price Prop Feature

MRS. VAUGHN RECALLS ARRIVAL IN COVERED WAGON

Lubbock Mother Marking 55th Year On Plains

H-Bomb Explosion Is Postponed Again

TECH IN THE SWC:

It's Wonderful!

GOOD MORNING

In Today's Paper

The WEATHER

KFYO CBS Radio

May 1956 headlines announcing Tech entry into the Southwest Conference.

Construction of Jones Stadium is delayed due to a fire in the east bleachers during concrete forming that destroys most of the east side.

had large stadiums. Rice, with an enrollment half the size of Texas Tech, had recently built a two-tier seventy-thousand-seat stadium that would one day host a Super Bowl. Suddenly, Jones Stadium appeared more as a liability for the program's entry into SWC play than the gleaming new complex opened only nine years earlier. To ensure equitable conference-wide gate revenue, the SWC stipulated that Texas Tech must have a stadium with a capacity of forty thousand seats or more before the Red Raiders could enter conference play. Tech administrators agreed to the prerequisite seating demands, but leadership was left with a head-scratcher. Nolan Barrick's 1957 Master Plan for the college, really a laundry list of upcoming projects slated for construction, included a cursory vision for Jones Stadium expansion with enclosed north and south end zones, replete with cantilevered upper-deck seating tiers, much like the types of upper-deck expansions that the University of Tennessee, LSU, and TCU were then

The west bleachers and press box to the Clifford B. and Audrey Jones Stadium, shortly before opening, November 1947.

Extract from the 1957 Texas Technological College Master Plan illustrating a financially infeasible superstructural expansion to Jones Stadium.

undertaking. But the question remained one of money, as the college had barely scraped together funds to make the original 1947 stadium a reality, and despite strong attendance and gate revenue with the existing stadium, Tech had barely done more than add a four-section seating expansion in 1953. They needed a solution that achieved the seating count within the college's meager budgetary resources, and in another irony of Texas Tech history, it just so happened that a Texas A&M alumnus had a solution in mind.

RED RAIDER FOOTBALL in the 1940s had few standing traditions, but one unwanted tradition was that Tech's football stadium could always be counted on to catch fire. Such was the fate of old Tech Field, which lost about six hundred seats in the northwest corner of its wood-framed horseshoe in an April 1944 fire.[5] The blaze was thankfully stopped before destroying the horseshoe outright, but signaled to Tech leadership that it was time for a new home. As President Emeritus, Clifford Jones's role did contain some major responsibilities, and between 1944 and 1946, while Jones fought bouts of angina, the former president also fundraised for the new stadium. The initial $396,700 new stadium budget was anchored by a $100,000 trust personally bequeathed by Clifford and Audrey Jones. Unfortunately, the project would run almost $100,000 over budget, requiring the Tech Board to issue revenue bonds not once but twice to finance the project.[6] Even with the overage, the new stadium was a spartan design—built of exposed ferroconcrete and largely devoid of architectural ornament.

In a shift from the usual commissioning of Wyatt Hedrick, Tech hired Haynes & Kirby as stadium architects, with the new engineering firm of Parkhill, Smith & Cooper for the project, which included a field house and offices under the southeast visitor bleachers.

Bill McMillan (top right), who was a prolific hunter, with wife and son, as they depart for a safari abroad.

Based upon McMillan's expansion scheme, a preliminary stadium rendering is developed by Nolan Barrick's office for the College Board of Directors' consideration prior to the addition of Hedrick's office to the project, 1958.

Consisting of ten sections of approximately 2,200 seats each including a west press box and a six-row set of steel overflow bleachers running along the north and south end zones, Haynes & Kirby had proposed a series of cast-in-place concrete ogee trims and water tables to the stadium's concrete columns to provide some minimal salute to the architecture of the campus, only to have the details value engineered out due to cost overruns. In the end, there was barely even a budget for a perimeter fence, let alone any paving on site whatsoever when construction began in March 1947.

While framing the concrete superstructure, wood coffer forms had been set in place by the contractor, Oldt Construction, and a concrete pour was underway on a windy June 26, when an uncontrollable fire broke out in the east bleacher formwork. Firefighters were helpless in combatting the blaze, and three of the five east sections were destroyed.[7] Tech administration was forced to announce that the already fire-scarred Tech Field would remain the Red Raiders' home venue until the delayed construction completion date in November. It was not until the final 1947 matchup, a November 29, 14 to 6 victory over Hardin-Simmons, that the Red Raiders were able to baptize the new facility with a victory and celebrate their third Border Conference football championship. At the game, Tech fans gave President Emeritus Jones a standing ovation as President Whyburn announced the new venue would be named the Clifford B. and Audrey Jones Stadium.[8]

ONE FALL FRIDAY EVENING in 1956, Bill McMillan was at Jones Stadium watching a Lubbock High School matchup dressed in the sailor-like football referee uniforms of the day as a part of a backup officials crew. Seated above McMillan was Agricultural Dean

The first section of east bleachers moves uneventfully at the hands of engineers and technicians from the Indiana firm LaPlant-Adair, 1959.

Wenzel L. "Runt" Stangel and his wife. McMillan, usually a rowdy sort at football games, sat still and quiet for over an hour with a painful, contemplative look on his face as he stared into space. Stangel, who knew McMillan well, started to get concerned, and finally tapped on McMillan's shoulder asking, "Bill, are you alright?" McMillan turned around; his blank stare gone, blurting out, "I think I know how we can expand Jones Stadium!" [9] As the Lubbock High Westerners played on that evening, McMillan excitedly outlined for Stangel and his wife a bold idea of how he thought Jones Stadium could be expanded without breaking the bank.

Though a Texas A&M graduate and letterman, spending the last thirty years in Lubbock had made McMillian as partisan a Red Raider

Circa-1959 rendering of the west press box expansion and improvements; Wyatt C. Hedrick, architects.

as any. Recalling a trade journal article he had read recently on an eight-story telephone exchange building that was moved several city blocks in New York City,[10] McMillan proposed first cutting the building frame of the east bleachers of Jones Stadium from its foundations and then using hydraulic jacking to push the structure slowly to its new destination. Once moved, a bowl would then be excavated to add as many as fifteen thousand new seats situated around a new subgrade field. It was a radical scheme, but saving seven sections of existing ferroconcrete risers and building expansion seating into an earthen bowl certainly seemed a cheaper proposition. McMillan had never worked on such a project before, but the old Aggie practically chained himself to his drafting desk over the next several weeks, slaving over a design for making the Jones Stadium expansion possible. Little did he know that he had only a short time to live.

Barrick too had never worked on such a project before, but he realized the college's funding limitations and thus objectively entertained McMillan's concept when President Jones approached him about it.

Excavation of the lower bowl continues as construction of the west press box and new pair-tower light standards completes to the west, early 1960.

An expanded Jones Stadium opens for the start of the 1960 season on September 17 against West Texas State College, winning 38 to 14.

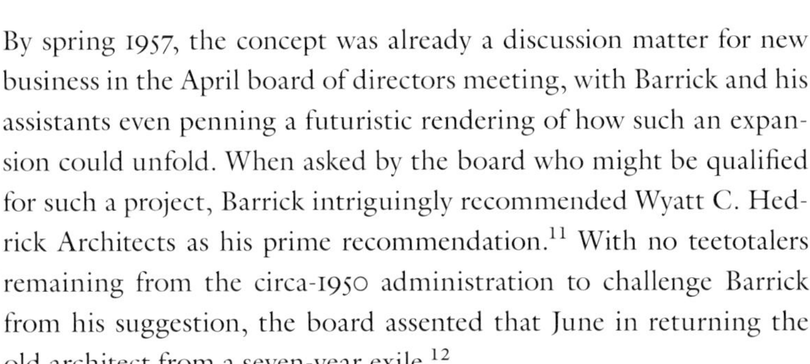

By spring 1957, the concept was already a discussion matter for new business in the April board of directors meeting, with Barrick and his assistants even penning a futuristic rendering of how such an expansion could unfold. When asked by the board who might be qualified for such a project, Barrick intriguingly recommended Wyatt C. Hedrick Architects as his prime recommendation.[11] With no teetotalers remaining from the circa-1950 administration to challenge Barrick from his suggestion, the board assented that June in returning the old architect from a seven-year exile.[12]

Barrick, Dewitt Weaver, and Pennington traveled to Fort Worth to consult with Hedrick on the expansion scheme in April, meeting in Hedrick's spacious wood-paneled office. Hedrick's burled pecan desk was almost devoid of accoutrements, though Barrick was fascinated with a row of electric buttons that ran along the edge of the desk.[13] When Hedrick pushed one button, instantly a secretary appeared with sketch paper and a red China pencil, signaling that the Lord Calvert fiasco had not hurt the architect too badly. Hedrick proposed teaming with Parkhill, Smith & Cooper as local civil engineer, given their familiarity with the original stadium, while also suggesting LaPlant-Adair of Indianapolis for the hydraulic relocation of the east bleachers. LaPlant-Adair was the obvious choice—they were the talk of the engineering world when three years earlier they moved the captured World War II German U-boat U-505 from Lake Michigan across Lakeshore Drive onto the front doorstep of the Museum of Science and Industry in Chicago.[14] Surely, sections of a concrete stadium were easier to move a few hundred feet than a German U-boat?

Back in Lubbock, unaware of Hedrick's commission, Bill McMillan had dreamed up a monster. Having developed a plan of mounting

Preliminary expansion concept rendering developed by MWM Architects in 1997 for the "Horizon" Campaign.

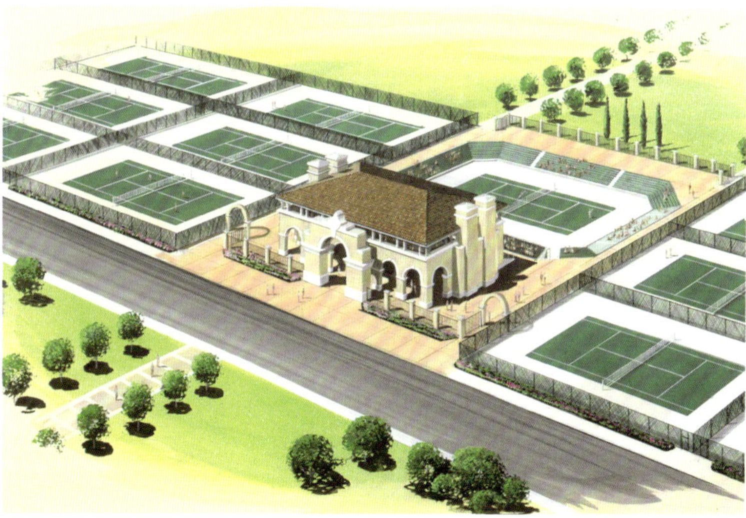

Included in visioning imagery for the "Horizon" Campaign was an MWM Architects preliminary design for the new Tennis Center.

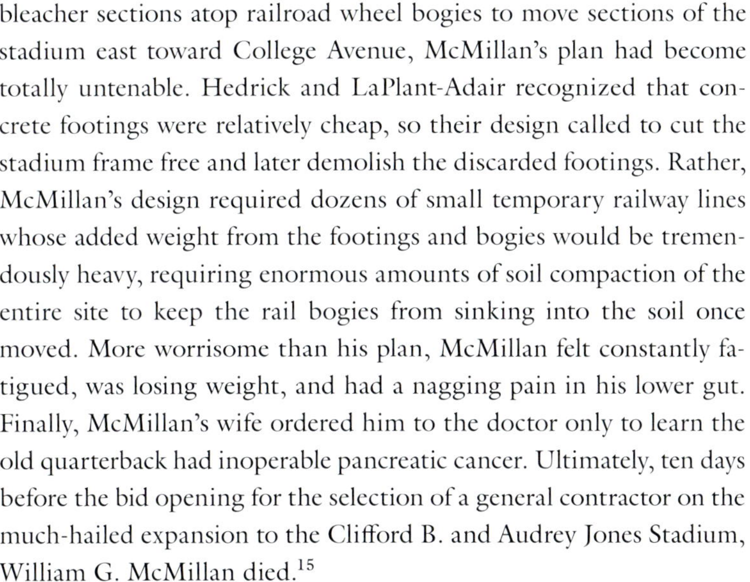

bleacher sections atop railroad wheel bogies to move sections of the stadium east toward College Avenue, McMillan's plan had become totally untenable. Hedrick and LaPlant-Adair recognized that concrete footings were relatively cheap, so their design called to cut the stadium frame free and later demolish the discarded footings. Rather, McMillan's design required dozens of small temporary railway lines whose added weight from the footings and bogies would be tremendously heavy, requiring enormous amounts of soil compaction of the entire site to keep the rail bogies from sinking into the soil once moved. More worrisome than his plan, McMillan felt constantly fatigued, was losing weight, and had a nagging pain in his lower gut. Finally, McMillan's wife ordered him to the doctor only to learn the old quarterback had inoperable pancreatic cancer. Ultimately, ten days before the bid opening for the selection of a general contractor on the much-hailed expansion to the Clifford B. and Audrey Jones Stadium, William G. McMillan died.[15]

McMillan's funeral at the Lubbock Memorial Cemetery was a grand affair. All of Lubbock's finest were in attendance to pay tribute to the burly old Aggie who had, quite literally, grown up with Texas Tech since its beginning. McMillan's best friend and scion academician of Texas Tech, William Curry Holden, was a pallbearer. One of the grandest floral tributes at the gravesite was a bilious wreath of red roses with a memento, "With Deepest Sympathies—Wyatt C. Hedrick," in thanks to the man who had a hand in returning Hedrick to one of his landmark clients. The *Lubbock Evening Journal* declared McMillan, " [the] ingenious man whose proposed idea helped to make the expansion of Jones Stadium a reality." [16]

LaPlant-Adair's engineering chief Kenneth Adair proposed an expansion plan that may have loosely resembled Bill McMillan's vision, but vastly simplified. Each of the seven seating sections would be cut into individual units, columns would be saw-cut from their foundations, secured to a temporary roller assembly, and then moved over timber blocking to the new location to be attached to a new set of identical foundation footings being poured farther east. Then the original spread footings would be excavated and demolished. The general scheme was so simple, it begged to wonder why anyone thought it was so revolutionary to begin with.

As time for the east bleacher relocation neared, dissent toward the radical plan began to surface, as public speculation and rumor mongering led to questioning if the concrete tiers could survive a 150-foot move. Nolan Barrick later remarked that much of the commotion may have emerged from a disapproving structural engineering professor in the Engineering Division, "an old Chicago steel bridge man who had no faith in concrete," Barrick later recalled.[17] Thankfully, Athletics or Tech administration were neither interested in dissent or delaying LaPlant-Adair's schedule. Tracks, blocking, and rollers were set, and on March 15, 1959, Seating Section O—today known as Section 119—was cut from its foundations and braced to move. Hundreds of students and locals arrived half-expecting to see a spectacular collapse of concrete onto the east stadium parking lot.[18] A flagman signaled to engage the hydraulic pistons, and at first it looked as if nothing was happening. A shadow began to appear at the edge of the adjacent section—the section *was* indeed moving. But following a shift of only six inches, the flagman halted work, then turned to the assembled audience and said, "That's it, folks. This was just a test to make sure everything is working." Someone in the audience shouted, "Is that all?," and within minutes the deflated crowd dispersed.[19] Though a slow process, within a matter of months, all seven of the East Bleacher sections had been moved. The McMillan plan had worked.

With the most radical phase of the project complete, the most time-consuming component of the stadium expansion now began—the excavation of well over a million cubic yards of earth to form a below-grade bowl with an additional 14,500 seats for Jones Stadium. As excavation continued, work began on a steel superstructure for the new west press box, the first in the Southwest Conference to feature an elevator. The *Toreador* featured weekly updates on stadium progress with front-page photographs purposely taken in an exaggerated

Rendering of the West Stadium Expansion to Jones SBC Stadium (now Jones AT&T Stadium), 2001 (completed 2003); Ellerbe-Becket Architects, with MWM architects.

portrait view to make the new press box superstructure appear gigantic.[20] New athletics offices were constructed south of the bowl, clad in a nondescript modernist aluminum-framed grid of glass and metal panels, which signaled the aesthetic disconnect that still existed then between large athletics venues and the general architectural style of a university campus. With a capacity 1,500 seats greater than the SWC mandate, the newly expanded Jones Stadium opened to a 38 to 14 win on September 17, 1960, in a nonconference match against West Texas State College.[21] Nolan Barrick would come to regret having had an elevator installed in the Jones press box, as he along with the Physical Plant Office would be plagued for years to come with constant servicing requests to fix the elevator's flaky traction drive.[22]

OVER THREE DECADES LATER, Texas Tech's invitation to join the Big XII Conference was as much an opportunity to leap into a new realm of national athletics prominence as it was for the university to reevaluate Jones Stadium's future. Tech now entered a conference

Circa-2014 aerial photograph looking north at Jones AT&T Stadium showing north seating, colonnade, and audio/visual improvements.

whose competitors boasted even larger venues than Tech's old SWC foes, and consistently filled them to capacity. Since the 1958–1960 expansion, little had changed at the Jones Stadium. A SWC ban of live mascots on the field in the late 1960s ended the colorful tradition of the Masked Rider galloping up and around the concrete Double T installed above the north end zone. A 1972 seating expansion to the north bowl expanded seating to forty-seven thousand and resulted in installing a perimeter retaining wall around the field as Texas Tech entered its AstroTurf era of playing surfaces. A concrete block-clad ticket office and Letterman's Lounge was added overlooking the north end zone in 1979, followed by a south end zone office expansion in 1991. Even Bill McMillan's son—Bill Jr.—added a distinctive moniker to the stadium's west façade with a two-story neon Double T donated in 1989 to complement the old 1938 historic Double T neon sign that had been installed on the east side.[23] It was during Tech's transition into the Big XII that a national trend was underway—a bevy of major college football stadium renovations and additions—many of which highlighted efforts to transform stadiums into large-scale manifestations of their institution's broader architectural style.

Following completion of the 1997 Master Plan, John Montford had enlisted FP&C to develop a simple but persuasive glossy visioning document that focused on the two-dozen capital projects envisioned

Photograph of the north entry façade to the Sports Performance Center; Gensler, architects, completed 2017.

in the master plan as centerpiece to Montford's "Horizon" Campaign. FP&C enlisted MWM Architects—successor to longtime Tech design firm staple SRMJ—to rapidly develop an expansion vision for the stadium, as well as Dan Law Field and a host of other new athletics venues. With only a week-and-a-half available, MWM partner Jeff Whitaker and architect Stephen Faulk frantically churned out a fleet of renderings for the vision document, including a stadium expansion that increased seating to a 60,500 capacity, added forty suite boxes, and five hundred indoor club seats.[24] MWM also hurriedly developed visions for a Spanish Renaissance–clad expansion to Dan Law Field, and similar visions for the new Women's Softball and Tennis facilities.

Continuing into 1998, Athletics Director Gerald Myers further raised expectations in tasking MWM and Atlanta-based sports design magnate Ellerbe Becket to further master plan stadium expansion to an eventual eighty-thousand-seat capacity.[25] The design team quickly realized that the Jones Stadium site had become significantly constrained, as an early south stadium expansion scheme was tabled when it was realized how critical 6th Street—the roadway between Jones Stadium and the Indoor Practice Facility—had become to campus utilities and drainage. Engineers projected that rerouting utilities away from 6th Street alone would cost over $30 million. Rather, Tech focused on fundraising for much-needed general renovations to the stadium, as well as the West Stadium expansion championed in MWM's inspiring 1997 "Horizon" Campaign rendering. Even Chancellor Montford dived into the effort, inviting former Board Chairman Ed Whitacre to lunch at the Lubbock Club in 2000 specifically to recruit Whitacre's company Southwestern Bell—recently renamed SBC—as a flagship donor to the project. Even Montford, the adroit politician, was apprehensive of asking his former board boss for a $20 million gift, but when he pitched Whitacre, the CEO said yes. After lunch, as the two made their way to the elevator, Montford had to hold his jaw shut when Whitacre quipped, "You know, that went well. I was worried you were going to ask for thirty million, and I wasn't going to give any more than twenty-five."[26]

With concourse renovations underway to what had been renamed Jones SBC Stadium, the Ellerbe Becket/MWM design team charged ahead with design of the West Stadium expansion. Even the western stadium expanse was not without challenges, as Boston Avenue, which bound Jones Stadium, was on Tech property, but the city retained usage easements that had to be relinquished prior to construction. To accommodate an entire club level of seating plus three additional stories of suites, the west stadium expansion would stand at over 120 feet tall with a ground floor colonnade whose arches alone were thirty feet high—massively taller than the vision portrayed in MWM's initial 1997 rendering. The main club level access lobby consisted of a bank of escalators and a two-story stained glass Double T installed high over the curtain wall of the main entrance. The Spanish Renaissance exterior would be the tallest application of the style in Texas Tech history. But the added cost of Plateresque motifs onto the stadium expansion did not sit well with everyone involved.

At one design presentation to Tech leadership in early 2001, Ellerbe Becket and MWM representatives presented the façade design concept

The sheer scale of the Sports Performance Center interior volume can be seen here with both a regulation football field and track seen side-by-side.

to attendees. Following the presentation, Coach Mike Leach paused with a pained look on his face, and then dryly announced, "All those doo-dads on the stadium won't make a better football team." [27] To break the awkward silence that followed, Chancellor Montford asked, "Coach, what do you mean?" Leach explained that regardless of the impressive design of the proposed West Stadium expansion, his football team languished in outdated locker rooms and support spaces, and that improving those spaces would accomplish far more for recruiting and team building value than any amount of Plateresque-revival folderol. A compromise emerged, where $10 million would be set aside from the $90 million stadium budget to design and build a separate Football Training Facility nearby that met Leach's needs. Aside from a $1 million scope increase requested by the Athletics Department for a hydrotherapy space in the new training facility, the Ellerbe Becket/MWM kept the entire project within budget, and the renovated stadium opened to a ribbon cutting on the afternoon of August 30, 2003, only hours before kickoff in a Red Raider win against SMU.[28]

IN THE SUMMER OF 2013, motorists driving on US Highway 87 south of Lubbock scratched their heads at the sight of semitrailers hauling gigantic tortilla chip–shaped masses of precast concrete the size of houses northward to Lubbock. The panels—each half-arcature was eleven feet tall simply to fit under highway overpasses—were destined for a massive new precast concrete colonnade under construction that would encircle the north end of the stadium,[29] yet another expansion to what had been renamed Jones AT&T Stadium after SBC's merger with the communications giant in 2005. Tech had steadily continued with a series of renovations, additions, and upgrades to the Jones into the late 2000s and beyond, including retiring the crowned AstroTurf field in 2006 in lieu of a more flat-profile "Air Raid" friendly field-turf surface, which was surrounded by a brick-and-stone façade installed over the old circa-1972 retaining wall. Following a momentous 2008 football season, Lee Lewis Construction began construction on a $34.9 million East Stadium expansion designed in partnership between Heery International of Atlanta and MWM, which increased the total complement of suites to eighty-nine and itself included another club level similar to the West addition.[30] In a partnership with country club management conglomerate ClubCorp, Texas Tech opened the Texas Tech Club on the east club level following the opening of the East expansion for the 2010 football season, which provided year-round dining options for members, in addition to further suites and club-level seating. Additional upper-tier and loge seating added in 2009 and again in 2013 would expand seating capacity to more than sixty thousand spectators.

But perhaps it was the installation of an $11 million jumbotron and sound system[31]—a system over five times the size of the previous board, which resided over the new north end zone colonnade that symbolically reflected a new era for the Jones that was logarithmically ahead of the stadium's humble beginnings over sixty-five years earlier. A typical gameday experience now included fireworks fired from atop the jumbotron following Red Raider touchdowns, complemented by rows of vividly colorful LED ribbon displays. By August 2014, an aggregate of $145.8 million in expansion and renovation work had been completed to the Jones over a fifteen-year period, while that same year, Athletics Director Kirby Hocutt announced plans for an even more ambitious $185 million expansion plan for Jones AT&T Stadium, nearby facilities, and other Red Raider athletics venues.[32]

J. Fred Bucy's two worst fears were realized in 2015—first on New Year's Eve as Lubbock received over ten inches of snowfall—the weight of which tore open a seam in the old Indoor Practice Facility roof, promptly collapsing it that night. The anticlimactic disaster was just as soon forgotten as four months later, the entirety of the old Bubble was demolished to make room for a massive new Gensler-designed Sports Performance Center extension to the Football Training Facility as a home to both football and track programs at Texas Tech. Bucy's other fear would come to light as the insistence that the core campus remain visible from Jones Stadium was dashed thanks to the Sports Performance Center's 185-foot-tall dynamic curving roof,[33] certainly an outlier curiosity in Spanish Renaissance architecture, but a feature that would easily catch the attention of any high school recruit. The $48 million facility—part of the recently renamed Edward E. Whitacre Jr. Athletic Complex—included a separate indoor running track and space for two full tandem football fields, that when connected to the existing Football Training Facility made the complex the single largest footprint of any building on the Tech dampus, save the main HSC Complex. For an institution whose Athletics Department at one time had to ask permission to make a long-distance phone call, Texas Tech had come very far.

22

SPANREN

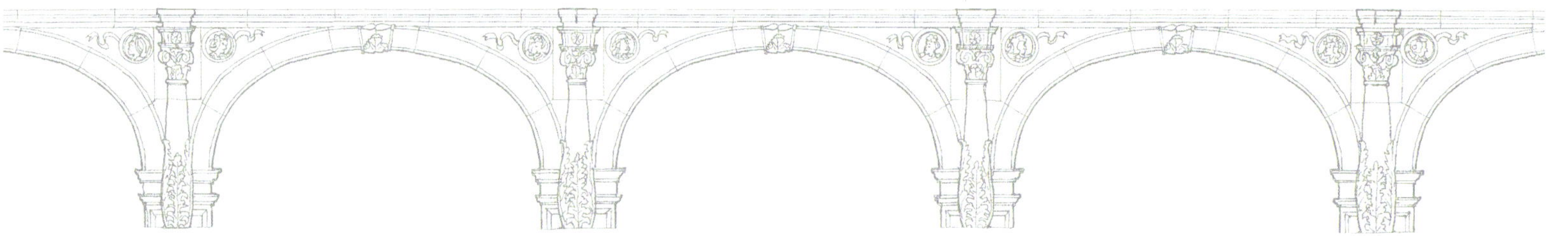

On the afternoon of Tuesday, December 3, 2002, Associate Dean Dr. Donald Clancy hurried into the final semester lecture of his graduate managerial accounting class late, but glowing. After apologizing for his tardiness he announced: "We have just finished the kickoff meeting for the new Jerry S. Rawls College of Business Administration! And soon, we hope to have a new home for this great college." [1] By "soon," Clancy meant nine years' time. With a nearly $70 million price tag—when adjusted for inflation was more money than had been spent on construction in the first twenty years of Texas Tech's existence—it was simply the most complex academic new facility the university had ever undertaken to build.

The year 2001 had proven to be a momentous year for the College of Business Administration with the appointment of Houston oil executive Allen T. McInnes as dean of the college, and the announcement that Jerry S. Rawls had donated $25 million to the college, spurring the rechristening of the Jerry S. Rawls College of Business Administration. It was during this bullish time that McInnes decided that the circa-1969 "BA" building was far outdated and incapable of serving the surging college in the twenty-first century. Despite having nearly one-in-six Tech students enrolled in the college in a more than two-hundred-thousand-square-foot complex, nearly a quarter of the classrooms sat obsolete and unused. Faux-walnut plastic laminate paneling in hallways was peeling away, and restrooms consistently stank. In late 2001, FP&C selected Boston atelier Goody Clancy & Associates (GCA) as design architect for a new home for Business Administration with PSC as local architect-of-record for the project. Following Clancy's late 2002 announcement, two years would pass as the college focused on fundraising before the PSC/GCA team was released into site analysis, programming, and schematic design work for a new facility. FP&C leadership viewed COBA—the project's popular acronym moniker—as an excellent opportunity to infill new construction into more sparse zones of the campus core as intended in the 1997 Master Plan. Early concepts prepared by GCA proposed demolishing the unimpressive single-story CASNR Annex and Range and Wildlife Building located north of 15th Street, which would allow

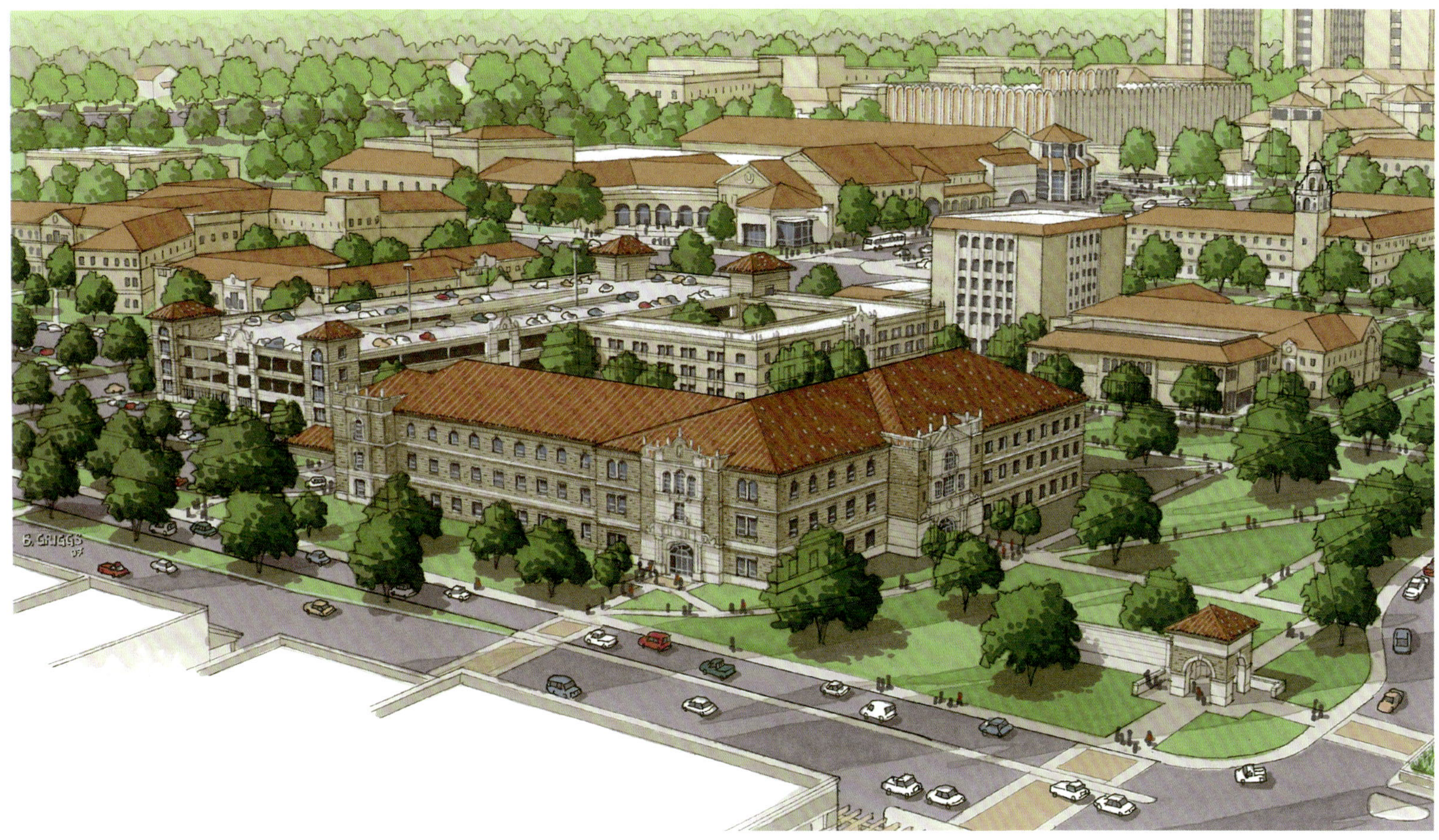

The Rawls College of Business and FP&C had experimented with multiple potential project sites between 2004 and 2008, including the potential demolition of Weeks Hall along the Broadway campus entrance, as seen in this rendering.

the new COBA to bound the yet undefined western campus mall proposed in the 1997 Master Plan.

McInnes roiled at what he perceived as the university's premiere college being buried deep within the campus core in early siting concepts, lamenting that VIPs and potential students would get lost just trying to find the building. Rather, COBA leadership proposed alternative sites including the grounds south of the Merket Alumni Center or the site northwest of the 19th Street–Indiana Avenue intersection. In time, FP&C added the site of the then-unused Weeks Hall dormitory astride the Broadway campus entrance to the discussion, but none of the options seemed to satisfy all stakeholders. Between 2005 and 2007, the project hovered in site selection purgatory while the College of Business continued fundraising.

In late 2007, a potential compromise appeared. Tech was due

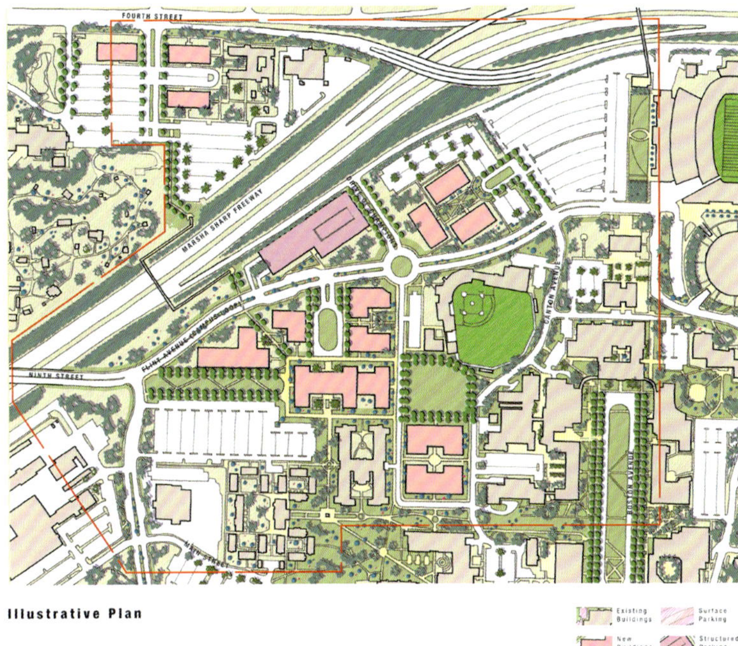

The North Campus Gateway master plan would establish the location of the Rawls College of Business, as well as any future academic building expansion in the area.

to decommission and demolish the old Quack Shack—the former SRMG-designed Thompson-Gaston Hall student clinic and former dormitory located southwest of the Lubbock Municipal Coliseum. Work was underway on Phase II of the Marsha Sharp Freeway nearby, with Texas Department of Transportation (TxDOT) planning to maintain a prominent eastbound offramp access point onto campus from the new freeway at the nearby Drive of Champions. When BOKA-Powell's Grover Murray Residence Hall was completed in 2005, the H-shaped complex did not provide the terminus to the proposed western pedestrian mall as originally envisioned in the 1997 Master Plan, but rather sat astride the mall axis. FP&C quickly convened a regional master planning team with PSC, former Sasaki planner Robert Sabbatini, and COBA and university representatives to plan what became the North Campus Gateway Precinct Plan. Completed in April 2008, the 130-acre plan amended the 1997 Master Plan by establishing how the Drive of Champions, 9th Street, and surrounding facilities could define what had long been regarded as a campus backdoor, as the Rawls College of Business would now become that front door. Concurrently, the new COBA Building would also serve as the terminus for the north-south pedestrian mall proposed in the 1997 Master Plan.

Based on the North Campus Gateway Plan, GCA and PSC charged ahead with facility design, unaware that the evolved product of the C-shape building plan that emerged from Watkin's original vision for cloistered courtyards had truly become a commonplace building footprint at Tech. COBA's plan was no more than two feet different in any dimension from the final post-1951 building footprint for the Administration Building. COBA had the distinction of being Tech's first LEED™ gold-certified sustainable facility as established by the US Green Building Council, featuring a range of sustainable strategies that signaled the broader national transformation in design and construction technology underway. In the summer of 2009, Thompson-Gaston Hall was abated and demolished so that 1,600 tons of her concrete and masonry could be pulverized into recycled aggregate for new concrete poured for the new building, while the steel superstructure and rebar were recycled and recast for reuse as well. GCA and PSC's design represented a fascinating compromise between an externally traditional Spanish Renaissance–inspired façade with a south courtyard that was comparably contemporary in appearance, replete with butt-jointed curtain wall glazing and sleek anodized sunshade devices over windows. COBA was the largest new academic building built at Tech in decades at over 147,000 gross square feet in total. Hailed by COBA leadership as the "Big Dig," over two years would pass before the Rawls College of Business was completed, along with a separate $20 million renovation to the existing BA Building, which would become home to the newly renamed College of Media and Communication in August 2012.

When completed, COBA represented a quantum shift in academic

North entrance façade, Jerry S. Rawls College of Business Adminstration; Parkhill, Smith & Cooper, with Goody Clancy architects, 2012.

classroom design at Texas Tech as compared to the fleet of older Tech academic facilities built three or four decades earlier. LED doorway displays provided students the days' class schedule for each classroom. The building could host its own dinner engagements and receptions from the new Dennis P. McCoy Conference Center—a fireplace-ensconced first-floor commons area enclosable through the use of stowable mahogany-paneled operable partitions. When completed in December 2011, the very nature of the facility reflected a new era at Texas Tech. National press took note of the opening. Curiously, eight months after the new COBA opening, UT System Regents just happened to approve plans for a new Graduate Business Education Center addition to the McCombs School of Business in Austin.[2] Though UT would never admit it, the Longhorns could never countenance being upstaged by a West Texas institution that had already proven they could do more with less.

IN THE SIXTEENTH CENTURY, Fernando de los Cobos y Molina had served with distinction as the court secretary of state to Spanish King and Holy Roman Emperor Charles V during the emergence of the Imperial Spanish era. In 1545, Cobos ceded his role to his nephew, Juan Vázquez de Molina, who continued the role with similar distinction during the reign of Phillip II.[3] Both were natives of Úbeda in Andalusia—a city that enjoyed a healthy patronage from the hidalguía of the Molina Family. Today, Úbeda is recognized as an UNESCO World Heritage Site thanks in large part to the celebrated Vázquez de Molina Square—one of the only predominantly Plateresque urban centers in all of Spain, and the world for that matter.[4] It is held that the younger Molina overruled the influence of the austere court architect Juan de Herrera and continued to direct his maestros mayores to complete work in the estilo plateresco well into the 1570s—long after Herrera eschewed the Plateresque style in lieu of a national policy of

Undated evening image of the south courtyard of the Rawls College of Business illustrating the more contemporary detailing of that façade.

Building massing and detail concept sketch of the Kent R. Hance Chapel, 2011 by Al York, FAIA, McKinney-York architects.

(*Left*) A grid of scallop shells on the south façade of the Casa de las Conchas, Salamanca, a pattern that would inspire architect Al York in the frontispiece panel to the Kent R. Hance Chapel, completed in 2012 (*below*).

instituting his far more austere, sober iteration on the Renaissance. So it came with a measure of historical irony that a likely distant descendant of the same Úbedan Molinas who championed the Plateresque style in the latter half of the sixteenth century would in late 2009 be named the third vice chancellor of Facilities Planning and Construction for the Texas Tech University System.

Michael Molina was the first Texas Tech alumnus to advance to the helm of FP&C following Mike Ellicott's retirement in September 2009. An Irving native and 1991 Tech alumnus and architect, Molina, who had previously led facilities for over a decade at United Supermarkets, was an adroit team builder, communicator, and marketer.[5] In an era when even FP&C had their own social media presence, having to constantly mention Spanish Renaissance architecture in speeches led Molina to adopt the more Twitter friendly term *SpanRen*.[6] While Molina continued to champion the campus master plan and Spanish Renaissance style just as Ellicott and Mann before him, Chancellor Hance had challenged Molina to tackle a range of additional

The Texas Tech University Innovation Hub, by Kirksey Architects, completed 2015.

issues—namely the rising cost of construction, and efficiency and operating expenses of the FP&C team. FP&C had grown significantly since the establishment of the University System, and prior to 2009, FP&C continued to internally design much of the landscape architectural and interior design scope in Tech projects. Hance challenged Molina to transition all project design roles to the firms that the University System had already hired to execute design services, while finding solutions to the ongoing challenge of controlling construction costs that many viewed as out-of-control.[7] These challenges emerged amidst a still-surging period for the University System. Angelo State University had left the Texas State University System in late 2007 to become the third academic body of the Texas Tech University System, while efforts were underway in institutional advancement that made even the substantial work of the Montford administration pale in comparison. Research funding was on the rise across the university system, with annual research funding for the TTUHSC alone having quadrupled from $15 million in 2006 to over $60 million in 2012.[8] In 2001, Texas Tech University had just under $43.4 Million in annual spending on research across the institution, growing annually at a pedestrian pace of just under 4 percent per year.[9] Beginning in the late 2000s however, that growth rate exploded, including one year, from 2009 to 2010, seeing nearly $40 million dollars in funding growth over the previous academic year alone.[10] In that same year, Tech rocketed past all other public universities in Texas, minus UT and A&M,

Entry archway to the Trait Development Headhouse & Greenhouse Building to the Bayer CropScience Seeds Innovation Center; PSC, architects, completed 2015.

with research expenditures higher than the Universities of Arkansas, Oklahoma, Louisville, or South Carolina. This growth could be attributed to many factors, and of course the dedicated efforts of faculty and leadership alike. That being said, much of the emphasis upon institutional advancement could be attributed to Hance himself. Always bearing the public face of a warm smile, and quick to unload a gamut of jokes at anyone listening, Hance understood and instilled in his team the unequivocal power of fundraising in advancing an emerging national institution.

Kent Hance too was a philanthropist, namely as majority donor for a new 250-seat, $3.5 million nondenominational chapel sited east of the recently renamed McKenzie-Merket Alumni Center in the southeast corner of campus. Completed in spring 2012, the Kent R. Hance Chapel, designed by Austin-based atelier McKinney/York

The Bayer Plant Science Addition and Renovation Project, funded through TRUF matching funds; designed by Smith Group+JJR, completed 2015

The south entry façade to the Texas Tech University System Office Building, completed spring 2017; PSC, architects.

Architects, became the first Tech building to introduce a single-bell *campanario* set astride a simple, but elegantly detailed cruciform plan. Architect Al York was drawn to the Spanish Isabelline penchant for adorning buildings with a diagonal grid of raised ornaments, like the Saint James–inspired scallop shells of the Casa de las Conchas in Salamanca, or Guadalajara's remarkable Palacio del Infantado. In the chapel's west façade, York incorporated a similar grid of rectangular stone protrusions in a subtle but twenty-first-century form of neoclassical Spanish vernacular.[11]

By the late 2000s, the growing public perception was that construction costs at Texas Tech, and higher education in general, were exorbitant. Much of the often $300-per-square-foot or higher construction costs came with demands that new facilities be built to last for a century or longer, while being outfitted with a bevy of modern technologies such as audio/visual, security and data connectivity technology. FP&C leadership like Billy Breedlove and John Russell investigated alternative construction methods, project management options, and new materials such as insulated concrete form (ICF) wall construction, precast concrete floor planking, and variable refrigerant flow (VRF) technology in HVAC systems as alternatives that could accelerate and reduce cost to construction. Many are typically used today.[12]

Innovations and the organizational transformation of FP&C came about during a continued explosion of growth in millennial-era student enrollment at Texas Tech, while new construction and campus development left Tech almost unrecognizable from its appearance even two decades prior. It was during that same period that the University System would grow its cumulative endowment value by $857 million—more than double where stood in 2006—to an endowment value of $1.33 billion in late 2018.[13] Much of this growth came with the success of the "Vision and Tradition: The Campaign for Texas Tech" initiative—launched by Chancellor Kent Hance in the late 2000s. The endowment value of the Texas Tech University System

Plateresque-revival archway from main lobby into the Board of Regents Lobby, Texas Tech University System Office Building.

has now outpaced other Association of American University member institutions such as the University of Colorado–Boulder and Iowa State University, to name only a few.

With growth not only in annual research expenditures and the systemwide endowment, Texas Tech University in particular would require a range of new and more specialized research facilities to house a growing range of scientific, biomedical, and engineering experimentation spaces. The 2013 launch of the Research and Technology Park at Texas Tech University, located west of the Health Sciences Center campus and the 2015 completion of the Seeds Innovation Center—a partnership with Bayer CropScience situated south of the International Cultural Center—are examples of Tech's strategy of seeking private-entity partnerships for research opportunity and innovation. (In 2018, in response to issues stemming from regulatory concerns over Bayer AG's purchase of Monsanto, Bayer sold their FiberMax cotton brand and other assets to German chemical magnate BASF Group, resulting in the renaming of the facility as the BASF Seeds Innovation Center.) The forty-thousand-square-foot Phase I Innovation Hub to the Research and Technology Park, designed by Kirksey of Houston, features leasable modular laboratory bays available to private-industry partners who in turn have the ability to staff labs and workspaces with emerging talent from the Texas Tech student body. The seventy-five-thousand-square-foot Seeds Innovation Center complex, designed by PSC, includes what the German leadership of Bayer AG would later jokingly refer to as the world's first Spanish-Renaissance automated greenhouse complex.[14] Within the Seeds Innovation Center, PSC based the entry arch to the new Trait Development Building upon of the Romero Gate—the entry portal to the circa-1526 Hospital Real in Burgos, which originally served as a waypoint on the Way of Saint James, and today serves as the campus entry to the University of Burgos. Even ninety years following William Ward Watkin's case study–inspired design work at Tech, architects engaged in work at Tech were finding new case studies to inspire present-day additions to the campus fabric.

To manage such frenetic systemwide growth, one particular facility was needed to establish a collaborative environment and smooth operational functions for the Texas Tech University System. Despite having a key role in over fifteen years of phenomenal growth in facilities, resources, and funding, the operational organs of the University System remained spread across a half-dozen buildings on the Tech campus. Visitors might easily confuse the University President's Office on the ground floor of the Administration Building with the System Chancellor's Office located on the southeast wing of the same building. Audit Services conducted their business out of converted dorm rooms in Drane Hall, while Institutional Advancement toiled away in their fundraising activities working out of four different buildings, one of which was a former daycare building. Other more established system-structured institutions such as the UT and A&M Systems possessed system-level, stand-alone headquarters buildings. The Texas Tech University System required a similar facility and began work in

West Village—Texas Tech's first ICF and structural plank-constructed residence hall, as looking southeast into one of the commons spaces; BGK, with Mackey-Mitchell architects, completed 2015.

fall 2014 for the design of a new System Headquarters to be located at the western edge of the Tech campus. Designed by PSC and completed by Vaughn Construction in March 2017, the nearly eighty-thousand-square-foot, three-story System Office Building serves as the home to the Board of Regents, as well as all ten departments that manage the University System.

DESPITE THE apartment housing infusion underway at nearby Overton Park—rampant enrollment growth in the 2000s required massive expansion of student housing on the Tech campus. Comparatively speaking, total enrollment at Texas Tech had grown almost the identical amount in the twenty-three years between 1976 and 1999 compared to the two years between 2012 and 2014.[15] Tech could not

Honors College Residence Hall, another ICF/concrete structural plank-framed residence hall; designed by BGK, with Mackey-Mitchell, and completed in summer 2017.

continue to construct more comparably expensive low-density multi-building complexes like the Carpenter-Wells Village of the late 1990s. Soon, student luxuries such as two-bed dorm rooms being rented by a single student would become distant memories. By the late 2000s, University Housing would have to bring one four- to five-hundred bed complex online every two years simply to maintain a baseline 25 percent on-campus housing rate. Enrollment growth-imposed demands have been particularly stressing upon Housing and Dining since 2013, as housing utilization rates came very near 100 percent in fall semesters. In 2015, demand was outpacing supply to the point that Housing and Dining resorted to draconian adaptive reuse measures of renovating study hall rooms in the towers of the Wiggins Complex into multibed temporary dorm rooms. Newer residence halls such as BOKA-Powell's 2005 Grover Murray Hall and 2012 Talkington Hall, and the 455-bed West Village Complex, completed in August 2014 in a design-build partnership between Whiting-Turner Construction, Barnes Gromatsky Kosarek Architects of Austin, and Mackey-Mitchell Architects of Kansas City, are consistently filled to capacity with waiting lists to follow. Unlike the enrollment boom of the 1960s, which ebbed following a fifteen-year period, Tech was facing the seemingly endless challenge of perpetual growth, and new strategies would be required beyond capital construction alone to equip the university to meet their housing needs, student life needs, and academic instructional capacity. Tech needed to revisit their beloved Master Plan.

23

FINIS CORONAT OPUS

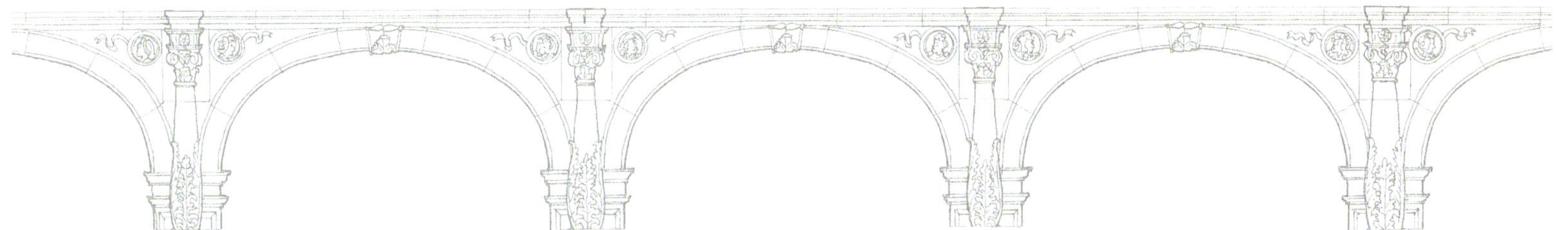

In July 2014, Theresa Drewell and FP&C staff were feverishly compiling estimates to proposed projects to be built throughout the University System over the next decade—a state-mandated report to Texas Higher Education Coordinating Board (THECB) known within institutional parlance as the "MP-1." The final tabulation was impressive, if not frightening. By 2024, the University System planned some $1,185,214,315 in new construction and renovation, representing a 1.6-million-square-foot addition to both the University and the Health Sciences Center in Lubbock.[1] It was a scale of expansion that would have sent founding fathers like Horn or Knapp into a fainting spell. When adjusted to 1925 dollars, the dollars proposed to be expended in the MP-1 would have been enough to construct all of Watkin's original master plan for Texas Technological College three-and-a-half times over!

Even more incredible was that the MP-1 projection did not account for myriad additional conceptual projects large and small that were being incorporated into the University System's update to the 1997 Campus Master Plan. Since 2014, numerous capital projects—many whose scale are two-, four-, or five-fold greater in magnitude to what were considered major Tech projects only a decade before—were underway in various stages of planning, fundraising, design, or construction. The College of Visual and Performing Arts began contemplating a more than $100 million Performing Arts Facility and another $105 million addition and renovation to the Music Building. In August 2018, the Museum of Texas Tech University announced the bold move to hire award-winning architects Thom Mayne and Arne Emerson of Morphosis Architects to design a $105 million Universiteum expansion to their complex. In January 2019, Tech Athletics leadership celebrated the groundbreaking on a $29.5 million Dustin R. Womble Basketball Center. Named in honor of the project's lead $10 million benefactor, "The Womble," designed by Kansas City–based Populous Architects, would form a western flank across Indiana Avenue from the United Supermarkets Arena as a nationally premiere athletics training and practice facility for Red Raider and Lady Raider basketball programs. None of these projects even appeared in the 2014 MP-1. Beyond that, further roadway improvements, structured

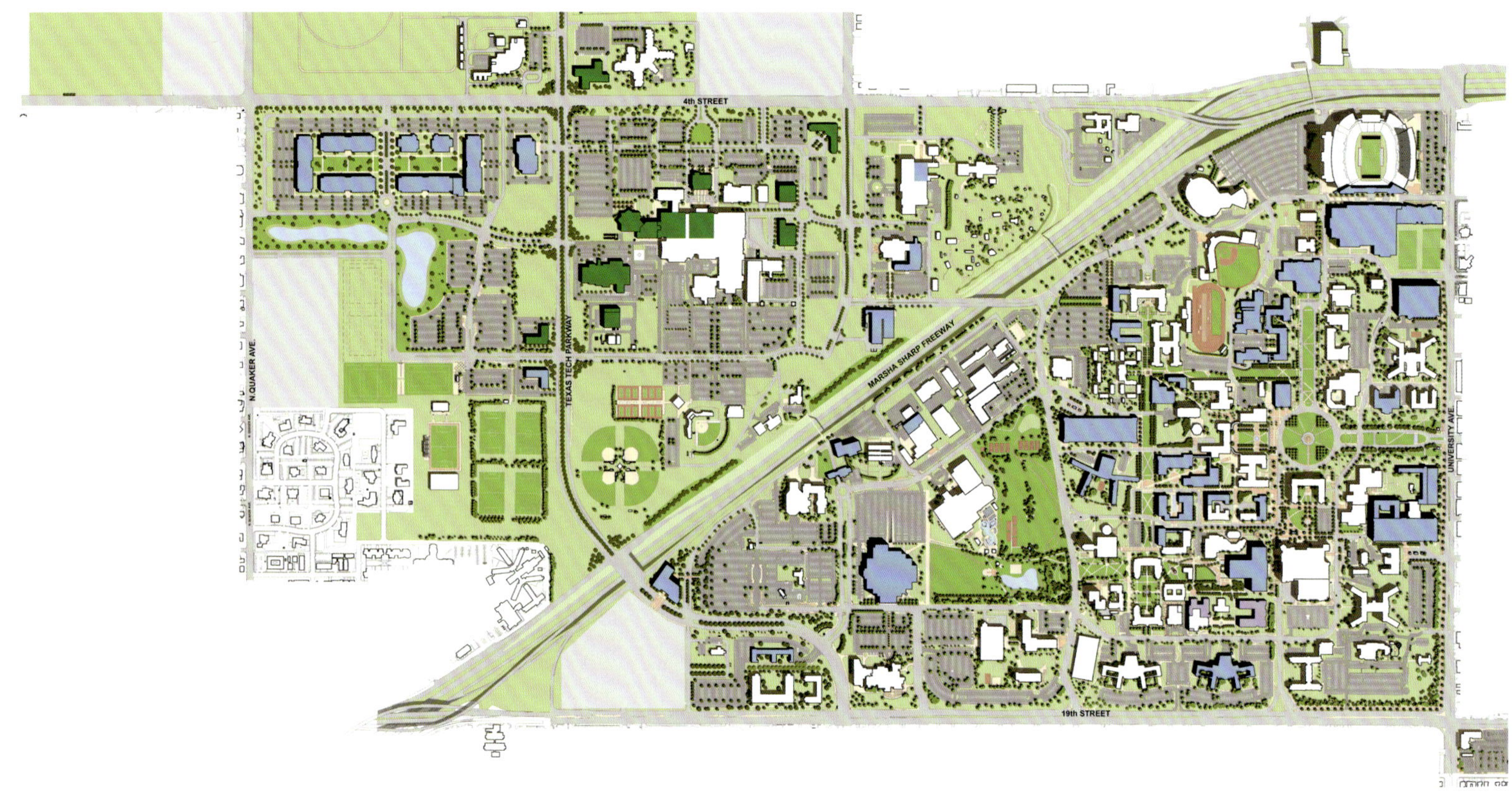

Vision 2024 Plan, 2014 Master Plan Update—Texas Tech University and TTUHSC Lubbock campus—Design Workshop, RCLCO, and PSC, planners.

parking for thousands of cars, and countless small-scale improvements to the campus landscape were being contemplated, but two did not even appear on the MP-1. Robert Duncan, the former state senator who was appointed chancellor following Kent Hance's retirement and elevation to chancellor emeritus status in 2014, only seemed to continue the status quo cavalcade in fundraising and advancement across the University System. In all, the true value of what lay beyond the horizon for Texas Tech in the decade prior to its approaching centennial could easily eclipse $2 billion worth of construction.

The hugely successful 1997 Master Plan, though over fifteen years old, had largely been implemented. In the years since its adoption, System and University leadership praised its planning objectives, but lamented that the document did not more thoroughly establish a deeper understanding of the identity and human-scale image of the institution. A broader national field of architects was now designing work at Texas Tech, and FP&C found themselves realizing the Architectural Guidelines included in the 1997 Master Plan focused on specific material requirements, but did not impart any understanding to the complex and subtle nuances of the Spanish Renaissance style. With so much work anticipated in the coming years, and a fear that

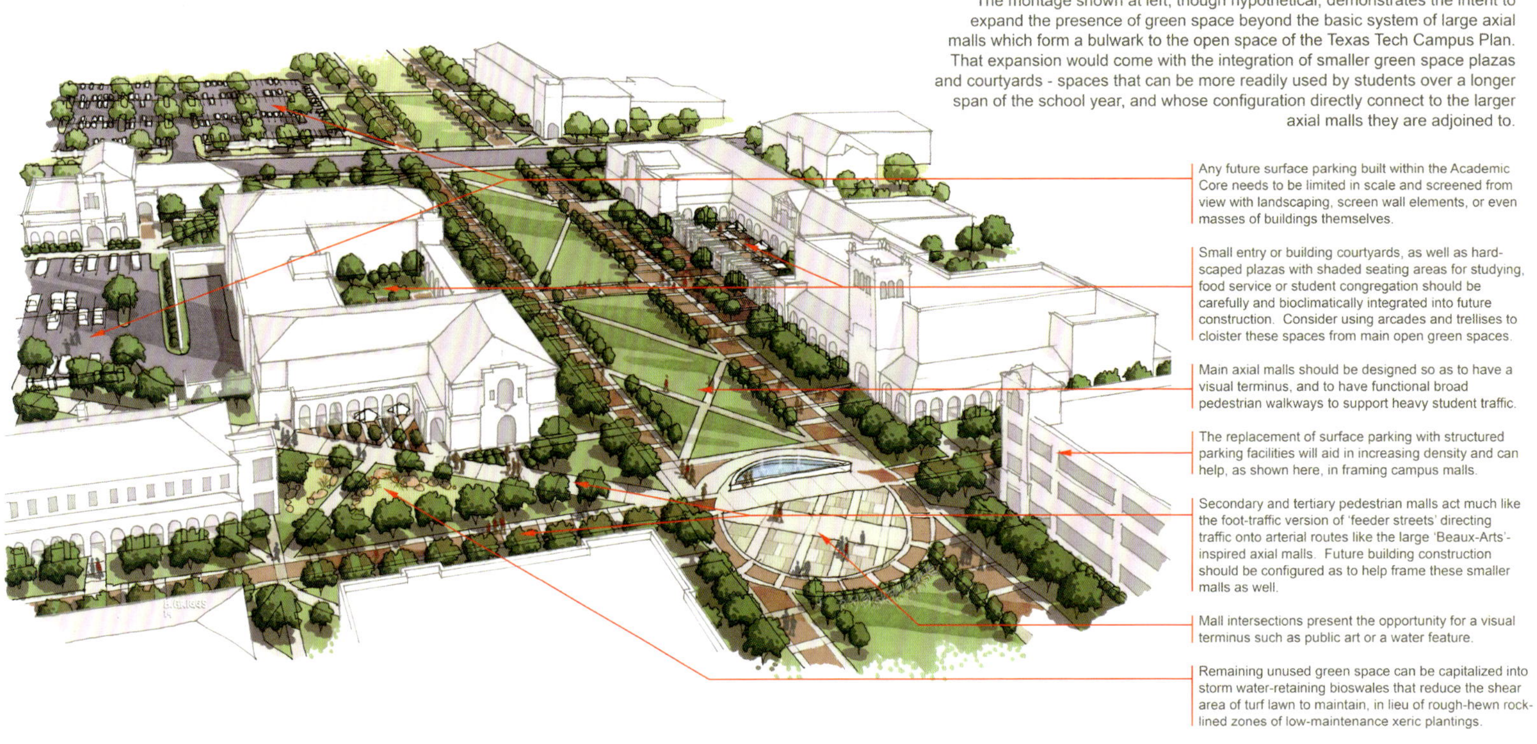

Stereotypical campus development strategy rendering, demonstrating best practices for future expansion within the Lubbock campus.

without more structured guidance from FP&C, design firms could lose sight of adhering to the Plateresque "Spirit of Place" so engrained at Texas Tech, the Board of Regents authorized Michael Molina and the FP&C team to execute an update to Tech's much-vaunted Master Plan.

In 2012, FP&C selected Austin-based real estate planning firm Robert Charles Lesser Company (RCLCO) and Design Workshop, a landscape architectural and planning firm, to execute what became known as Master Plan Update, or MPU. A year later, PSC was added to the team and tasked to focus on campus heritage, aesthetics, and architectural guidelines. Beyond a reaffirmation of the 1997 Plan, the MPU addressed new problems generated by the expectation of an anticipated 40,000-plus student enrollment by 2020, identifying facility-based solutions to improving academic stature of the university and HSC, further establishing an architectural identity to the campus perimeter and entry points, and providing a greater understanding of the Spanish Renaissance style.

Development of the MPU emerged amidst a fever-pitch furor among system, university, and even HSC leadership in favor of the Spanish Renaissance aesthetic, with the Board of Regents standing at the forecastle of that furor. In 1997, SpanRen had been largely confined to the Lubbock campus, and even then only to the university grounds southeast of the Brownfield Highway. Aesthetic outliers like the austere HSC campus, the "Mesa-modernist" Museum, or the

Prototypical entry gateway concept developed for the Master Plan Update. One objective of the MPU was to significantly increase campus perimeter identity and a "sense of arrival" to the institution.

ranch-inspired National Ranching Heritage Center were generally regarded as acceptable outliers. Within little more than a decade, the prevailing mindset had totally changed. HSC leadership had toyed with the introduction of a free-standing Spanish-revival colonnade at the initial concepts for the PSC-designed Academic Classroom Building at HSC as early as 2000, but the concept was deemed cost prohibitive.[2] But beginning in 1999, Spanish Renaissance–revival expansion projects were being designed and built at HSC campuses in Amarillo, El Paso, and later Abilene and Odessa, as the estilo plateresco was becoming the signature identity of not only the university, but the broader system. Inevitably, both HSC leadership and the Board of Regents pressed for a change included in the MPU where future Lubbock HSC construction would too be dictated in the Spanish-Renaissance style, a tectonic shift from HSC's long history of tinted curtain wall, cast-in-place concrete, and dark anodized bronze paneling. Then-HSC President Dr. Tedd Mitchell (who would later be appointed in 2018 as the fifth chancellor of the TTU System) was eager to visually rebrand his institution from a look he often described in speeches as "Soviet architecture" to a more Plateresque appearance.[3] Perkins's and Will's 2017 design for a Spanish Renaissance HSC University Center situated north of Pod B clearly announced that the future of facilities growth at the HSC Lubbock campus would be SpanRen. Corners to the north façade to the Welcome Center would feature none other than Palacio de Monterrey–stylized tower forms. By 2016, Angelo State University was the only remaining system institution untouched by the Spanish invasion.

Texas Tech's architectural stylistic orthodoxy had endured criticism in architectural circles as being kitschy and disingenuous, as contemporary designers argued that projects built on campus since 1997 appeared to have Plateresque ornament wallpapered on their façades indiscriminately, rather than developing facility designs that adhered to the formative, proportional, and detailing dictums that originated from the sociocultural and bioclimatic origins of Renaissance-era Spain. Others pointed to contrasting avant-garde contemporary planning and design solutions underway at previously neoclassicist institutions like the University of Cincinnati, MIT, and even in the peripheral campus at Stanford University, arguing that such solutions were more appropriate for the present-day, millennial-era student. Their arguments failed to account for the inherent subjective nature of stylistic penchants at American universities, as just as many noted institutions—the University of Virginia, Oklahoma State, and SMU, among many others—continued to embrace their neoclassical roots. After its adoption in December 2014, the MPU would bring architects nationwide into a deeper understanding of Texas Tech's Plateresque-revival aesthetic.

Criticism aside, the staunch affection system and university leadership continue to hold toward the estilo plateresco is both a testament to William Ward Watkin's vision and the merits of an aesthetically pleasing style. From a branding perspective, it is Texas Tech's differentiating wild card. As of 2017, only two other US universities out of over 2,700 accredited institutions—the University of San Diego[4] and New Mexico State University[5]—have an adopted policy of Spanish Renaissance architecture as their campus style. Mountains of survey feedback from students, parents, and alumni have confirmed that the

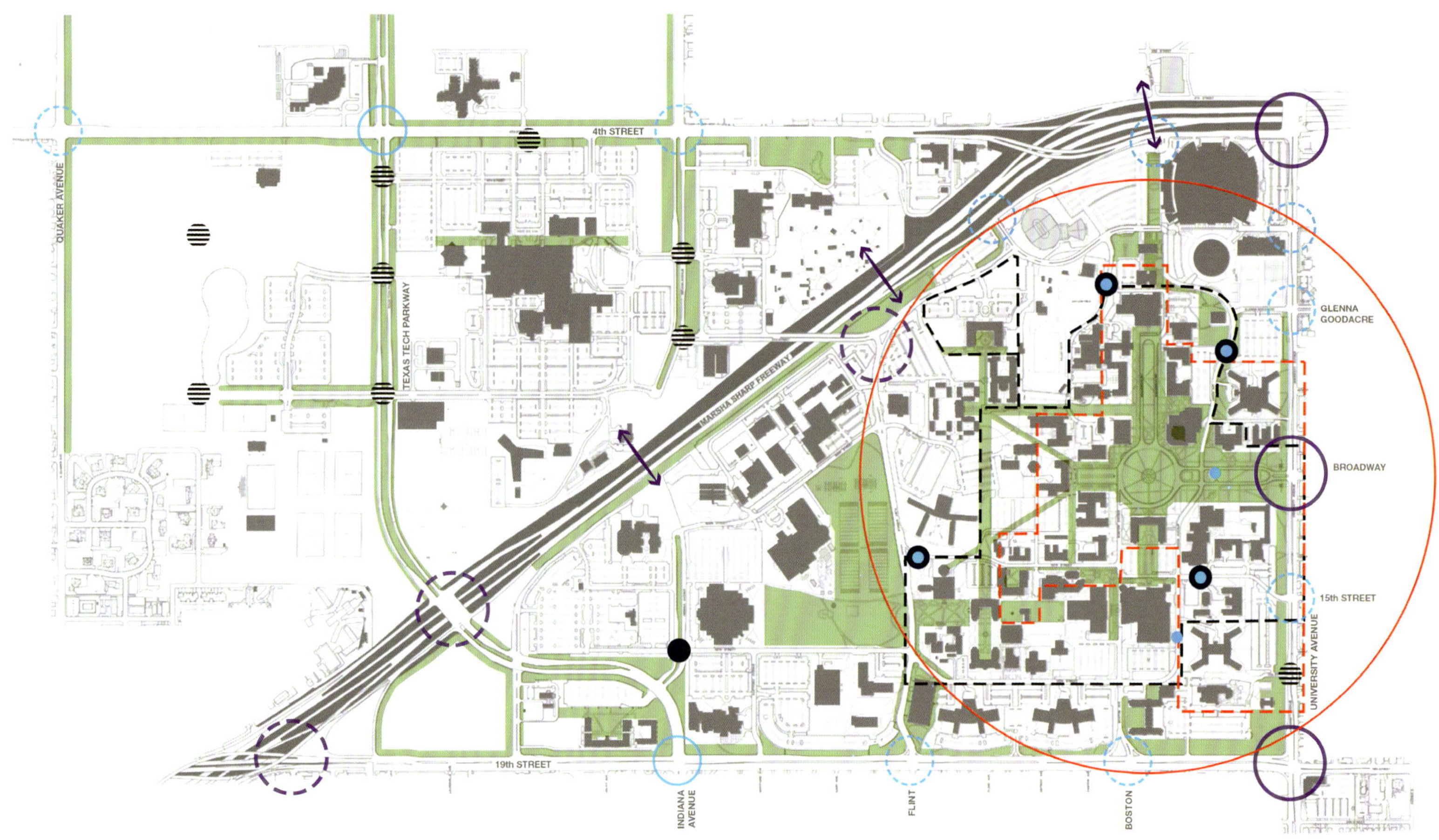

Campus diagram from the MPU affirming both defined areas of green spaces, malls, and need for defining entry features at vehicular entry points onto campus.

continued use of the Spanish-revival Beaux-Arts style is well received, exuding an environment of stability and prosperity to the public at large. That perception, and the intrinsic recruiting value that comes with it cannot be understated, as rising competition from rival and neighboring institutions—a key contributing factor to the malaise at Tech of the 1980s—is if anything a more acute issue today. Whether perceived as kitschy or not, SpanRen has been an unquestionably successful marketing component of the university. But architectural style aside, the ultimate aspiration of Tech leadership has not been as much enrollment growth, research expenditures, increased endowment, or higher academic rankings, as much as it has been focused on the cumulative result of all those factors—a buzzword term that remains frontispiece at Texas Tech—*Tier One.*

The quest for Tier One status at Texas Tech accelerated with the passing of House Bill 51 in 2009 establishing the National Research University Fund (NRUF) for emerging public research universities

The Burkhart Center for Autism Education and Research further infilled campus density along the northern boundary of 18th Street upon its completion in 2013; SHW Design (now Stantec), architects.

The Terry Fuller Petroleum Engineering Research Building, situated at the northeast corner of the Engineering Key; completed in 2014, Kirksey Architects.

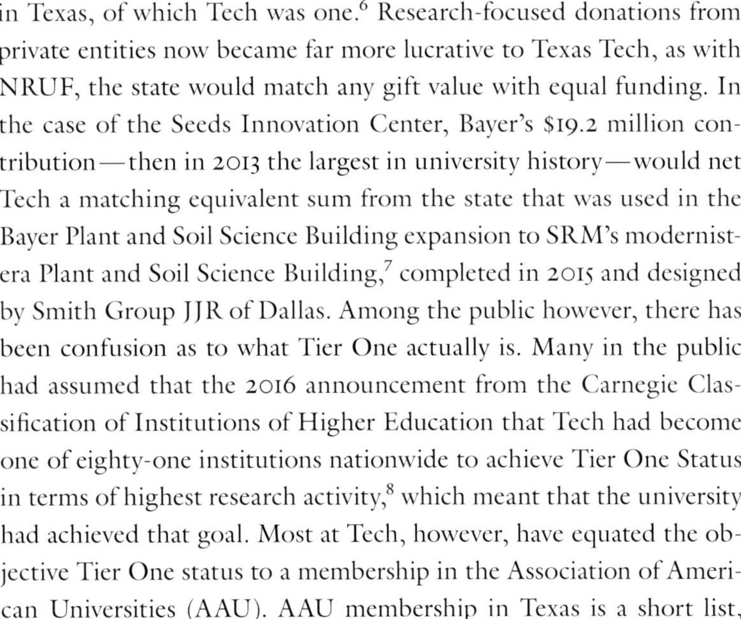

in Texas, of which Tech was one.[6] Research-focused donations from private entities now became far more lucrative to Texas Tech, as with NRUF, the state would match any gift value with equal funding. In the case of the Seeds Innovation Center, Bayer's $19.2 million contribution—then in 2013 the largest in university history—would net Tech a matching equivalent sum from the state that was used in the Bayer Plant and Soil Science Building expansion to SRM's modernist-era Plant and Soil Science Building,[7] completed in 2015 and designed by Smith Group JJR of Dallas. Among the public however, there has been confusion as to what Tier One actually is. Many in the public had assumed that the 2016 announcement from the Carnegie Classification of Institutions of Higher Education that Tech had become one of eighty-one institutions nationwide to achieve Tier One Status in terms of highest research activity,[8] which meant that the university had achieved that goal. Most at Tech, however, have equated the objective Tier One status to a membership in the Association of American Universities (AAU). AAU membership in Texas is a short list, with only Rice, Texas A&M, and the University of Texas at Austin as current members.

What roles will architecture and campus planning play in Tech's pursuit of an AAU membership? For one, if enrollment and university-wide research activity increases, then equipping Texas Tech with modern research space that aligns with the aspirational goals of the MPU becomes critical. It is not surprising that over 70 percent of Tech's nonstudent life facility growth since 2012 has been research-based rather than instructional-classroom based.[9] The Burkhart Center for Autism Education and Research, completed in November 2013 and designed by SHW (now Stantec) of Dallas, the Terry Fuller Petroleum Engineering Research Building, completed in January 2014 and designed by Kirksey of Houston, and the aforementioned Bayer Plant and Soil Science Building are all examples of academic facilities that are sparse in classrooms, but abundant in esoteric research space.

House Bill 100, signed into law by Governor Greg Abbott in July 2015, injected approximately $3 billion in much-needed tuition revenue

Still under construction at the time of publication, TreanorHL's (with Ayers Saint Gross) massive new Experimental Sciences Building II will be key in completing the framing of the northwest campus pedestrian mall intersection originally envisioned in the 1997 Master Plan.

bond (TRB) funding into Texas higher education,[10] which included an $83 million expansion to facilities at the Lubbock TTUHSC campus, and a $77 million Experimental Sciences Building II Building at Texas Tech.

Experimental Sciences Building II, designed by TreanorHL, is representative of the growth strategy university leadership hoped to capitalize upon in relocating research activities into new, institution-competitive spaces like the ESBs, while investing additional capital into the modernization of older facilities for undergraduate and graduate instruction. Both Molina and Tech President Lawrence Schovanec have stressed the positive ripple effect of projects like the ESB II frees up tens of thousands of square feet of former research spaces in older facilities that can then be renovated into state-of-the-art general instructional and office space.[11] The Biology Tower and Complex, renovated in 2013, and former Mass Communications Building—now the Maddox Engineering Research Center—whose renovation was designed by Condray Design Group in 2015, are examples of this strategy in action. In historic areas like the Mathematics and Science

While Tech leadership remains committed to goals affirmed in the 1997 and 2014 Master Plan documents, visions to remove parking in key areas of the campus core, in lieu of green space like the above 1997 "Horizon" Campaign vision for the campus core are yet unrealized.

Quadrangle, the desire that research space migration and subsequent existing space renovations will generate the impetus for the removal of surface parking out of the Court of Honor once and for all, as intended by Watkin over ninety years ago. Unsurprisingly, $164 million in projects listed in the 2014 MP-1 is research-centric construction[12], opening the doors to allowing other funding like HEAF to be allocated on displaced existing campus building renovations.

When asked in March 2016 about which project he personally wants to see implemented at Tech, Michael Molina had a quick answer—largely eliminate parking south of the Administration Building.[13] Watkin had envisioned a semiformal park south of Administration—a vision that was slowly lost with the construction of the Student Union and Music Building, but mainly with the pestilential rise of the automobile at Tech. The sea of asphalt and fenders glaringly visible between Administration and the Student Union has been particularly unsightly, especially given that James Atcheson's circa-1952 Student Union design included a handsome, mildly Romanesque entry arch aligned with the Administration Building salle-porte to the north. That connection remains totally lost on students and the public today. Preliminary designs developed in 2013 include a compromise solution with a landscaped central mall south of Administration, but retains limited surface parking south of the Administration East Wing. But that plan is yet to be funded or implemented.

Parking remains a challenge today, though statistics from TTU Traffic and Parking indicate that parking provisions at Texas Tech are superior in both options and quantity than any number of other peer institutions. The university has evolved greatly from the early 1950s when Nolan Barrick observed the maddening spectacle of vehicular traffic clogging roadways around Memorial Circle. It is no surprise that three of the six core planning principles in the 2014 Master Plan Update recommend the removal of surface parking as an objective toward strengthening the campus core, enhancing campus identity, and developing more beautiful open spaces. Increasing campus core density, also indicated in both the 1997 Master Plan and the MPU's Vision 2024 Plan, will by default require the displacement of hundreds, if not thousands of existing parking stalls, particularly west of the Mathematics and Science Quadrangle. In the MPU, three sites around the perimeter of the Tech campus core were identified as potential locations for parking garage facilities with one-thousand-car capacities or greater. As seen with the Flint Avenue Parking Facility, achieving Texas Tech's planning aspirations from a parking standpoint will be an expensive endeavor. A 2014 report by parking design firm Carl Walker indicated that though cost for structured parking in Texas was lower than the $18,000 per space national average,[14] a 1,200-car Plateresque-detailed parking garage at Tech could still cost upward of $19 million in present-day dollars. Unlike the Flint Avenue Facility, future garages at Tech will likely feature more student friendly intermodal bus stops designed to centralize Citibus student commuter traffic through a single location, and may potentially incorporate other features like café-style retail and dining venues. Implementation of the structured parking goals of the MPU alone could even further fundamentally change the face of Texas Tech.

PUBLIC-PRIVATE PARTNERSHIPS, or P3s—a hugely popular topic today in higher education—was a concept that too was integrated into the 2014 Master Plan Update. One of the core principles outlined in the MPU centered around the concept of "land endowment" to better use many unused swaths of the 1,839-acre campus. Of the more than four hundred acres of Tech property that remain unused or are used in a low-impact function such as crop research, many parcels are ideally suited for commercial or governmental partnerships that could provide teaching, clinical, or research synergies with either the university or HSC. In spring 2017, the US Department of Veteran's Affairs commenced soliciting for design-build services for a new Lubbock Clinical Building anticipated to be built beginning in 2019,[15] while the US Department of Agriculture is undertaking a second cotton laboratory facility that began construction the same year. Other land lease opportunities lend themselves as ideal for low-rise, mixed-use retail space and student-centric entertainment venues. Proposed privately maintained housing envisioned on the western or southwestern perimeters of the campus could potentially generate similar synergy just as with Overton Park in the 2000s by providing thousands of apartment lease spaces situated on Tech property to students.

While many higher education institutions in Texas have incorporated P3 solutions to address housing needs that more often than not used residential-grade construction methods, Texas Tech and FP&C have remained adamant—as far as Tech-owned housing is concerned—that future construction would comply with FP&C's rigorous institution-grade construction standards. Recent housing projects designed in partnership between BGK and Mackey-Mitchell—the West Village Complex and more recently completed Honors College Residence Hall—continue the practice of highest quality institutional construction and Spanish Renaissance exterior detailing. Such commitment is fiscally daunting for Tech, as continued enrollment requires the addition of some three to five hundred beds to the university physical plant every two years simply to keep pace, while over $100,000 per bed has been spent for housing constructed since 2013.

THE ROMAN POET OVID once wrote "Finis coronat opus"—the end completes the work. Ovid could not have been speaking of American higher education, and certainly not of Texas Tech. Like Gilbert Stuart's *Athenaeum*, the Texas Tech University campus today remains incomplete as it continues to undergo transformative change while its architectural image and legacy continue to grow. But if ongoing changes at Tech are impressive enough, more impressive still is how a rural college established in an oft-ridiculed place chided for its flatness, dust, and incessant wind—one of the last-settled regions of the Great American Desert—has managed to grow forty-fold in less than a century into a nationally ranked institution. Further, it is arguable that no other college or university in American history has grown from a small-town rural environment in such meteoric fashion as Texas Tech University. Scores of fine institutions situated in far-flung small towns ranging from Boone, North Carolina, and Dickinson, North Dakota, to Goodwell, Oklahoma, and Pullman, Washington, were established years if not decades prior to the establishment of Texas Technological College, yet many if not most have never grown to even a fraction of the size of Tech. This phenomenon begs to question what factors have led to Tech's remarkable growth in less than a century's time. In part, that question can be answered through the growth swells of three successive American generations of college-age students—the post–Great War generation who attended Tech in its founding years, the post–World War II and baby boomer generations who swelled Tech's enrollment past the 1960s, and finally the Generation X and millennial generations whose presence is still being felt at Tech today. Over the course of those generations, the national predisposition toward higher education has transformed alongside an American workforce that is so contrastingly technology-centric and services-oriented than the agricultural- and manufacturing-based economy that existed during Texas Tech's founding. Quite simply put, most American children, teenagers, and young adults today want, and often *expect* a college education. In 2010, the US Department of Education reported some 21,016,126 college or university students

Present-day aerial image of Memorial Circle looking south toward the Administration Building.

in the United States—nearly two out of every three persons of college age—with expectations that number will increase by over 25 percent in the next decade.[16] Even today, that data equates to a larger cumulative student population than the national cadre of colleges and universities could realistically support. Simply put, Tech's enrollment will continue to grow, and therefore its facilities and campus with it. While ongoing debate continues about myriad postsecondary dilemmas—the rising cost of college education, growing student debt, the reality that many college-age students are more ideally suited for technical vocational training than a four-year college education, and the future role of online education, among others—there will remain a bulwark place in the future for public research universities like Texas Tech. Frenetic population growth in Texas alone is reason enough to expect future enrollment growth at Texas Tech.

But evidence points to other factors—perhaps the growing number of successive family generations attending Tech, or the perception of the workmanlike attitude held toward Tech students, faculty, and alumni—a trait valued by prospective employers and the public at large. Beyond those reasons is a fundamental underlying factor that has contributed most greatly to the foundational fabric of Texas Tech, which was and remains today its architecture. Flamboyant in detail, reserved in color, and well adapted to the harsh Castilian- and Andalusian-like climate of West Texas, the Plateresque Spanish Renaissance–revival architecture of Texas Tech remains a subconscious signature livery to an institution whose existence and flourishing is a hard-fought accomplishment. What William Ward Watkin fashioned in style and plan nearly a century ago helped to define an institution in ways that are unfolding even today. Even had those more fortuitous "What ifs?" of Tech's past had come to a reality—Watkin's return to Texas Tech in the 1950s, the construction of a monumental Alamo Commencement Hall, a nuclear engineering program, or a presidential library—they would have only marginally brightened an overarching architectural fabric of great richness and splendor. Even modern "What ifs?" abound regarding Tech's more recent architectural history. Had Tech administrators not built such an impressive (and at the time somewhat controversial) United Spirit Arena in the late 1990s, would Texas Tech have been as successful in hiring Bob Knight as their men's basketball coach in 2001, and therefore would Tech have been able to hire former Knight assistant and current men's coach Chris Beard? Speculation aside, our architectural heritage still remains. All of the massing, ornament, finials, colonnades, and landscapes of the Tech campus today can be compared as something akin to Johann Wolfgang von Goethe's oft-clichéed description of architecture as "frozen music."[16] If Goethe's analogy holds true, whereas a movement serves as a self-contained portion to a musical composition, and a concerto often describes a collection of three or more movements, an opus represents the catalogue of an artist's life works.

In Lubbock, Texas, at Texas Tech University, today stands an *opus in brick and stone.*

EPILOGUE

A REQUIEM FOR TEMPLES AND TITANS

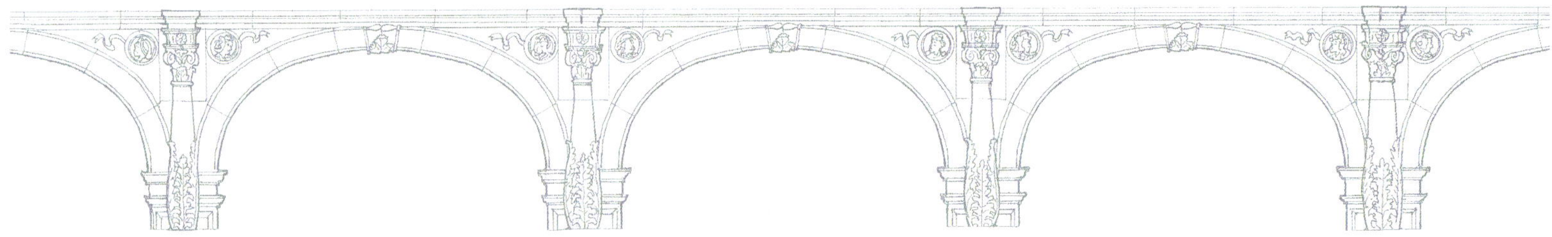

By October 1905, the turnstiles stood still as the little white city of Spanish-revival buildings in Portland, Oregon, had officially closed. Like so many world's fairs of the era, in short time, very little would remain of the Lewis & Clark Centennial Exposition. Most buildings of the exposition would be razed within the year, as their plaster-and-staff construction would not long survive the Pacific Northwest climate. Even the handsome twin towers and curved colonnades of the US Government Complex could not escape demolition with their Vanduzen-crafted bells disappearing to history. Guild's Lake would eventually be drained and the island leveled to accommodate industrial growth of Northwest Portland.[1] Today, few know of the history of the Lewis & Clark Centennial Exposition, as names for the buildings and streets of the former exposition site draws far more interest from the public today, given that beginning in the late 1980s they would inspire character names developed by Portland local Matt Groening for his new animated show *The Simpsons*. America's first Spanish-revival world's fair had simply disappeared.

Bertram Goodhue had been adamant that only the California State Building—the present-day San Diego Museum of Man—be retained after closing of the Panama-California Exposition in San Diego, while the rest of the park be left to weather into a state of ruins, with the gardens allowed to grow lush around them.[2] But for that to happen, the exposition would have to close, which it never did. Former President Theodore Roosevelt—no longer concerned of suffering the same fate at a World's Fair as his predecessor—attended the San Diego Exposition in July 1915. While there, he addressed a crowd with the following plea: "[Balboa Park] is so beautiful that I wish to make an earnest plea. . . . I hope that not only will you keep these buildings running for another year but you will keep these buildings of rare, phenomenal taste and beauty permanently."[3] San Diego thankfully listened to Roosevelt rather than Goodhue.

Balboa Park remains today an iconic feature in the San Diego landscape, and perhaps one of the most lasting and successful world's fairgrounds in world's fair history. Little would change over the decade following the first exposition other than the novel idea by a local

Present-day view of the San Diego Museum of Man as seen from the Plaza de California, Balboa Park, San Diego.

doctor to convert fruit orchards planted north of the exposition into what is known today as the world-renowned San Diego Zoo. Balboa Park was such a pinnacle exposition design that it would host two more world's fairs in 1935–36 and 1953. Sadly, Carleton Winslow's Top of the World Restaurant and Home Economy Building, situated on the Plaza de Panama and like Tech's Chemistry Building inspired by Hontañon's pivotal Palacio de Monterrey, were razed in the early 1960s to make way for the modernist Timken Museum of Art. Ironically, in the final days of 2004 and again in 2013, thousands of Texas Tech fans visiting San Diego to attend the Holiday Bowl visited Balboa Park. Walking the grounds of the 1915 Panama-California Exposition much like Amon Carter, Paul Horn, and Carl Staats had done eight decades before, Tech fans were unaware of what monumental impact that place of beauty had upon their alma mater.

For Bertram Goodhue, the success of the Panama-California Exposition unlocked reams of new commissions as he left his partnership with Ralph Adams Cram for independent practice. Spanish-colonial-revival residences in California, new buildings for the California Institute of Technology, and the Nebraska State Capitol, all added to East Coast commissions that kept Goodhue busy. For a chain smoker with a heart murmur who never really handled stress well, the frenetic pace was not good for the architect. His eyesight had begun failing as well by the San Diego commission, and by 1918 the titanic delineator reported to his client that his drawings for the planned Spanish-revival community for Tyrone, New Mexico, that the enclosed renderings would be his last.[4] In Goodhue's design for Tyrone—a picturesque Spanish-revival company mining town beloved by its employees—paradise would be short-ived. Copper demand after the Great War plummeted, and in 1921 Phelps-Dodge closed the mine and town. Tyrone, New Mexico, would sit empty for the next forty years until copper demand skyrocketed in the 1960s. Phelps-Dodge only then realized that the richest copper deposits lay directly under Tyrone, prompting the company to raze the entire town in the late 1960s as a precursor to an open-pit mining operation that is still operational. Today, the former site of America's finest master planned

Undated but recent aerial view image of the copper mine at Tyrone, New Mexico, whose gargantuan excavations had long since wiped out the former Goodhue-planned mining community.

The Julia Ideson Library, following its restoration and expansion; image dated fall 2014.

Spanish-revival community east of California is nothing more than a great one-hundred-meter-deep maw in the earth visible from outer space.

Goodhue's health continued to deteriorate and on the night of April 23, 1924, a badly ill Goodhue was forced to leave a New York City theater performance early. Upon returning to his apartment he would die of an apparent heart attack.[5] Five years after his death, Goodhue's friends and colleagues raised funds for a gray marble memorial at the Church of the Intercession in New York City where his body was interred. A knight-like effigy of Goodhue's lay over his tomb, and the overhead arch to the memorial was inscribed with a sentiment in Latin: NIHIL TETIGIT QUOD NON ORNAVIT—*He touched nothing with which he did not adorn.*[6] Also carved over his tomb was a collection of Goodhue's greatest works—the Chapel at West Point, the Nebraska State Capitol, the Rockefeller Memorial Chapel, among others. Over his heart sits the California State Building at Balboa Park.

Ralph Adams Cram would helm Cram and Ferguson successfully through the 1920s, even gracing the cover of *Time* magazine in late 1926. But the rise of modernism and the effects of the Great Depression had their impact on Cram and his firm. The elderly architect soldiered on, even finding time to host a young Nolan Barrick and his wife Rosemary, who in summer 1942 visited Cram at his home in Sudbury for dinner while Barrick was in training at the Naval Cartography School at Harvard.[7] Cram, like Goodhue, faced declining health in his final years and was half blind when he visited the unveiling of his Gothic-revival masterpiece—Saint John the Divine in New York City—in late 1941.[8] On September 22, 1942, Ralph Adams Cram died at the age of seventy-eight.[9] Thankfully, Cram's greatest contribution to the Spanish-revival architectural movement—the Julia Ideson

Library in downtown Houston—has survived well, even with the recent flooding threat of Hurricane Harvey. Today, the Ideson Library is a special collections library that was expanded through a 2011, $32 million Gensler-designed renovation and expansion project. To this day, visitors remain largely unaware what inspiration Ralph Adams Cram and the Ideson indirectly had upon Texas Tech.

WHERE WOULD Plateresque-revival architecture in the United States be without the work of Arthur and Mildred Stapley Byne? Prolific writing on Spanish architecture and furniture brought the Byne's financial sustenance, but their expensive Plateresque-revival home in Madrid and lifestyle required that the Byne's role expand from architectural historians to brokers of Spanish antiquarian artwork, furniture, and architectural features. The political disorganization of 1920s and 1930s Spain proved a ripe time for dealers like the Byneses to flourish. The Spanish-revival movement was rampant in the United States and California architect Julia Morgan and her client, William Randolph Hearst were noted buyers. Arthur Byne's acquisitions over time blurred into the outright pillaging of Spanish architectural artifacts that were bought on the cheap, dismantled, and shipped to America. Morgan incorporated many Byne-procured *antiquarios* into the mammoth Hearst Castle project then under construction. Byne even sold Hearst two whole Spanish monasteries that were dismantled stone-by-stone and shipped to the United States. Never rebuilt by Hearst, they sat for decades sharing space in a New York City warehouse with countless other Hearst acquisitions[10]—including a circa-1688 globe crafted by Italian cartographer Vincenzo Coronelli.[11] That Coronelli globe would later come into the possession of none other than Texas Technological College. Tech acquired the globe in 1968 to commemorate the one-millionth acquisition of the College Library, and following an extensive restoration resides today in its own rotunda of the Southwest Special Collections Library, thanks to a generous contribution by Jim Sowell.

Effects of the Spanish Civil War upon great works of the Renaissance; one of the corner statuaries of the tomb of Cardinal Cisneros, decapitated by bomb shrapnel from a 1937 bombing of the Cathedral of Alcalá.

Also caught in the grips of the Great Depression, the Bynes were forced to sell off some of their own considerable collection of art, furniture, and architectural artifacts, while Don Arturo Byne, as many Spaniards referred to him, continued in his illicit trade, despite growing public disdain for him and his business. The Byneses were en route back from buying such an antiquario on a road in northern Andalusia on the evening of July 16, 1935, when their sedan collided with a truck.[12] Arthur Byne was killed instantly, though amazingly, or perhaps by intentional design, Mildred was not even injured. Some speculate today whether Byne was the victim of a targeted attack—retribution for a greedy American who had pillaged Spain of its architectural beauty for over a decade. After Arthur's death, Mildred Stapley Byne would leave Spain and not return until after the Spanish Civil War, dying on Christmas Eve 1941 in Madrid.

Spain's collection of beautiful cities and towns had thankfully escaped destruction during the War of Succession, as well as the Napoleonic Peninsula War, with Salamanca even narrowly avoiding bombardment during the 1812 battle fought near there. Perhaps most destructive was the Great Lisbon Earthquake, which struck on All Saints' Day 1755. Even three hundred miles away from the earthquake's epicenter, in Córdoba, the quake nearly shattered the iconic Torre del Alminar, which would require three years to repair.[13] But the effects of the Spanish Civil War was something altogether different.

The bitter war between Franco, his fascist Nationalists, Falangists, and fascist allies in Germany and Italy against the remnants of the Republic and their often-fanatical leftist forces tore the nation asunder, with many great works of Spain's estilo plateresco lost in the process. The siege of Madrid, lasting between 1936 and 1939, resulted in the destruction of much of its Renaissance-era architecture. On December 6, 1936, pro-Nationalist aircraft of the Italian Regia Aeronautica bombed Guadalajara, destroying the famed Isabelline Palacio del Infantado.[14] In spring 1937, Republican aircraft bombed Córdoba, fortunately missing the cathedral/mosque and Torre del Alminar, but prompting retaliation by Nazi bombers of the German Condor

Detail view of the southeastern façade of Sigüenza Cathedral's two bell towers, highlighting spall damage around openings from gunfire and shelling received during the 1936 battle and siege.

Legion over the Republican-held city of Jaén, thankfully sparing the city's cathedral, the only Plateresque Spanish Renaissance cathedral in the world.

Sigüenza Cathedral was an early victim, overrun in the summer of 1936 by a radical Marxist faction of the Republican Army, who proceeded to execute the cathedral clergy and attempted to torch the cathedral itself. Ironically, Republican forces were forced to barricade themselves in the cathedral once Nationalist forces arrived in early August to retake the town. Lack of supplies and potential starvation finally led to the surrender of Republican forces on October 15, largely sparing the cathedral from destruction, though much of the cathedral's upper works and groin vaults were severely damaged.[15] Thankfully, the ornate entry portals of the cathedral cloister and its many chapels—most notably the Capilla de Santiago de Zebedeo—survived, as the cathedral itself would be restored in the 1940s to its earlier beauty. But even today, scores of bullet holes and cannon spalls gouged into the Piedra de Villamayor–clad walls of the cathedral tower mark the horrors of 1936.

Less fortunate was the Palacio Arzobispal, the former seat of the Archdiocese of Alcalá de Henares, which had served as the central archives of Spain, only to be requisitioned as a barracks and munitions storehouse by the Nationalist Army during the war. On August 11, 1939, an ammunition fire—suspected by some as an intentional act—broke out and blazed out of control destroying over half of the palace, including its entry façade and iconic stairway.[16] Though the entry façade would eventually be rebuilt in 1996, the Covarrubias-designed grand stair—the inspiration for the twin grand stairways at the Texas Tech Administration Building—was lost save for two ornate rusticated stone panels that today reside in Alcalá's Cathedral Museum. Other more modern works of architecture survived the civil war intact, including Sevilla's Parque Maria Luisa—the site of the last of so many Beaux-Arts-era world's fairs. The Ibero-American Exposition which nearly bankrupted the already floundering Spanish government survives today as an architectural and planning gem to Sevilla, particularly the Plaza de España. Aside from the cathedral/mosque of Córdoba and the Museo del Prado in Madrid, the Plaza de España remains one of Spain's most visited architectural landmarks, and is a particular favorite for filming Hollywood movies, ranging from *Lawrence of Arabia* to *Star Wars*.

Today, the spirit of restoration that led to rebuilding the Palacio del Infantado and the Palacio Arzobispal has swept across Spain, as scores of Plateresque-era façades undergo restoration—most notably Rodrigo Gil de Hontañon's pivotal Colegio Mayor de San Ildefonso façade to the Universidad de Alcalá and the Palacio de Monterrey in Salamanca, whose restorations were both completed in 2017. Each year, millions of international tourists travel to Salamanca, Alcalá de Henares, Sevilla and elsewhere to see those buildings of the estilo plateresco that remain handsome manifestations of Spain's golden age.

WORK VOLUME at Wyatt Hedrick's firm waned in the 1950s, largely because so many of Hedrick's former employees had left the firm to establish successful firms of their own. Though partially retired by the early 1960s, Hedrick continued to keep busy in securing occasional commissions and checking in on staff. Wyatt and Mildred Hedrick were in Houston when Hedrick fell ill in late April 1964. Taken to Memorial Hermann Hospital, Hedrick was admitted to a hospital building only short walk from his pinnacle commission, the Shamrock Hotel.[17]

The hotel that had indirectly killed Hedrick's one-time design collaborator William Ward Watkin had proven to be a boondoggle. Long since sold off by Glenn McCarthy, the Shamrock was bought by Hilton Hotels and soldiered on into the 1980s, and though once perceived as being in the fringe of South Houston, it was now located next to one of the largest medical districts in the world. No longer a modern, first-line hotel, anticipated renovation costs and rising land values due to the nearby medical district conspired to kill the behemoth. Despite an eleventh-hour outcry by Houston preservationists

Workers install new lead flashing and continue restoration work to the Piedra de Villamayor filigree of the famed Palacio de Monterrey in Salamanca, 2017.

to save the building, Hilton sold the Shamrock in 1987, and the monstrous hotel, save its parking garage, was demolished by wrecking ball that June.[18]

Back in hospital that spring in 1964, even at seventy-five, Hedrick could not sit still. Memorial Hermann had a long-standing policy not to provide outside phone lines for patients, despite the myriad oil tycoons, businessmen, and politicians who had demanded otherwise. In a final example of his "Virginia gentleman" skills of persuasion, Hedrick convinced staff to bend rules, and got a phone line so he could continue business with the Fort Worth office.[19] But on May 5, 1964, Wyatt Cephas Hedrick would succumb to his illness, and after a long and successful career, Hedrick's energy quotient finally fell to zero.

ON APRIL 8, 2019, following completion of its last dirt-floor rodeo event the day before, demolition teams arrived at the Lubbock Municipal Coliseum and Auditorium to commence work on abating and demolishing the old behemoth to make room for new student athlete housing. Four months earlier, the Texas Tech Red Raiders men's basketball team played a final ceremonial game in the coliseum as they defeated Abilene Christian University, but it so happened that on April 8, the Red Raiders were 1,134 miles to the north, playing in the final NCAA men's basketball game of the year. As with so many Texas Tech stories rich with irony, the physical end of one era coincided with the physical beginning of another. At the US Bank Stadium in Minneapolis that evening, the Texas Tech Red Raiders battled the University of Virginia Cavaliers for the NCAA National Championship in Division I men's basketball, hoping to equal the magic of Marsha Sharp's vaunted Lady Raiders twenty-six years earlier. Though Coach Beard's team was ultimately unsuccessful, with a lineup lacking in blue-chip recruits but abounding in skill, athleticism, and determination, the Red Raiders team fought the Cavaliers into overtime and proved yet again that Texas Tech could always do more with less.

THE YEAR 1978 WOULD MARK twenty-five years of service at Texas Tech for Nolan Barrick, who retired as chair of the Architecture Department that year to focus on designing custom stained-glass fabrications—a Beaux-Arts–era craft imparted by his mentor William Ward Watkin. Barrick would also work with his wife Rosemary on research and writing a book on the origins of Texas Tech's architectural heritage. That book—*Texas Tech: The Unobserved Heritage*—was nearing completion in 1984 when Rosemary Watkin Barrick suffered a fatal heart attack. A devastated Barrick would dedicate his book published a year later to his late wife and daughter of William Ward Watkin. Nolan later remarried and remained a staple at annual AIA Lubbock gatherings into the 1990s and 2000s, outliving his former CPC colleagues Flo Urbanovsky, who died in July 1988 after battling

Nolan and Betty Barrick at an AIA Lubbock event, August 2006.

a long illness,[20] and most tragically Haskell Taylor, who was killed in an apparent home invasion robbery at his Lubbock apartment in October 1996. His murder today remains unsolved.[21] Barrick and his wife Betty remained in touch with Tech, and in 2003 the couple toured the new West expansion of Jones SBC Stadium, thoroughly impressed with the bank of luxury elevators that were a quantum improvement over the pesky press box elevator that haunted him in his final years as college architect.[22] Nolan Ellimore Barrick passed away fewer than four months shy of his one hundredth birthday, on Independence Day 2013. Albeit not a Texas Tech alumnus, the university was more than obliged to lower Memorial Circle flags to half-staff in honor of his passing, and for good reason. If not for Nolan Barrick, Memorial Circle might not exist today.

APPENDIX A | INDEX OF BUILDINGS

THE FOLLOWING INDEX reflects major capital projects constructed at Texas Tech University, the former Texas Technological College, and the Lubbock Main Campus of the TTU Health Sciences Center, from 1924 to the date of publication (projects still in design or under construction at the date of publication are not listed). Projects are listed in chronological order. For adaptive reuse projects, original building names appear first, followed by their present-day name or use in italics. Subsequent large-scale, capital renovations and/or expansions (excluding life safety upgrades) are listed below each project in italics. Only the architecture firm (or multidisciplinary firm) responsible for design, followed by the architect-of-record is listed, and named as their firm name appeared at the date of building completion. Buildings since demolished are indicated by †.

Information for building names, architects, and dates are from the following sources: "Appendix I," *The First Thirty Years,* by Ruth Horn Andrews; "Higher Education Facilities Inventory for Institution #003644, Texas Tech University," as prepared by the Texas Higher Education Coordinating Board; drawing files of the Texas Tech University Physical Plant, Office of Engineering Services; multiple editions of the "Brick and Mortar Report," as periodically submitted by TTU System Facilities Planning and Construction to the TTU System Board of Regents; and University Archives, Southwest Collection, Holdings U1.5, U1.6, and U202.1.

Texas Tech University (Prior to September 1, 1969; Texas Technological College)

NAME	ARCHITECT	YEAR
President's House	W. W. Watkin/Sanguinet, Staats & Hedrick	1925
Merket Alumni Center Additions	*H. Duane Pierce Architects*	*1995*
McKenzie/Merket Addition	*JDMA Architects*	*2010*
Administration Building	W. W. Watkin/Sanguinet, Staats & Hedrick	1925
Administration Wing Expansion	*Wyatt C. Hedrick*	*1951*
Livestock Judging Arena	W. W. Watkin/Sanguinet, Staats & Hedrick	1925
Textile Engineering *(Industrial Engineering)*	W. W. Watkin/Sanguinet, Staats & Hedrick	1925
Mechanical Engineering Expansion		*1999*
Dairy Barn	Sanguinet, Staats & Hedrick	1925
Home Economics *(Human Sciences)*	W. W. Watkin/Sanguinet, Staats & Hedrick	1925
Home Economics Expansion	*Haynes & Kirby*	*1951*
Home Economics Expansion II	*Architects III Joint Venture*	*1973*
Food Sciences Tower	*Tisdel & Adling*	*1977*
Child Research Development Center	*SHW Group*	*2006*
Agriculture *(Speech)* †	W. W. Watkin/Sanguinet, Staats & Hedrick	1926
Cafeteria *(Bookstore)* †	Sanguinet, Staats & Hedrick	1926
Gymnasium *(Old Gymnasium)* †	Sanguinet, Staats & Hedrick	1926
Baseball Field *(Dan Law Field at Rip Griffin Park)*	N/A	1926
Dan Law Field Renovation		*1996*
Renovations and Additions	*Ellerbe Becket/MWM Architects*	*2001*
Rip Griffin Park Renovation	*MWM Architects*	*2012*
Home Management House	W. W. Watkin/Wyatt C. Hedrick	1927
West Engineering *(Electrical Engineering)*	W. W. Watkin/Wyatt C. Hedrick	1928
Chemistry	W. W. Watkin/Wyatt C. Hedrick	1929
Chemistry Expansion	*Pitts, Phelps, Saxe & White*	*1970*
Heating Plant No. 1 *(Old Power Plant)* †	W. W. Watkin/Wyatt C. Hedrick	1930
Men's Dormitory No. 1 *(West Hall)*	Wyatt C. Hedrick	1934
West Hall Visitors Center	*Adling Associates*	*2001*

Texas Tech University (Prior to September 1, 1969; Texas Technological College) (*continued*)

NAME	ARCHITECT	YEAR
Women's Dormitory No. 1 *(Doak Hall)*	Wyatt C. Hedrick	1934
Doak Hall Conference Center	*Adling Associates*	*1994*
Library *(Mathematics and Statistics)*	Wyatt C. Hedrick	1938
Men's Dormitory No. 2 *(Sneed Hall)*	Wyatt C. Hedrick	1938
Women's Dormitory No. 2 *(Drane Hall)*	Wyatt C. Hedrick	1938
Press Building *(Journalism)*	Wyatt C. Hedrick	1941
National Wind Institute	*Condray Design Group*	*2016*
Agriculture *(Agricultural Sciences)*	Wyatt C. Hedrick	1942
Men's Dormitories Nos. 3 & 4 *(Bledsoe-Gordon Halls)*	Wyatt C. Hedrick	1947
Women's Dormitories Nos. 3 & 4	Wyatt C. Hedrick	1947
Clifford B. and Audrey Jones Stadium *(Jones SBC Stadium/Jones AT&T Stadium)*	Haynes & Kirby	1947
Seating Expansion	*Haynes & Kirby*	*1953*
East Seating Relocation & Bowl	*Wyatt C. Hedrick/LaPlant-Adair*	*1960*
North Ticket Office	*Tisdel & Adling*	*1979*
Jones SBC Stage I Renovations	*Ellerbe Becket/MWM Architects*	*2001*
West Stadium and Club Expansion	*Ellerbe Becket/MWM Architects*	*2003*
East Stadium and Texas Tech Club	*Heery International/MWM Architects*	*2010*
North Jumbotron and Renovation	*MWM Architects*	*2013*
Heating Plant No. 2 †	Wyatt C. Hedrick	1947
Museum of West Texas	O. R. Walker	1949
Holden Hall Expansion	*Harper & Kemp*	*1975*
Petroleum Engineering	Wyatt C. Hedrick	1950
Petroleum Engineering Renovation Phase I	*Dekker/Perich/Sabbatini*	*2018*
Music Building *(Part of SUB/Allen Complex)*	Walsh & Hazelwood	1951
East Engineering *(Civil Engineering)*	Atcheson & Atkinson	1951
Civil Engineering Expansion	*Atcheson, Atkinson & Cartwright*	*1972*
Television and Radio Station	Wyatt C. Hedrick	1951
Agricultural Engineering and Annex	Haynes & Kirby	1951

Texas Tech University (Prior to September 1, 1969; Texas Technological College) (*continued*)

NAME	ARCHITECT	YEAR
Animal Sciences *(Landscape Architecture Annex)*	Haynes & Kirby	1951
Wildlife and Fisheries	*Haynes & Kirby*	*1961*
Science Building	Wyatt C. Hedrick	1951
Student Union Building	Atcheson & Atkinson	1953
Student Union Expansion	*Atcheson, Atkinson & Cartwright*	*1962*
University Center/Allen Theater	*Atcheson, Atkinson & Cartwright*	*1973*
Student Union Building Expansion	*HHPA Architects*	*2005*
Len and Harriet McClellan Memorial Infirmary		
Len and Harriet McClellan Memorial Hall	Butler-Brasher Company	1956
Weeks Hall	Atcheson, Atkinson & Cartwright	1957
Adaptive-Reuse Renovation	*Dekker/Perich/Sabbatini*	*2019*
Men's Gymnasium	Herbert Brasher & Associates	1957
Creative Movement Studio	*Condray Design Studio*	*2013*
Men's Dormitories Nos. 5, 6 (*Carpenter-Wells Hall*) †	Associated Architects & Engineers of Lubbock	1958
Women's Dormitories Nos. 5, 6		
(Thompson-Gaston Hall) †	Associated Architects & Engineers of Lubbock	1958
School of Medicine/Student Clinic	*SRMJ Architects*	*1971*
Classroom and Office Building *(English and Philosophy)* †	Butler-Kimmel Company	1960
Architecture/Computer Building *(Engineering Center)*	Haynes & Kirby	1961
Chemical and Nuclear Engineering *(Engineering and*		
Technology Labs)	Associated Architects & Engineers of Lubbock	1961
Livermore Engineering Laboratory	*F&S Partners*	*2007*
Center for Pulsed Power & Power Electronics	*F&S Partners*	*2009*
Agricultural Plant Sciences	Smith, Roberts & Messersmith	1961
Goddard Range and Wildlife Addition	*SRMJ Architects*	*1975*
Bayer Plant and Crop Sciences Lab	*Smith Group/JJR*	*2015*

Texas Tech University (Prior to September 1, 1969; Texas Technological College) (*continued*)

NAME	ARCHITECT	YEAR
Physical Plant Building	Atcheson, Atkinson & Cartwright	1961
Physical Plant Annex	*Davis, Foster & Thorpe*	*1969*
Exercise and Sports Science	*Condray Design Group*	*2012*
Women's Auxiliary Gymnasium †	Brasher, Spencer & Goyette	1961
Library	Pitts, Mebane & Phelps	1962
Library Expansion	*SRMJ Architects*	*1975*
Library Renovations	*Parkhill, Smith & Cooper*	*2000*
Wall-Gates Hall	Associated Architects & Engineers of Lubbock	1963
Psychology Building	Stiles, Roberts & Messersmith	1964
Psychology Addition	*Architects III Joint Venture*	*1975*
Charles E. Maedgen Jr. Theater	Stiles, Roberts & Messersmith	1964
College of Visual and Performing Arts	*HGA/Brown Reynolds Watford*	*2019*
Stangel-Murdough Hall	Associated Architects & Engineers of Lubbock	1964
The Market at Stangel-Murdough Hall	*Adling Associates*	*1999*
Hulen-Clement Hall	Associated Architects & Engineers of Lubbock	1964
Central Food Warehouse	Associated Architects & Engineers of Lubbock	1964
Art 3D Annex	*Team HAAS/Parkhill, Smith & Cooper*	*2010*
Foreign Languages	Pitts, Mebane & Phelps	1966
The Wiggins Complex		
Chitwood, Weymouth, and Coleman Halls		
Wiggins Central Dining Facility	Stiles, Roberts & Messersmith	1967
Housing and Dining Offices	*JDMA Architects*	*2008*
Central Heating & Cooling Plant (CHACP I)	Pitts, Mebane, Phelps & White	1968
Business Administration	Page Southerland Page	1969
College of Media and Communications	*Parkhill, Smith & Cooper*	*2012*

Texas Tech University (Prior to September 1, 1969; Texas Technological College) (*continued*)

NAME	ARCHITECT	YEAR
School of Law	Harrell + Hamilton	1969
Mark and Becky Lanier Professional Development Center	*SHW Group*	*2008*
Biology *(Biological Sciences)*	Pierce & Pierce	1969
Museum of Texas Tech University	SRMJ Architects	1970
Natural Sciences Research Laboratory Addition	*MWM Architects*	*2005*
Art and Architecture Complex	Ford Powell & Carson	1970
Interdisciplinary Design + Fabrication Lab Expansion	*Parkhill, Smith & Cooper*	*2018*
Track Dressing Room	Schmidt & Associates	1971
Track Team Building Renovations	*MWM Architects*	*2014*
Livestock Pavilion and Meat Judging Lab	SRMJ Architects	1973
Animal and Food Sciences	*Parkhill, Smith & Cooper*	*2005*
Mass Communications	Calhoun, Tungate & Jackson	1976
Maddox Engineering Research Center	*Condray Design Group*	*2016*
National Ranching Heritage Center—DeVitt & Mallet Ranch Building	Tisdel & Adling	1976
Christine DeVitt Wing Expansion	*Adling Associates*	*2006*
NRHC North Addition	*Adling Associates*	*2011*
Robert H. Ewalt Student Recreation Center	Jarvis Putty Jarvis	1980
Recreation Center Expansion	*Brown Reynolds + Watford*	*2001*
Leisure Pool Expansion	*Brinkley Sargent Architects*	*2009*
Athletics Training Center †	Spencer Associates/JDMA Architects	1986
Southwest Special Collections Library	Komatsu/Rangel/AC Associates	1995
International Cultural Center	JDMA Architects	1997
Carpenter-Wells Residential Hall Complex	Lotti Krishnan Short	1998
Frazier Alumni Pavilion	H. Duane Pierce Architects	1998
Pavilion Addition	*JDMA Architects*	*2019*

Texas Tech University (Prior to September 1, 1969; Texas Technological College) (*continued*)

NAME	ARCHITECT	YEAR
United Spirit Arena *(United Supermarkets Arena)*	Rosser International/JDMA Architects	1999
Interior/Locker Room Renovations	*Parkhill, Smith & Cooper*	*2016*
Flint Avenue Parking Facility	Walker Parking Consultants/Adling Associates	2002
English-Philosophy & Education Complex	Hellmuth, Obata + Kassabaum	2002
Marsha Sharp Center for Student Athletes	MWM Architects	2004
Football Training Facility	Ellerbe Becket/MWM Architects	2004
Grover E. Murray Residence Hall	BOKA-Powell	2005
Experimental Sciences Building *(Experimental Sciences Building I)*	CO Architects	2005
Student Wellness Center	F&S Partners	2006
Outreach and Extended Studies Building	Adling Associates	2006
Bayer CropSciences Seeds Innovation Center—Research and Development	*Parkhill, Smith & Cooper*	*2015*
Softball Team Facility	Heery International/Parkhill, Smith & Cooper	2010
Jerry S. Rawls College of Business Administration	Goody Clancy/Parkhill, Smith & Cooper	2012
Rawls College of Business Expansion	*Parkhill, Smith & Cooper*	*2016*
Kent R. Hance Campus Chapel	McKinney/York Architects	2012
Talkington Residence Hall and the Commons	BOKA-Powell	2012
Cash Foundation Clubhouse Don-Kay-Clay and Cash Family Team Facility at the Rawls Course	JDMA Architects	2012
Gerald Myers Indoor Soccer Facility	Wilson Architects	2012
Burkhart Center for Autism Education and Research	SHW Group (now Stantec)	2013
Terry Fuller Petroleum Engineering Research Building	Kirksey	2014
West Village Residential Complex	Barnes Gromatzky Kosarek/Mackey-Mitchell Architects	2014
Bayer CropScience Seeds Innovation Center Trait Development Building	Parkhill, Smith & Cooper	2015
TTU Research and Technology Park—Phase I	Kirksey	2015

Texas Tech University (Prior to September 1, 1969; Texas Technological College) (*continued*)

NAME	ARCHITECT	YEAR
United Spirit Arena *(United Supermarkets Arena)*	Rosser International/JDMA Architects	1999
University System Office Building	Parkhill, Smith & Cooper	2017
Honors Residence Hall Project	Barnes Gromatzky Kosarek/Mackey-Mitchell Architects	2017
Sports Performance Center within the Edward E. Whitacre Jr. Athletic Complex	Gensler	2017
Experimental Sciences Building II	TreanorHL Architects/Ayers Saint Gross	2019
Athletics Dining Facility	MWM Architects	2019

Texas Tech University Health Sciences Center Lubbock Campus (Prior to September 1, 1979; the Texas Tech University School of Medicine)

NAME	ARCHITECT	YEAR
School of Medicine Phase IA *(Pods A/B/C)*	CRS/Harwood K. Smith Architects	1975
Phases II and III Finish-Out	*Harwood K. Smith Architects*	*1979*
F. Marie Hall Synergistics Center	*Parkhill, Smith & Cooper*	*2003*
The F. Marie Hall SimLife Center	*F&S Partners*	*2010*
HSC 4C Cancer Research Labs	*F&S Partners*	*2010*
Central Heating and Cooling Plant (CHACP) II	Harwood K. Smith Architects	1976
Preston Smith Library of the Health Sciences	Parkhill, Smith & Cooper	1999
Academic Classroom Building	Parkhill, Smith & Cooper	2003
Lubbock Clinical Pavilion	FKP Architects	2007
Messer/Racz Pain Center	FKP Architects	2009
Lubbock Education, Research and	Perkins+Will	2019
Technology + West Expansion TTUHSC University Center	Perkins+Will	2019

APPENDIX B | GLOSSARY OF ARCHITECTURAL TERMINOLOGY

Definitions are taken from either the *Illustrated Dictionary of Historic Architecture*, Cyril M. Harris, ed.; *Imperial Spain: 1469–1716*, first edition, by John Huxtable Elliott; or interview materiel provided by Dr. Javier Rivera Blanco, Sarai Herrera, and José Javier Lopez Martín during research travels in Spain. *Italic* terms in the definitions are also defined in this glossary.

acanthus A Mediterranean plant, whose leaves are most commonly stylized in *Corinthian* capitals, or as a raised ornament found commonly in *neoclassical* architecture.

aedicule A door or window framed by columns or pilasters and framed with a pediment set atop flanking columns or pilasters.

aileron A convex scroll often resting astride and flanking a façade or detail feature.

ancon A scrolled bracket that supports a cornice or entablature over a door or window.

arabesque In *Plateresque* architecture, an intricate overall pattern of stylized plants and figures either painted, inlaid, or carved in raised or low relief.

Araeostyle A form of column spacing (or intercolumniation) common in *colonnades* at Texas Tech where the spacing ration between the width of opening between columns and width of a column varies between 4:1 and 5:1.

arcade A covered walk with a line of arches (a *colonnade*) along one or both sides of the walkway.

arco carpanel Spanish term for a *baskethandle arch*; an elliptical or semielliptical arch where the line of arch parabolically transitions into the edge-of-column without a sharp angle at the *springline*.

artesonado Spanish term for a form of often-intricate *Mudéjar* woodworking applied in ceilings in which a combination of coffering, intricate geometric patterning, and/or *arabesques,* often with fastened connections executed without nails or traditional fasteners.

balconette A pseudo-balcony where a low ornamental sill or railing, often a fabricated *reja* in Spanish architecture, is applied to a window or upper-floor opening.

balustrade An entire railing composition, often fabricated in stone consisting of a top rail set atop a row of balusters, divided and/or bounded by pedestals.

Baroque A European style of architecture and decoration that developed in seventeenth-century Italy, expounded upon late Renaissance and Mannerist forms, often more conspicuously ornamented and sculpted than earlier Renaissance classicism.

baskethandle arch An elliptical or semielliptical arch where the line of arch smoothly transitions into the edge-of-column without a sharp angle at the *springline*.

Beaux-Arts A nineteenth- and twentieth-century movement espousing historicistic and eclectic neoclassical design, named for the *École des Beaux-Arts* in Paris, the influential progenitor of the style during that era.

campanario A Spanish simplification of a *campanile* consisting of an unenclosed tower form, traditionally distinguished by an arched opening for a bell with buttressed corners or multiple arched openings diagonally stacked. *Campanarios* were a common and a less expensive substitution for *campaniles* in Spanish mission architecture of the Southwestern United States.

campanile (or *carillon*) An enclosed and roofed bell tower commonly found in the cathedral, church, and monastical architecture of Spain.

cantilever A beam, girder, truss, or architectural form that projects beyond its supporting wall or column.

capital The top-most member, usually decorated of a column or pilaster that connects the column to the *entablature* above. At Texas Tech, and in Plateresque architecture, most often capitals are in the *Corinthian* order.

Churrigueresque The lavishly ornamented Spanish Baroque style of the early eighteenth century, named after the Spanish *maestro mayor* José Benito de Churriguera (1665–1725); a popular style in New Spain, particularly in Mexico.

cloister A covered walk surrounding a court or courtyard, usually linking a church or cathedral to other buildings of a monastery.

colonnade A number of columns arranged in order at a common interval, often supporting either an entablature, a series of arches in *arcade*, and/or one side of a roof.

conch A semicircular niche, usually covered with a half-dome relief. Often in Plateresque architecture, the dome form is fashioned in the form of a scallop shell.

corbel (or corbeling) A piece—usually brick or stone—jutting from a wall to carry a superincumbent weight above, sometimes in repetitive patterns.

Corinthian Either column or capital, the most slender and ornate of the three classical Greek orders of columns, characterized by an inverted-bell-shaped capital with volute scrolls at its upper corners, with two rows of *acanthus* leaves below it. Originally used profusely by the Romans, its ornate appearance made it popular with *maestros mayores* and patrons alike of the Spanish Renaissance.

drip edge (or *drip cap*) A horizontal molding originally prevalent in the *Gothic* style, usually of carved stone in an *ogee* or similar profile, set over a door, arch, or window frame to divert water away from the opening.

engaged column A column, partially built into the façade behind it, either in entirety or connected at pedestal and entablature, but not freestanding.

enjabalgadura A Spanish term for a form of *Mudéjar* wall detailing where corner or in-wall brick masonry *quoining* alternates with flush panels of stucco, which are horizontally broken by courses of brick masonry. A wall style commonly found in Castilian and Aragonese cities such as Alcalá de Henares and Zaragoza.

entablature The elaborated beam member carried by either columns or pilasters below and whose height is dictated by the classical order of columns used (which in *Plateresque* architecture is most often the *Corinthian* order).

escudo A raised or relief-carved shield in Spanish architecture; often either representative of a noble family (*hidalguía*), or denoting the crown or head of state.

escutcheon In the context of stone work, a traditionally raised carved ornamental detail surrounding a shield (*escudo*), bust, or other small detail.

Estilo Plateresco Hispanicization of the term *Plateresque* style. See *Plateresque*.

estípite An *engaged column* or *pilaster* found in *mannerist* or *Baroque*-era architecture (but not found in *Plateresque* or *Herreran* styles) in Spain and New Spain, typified by the presence of an inverted obelisk.

fascia Any flat horizontally oriented vertical surface, panel, or molding either set in cantilever above a wall or resting below the eave of a roof.

filigree In *Plateresque* architecture, a perforated *parapet* formed of often-symmetrical animals, figurines, or floral patterns carved in florid detail and divided by pedestals or *finials* in a similar fashion to balustrades.

finial An ornamental spire rising from an eave or pedestal, crafted in carved stone, which in *Plateresque* architecture is an evolution from its florid *Gothic* ancestor, the spire, found commonly atop the towers of flying *buttresses* on churches or cathedrals.

Flemish bond In brickwork, a bond in which each horizontal course consists of headers (the longest, most slender face of brick) and stretchers (the end face of the brick laid flattest) are laid alternatively, with horizontal courses laid with headers centered to stretchers above or below it.

frieze The middle, often tallest, horizontal segment of a classical *entablature* and the most common surface in *neoclassical* architecture to find a carved or raised inscription.

frontispiece The decorated front wall or bay of a building.

gable The vertical triangular portion at the end of a building façade that terminates a double-sloping roof.

glazier A tradesperson whose skill is in the fabrication of building glass (or glazing), and unit windows for building openings.

Gothic style An architectural style of the High Middle Ages in Western Europe that first emerged in France in the latter twelfth century. The *Gothic style* remained a popular and dominant style in Spain through the end of the fifteenth century, and many elements of *Gothicism* inherently became a elements of the later *Plateresque* stylistic vocabulary.

header The masonry form, or composition of masonry details, which reside directly above the opening in a façade, such as a door or window.

heraldry The design, display, and study of coats-of-arms used for the identification of kingdoms, royal houses or families, and noble families.

Herreran style The prevailing style of architecture in the latter half of the sixteenth century, which supplanted the *estilo plateresco*, defined by the near elimination of ornament in favor of a proportionally—and mathematically more precise Renaissance style. Named for its progenitor, Spanish *Corte Real* architect Juan de Herrera (1530–1597).

hidalgo (or *hidalguía*) A Spanish term for a nobleman, or noble class of people, officially declared as such by the Spanish Royal Court or *Cortes Real*.

hypostyle hall A large space with a flat roof supported by a grid of columns. Though originally used by the Egyptians and Persians, it was also used as the primary structural system for the Great Mosque of Córdoba.

Isabelline Named for Queen Isabella of Spain (1451–1504), a transitional architectural style between the *Gothic* and *Plateresque* periods dating between 1480 and 1504, marked by the absence of Italian Renaissance ordering, but still containing the same florid details seen in the *Plateresque* style.

maestro mayor A Spanish term that combined the role of architect, chief foreman of construction, and chief craftsman, all in one person.

mannerism (or *mannerist*) Transitional style in Renaissance architecture and the arts during the sixteenth century, typified by the unconventional use of classical elements.

mihrab A niche or opening in the wall of a mosque, at the point nearest to Mecca, used to orient one for prayer.

mudéjar A broad range of details, construction methods, and styles developed by Moorish craftsmen of the Nasrid Dynasty in Islamic-ruled Spain dating back to the eighth century AD, but retained and integrated into later styles and periods of Spanish architecture following the *Reconquista*.

neoclassical The final phase of European classicism that extended into the twentieth century into the Western Hemisphere, characterized by monumentality and strict use of Greco-Roman orders.

ogee The cross section of a double curve, formed by the union of a convex and concave line, resembling an S-shape, and used most frequently in the molding, cornices, and belt coursing of classical architecture.

Oxbridge A portmanteau of the institutional names Oxford and Cambridge describing the highly organic monastic-styled architecture of English, and more broadly European collegiate construction prior to the Jeffersonian era of campus planning.

Palladian stair A Roman-inspired, classically detailed, and symmetrical stair, consisting of a combination of divergent and/or convergent series of stair risers that converge at one or multiple intermediate landing(s), or connect to a central perpendicular series of stair risers. Named for the formalist Roman-revival Renaissance style of Andrea Palladio (1508–1580).

parapet A low-guarding wall separating the edge of the roof, balcony, or terrace.

pediment In classical architecture, the triangular end of a roof, or architectural feature set above a doorway, window, or entry feature, which has been enclosed with the traditional features of two diagonal raking cornices set over a horizontal cornice.

peristyle An enclosing or radially connecting colonnade, situated between two buildings or arcades.

piano nobile A classical term for the first floor above the ground floor, from which the system of European floor numbering still used today derives.

Piedra de Villamayor A name applied to one of two types of golden-hued stone quarried in and around the municipality of Villamayor in the province of Salamanca; one a softer sandstone-like stone, and the other more limestone-like and ideal for fine carving, which was commonly used in *Plateresque*-era architecture in Castile and Andalusia.

pilaster An engaged pier or pillar, often including a capital or base.

piso de hidalguía A common design feature in *Plateresque* architecture that defies common precepts of Renaissance architecture, where the upper-most floor of a building façade receives the most ornate and articulated detail, often corresponding with the floor containing living and/or working spaces of Spanish nobility (*hidalguía*).

Plateresque A term applied to describe the prevailing style of architecture in Spain in the first half of the sixteenth century, comparing the profuse use of ornament in the style with the popular ornate silver jewelry (or *plata*) of the period. First use of term was made by Renaissance essayist Cristóbal de Villalón in 1539 and later applied by historian Diego Ortiz de Zúñiga in the seventeenth century.

quoin In masonry construction, an articulated stone or brick used at building corners to reinforce that corner or edge, or for decorative purposes.

reja (or *rejería*) A Spanish term for a wrought-iron grille, or for the field of wrought-iron craftsmanship.

Romanesque The style emerging in Western Europe beginning in the early eleventh century, based on Roman and Byzantine elements, and characterized by massive articulated walls and round arches, only to later be superseded by the *Gothic* movement. A popular *Romanesque*-revival movement would later take place throughout the British Empire and the United States in the nineteenth century.

roundel A small circular panel or raised detail, including *escudos*, busts, or florid details, often carved into stone.

rowlock A brick laid on its edge so that its end is visible. Sometimes, *rowlock* coursing is set to project from a façade, or is laid in multiple *rowlock* courses about an arch, producing a *rowlock* arch.

rusticated In classical architecture, a masonry technique where the face treatment or joint articulation of masonry low to the ground on a façade is pronounced so as to accentuate the base form of the building.

salle-porte A through-building passageway, often articulated by arched opening or other details, allowing transit without having to enter the building.

soffit The exposed undersurface of any overhead component of a building, such as a roof overhang, balcony, or cornice.

soldier course A brick masonry course, often interrupting a traditional series of running bond courses, where a course of brick stretchers have been set vertically.

Spanish-colonial revival A stylistic movement, particularly popular in California during the early twentieth century, which adapted the simple stucco- and stone-clad motifs of the Spanish-colonial era in the Southwestern United States in the sixteenth and seventeenth century to modern building types.

springline The elevation at which a column or jamb transitions into the curve of an arch or vault.

transom A glazed light (window) or opening set over a door.

voussoir A wedge-shaped masonry unit in an arch or vault whose converging sides are cut as radii of one of the centers of the arch or vault.

water table An articulated masonry base, or change in masonry treatment, set at the base of a building anywhere from a few feet in height up to the full height of the first floor.

APPENDIX C | IMAGE CREDITS

Images not credited herein, or not in the public domain, are by the author. Pages with multiple images are credited from top to bottom.

FRONTISPIECE: "Illustration: Spanish Renaissance Styles", from THE STORY OF ARCHITECTURE IN MEXICO by Trent Elwood Sanford. Copyright 1947 by W. W. Norton & Company, Inc. Used by permission of W. W. Norton & Company, Inc.

xviii Reprinted by permission of Texas Tech University.

xxi Chicago History Museum, Image# ICHi-064414.

4 Image MSS0187-0614, Houston Public Library, HMRC.

5 Woodson Research Center, Fondren Library, Rice University.

5 Image LC-DIG-ds-08213, US Library of Congress Prints & Photographs Online Catalog.

6 J. E. Stout, Photographer, USDA Agricultural Research Service.

7 Image #0010108, Texas Tech University Blueprint Collection, Southwest Collection/Special Collections Library, Texas Tech University.

10 La Rendición de Granada (1882), Francisco Pradilla y Ortiz. Palacio del Senado, Madrid, Spain.

12 Architect of the Capitol.

20 Oregon Historical Society.

21 Courtesy of Special Collections, Schaffer Library, Union College.

22 Stanford University Print Collection, Image #SC1039.

22 Oregon Historical Society.

24 Used with the permission of the Panama-California Exposition Digital Archive, The Committee of One Hundred, San Diego, California.

25 James Riely Gordon collection, Alexander Architectural Archives, University of Texas Libraries, The University of Texas at Austin.

32 Courtesy of Panhandle-Plains Historical Museum, Canyon, Texas.

32 Woodson Research Center, Fondren Library, Rice University.

33 Woodson Research Center, Fondren Library, Rice University.

34 Image #E3128, Heritage Club Collection, Southwest Collection/Special Collections Library, Texas Tech University.

34 Courtesy, Fort Worth *Star-Telegram* Collection, Special Collections, The University of Texas at Arlington Libraries.

37 Courtesy of Ames Fender, AIA, Architect.

37 Image # SWCPC57(Z)-E27.37, Lubbock History Collection, Southwest Collection/Special Collections Library, Texas Tech University.

42 Courtesy of The Redfern Gallery, Laguna Beach, California.

43 John Nolen Collection, The Architectural Archives, University of Pennsylvania.

43 Image Key Number 3793, Houston Public Library, HMRC.

44 Woodson Research Center, Fondren Library, Rice University.

44 Woodson Research Center, Fondren Library, Rice University.

45 Woodson Research Center, Fondren Library, Rice University.

49 Courtesy of the Iowa Barn Foundation.

55 Image #549, Lubbock Pictorial Collection, Southwest Collection/Special Collections Library, Texas Tech University.

56 Woodson Research Center, Fondren Library, Rice University.

61 Image #C1077, Heritage Club Collection, Southwest Collection/Special Collections Library, Texas Tech University.

62 Image ID# President's Home, Heritage Club Collection, Southwest Collection/Special Collections Library, Texas Tech University.

62 Image ID# Agriculture Pavilion, Heritage Club Collection, Southwest Collection/Special Collections Library, Texas Tech University.

62 Image # wr.c.4.5.12.3.2, Winston Reeves Photograph Collection, Southwest Collection/Special Collections Library, Texas Tech University.

64 Courtesy of the University of Massachusetts Lowell.

66 Image # wr.c.4.2.19.2.1, Winston Reeves Photograph Collection, Southwest Collection/Special Collections Library, Texas Tech University.

66 Image # SWCPC57(T)-E6.19, Lubbock History Collection, Southwest Collection/Special Collections Library, Texas Tech University.

68 Image # SWCPC57(T)-E6.42, Lubbock History Collection, Southwest Collection/Special Collections Library, Texas Tech University.

70 Image ID# Aerial of Texas Tech, Heritage Club Collection, Southwest Collection/Special Collections Library, Texas Tech University.

70 Image # wr.c.1.1.3.4.1, Winston Reeves Photograph Collection, Southwest Collection/Special Collections Library, Texas Tech University.

74 Courtesy of the San Diego History Center.

77 University of Texas Buildings Collection, Alexander Architectural Archives, University of Texas Libraries, The University of Texas at Austin.

77 Courtesy of Chris Cooper, Fisher-Heck Architects, San Antonio, Texas.

79 Courtesy of Brandon Young, AIA.

84 Image ID# Library, Red Raider Retrospectives, 1923–Present Collection, Southwest Collection/Special Collections Library, Texas Tech University.

84 Image #C134-14, Heritage Club Collection, Southwest Collection/Special Collections Library, Texas Tech University.

85 Image #C130-5, Heritage Club Collection, Southwest Collection/Special Collections Library, Texas Tech University.

88 Image # wr.c.4.2.19.4.1, Winston Reeves Photograph Collection, Southwest Collection/Special Collections Library, Texas Tech University.

93 Image ID# Home Management House, Red Raider Retrospectives, 1923–Present Collection, Southwest Collection/Special Collections Library, Texas Tech University.

93 Image ID# Boiler Plant, Red Raider Retrospectives, 1923–Present Collection, Southwest Collection/Special Collections Library, Texas Tech University.

95 Woodson Research Center, Fondren Library, Rice University.

95 Woodson Research Center, Fondren Library, Rice University.

98 Parkhill, Smith & Cooper, Inc.

98 Parkhill, Smith & Cooper, Inc.

99 Image #P943-1, Heritage Club Collection, Southwest Collection/Special Collections Library, Texas Tech University.

100 Image ID# Dormitories, Heritage Club Collection, Southwest Collection/Special Collections Library, Texas Tech University.

101 Image # wr.c.93P.5.20.14.1, Winston Reeves Photograph Collection, Southwest Collection/Special Collections Library, Texas Tech University.

101 Woodson Research Center, Fondren Library, Rice University.

103 Image ID# Dairy Barn, Red Raider Retrospectives, 1923–Present Collection, Southwest Collection/Special Collections Library, Texas Tech University.

104 Sanguinet, Staats, and Hedrick Records, Alexander Architectural Archives, University of Texas Libraries, The University of Texas at Austin.

104 Sanguinet, Staats, and Hedrick Records, Alexander Architectural Archives, University of Texas Libraries, The University of Texas at Austin.

105 Image # wr.c.5.6.13.2.2, Winston Reeves Photograph Collection, Southwest Collection/Special Collections Library, Texas Tech University.

105 Image # wr.c.4.4.1.1.1, Winston Reeves Photograph Collection, Southwest Collection/Special Collections Library, Texas Tech University.

108 Image ID# Agriculture Building, Red Raider Retrospectives, 1923–Present Collection, Southwest Collection/Special Collections Library, Texas Tech University.

108 Image # wr.c.4.5.3.3.2, Winston Reeves Photograph Collection, Southwest Collection/Special Collections Library, Texas Tech University.

111 Image # wr.c.37P.1.2.4.1, Winston Reeves Photograph Collection, Southwest Collection/Special Collections Library, Texas Tech University.

112 Image # SWCPC57(X)-E2.14, Lubbock History Collection, Southwest Collection/Special Collections Library, Texas Tech University.

113 Image ID# Journalism, Public Information, 1928–1968 Collection, Southwest Collection/Special Collections Library, Texas Tech University.

114 Courtesy of E. Paul Koeppe, AIA.

114 Image ID# Cadets, Red Raider Retrospectives, 1923–Present Collection, Southwest Collection/Special Collections Library, Texas Tech University.

115 Image ID# Faculty Club, Public Information, 1928–1968 Collection, Southwest Collection/Special Collections Library, Texas Tech University.

115 Image # wr.c.19.14P.9.5.1.1, Winston Reeves Photograph Collection, Southwest Collection/Special Collections Library, Texas Tech University.

116 Image # wr.c.56P.2.2.6.1, Winston Reeves Photograph Collection, Southwest Collection/Special Collections Library, Texas Tech University.

116 Image ID# Petroleum Engineering, Red Raider Retrospectives, 1923–Present Collection, Southwest Collection/Special Collections Library, Texas Tech University.

116 Image ID# Administration Building, Public Information, 1928–1968 Collection, Southwest Collection/Special Collections Library, Texas Tech University.

120 Courtesy of Luxco, Inc.

120 Image MSS0114-2161, Houston Public Library, HMRC.

120 Woodson Research Center, Fondren Library, Rice University.

121 Image ID# Home Economics Building, Heritage Club Collection, Southwest Collection/Special Collections Library, Texas Tech University.

124 Image # wr.c.56N.2.2.4.1, Winston Reeves Photograph Collection, Southwest Collection/Special Collections Library, Texas Tech University.

127 Image ID# Museum, Public Information, 1928–1968 Collection, Southwest Collection/Special Collections Library, Texas Tech University.

127 Image ID# Nolan Barrick 3, Texas Tech People Collection, Southwest Collection/Special Collections Library, Texas Tech University.

190 Image # wr.c.42P.3.1.3.1, Winston Reeves Photograph Collection, Southwest Collection/Special Collections Library, Texas Tech University.

190 Image # wr.c.126P.2.36.1.1, Winston Reeves Photograph Collection, Southwest Collection/Special Collections Library, Texas Tech University.

192 Image ID# Civil Engineering, Winston Reeves Photograph Collection, Southwest Collection/Special Collections Library, Texas Tech University.

195 Image # wr.c.38P.5.1.3.1, Winston Reeves Photograph Collection, Southwest Collection/Special Collections Library, Texas Tech University.

195 Image # wr.c.87P.2.11.1.1, Winston Reeves Photograph Collection, Southwest Collection/Special Collections Library, Texas Tech University.

195 Image # wr.c.88P.1.15.2.1, Winston Reeves Photograph Collection, Southwest Collection/Special Collections Library, Texas Tech University.

196 Image # wr.c.38P.5.1.4.1, Winston Reeves Photograph Collection, Southwest Collection/Special Collections Library, Texas Tech University.

197 Image #C1223, Heritage Club Collection, Southwest Collection/Special Collections Library, Texas Tech University.

197 Image # wr.c.115P.2.13.1.1, Winston Reeves Photograph Collection, Southwest Collection/Special Collections Library, Texas Tech University.

200 Image ID# English Building, Red Raider Retrospectives, 1923–Present Collection, Southwest Collection/Special Collections Library, Texas Tech University.

200 Image ID# Architecture-Computer Building, Heritage Club Collection, Southwest Collection/Special Collections Library, Texas Tech University.

201 Image ID# Aerial of Texas Tech, Red Raider Retrospectives, 1923–Present Collection, Southwest Collection/Special Collections Library, Texas Tech University.

202 Image # wr.c.117N.3.15.1.1, Winston Reeves Photograph Collection, Southwest Collection/Special Collections Library, Texas Tech University.

202 Image # wr.c.117N.3.15.4.1, Winston Reeves Photograph Collection, Southwest Collection/Special Collections Library, Texas Tech University.

206 Armstrong, R. H.; Kolb, W. L.; Lennox, D. H.; Kelber, C. N.; Selep, Andrew & Spinrad, B. I. Engineering, Construction and Cost of the Argonaut Reactor, report, March 1957; Lemont, Illinois. (https://digital.library.unt.edu/ark:/67531/metadc67185/: accessed September 9, 2019), University of North Texas Libraries, Digital Library, https://digital.library.unt.edu; crediting UNT Libraries Government Documents Department.

207 Image ID# University Theater 3, Red Raider Retrospectives, 1923–Present Collection, Southwest Collection/Special Collections Library, Texas Tech University.

210 Image Serial No. 854-2A-WH65, LBJ Library Photo by Frank Wolfe, Courtesy of The Lyndon Baines Johnson Presidential Library.

211 Parkhill, Smith & Cooper, Inc.

212 Image ID# Weymouth, Red Raider Retrospectives, 1923–Present Collection, Southwest Collection/Special Collections Library, Texas Tech University.

212 Image ID# Proposed Central Heating and Cooling Plant, Public Information, 1928-1968 Collection, Southwest Collection/Special Collections Library, Texas Tech University.

213 Image #C340, Heritage Club Collection, Southwest Collection/Special Collections Library, Texas Tech University.

213 Image ID# Howard W. Schmidt, M. L. Pennington, Jerry Kirkwood, H. H. May, Public Information, 1928–1968 Collection, Southwest Collection/Special Collections Library, Texas Tech University.

215 Image ID# Artist's rendering of the new biology building, Public Information, 1928–1968 Collection, Southwest Collection/Special Collections Library, Texas Tech University.

216 Image ID# Moving temporary classroom, Public Information, 1928–1968 Collection, Southwest Collection/Special Collections Library, Texas Tech University.

218 Image ID# Museum, Red Raider Retrospectives, 1923–Present Collection, Southwest Collection/Special Collections Library, Texas Tech University.

218 Image ID# Museum Building, Photographic Services, 1969–Present Collection, Southwest Collection/Special Collections Library, Texas Tech University.

222 Courtesy of the Special Collections Research Center, University of Chicago Library.

223 Courtesy of the *Lubbock Avalanche-Journal*.

223 Image ID# Lubbock tornado, Heritage Club Collection, Southwest Collection/Special Collections Library, Texas Tech University.

224 Image ID# Architecture Building 1, Red Raider Retrospectives, 1923–Present Collection, Southwest Collection/Special Collections Library, Texas Tech University.

225 Image ID# Art Building, Red Raider Retrospectives, 1923–Present Collection, Southwest Collection/Special Collections Library, Texas Tech University.

225 Image ID# Museum, Public Information, 1928–1968 Collection, Southwest Collection/Special Collections Library, Texas Tech University.

225 Image # wr.c.52P.5.20.2.1, Winston Reeves Photograph Collection, Southwest Collection/Special Collections Library, Texas Tech University.

226 Image #C355, Heritage Club Collection, Southwest Collection/Special Collections Library, Texas Tech University.

226 Image ID# Museum, Public Information, 1928–1968 Collection, Southwest Collection/Special Collections Library, Texas Tech University.

227 Image #C341, Heritage Club Collection, Southwest Collection/Special Collections Library, Texas Tech University.

228 Image ID# Memorial Circle, Red Raider Retrospectives, 1923–Present Collection, Southwest Collection/Special Collections Library, Texas Tech University.

234 Image ID# Medical School, Red Raider Retrospectives, 1923–Present Collection, Southwest Collection/Special Collections Library, Texas Tech University.

234 Image # wr.c.93P.5.20.15.1, Winston Reeves Photograph Collection, Southwest Collection/Special Collections Library, Texas Tech University.

235 Courtesy of Jack DeBartolo, FAIA.

235 Courtesy of Jack DeBartolo, FAIA.

236 Courtesy of Jack DeBartolo, FAIA.

236 Image #05, Texas Tech University Blueprint Collection, Southwest Collection/Special Collections Library, Texas Tech University.

236 Courtesy of Jack DeBartolo, FAIA.

237 HKS, Inc.

237 HKS, Inc.

239 HKS, Inc.

240 HKS, Inc.

245 Image ID# Agriculture Building, Heritage Club Collection, Southwest Collection/Special Collections Library, Texas Tech University.

248 Parkhill, Smith & Cooper, Inc.

249 Courtesy of Mr. Kris Barton / Full Throttle RC.

252 HOK Group, Inc.

256 Parkhill, Smith & Cooper, Inc.

257 KSQ Design, Inc.

258 HOK Group, Inc.

259 HOK Group, Inc.

259 HOK Group, Inc.

260 HOK Group, Inc.

261 HOK Group, Inc.

261 HOK Group, Inc.

262 Parkhill, Smith & Cooper, Inc.

264 JDMA Architects.

265 JDMA Architects.

266 JDMA Architects.

268 HOK Group, Inc.

272 Photo by Evan Schiller / www.golfshots.com, courtesy of Renaissance Golf Design, Inc.

272 Photo by J. Ryan Montgomery, courtesy of Renaissance Golf Design, Inc.

273 Brown Reynolds Watford Architects.

274 Parkhill, Smith & Cooper, Inc.

275 Parkhill, Smith & Cooper, Inc.

275 Parkhill, Smith & Cooper, Inc.

276 Courtesy of William L. Adling, AIA.

280 Provided by Holzman Moss Bottino Architecture.

281 Provided by Holzman Moss Bottino Architecture.

282 Texas Tech University.

283 Parkhill, Smith & Cooper, Inc.

284 Parkhill, Smith & Cooper, Inc.

288 Image ID# Electra Waggoner Biggs, Texas Tech People Collection, Southwest Collection/Special Collections Library, Texas Tech University.

288 Image ID# Will Rogers Statue, Public Information, 1928–1968 Collection, Southwest Collection/Special Collections Library, Texas Tech University.

290 Reprinted by permission of Texas Tech University.

290 Reprinted by permission of Texas Tech University.

291 Image ID# Peter Hurd, Public Information, 1928–1968 Collection, Southwest Collection/Special Collections Library, Texas Tech University.

291 Reprinted by permission of The Daily Toreador, photo by Derrick Spencer.

291 Reprinted by permission of Texas Tech University Health Sciences Center.

292 Reprinted by permission of Texas Tech University.

293 Reprinted by permission of Texas Tech University.

294 Reprinted by permission of Texas Tech University.

298 Courtesy of the *Lubbock Avalanche-Journal.*

298 Image # wr.c.14.9.13.1.3, Winston Reeves Photograph Collection, Southwest Collection/Special Collections Library, Texas Tech University.

299 Image # wr.c.87P.2.15.1.1, Winston Reeves Photograph Collection, Southwest Collection/Special Collections Library, Texas Tech University.

299 Parkhill, Smith & Cooper, Inc.

300 Image # wr.c.11.8.15.1.1, Winston Reeves Photograph Collection, Southwest Collection/Special Collections Library, Texas Tech University.

301 Image ID# Jones Stadium, Public Information, 1928–1968 Collection, Southwest Collection/Special Collections Library, Texas Tech University.

301 Image ID# Jones Stadium, Public Information, 1928–1968 Collection, Southwest Collection/Special Collections Library, Texas Tech University.

302 Image ID# Jones Stadium, Heritage Club Collection, Southwest Collection/Special Collections Library, Texas Tech University.

302 Image # wr.c.108P.6.2.1.1, Winston Reeves Photograph Collection, Southwest Collection/Special Collections Library, Texas Tech University.

303 Courtesy of AECOM and MWM Architects, Inc.

303 Courtesy of AECOM and MWM Architects, Inc.

304 Courtesy of AECOM and MWM Architects, Inc.

305 Courtesy of Mr. Kris Barton / Full Throttle RC.

306 Courtesy of Dror Baldinger, FAIA.

307 Courtesy of Dror Baldinger, FAIA.

310 Parkhill, Smith & Cooper, Inc.

311 Parkhill, Smith & Cooper, Inc.

312 Parkhill, Smith & Cooper, Inc.

313 Parkhill, Smith & Cooper, Inc.

314 McKinney York Architects.

314 Courtesy of Dror Baldinger, FAIA.

315 Photograph Copyright Wade Griffith Photography / Architecture by Kirksey Architects, Inc.

317 SmithGroup, Inc.

317 Parkhill, Smith & Cooper, Inc.

318 Parkhill, Smith & Cooper, Inc.

319 Barnes Gromatzky Kosarek Architects with Mackey Mitchell Architects, Photograph by Alain Jaramillo.

320 Barnes Gromatzky Kosarek Architects with Mackey Mitchell Architects, Photograph by Alain Jaramillo.

322 Parkhill, Smith & Cooper, Inc.

323 Parkhill, Smith & Cooper, Inc.

324 Parkhill, Smith & Cooper, Inc.

325 Parkhill, Smith & Cooper, Inc.

327 Courtesy of TreanorHL and Ayers Saint Gross.

328 HOK Group, Inc.

330 Courtesy of Mr. Kris Barton / Full Throttle RC.

NOTES

CHAPTER 1. WHAT IF?

1. Patrick J. Nicholson, *William Ward Watkin and the Rice Institute* (Houston: Gulf Publishing Company, 1991), 316.

2. Ibid., 312.

3. "Architect, Prof[essor] at Rice Dies," *Houston Chronicle,* June 25, 1952, Obituary.

4. "Charles Arthur Bassett II." Last modified August 18, 2006, retrieved on September 4, 2017, http://www.arlingtoncemetery.net/cabasset.htm.

5. Donald K. Slayton, and Michael Cassutt, *Deke! U.S. Manned Space: From Mercury to the Shuttle*, 1st ed. (New York: St. Martin's Press, 1994), 167.

6. Jane Gilmore Rushing and Kline A. Nall, *Evolution of a University: Texas Tech's First Fifty Years* (Austin, Texas: Madrona Press, 1975), 156–158.

7. Nicholson, *William Ward Watkin and the Rice Institute*, 225–228.

8. Nolan Ellimore Barrick, "Interview with Author," December 18, 2010.

9. Drexel Turner, ed. *Lyceum to Landmark: The Julia Ideson Building of the Houston Public Library,* 1st ed. (Houston: Beasley, 1979), 2.

10. Mildred Hedrick Fender and Ames Fender, AIA, "Interview with Author," November 29, 2009.

11. Barrick, "Interview with Author," October 25, 2009.

12. "Grant of $67,000 for Texas Tech Stadium Is Cancelled," *Sunday Avalanche-Journal*, December 15, 1935, 1.

13. "Completion of the Administration Building for Texas Technological College, Job no. 1908," Wyatt C. Hedrick, Architect with William Ward Watkin, Associate Architects, drawn 1926. Texas Tech University Blueprint Collection, retrieved from https://swco-ir.tdl.org/handle/10605/60.

CHAPTER 2. 1492

1. J. H. Elliott, *Imperial Spain, 1469–1716,* 1st ed. (New York: St. Martin's Press, 1964), 19–24, 30–32.

2. Albert F. Calvert, *Spain*, vol. 2 (London: J. M. Dent & Sons, 1911), 831, 834, 837.

3. Javier Rivera Blanco, "Interview with Author [and Interpreter]," October 1, 2017.

4. Elliott, *Imperial Spain, 1469–1716,*, 117

5. Samuel Eliot Morrison, *Admiral of the Ocean Sea: A Life of Christopher Columbus*, 2nd ed. (Boston: Little, Brown and Company, 1970), 224–228.

6. Ibid., xiv.

7. Robert Bracey, Thomas Hockenhull, et. al., *Symbols of Power: Ten Coins That Changed the World* (New York: Columbia University Press, 2015), 130–145.

8. J. H. Elliott, *Imperial Spain, 1469–1716*, 1st ed. (New York: St. Martin's Press, 1964), 174–177, 263–264.

9. A. D. F. Hamlin, *A History of Ornament: Renaissance and Modern* (New York: The Century Company, 1923), 271.

10. J. B. Bury, "The Stylistic Term 'Plateresque,'" *Journal of the Warburg and Courtald Institutes,* vol. 39 (London: Warburg Institute, 1979), 202–204.

11. Coinage Act of April 2, 1792, sections 9 and 13, United States Mint Historical Documents. Last updated April 19, 2017, retrieved from https://www.usmint.gov/learn/history/historical-documents/coinage-act-of-april-2-1792.

12. Arthur Nussbaum, *A History of the Dollar* (New York: Columbia University Press, 1957), 56.

13. Elliott, *Imperial Spain, 1469–1716*, 174–177, 104–105.

14. José Andrés Miguel Benito, "Interview with Author [and Interpreter]," October 5, 2017.

15. Ludwig Pastor, *The History of Popes.* (London: K. Paul, Trench, Trübner & Co., Ltd., 1906), 416.

16. Bernard Bevan, *History of Spanish Architecture* (New York: Charles Scribner's Sons, 1939), 140.

17. Arthur Byne and Mildred Stapley, *Spanish Architecture of the Sixteenth Century* (New York: G. P. Putnam's Sons, 1917), 186.

18. Ibid., 12, 21, 67–75.

19. George Kubler and Martin Soria, *Art and Architecture in Spain and Portugal and Their American Dominions: 1500 to 1800* (Baltimore: Penguin Books, 1959), 55.

20. Manuel Nieto Cumplido, "Bell-Tower of the Mosque-Cathedral [English Guide Brochure]," Cabildo Catedral de Córdoba, 2015.

CHAPTER 3. WESTERN INSPIRATION

1. Carl Abbott, *The Great Extravaganza: Portland and the Lewis and Clark Exposition* 3rd ed. (Portland: Oregon Historical Society Press, 2004), 3–4.

2. "The Last Speech of William McKinley," Senate Document no. 268, 58th Congress, 2nd Session, (Washington, DC: Government Printing Office, 1904), 3–4.

3. Paul V. Turner, Marcia E. Vetrocq, and Karen Weitze, *The Founders and the Architects: The Design of Stanford University* (Palo Alto, CA: Stanford University Press, 1976), 11.

4. Abbott, *The Great Extravaganza*, 27.

5. Robertus Love, "The Lewis and Clark Fair," *The World's Work*, vol. 10, no. 4 (New York: Doubleday, Page & Co., August 1905), 6447–6449.

6. Abbott, *The Great Extravaganza*, 27–28.

7. Chris Meister, *James Riely Gordon: His Courthouses and Other Public Architecture* (Lubbock: Texas Tech University Press, 2011), 92–95.

8. Meister, *James Riely Gordon*, 99.

9. Robert W. Rydell, *All the World's a Fair: Visions of Empire at American International Expositions, 1876–1916* (Chicago: University of Chicago Press, 1987), 25, 110, 124.

10. Roger M. Showley, *Balboa Park: A Millennium History* (Carlsbad, CA: Heritage Media Corp., 1999), 23–24.

11. Richard W. Amero, *Balboa Park and the 1915 Exposition* (Mount Pleasant, SC: The History Press, 2013), 16.

12. Roger M. Showley, *Balboa Park*, 23–24.

13. Romy Wyllie, *Bertram Goodhue: His Life and Residential Architecture*, (New York: W. W. Norton, 2007), 19, 22.

14. Ibid., 25–26.

15. Douglass Shand-Tucci, *Ralph Adams Cram: An Architect's Four Quests,* (Amherst: University of Massachusetts Press, 2005), 247–251.

16. Winsor Soule [with introduction by Ralph Adams Cram], *Spanish Farm Houses and Minor Public Buildings* (New York: Architectural Book Publishing, 1924), ii.

17. Wyllie, *Bertram Goodhue*, 75.

18. Bertram Grosvenor Goodhue, *The Architecture and the Gardens of the San Diego Exposition* (San Francisco: Paul Elder and Company, 1916), 3.

19. George Kubler and Martin Soria, *Art and Architecture in Spain and Portugal and Their American Dominions: 1500 to 1800* (Baltimore: Penguin, 1959), 81.

20. Amero, *Balboa Park and the 1915 Exposition*, 53.

21. Ibid., 133.

22. Ibid., 106.

CHAPTER 4. WYATT, BILLY, AND CHIP

1. June Rayfield Welch, *The Colleges of Texas,* (Dallas: GLA Press, 1981), 144.

2. Ibid.

3. Patrick J. Nicholson, *William Ward Watkin and the Rice Institute* (Houston: Gulf Publishing Company, 1991), 174.

4. Herbert Eugene Bolton, *Coronado: Knight of Pueblo and Plains* (Albuquerque: University of New Mexico Press, 1949), 271, 273.

5. Nicholson, *William Ward Watkin and the Rice Institute*, 53, 64.

6. Ibid., 66–70.

7. Homer Dale Wade, *Establishment of Texas Technological College, 1916–1923* (Lubbock: Texas Tech Press, 1956), 93–96.

8. Arthur Byne and Mildred Stapley Byne, *Spanish Interiors and Furniture,* vol. 1 (New York: William Helburn Inc., 1922), v–vi, plate 24.

9. Welch, *The Colleges of Texas,* 144.

10. Correspondence from C. H. Page and Brother to Amon G. Carter, August 17, 1923.

11. Correspondence from Frank O. Witchell to A. G. Carter, May 28, 1923.

12. Correspondence from Guy A. Carlander to A. G. Carter, September 14, 1923.

13. Jay C. Henry, *Architecture in Texas 1895–1945*, (Austin, Texas: University of Texas Press, 1993), 57.

14. Ibid., 133.

15. "Sanguinet, Staats & Hedrick," Reference File, Alexander Architectural Archive, University of Texas at Austin, reviewed on January 22, 2010.

16. Deborah M. Liles, "Wyatt Cephas Hedrick: Builder of Cities," (Master's Thesis, University of North Texas, May 2008), 3–7.

17. Christopher Long, *Handbook of Texas Online*, "Clarkson, Wiley G.," retrieved November 14, 2018, http://www.tshaonline.org/handbook/online/articles/fclrg.

18. Correspondence from W. G. Clarkson to Amon G. Carter, October 26, 1923.

19. Multiple typed letter and telegraphic correspondences from Wyatt C. Hedrick, April 20, 1923, to May 30, 1923. Retrieved from Amon G. Carter Papers, Texas Tech University Southwest Special Collections, undated.

20. Wade, *Establishment of Texas Technological College*, 156.

21. Correspondence from Wyatt C. Hedrick [on behalf of Sanguinet, Staats & Hedrick] to Amon G. Carter [on behalf of the Texas Technological College Board of Directors], May 8, 1923.

22. Correspondence from William Ward Watkin to Amon G. Carter, September 14, 1923.

23. Ibid.

24. Telegram from Amon G. Carter to William Ward Watkin, September 19, 1923.

25. Correspondence from W. G. Clarkson to Amon G. Carter, October 26, 1923.

26. Correspondence from L. W. Robert to Amon G. Carter [with cc: to Wyatt C. Hedrick], December 8, 1923.

27. Correspondence from William Ward Watkin to Amon G. Carter, February 23, 1924.

28. Ruth Horn Andrews, *The First Thirty Years* (Lubbock: Texas Tech Press, 1956), 5–6.

29. H. Allen Anderson, *Handbook of Texas Online*, "Spade Ranch," retrieved March 5, 2019, http://www.tshaonline.org/handbook/online/articles/aps04.

30. Jane Gilmore Rushing and Kline A. Nall, *Evolution of a University: Texas Tech's First Fifty Years* (Austin: Madrona Press, 1975), 23.

31. Correspondence from Wyatt C. Hedrick to William Ward Watkin and L. W. Robert, Jr. [record example of many], dated August 9, 1927.

CHAPTER 5. ARMISTICE DAY

1. Patrick J. Nicholson, *William Ward Watkin and the Rice Institute* (Houston: Gulf Publishing Company, 1991), 162–163.

2. Correspondence from William Ward Watkin to Amon G. Carter, February 23, 1924.

3. Ibid.

4. "Board Minutes," March 28, 1924, meeting, Texas Technological College Board of Directors, vol. 1, 44.

5. Drexel Turner, ed. *Lyceum to Landmark: The Julia Ideson Building of the Houston Public Library*, 1st ed. (Houston: The Beasley Company, 1979), 2, 5–6.

6. Ibid., 6.

7. Telegram from A. G. Carter to William Ward. Watkin, May 10, 1924.

8. Correspondence from P. W. Horn to A. G. Carter [enclosing preliminary buildings budget], dated July 25, 1924.

9. Stephen Fox, *The General Plan of the William M. Rice Institute and Its Architectural Development*, "Architecture at Rice," Monograph 29 (Houston: Rice University School of Architecture, 1980), 9–10.

10. Fox, *The General Plan of the William M. Rice Institute and Its Architectural Development*, 13–14.

11. "Texas Tech University Campus Survey 1973," correspondence from Jerry Kirkwood to Bennett Reaves with attached exhibit of original land ownership tract description for Texas Technological College [later Texas Tech University and the Texas Tech University College of Medicine], dated April 8, 1974.

12. "School Will Be Most Beautiful in State, Claim," *Houston Chronicle*, September 14, 1924, 1.

13. Telegram from A. G. Carter to Wm. Ward. Watkin, May 10, 1924.

14. Ibid.

15. Ibid.

16. "Convention Will Complete Work Tonight," *Brownwood Bulletin*, Evening Edition, May 15, 1924, 1.

17. Correspondence from Carl G. Staats to Dr. P. W. Horn, June 13, 1924.

18. "School Will Be Most Beautiful in State, Claim," *Houston Chronicle*, September 14, 1924, 1.

19. Ruth Horn Andrews, *The First Thirty Years* (Lubbock: Texas Tech Press, 1956), 7.

20. Correspondence from P. W. Horn to A. G. Carter, dated July 25, 1924.

21. Correspondence from P. W. Horn to William Ward Watkin, dated May 5, 1924 [with enclosure of earlier correspondence from Raymond A. Pearson to Dr. P. W. Horn, dated May 2, 1924].

22. Correspondence from W. C. Hedrick to F. G. Pettibone, dated March 10, 1924.

23. Correspondence from W. R. Hendrickson to Messrs. Sanguinet, Staats & Hedrick, dated June 12, 1924.

24. Turner, ed. *Lyceum to Landmark*, 5.

25. Nolan Barrick, *Texas Tech . . . The Unobserved Heritage* (Lubbock: Texas Tech Press, 1985), 22.

26. Albert F. Calvert, *Spain,* vol. 2 (London: J. M. Dent & Sons, 1911), 676.

27. Manuel Nieto Cumplido, "Bell-Tower of the Mosque-Cathedral [English Guide Brochure]," Cabildo Catedral de Córdoba, 2015.

28. Arthur Byne and Mildred Stapley Byne, *Spanish Architecture of the Sixteenth Century* (New York: G. P. Putnam's Sons, 1917), 67–72.

29. "Board Minutes," June 27, 1924, meeting, Texas Technological College Board of Directors, vol. 1, 54.

30. Ibid., vol. 1, 53.

31. Ibid.

32. "School Will Be Most Beautiful in State, Claim," *Houston Chronicle,* September 14, 1924, 1.

33. *Jackson, J. Bedford–Carthage Stone v. Ramey*, 34 S.W.2d 387 (Tex. Civ. App. 1930).

34. William G. McMillan, Jr., "Interview with Author and Mike W. Moss," February 2, 2011.

35. Ibid.

36. "Board Minutes," August 27, 1924, meeting, Texas Technological College Board of Directors, vol. 1, 64.

37. Andrews, *The First Thirty Years*, 9.

38. Correspondence from William Ward Watkin to Dr. P. W. Horn, November 15, 1924.

CHAPTER 6. START WALKING

1. *Jackson, J. Bedford–Carthage Stone v. Ramey*, 34 S.W.2d 387 (Tex. Civ. App. 1930).

2. Ibid.

3. Correspondence from William Ward Watkin to Dr. P. W. Horn, dated December 4, 1924.

4. Ibid., dated December 15, 1924.

5. Lloyd C. and June-Marie F. Engelbrecht, *Henry C. Trost: Architect of the Southwest* (El Paso: El Paso Public Library Association, 1981), 69, and dust jacket overleaf.

6. Correspondence from William Ward Watkin to Dr. P. W. Horn, dated December 15, 1924.

7. Nolan Barrick, *Texas Tech . . . The Unobserved Heritage* (Lubbock: Texas Tech Press, 1985), 24.

8. "Board Minutes," January 6, 1925, meeting, Texas Technological College Board of Directors, vol. 1, 94.

9. Matthew J. Milliner, "The Princeton University Chapel." Pamphlet. (Princeton, NJ: Educational Technologies Center of Princeton University, 2007), 4.

10. Barrick, *Texas Tech . . . The Unobserved Heritage,* 28.

11. Patrick J. Nicholson, *William Ward Watkin and the Rice Institute* (Houston: Gulf Publishing Company, 1991), 213.

12. *Jackson, J. Bedford–Carthage Stone v. Ramey,* 34 S.W.2d 387 (Tex. Civ. App. 1930).

13. "Texas Trail & Highway Map, No. 17," Gulf Oil Company (Chicago: Rand McNally, 1924).

14. Correspondence from R. A. Ramey to Amon G. Carter, dated April 7, 1925.

15. Paul W. Horn, "President's Report to the Board of Directors," March 27, 1925, 1.

16. "Board Minutes," April 14, 1925, meeting, Texas Technological College Board of Directors, vol. 1, 47.

17. Correspondence from L. W. Robert, Jr. to Amon G. Garter, January 12, 1925.

18. Correspondence from Dr. P. W. Horn to Amon G. Carter, May 23, 1925.

19. Paul W. Horn, "The Appeal of Texas Technological College," *Bulletin of Texas Technological College,* vol. 4, no. 6, April 1928, 2. C.

20. Matlack Price, "The Panama–California Exposition. San Diego, California," *The Architectural Record*, vol. 37, January–June 1915, 236.

21. "Form S1—Application for Membership [for Llewellyn William Pitts, submitted April 10, 1943]," Archives of the American Institute of Architects, item 13.

22. Correspondence from P. W. Horn to Amon G. Carter, dated May 29, 1925 [with enclosed correspondence from K. K. Rockne to P. W. Horn, dated May 26, 1925].

23. Ruth Horn Andrews, *The First Thirty Years* (Lubbock: Texas Tech Press, 1956), 132.

24. Ibid., [referencing *Fort Worth Star–Telegram* editorial dated February 24, 1925].

25. "Board Minutes," July 18, 1925, meeting, Texas Technological College Board of Directors, vol. 1, 125.

26. Barrick, *Texas Tech . . . The Unobserved Heritage,* 30–31.

27. Arthur Byne and Mildred Stapley Byne, *Spanish Architecture of the Sixteenth Century* (New York: G. P. Putnam's Sons, 1917), 61.

28. "Board Minutes," April 14, 1925, meeting, Texas Technological College Board of Directors, vol. 1, 106.

29. Correspondence from William Ward Watkin to Judge Lewis T. Carpenter, dated October 7, 1925.

30. "Board Minutes," August 15, 1925, meeting, Texas Technological College Board of Directors, 1925, vol. 1, 130–131.

31. Jane Gilmore Rushing and Kline A. Nall, *Evolution of a University: Texas Tech's First Fifty Years* (Austin: Madrona Press, 1975), 86.

32. "The Texas Technological College," [Advertisement], *Lubbock Morning Avalanche*, September 27, 1925, 8.

33. "Fall Enrollment Since 1925," Texas Tech University Office of Institutional Research, last modified on October 4, 2017, retrieved from: https://www.depts.ttu.edu/irim/ARCHIVE/ENR/FALLENRL.php.

34. June Rayfield Welch, *The Colleges of Texas* (Dallas: GLA Press, 1981), 184.

CHAPTER 7. SPANISH TRIUMPH

1. Pamela G. Hollie, "Southern Pacific Takes on Bell," *The New York Times,* April 9, 1979, Business Day Section 1.

2. "Significant Earthquakes and Faults: Santa Barbara Earthquake," California Institute of Technology Southern California Earthquake Data Center, last updated on January 31, 2013, retrieved from: http://www.data.scec.org/significant/santabarbara1925.html.

3. "Quake Claims 9 Lives, City to Rebuild at Once!" *The* [Santa Barbara] *Morning Press,* June 30, 1925, 1.

4. Patricia Gebhard and Kathryn Masson, *The Santa Barbara County Courthouse* (Santa Barbara, CA: Daniel & Daniel, 2001), 20.

5. *The Architectural Digest,* vol. 6, no. 4, Fall 1925, 13–18, 21–27, 31–34, 56–69.

6. Larry Spain, "The Enchanted Ghost," *Desert* [Magazine], February 1966, 16–18.

7. Werner Hegemann and Elbert Peets, *The American Vitruvius: An Architects' Handbook of Civic Art* (New York: Princeton Architectural Press, 1988), 193.

8. Lawrence W. Speck and Richard L. Cleary, *The Campus Guide: The University of Texas at Austin* (New York: Princeton Architectural Press, 2011), 16–17, 53–54.

9. Austin Whittlesey, *The Renaissance Architecture of Central and Northern Spain* (New York: Architectural Book Publishing, 1920), xiii.

10. Jay C. Henry, *Architecture in Texas 1895–1945* (Austin, Texas: University of Texas Press, 1993), 151.

11. *The Architectural Digest,* vol. 6, no. 4, Fall 1925, 21–22.

12. William Davenport, *Fine Art Treasures in the West* (Menlo Park, CA: Lane Magazine & Book, 1966), *27–31.*

13. Richard W. Amero, "History of the Casa del Prado Building at Balboa Park," San Diego History Center Online Archives, Amero Collection, retrieved on December 14, 2017, from: http://www.sandiegohistory.org/archives/amero/casaprado/.

14. Henry, *Architecture in Texas, 1895–1945*, 173.

15. Ibid., 175.

16. Ibid.

17. J. Brantley Hightower, "Blog: Pioneering Shopping Malls," *Texas Architect*, Texas Society of Architects, March 1, 2013, retrieved from: https://texasarchitects.org/pioneering-shopping-malls/.

18. "Facilities: Municipal Auditorium," City of Big Spring Website, retrieved on December 8, 2017, from: http://www.mybigspring.com/Facility/Details/Municipal–Auditorium–8.

19. Lloyd C. Engelbrecht and June-Marie F. Engelbrecht, *Henry C. Trost: Architect of the Southwest* (El Paso, Texas: El Paso Public Library Association, 1981), 69–72.

20. Jerry Flemmons, *Amon: The Texan Who Played Cowboy for America* (Lubbock, Texas: Texas Tech University Press, 1998), 100, 154.

21. "New Houston Federal Land Bank," *Southern Architect and Building News,* January 1930, 14–15.

22. Drexel Turner, ed. *Lyceum to Landmark: The Julia Ideson Building of the Houston Public Library,* 1st ed. (Houston: Beasley Company, 1979), 19, 22.

23. "Architecture in Texas," Typewritten article draft for the *Times of*

London, February 1925. William Ward Watkin Papers, Woodson Research Center, Rice University.

24. William Ward Watkin, "Texas Technological College, Lubbock, Texas," *The American School and University*, 1928–1929 edition (New York: American School Publishing, 1928), 66–69.

25. Correspondence from Amon G. Carter to Dr. P. W. Horn, dated January 31, 1927.

26. "Board Minutes," April 18, 1927, meeting, Texas Technological College Board of Directors, vol. 1, 196.

27. Flemmons, *Amon*, 120–121.

28. Correspondence from Harold Hough [a.k.a. in letter as the "W.B.A.P. Boiler Room] to Dr. P. W. Horn, dated December 27, 1926.

29. Flemmons, *Amon*, 120.

CHAPTER 8. NO BED TO SLEEP IN

1. "Fall Enrollment Since 1925," Texas Tech University Office of Institutional Research, last modified on October 4, 2017, retrieved from: https://www.depts.ttu.edu/irim/ARCHIVE/ENR/FALLENRL.php.

2. Correspondence from E. Y. Freeland to Amon G. Carter, dated March 7, 1926.

3. P. W. Horn, "[Bulletin] to Prospective Students," undated [but based upon letterhead assumed issued in summer 1925], 3.

4. Correspondence from William Ward Watkin to H. T. Kimbrough [Kimbro], dated March 2, 1927.

5. Correspondence from William Ward Watkin to Wyatt C. Hedrick, dated June 20, 1927.

6. Ibid., dated September 1, 1927.

7. Correspondence from Mrs. Walter Wiley and Mrs. Ben Oatie [Scott–Dickson Chapter no. 197 of the Daughters of the Confederacy] to Amon G. Carter, dated September 28, 1925.

8. Correspondence from P. W. Horn to William Ward Watkin, dated August 31, 1927.

9. Correspondence from William Ward Watkin to Wyatt C. Hedrick, dated September 2, 1927.

10. Correspondence from William Ward Watkin to Dr. P. W. Horn, dated September 2, 1927.

11. Nolan Barrick, *Texas Tech: The Unobserved Heritage* (Lubbock: Texas Tech Press, 1985), 36.

12. Andrew Noble Prentice, *Renaissance Architecture and Ornament in Spain*, 1920 US Edition of 1893 Publication (New York: Architectural Book Publishing, 1920), plate 32.

13. Ángel Pérez López and Alberto Pascual de los Ángeles, *Colegio Mayor de San Ildefonso: Fábrica de la fachada (1537–1553) —Alcalá de Henares* (Alcalá de Henares: Ayuntamiento de Alcalá and Universidad de Alcalá, 1999), 182–183.

14. Correspondence from William Ward Watkin to E. W. Province [Provence], dated September 15, 1927.

15. Correspondence from P. W. Horn to William Ward Watkin, dated August 31, 1927.

16. Correspondence from William Ward Watkin to Dr. [William] Read, dated November 5, 1927.

17. Correspondence from E. W. Provence to William Ward Watkin, dated October 10, 1927.

18. Ibid.

19. José Andrés Miguel Benito, "Interview with Author [and Interpreter]," October 5, 2017.

20. Correspondence from William Ward Watkin to Clifford Jones, dated November 7, 1927.

21. Correspondence from William M. Craig to William Ward Watkin, dated July 7, 1923.

22. Ralph Adams Cram, *Black Spirits & White: A Book of Ghost Stories* (Chicago: Stone & Kimball, 1895), 133–150.

23. H. P. Lovecraft, *Supernatural Horror in Literature, 1927, 1933–1935*, "X: The Modern Masters," retrieved on September 14, 2017 from: http://www.yankeeclassic.com/miskatonic/library/stacks/literature/lovecraft/essays/supernat/supern00.htm.

24. Douglass Shand-Tucci, *Ralph Adams Cram: An Architect's Four Quests* (Amherst: University of Massachusetts Press, 2005), 520.

25. "Basil Valentine: A Seventeenth Century Hoax," *Popular Science Monthly*, vol. 81 (New York: The Science Press, December 1912), 591–594.

26. John Read, *From Alchemy to Chemistry*, 1st ed. (New York: Dover Publications, 1957), 29.

27. Adolph K. L. Claus, *Berichte über die Verhandlungen der Naturforschenden Gesellschaft zu Freiburg im Breisgau*, vol. 4 (Universitäts—Buchhandlung von J. Diernfellner, 1867), 317.

28. "Logos," American Chemical Society Website, retrieved on November 12, 2017 from: https://www.acs.org/content/acs/en/about/branding/logos.html.

29. "Chemical Corps," Office of the Administrative Assistant to the Secretary of the Army, the Institute of Heraldry Website, retrieved on

January 22, 2013 from: http://www.tioh.hqda.pentagon.mil/Branches/Chemical Corps.htm.

30. Dorman H. Winfrey and Elizabeth Howard West, *Handbook of Texas Online*, retrieved on December 2, 2017 from: http://www.tshaonline.org/handbook/online/articles/fwe32.

31. Correspondence from Elizabeth Howard West to Dr. P. W. Horn, dated March 29, 1928.

32. Ruth Horn Andrews, *The First Thirty Years* (Lubbock: Texas Tech Press, 1956), 48.

33. Correspondence from Elizabeth Howard West to Dr. P. W. Horn, dated March 29, 1928.

34. "Torreón de los Guzmanes," [Brochure], Tourism Office, Diputación de Ávila, 2010 Printing.

35. Correspondence from William Ward Watkin to Thomas E. Campbell, dated July 11, 1928.

36. Patrick J. Nicholson, *William Ward Watkin and the Rice Institute* (Houston: Gulf Publishing Company, 1991), 220–227.

37. Ibid., 228.

CHAPTER 9. FRIENDS IN HIGH PLACES

1. "President Horn Is Dead," *The Toreador*, vol. 8, no. 27, April 14, 1932, 1.

2. Jane Gilmore Rushing and Kline A. Nall, *Evolution of a University: Texas Tech's First Fifty Years* (Austin: Madrona Press, 1975), 45.

3. Correspondence from Bradford Knapp to Dr. Clarence Ousley, dated May 25, 1932.

4. Ruth Horn Andrews, *The First Thirty Years* (Lubbock: Texas Tech Press, 1956), 40.

5. Correspondence from Franklin D. Roosevelt to Bradford Knapp, dated January 11, 1933.

6. "We Ask You, West Texas Chamber of Commerce!" *The Toreador*, vol. 11, no. 56, May 2, 1936, 2.

7. Lonnie McCurry, "Interview with Author," dated November 24, 2009.

8. "National Industrial Recovery Act," Pub.L. 73–67, 48 Stat. 195, enacted June 16, 1933.

9. Deborah M. Liles, "Wyatt Cephas Hedrick: Builder of Cities," (Master's Thesis, University of North Texas, 2008), 88.

10. "Wyatt C. Hedrick Architects," Past Projects Listing, Undated.

11. "Board Minutes," December 9, 1933 meeting, Texas Technological College Board of Directors, vol. 3, 399–400.

12. Liles, "Wyatt Cephas Hedrick," 88.

13. Correspondence from Wyatt C. Hedrick to John A. Hulen, dated August 31, 1933.

14. "Board Minutes," December 9, 1933 meeting, Texas Technological College Board of Directors, vol. 3, 400.

15. Ibid., vol. 3, 398.

16. Liles, "Wyatt Cephas Hedrick," 45.

17. Liles, "Wyatt Cephas Hedrick," 84.

18. E. Paul Koeppe, "Interview with Author," dated August 31, 2013.

19. Jane Gilmore Rushing and Kline A. Nall, *Evolution of a University: Texas Tech's First Fifty Years* (Austin, Texas: Madrona Press, 1975), 52–53.

20. Ibid., 53.

21. Ibid., 53–54.

22. Floy Farrar Wilbanks, "The Life and Work of Dr. Bradford Knapp," (Master's Thesis, Texas Technological College, 1940), 90.

23. Wyatt C. Hedrick Architects, "Plan and Elevations—Dairy Manufacturing Building—Texas Technological College, PWA Project no. 1064," Oversize Vellum Drawing, Alexander Architectural Archives, University of Texas at Austin, undated.

24. "Board Minutes," August 15, 1925, meeting, Texas Technological College Board of Directors, vol. 1, 129.

25. Lonnie McCurry, "Interview with Author," dated November 24, 2009.

26. C. W. Short and R. Stanley-Brown, *Public Buildings: A Survey of Architecture of Projects Constructed by Federal and Other Governmental Bodies Between the Years 1933 and 1939* (Washington, DC: Government Printing Office, 1939), 323.

27. "Board Minutes," December 4, 1935, meeting, Texas Technological College Board of Directors, vol. 3, 553–554.

28. "Grant of $67,000 for Texas Tech Stadium Is Cancelled," *Sunday Avalanche-Journal*, vol. 10, no. 15, December 15, 1935, 1.

29. Wyatt C. Hedrick Architects, "Stadium Plan—Texas Technological College—PWA Project no. 1044," Oversize Vellum Drawing, Alexander Architectural Archives, University of Texas at Austin, November 15, 1935.

30. "Knapp Studies Stadium Plan," *The Toreador*, vol. 11, no. 56, May 2, 1936, 1.

31. "Index to Chimes by Vanduzen—Buckeye Bell Foundry / The E. W. Vanduzen Company, Cincinnati, Ohio, USA, 1894–1950," Tower Bells of America, retrieved on October 24, 2017 from: http://www.towerbells.org/data/IXfoundryVanduzen.html.

32. "Red Raiders Dedicate New Stadium Saturday; Play TCU," *The Toreador*, vol. 11, no. 4, September 23, 1936, 3.

33. Collier Parish, "Tech Stops Baugh, TCU in Stadium Dedication," [Reprint of original *Sunday Avalanche-Journal* September 27, 1936 article], *Greatest Moments in Texas Tech Football History* (Birmingham, AL: Epic Sports, 2001), 14.

34. Andrews, *The First Thirty Years*, 266.

35. Rushing and Nall, *Evolution of a University*, 55.

36. "Library Architect Continues Plans," *The [Summer Session] Toreador*, vol. 11, no. 68, July 23, 1937, 1.

37. Nolan Ellimore Barrick, "Interview with Author," December 18, 2010.

CHAPTER 10. THE X–BUILDINGS

1. Ruth Horn Andrews, *The First Thirty Years* (Lubbock: Texas Tech Press, 1956), 105.

2. "Fall Enrollment Since 1925," Texas Tech University Office of Institutional Research, last modified on October 4, 2017, retrieved from: https://www.depts.ttu.edu/irim/ARCHIVE/ENR/FALLENRL.php.

3. Jane Gilmore Rushing and Kline A. Nall, *Evolution of a University: Texas Tech's First Fifty Years* (Austin: Madrona Press, 1975), 78.

4. "Spacious Reading Rooms Planned for New Library," *The [Summer Session] Toreador*, vol. 11, no. 70, August 6, 1937, 1.

5. "Ruth Horn Andrews Papers, 1878–1979 and undated," [Arbor Day Celebration Notes], Southwest Collection/Special Collections Library, Texas Tech University, box 1, folder 30.

6. Opal McMahon, "Last Rites to Be Held Monday for Tech President," *Lubbock Avalanche-Journal*, June 12, 1938, 1.

7. Rushing and Nall, *Evolution of a University*, 76–79.

8. Ibid., 89.

9. Deborah M. Liles, "Wyatt Cephas Hedrick: Builder of Cities," (Master's Thesis, University of North Texas, 2008), 25.

10. E. Paul Koeppe, "Interview with Author," dated August 31, 2013.

11. "Ruth Horn Andrews Papers, 1878–1979 and undated," Southwest Collection/Special Collections Library, Texas Tech University, box 2, folders 10 and 26.

12. Mildred Hedrick Fender and Ames Fender, AIA, "Interview with Author," November 29, 2009.

13. Correspondence from William Ward Watkin to W. T. Strange, Jr., dated June 24, 1944.

14. Correspondence from William Ward Watkin to Clifford Jones, dated February 2, 1944.

15. Betty Lolana Lummus Thompson, *Clifford B. Jones: Third President of Texas Technological College* (Master's Thesis, Texas Tech University, 1982), 31.

16. Andrews, *The First Thirty Years*, 63.

17. Ibid.

18. "Fall Enrollment Since 1925," Texas Tech University Office of Institutional Research, last modified on October 4, 2017, retrieved from: https://www.depts.ttu.edu/irim/ARCHIVE/ENR/FALLENRL.php

19. "College Building Amendment Election Set For Saturday, August 23," *The Hereford Brand*, August 14, 1947, 1.

20. Andrews, *The First Thirty Years*, 67–68.

21. "20 Surplus Buildings Now on Tech Campus," *The Toreador*, vol. 21, no. 33, June 27, 1947, 1.

22. "Ruth Horn Andrews Papers, 1878–1979 and undated," Southwest Collection/Special Collections Library, Texas Tech University, box 1, folders 28 and 30, and box 2, folder 26.

23. Andrews, *The First Thirty Years*, 72.

24. Correspondence from William Ward Watkin to Amon G. Carter, dated February 15, 1926.

25. "CPI Inflation Calculator," U.S. Bureau of Labor Statistics Website, retrieved on May 20, 2017 from: https://data.bls.gov/cgi-bin/cpicalc.pl.

26. Deborah M. Liles, "Wyatt Cephas Hedrick: Builder of Cities," (Master's Thesis, University of North Texas, 2008), 100.

27. Ibid., 101.

28. Frances Hallam Hurt, "Interview with Author," March 13, 2012.

29. Mildred Hedrick Fender and Ames Fender, AIA, "Interview with Author," November 29, 2009.

CHAPTER 11. LORD CALVERT

1. "For Men of Distinction. . . Lord Calvert," [Advertisement], *Life*, vol. 26, no. 47, November 21, 1949, 140.

2. Stephen Fox, *Handbook of Texas Online*, "Shamrock Hotel," retrieved December 4, 2017 from: http://www.tshaonline.org/handbook/online/articles/ccs05.

3. Ibid.

4. Choc Hutcheson, "Big Crowd Greets Movie Stars During Brief Visit in Lubbock," *Lubbock Morning-Avalanche,* March 16, 1949, 1.

5. Glenhall Taylor, *Before Television: The Radio Years* (New York: A. S. Barnes 1979), 139–146.

6. Diane Cowen, "Frank Lloyd Wright's Legendary Architecture Lives on in Houston," *Houston Chronicle*, June 2, 2017, retrieved on November 30, 2017, from: https://www.houstonchronicle.com/life/home/design/article/Frank-Lloyd-Wright-s-legendary-architecture-lives-11192296.php.

7. Robert Adams Ivy, Jr., *Fay Jones* (Washington, DC: AIA Press, 1992), 17.

8. E. Paul Koeppe, "Interview with Author," dated August 31, 2013.

9. "Frank Lloyd Wright Accepts 1949 AIA Gold Medal," [Audio Recording Only], YouTube, retrieved on July 10, 2017 from: https://www.youtube.com/watch?v=UPL_8MhCi8M.

10. Patrick J. Nicholson, *William Ward Watkin and the Rice Institute* (Houston: Gulf Publishing Company, 1991), 265.

11. "$21 Million Hotel Opens," *Life,* vol. 26, no. 13, March 26, 1949, 27–31.

12. Deborah M. Liles, "Wyatt Cephas Hedrick: Builder of Cities," (Master's Thesis, University of North Texas, 2008), 101.

13. "Armstrong Browning Library and Museum: History," Baylor University Website, retrieved on November 8, 2018, from: https://www.baylor
.edu/browninglibrary/index.php?id=942624.

14. Ibid.

15. "For Men of Distinction . . . Lord Calvert," [Advertisement], *Life,* March 13, 1950, 138.

16. "Baccalaureate Speaker Announced," *The Toreador,* vol. 24, no. 44, March 18, 1950, 1.

17. Gary Wooten Smith, "Sylvan Blum Haynes: The Dean of West Texas Architects," (Master's Thesis, Texas Tech University, 1993), 128.

18. Jeff Townsend, "Interview with Nolan and Rosemary Barrick," [Oral History], Southwest Collection/Special Collections Library, Texas Tech University, November 30, 1973.

19. Jim C. Doche, "Interview with Author," dated September 20, 2012.

20. Townsend, "Interview with Nolan and Rosemary Barrick."

21. Nolan Ellimore Barrick, "Interview with Author," December 18, 2010.

22. Ibid., October 25, 2009.

CHAPTER 12. SHEER MADNESS

1. "Fall Enrollment Since 1925," Texas Tech University Office of Institutional Research, last modified on October 4, 2017, retrieved from: https://www.depts.ttu.edu/irim/ARCHIVE/ENR/FALLENRL.php.

2. Jeff Townsend, "Interview with Nolan and Rosemary Barrick," [Oral History], Southwest Collection/Special Collections Library, Texas Tech University, November 30, 1973.

3. Ruth Horn Andrews, *The First Thirty Years* (Lubbock: Texas Tech Press, 1956), 7.

4. "14. Campus Plot Plan," Meeting Minutes, Campus Planning Committee, Texas Technological College, January 27, 1957.

5. Correspondence from Lawrence Wood "Chip" Robert Jr. to Nolan Barrick, dated October 19, 1953.

6. Nolan Ellimore Barrick, "Interview with Author," October 25, 2009.

7. Ibid., December 18, 2010.

8. James E. Brink, "Caprock Chronicles: Texas Tech's Infirmary-Turned-Honors College Named for Ranchers Len and Harriett McClellan," *Lubbock Avalanche-Journal,* April 29, 2017, retrieved on November 4, 2017, from: https://www.lubbockonline.com/caprockchronicles/20170429/caprockchroniclestexas-tech-s-infirmary-turned-honors-college-named.

9. Lawrence L. Graves, ed., *A History of Lubbock* (Minneapolis: Lund Press, 1962), 574.

10. Waggoner Carr and "House Bill No. 478, An Act Amending Chapter 185, Acts of the Regular Session of the 48th Legislature, 1943," 53rd Regular Legislative Session, Texas Legislative Reference Library.

11. "Demolition Coliseum Plan—Sheet DA101, and Demolition Auditorium Plan—Sheet DA102," Lubbock Municipal Coliseum and Auditorium Abatement and Demolition, Parkhill, Smith & Cooper, Inc., drawings issued November 19, 2018.

12. Barrick, "Interview with Author," December 18, 2010.

13. Townsend, "Interview with Nolan and Rosemary Barrick."

14. Barrick, "Interview with Author," October 25, 2009.

15. "Building No. 218—Recreation Annex [Formerly Women's Gymnasium]," Drawing Flat File, Texas Tech University Physical Plant, Office of Engineering Services, retrieved on January 14, 2010.

16. "23. Housing," Meeting Minutes, Campus Planning Committee, Texas Technological College, October 15, 1958.

17. David Messersmith, "Interview with Author," dated September 2, 2016.

18. "51. Dorms, New Men's," Meeting Minutes, Campus Planning Committee, Texas Technological College, October 1, 1958.

CHAPTER 13. RADIATORS AND REACTORS

1. Kent Hance, speech given, "Jerry S. Rawls College of Business Administration Grand Opening," January 17, 2012.

2. "Building No. 199—English and Philosophy [Formerly Classroom and Office Building]," Drawing Flat File, Texas Tech University Physical Plant, Office of Engineering Services, retrieved on January 14, 2010.

3. Jane Gilmore Rushing and Kline A. Nall, *Evolution of a University: Texas Tech's First Fifty Years* (Austin: Madrona Press, 1975), 121.

4. W. M. Pearce, "Report on Projected Enrollment at Texas Technological College," June 11, 1960, President's Office: An Inventory of Its Records, 1916–1968 and undated, Southwest Collection/Special Collections Library, Texas Tech University.

5. "Texas Technological College Institutional Self-Study," Report to Commission on Colleges / Southern Association of Colleges and Schools, September 1962, 8–25.

6. Ibid., 25.

7. E. Paul Koeppe, "Interview with Author," dated August 31, 2013.

8. "Board Minutes, Item #921," December 10, 1960 meeting, Texas Technological College Board of Directors.

9. Edward Durell Stone, *The Evolution of an Architect* (New York: Horizon Press, 1962), 138.

10. Nolan Ellimore Barrick, "Interview with Author," December 18, 2010.

11. Nolan Barrick, *Texas Tech: The Unobserved Heritage* (Lubbock: Texas Tech Press, 1985), 20.

12. Correspondence from R. C. Janeway to Dr. E. N. Jones, dated September 26, 1958 [Enclosed as exhibit "Attachment No. 4 to Campus Planning Committee Meeting Minutes," dated October 8, 1958].

13. "Biographical Sketch Record for Llewellyn William Pitts," undated. Archives of the American Institute of Architects, 2.

14. Correspondence from Llewellyn W. Pitts to Nolan Barrick, dated January 6, 1959.

15. Stephen Fox, *The General Plan of the William M. Rice Institute and Its Architectural Development*, "Architecture at Rice," Monograph 29 (Houston: Rice University School of Architecture, 1980), 78.

16. Nolan Ellimore Barrick, "Interview with Author," October 25, 2009.

17. "Tech Board Passes on Construction," *Tex Talks*, vol. 11, no. 3, July 1960, 1.

18. Richard P. Dober, *Campus Planning* (New York: Reinhold Publishing, 1964), 84.

19. "Tech Directors Approve Ag Science Building," *Tex Talks*, vol. 11, no. 1, January 1960, 4.

20. "97. Chemical Engineering and Nuclear Reactor Building," Meeting Minutes, Campus Planning Committee, Texas Technological College, October 29, 1958.

21. "Argonne National Laboratory Naught Power Reactor," Proceedings of the Second United Nations International Conference on the Peaceful Uses of Atomic Energy, No. 58, 9. 2. (London: United Nations Publications, 1958), 265–269, 531–537.

22. "97. Chemical Engineering and Nuclear Reactor Building," Meeting Minutes, Campus Planning Committee, Texas Technological College, October 29, 1958.

23. Barrick, "Interview with Author," October 25, 2009.

24. "Fall Enrollment Since 1925," Texas Tech University Office of Institutional Research, last modified on October 4, 2017, retrieved from: https://www.depts.ttu.edu/irim/ARCHIVE/ENR/FALLENRL.php.

25. Correspondence (and attachment) from Nolan E. Barrick to Dr. R. C. Goodwin, dated November 1, 1962.

26. Correspondence (with attached memorandum) from E. Hoyse McMurtry to Nolan E. Barrick, dated May 1, 1963.

27. "Summary of Proposed Methods to Provide Housing," March 18, 1965. Attachment for distribution at Campus Planning Committee Meeting No. 242, March 18, 1965.

CHAPTER 14. GOING VERTICAL

1. Lyndon B. Johnson, "Remarks at Southwest Texas State College Upon Signing the Higher Education Act of 1965." Transcript dated November 8, 1965, retrieved January 14, 2011, from: http://www.lbjlib.utexas.edu/johnson/lbjforkids/edu_whca370–text.shtm.

2. Kenneth May, "Public Support Needed for Tech Progress, Dr. Goodwin Reports," *Lubbock Avalanche-Journal*, June 14, 1964, 2–A.

3. "Amendment One Passage Called Tech 'Salvation,'" *Lubbock Avalanche-Journal*, November 4, 1965, 1–A.

4. Editorial, "What's the Future for Texas Education?" *The Daily Toreador*, September 23, 1965, 4.

5. Campus Planning Committee Records, miscellaneous memoranda, minutes, and letters, 1965–1968, and undated, Southwest Collection/Special Collections Library, Texas Tech University.

6. "Building No. 273—Central Heating and Cooling Plant [1]." Drawing Flat File, Texas Tech University Physical Plant, Office of Engineering Services, retrieved August 20, 2015.

7. Nolan Ellimore Barrick, "Interview with Author," December 18, 2010.

8. Jeff Townsend, "Interview with Nolan and Rosemary Barrick," [Oral History], Southwest Collection/Special Collections Library, Texas Tech University, November 30, 1973.

9. Correspondence from Nolan E. Barrick to Haskell Taylor, dated August 19, 1968.

10. Correspondence from H. L. Bevis to George Heather, dated July 30, 1956.

11. David Messersmith, "Interview with Author," dated September 2, 2016.

12. "Part A—Higher Education Facilities Inventory For—003644 Texas Tech University." Prepared by the Texas Higher Education Coordinating Board, March 4, 2002, edition.

13. "Board Minutes, Items H395–H397 and H500." June 3, 1967, meeting, Texas Technological College Board of Directors.

14. "Groundbreaking Ceremony Brochure," School of Law, Texas Technological College, July 20, 1968.

15. "Temporary Tech Classrooms Due to Arrive Today," *Lubbock Avalanche-Journal,* May 10, 1966, 1-A.

16. Editorial, "Indiana Still 50-50 Proposition," *Lubbock Avalanche-Journal,* August 22, 1972, 4-A.

17. Memorandum from Jerry Kirkwood to Campus Planning Committee, plus Mr. Howard Schmidt, dated April 18, 1968.

18. "Groundbreaking Ceremony Brochure." School of Law, Texas Technological College, July 20, 1968.

19. "Attachment No. 743: Project Summary for Project 4-7-00076-0 (4-1684 & 2-1684)—Biology Building," dated November 22, 1967. Presented December 5, 1967, Campus Planning Committee meeting.

20. Correspondence from Robert White to Howard Schmidt, dated February 21, 1968.

21. Jane Gilmore Rushing and Kline A. Nall, *Evolution of a University: Texas Tech's First Fifty Years* (Austin: Madrona Press, 1975), 151–154.

22. Stephen Faulk, "Interview with Author," dated August 29, 2016.

23. David Messersmith, "Interview with Author," dated September 2, 2016.

CHAPTER 15. THE FORGOTTEN MASTER PLAN

1. Tim Marshall, "A Tribute to Dr. Ted Fujita," Stormtrack website, retrieved on August 30, 2017, from: https://www.stormtrack.org/library/people/fujita.htm.

2. "NWS Lubbock, TX Local Weather Events: The 1970 Lubbock Tornado," retrieved on December 5, 2017 from: https://www.weather.gov/lub/events-1970-19700511.

3. Ibid.

4. Ibid.

5. Correspondence from Grover Murray to Haskell Taylor, dated October 5, 1967.

6. "Texas Technological College Master Plan," Office of the Supervising Architect, 1957.

7. Correspondence from Grover Murray to Haskell Taylor, dated January 17, 1968.

8. Memorandum (with "Long—Range Plan for Record Purposes" meeting minutes attached) from Haskell Taylor to Campus Planning Committee and Howard Schmidt, April 6, 1970.

9. Correspondence from Haskell G. Taylor to Dr. Gerald W. Thomas, dated April 5, 1968.

10. "Fall Enrollment Since 1925," Texas Tech University Office of Institutional Research, last modified on October 4, 2017, retrieved from: https://www.depts.ttu.edu/irim/ARCHIVE/ENR/FALLENRL.php.

11. Correspondence from Glenn E. Barnett to Elmer D. Cain, dated December 2, 1968 [as Attachment no. 21 to January 18, 1969 Campus Planning Committee Meeting Minutes].

12. Nolan Ellimore Barrick, "Interview with Author," December 18, 2010.

13. Memorandum from Glenn E. Barnett to Haskell Taylor, dated September 2, 1969.

14. Correspondence from Norman Igo to Andrew Perez III, dated November 7, 1969.

15. Correspondence from Andrew Perez to Alan Farnsworth, dated April 1, 1969.

16. "Texas Tech Architecture Building," WJE, Inc., https://www.wje.com/projects/detail/texas-tech-architecture-building, accessed on July 30, 2019.

17. John T. White, "Story Communicated to Author," dated April 20, 2015.

18. Memorandum from Glenn Barnett to Haskell Taylor, dated February 10, 1969.

19. Ibid., dated June 4, 1969.

20. "Recommendations of Space Committee Temporary Buildings," undated (assumed based on information in document to be summer 1972).

21. Memorandum from F. J. Wehmeyer to Dr. Glenn E. Barnett, dated April 9, 1975.

22. Jane Gilmore Rushing and Kline A. Nall, *Evolution of a University: Texas Tech's First Fifty Years* (Austin: Madrona Press, 1975), 67.

23. "Tech Board Passes on Construction, and Plans Near Completion for Union Extension," *Tex Talks,* vol. 11, no. 3, July 1960, 1, 4.

24. Kenneth May, "Tech Regents Push Building Program," *Lubbock Avalanche-Journal,* May 13, 1972, 1-A and 5-A.

25. "Mass Comm Building set for 1975," *The University Daily,* April 11, 1973, 1.

26. David Messersmith, "Interview with Author," dated September 2, 2016.

27. Ibid.

28. "Building no. 325—College of Human Sciences [Formerly Food Technology]," Drawing Flat File, Texas Tech University Physical Plant, Office of Engineering Services, retrieved on August 20, 2015.

CHAPTER 16. PLENTY OF COTTON BALE STORAGE

1. Delwin Jones, "House Bills 920 through 925, Regular Session of the 61st Legislature, Texas Legislative Reference Library.

2. "A Pictorial History of the Texas Tech Seal," Southwest Collection Archive, Special Collections Library, Texas Tech University, blog posted August 14, 2018, retrieved on January 20, 2019, from: https://southwestcollection.wordpress.com/2018/08/14/a-pictorial-history-of-the-texas-tech-seal/.

3. Jane Gilmore Rushing and Kline A. Nall, *Evolution of a University: Texas Tech's First Fifty Years* (Austin: Madrona Press, 1975), 141.

4. "Hospital Board Okays New Bid To Get Funds," *Lubbock Avalanche-Journal,* May 15, 1972, 1, 16.

5. Jack DeBartolo, "Interview with Author," dated September 16, 2016.

6. "TECH1: Schematic Design Program, Texas Tech University School of Medicine," Caudill Rowlett Scott Architects, March 15, 1971, 8, 55–64, 91.

7. Ronald Skaggs, "Interview with Author," dated August 23, 2016.

8. Jack DeBartolo, "Interview with Author," dated September 16, 2016.

9. "TECH1: Schematic Design Program, Texas Tech University School of Medicine," 4.

10. Rick McCarty, "Press Release," Texas Tech University School of Medicine Groundbreaking, January 31, 1973.

11. W. Eugene Smith, "Freeway Removal Opposed," *Lubbock Avalanche-Journal,* August 18, 1973, 1, 16.

12. Celeste Loucks, "Med School Project 'Big Time,'" *Lubbock Avalanche-Journal,* June 16, 1974, 1, 8.

13. Eric Williams, "Interview with Author," dated September 13, 2010.

14. Ibid.

15. Ronald Skaggs, "Interview with Author," dated August 23, 2016.

16. Oscar H. Mauzy, "A Bill Entitled to Be an Act Relating to the Texas Tech University Health Sciences Center" Senate Bill No. 371, Regular Session of the 66th Legislature, Texas Legislative Reference Library.

CHAPTER 17. MALAISE

1. "Degrees Conferred Since 1927," Texas Tech University Office of Institutional Research, last modified on October 4, 2017, retrieved from: https://www.depts.ttu.edu/irim/ARCHIVE/DEGAWD/DEGFR27.php.

2. "Fall Enrollment Since 1925," Texas Tech University Office of Institutional Research, last modified on October 4, 2017, retrieved from: https://www.depts.ttu.edu/irim/ARCHIVE/ENR/FALLENRL.php.

3. "Vital Statistics of the United States, 1939–1964 and 1965–1979," National Center for Health Statistics, Centers for Disease Control and Prevention, last updated on February 27, 2013, retrieved from: https://www.cdc.gov/nchs/products/vsus.htm.

4. Thomas D. Snyder, ed., *120 Years of American Education: A Statistical Portrait* (Washington, DC: National Center for Education Statistics, US Department of Education, 1993), 66.

5. "Fall Enrollment Since 1925," Texas Tech University Office of Institutional Research, last modified on October 4, 2017, retrieved from: https://www.depts.ttu.edu/irim/ARCHIVE/ENR/FALLENRL.php.

6. Memorandum from J. Knox Jones, Jr. to Dr. Glenn E. Barnett, dated November 8, 1975.

7. "Texas Tech University Five-Year Campus Development Plan," Texas Tech University Office of Planning, October 1985, 36.

8. "Overview: Permanent University Fund (PUF) and Higher Education Fund (HEF), Office of External Relations, Texas Higher Education

Coordinating Board, February 2009, retrieved on April 7, 2016, from: www.thecb.state.tx.us/reports/pdf/1627.pdf.

9. Memorandum from J. Knox Jones, Jr. to Dr. Glenn E. Barnett, dated October 2, 1976.

10. Memorandum from Glenn E. Barnett to Dr. William Johnson, dated June 6, 1975.

11. "Space Committee Minutes," Item 7, dated April 11, 1977, 2.

12. Ibid., Item 6a, dated August 29, 1977, 2.

13. Ibid., Item 6b, dated August 29, 1977, 2.

14. Memorandum from Robert Bray to Robert Meyer, dated March 22, 1987.

15. Memorandum from Robert Bray to Lauro Cavazos, dated August 8, 1984.

16. "Texas Tech University Central Campus Preliminary Master Landscape Plan," 3D/International, February 1984, 3, 7–8, 10, 16–22, 35–36.

17. "Texas Tech University Central Campus Preliminary Master Landscape Plan," 3D/International, February 1984, 38–39.

18. Correspondence from William Ward Watkin to Messrs. Sanguinet, Statts [Staats] & Hedrick, dated June 22, 1925.

19. Memorandum from Glenn E. Barnett to Mr. Thompson and Drs. Jones, Ewalt, and Hardwick, dated July 27, 1977.

20. Correspondence from Glenn Hill to Lauro F. Cavazos, dated April 29, 1983.

21. Lynn Whitfield, "Caprock Chronicles: Elo J. Urbanovsky: Early architect of the Texas Tech campus," *Lubbock Avalanche-Journal,* December 8, 2018, retrieved from: https://www.lubbockonline.com/news/20181208/caprock-chronicles-elo-j-urbanovsky-early/.

22. "The Roof of the Pontiac Silverdome, Home of the Detroit Pistons and the Detroit Lions, Collapsed," United Press International [UPI Archives], March 4, 1985, retrieved on August 30, 2017, from: https://www.upi.com/Archives/1985/03/04/The-roof-of-the-Pontiac-Silverdome-home-of-the/7866478760400/.

23. Joe D. McKay, "Interview with Author," September 19, 2016.

24. Ibid.

25. William L. Adling, "Interview with Author," September 5, 2017.

CHAPTER 18. SYZYGY

1. Mel Greenberg, "Swoopes' 47 Carry Texas Tech to Title Ohio State Fell, 84–82, As The Raiders' Unstoppable Forward Snapped a Slew of Tournament Records," *The Philadelphia Inquirer,* April 5, 1993.

2. Michael B. Baker, "Story Communicated to Author," dated August 4, 2010.

3. "Doug Hensley, "Lubbock's Triumphs and Troubles of the '90s," *Lubbock Avalanche-Journal*, December 30, 1999, retrieved on September 6, 2014, from: http://lubbockonline.com/stories/123099/loc_123099088.shtml.

4. Brian Davis, "How Baylor Got into the Big 12," *The Dallas Morning News,* August 30, 2006, retrieved on September 6, 2014, from: http://www.dallasnews.com/sharedcontent/sportsday/bf22e33.html.

5. Brad Townsend, "SWC's Dying Days," *The Dallas Morning News*, September 4, 2015, retrieved on July 29, 2017, from: http://interactives.dallasnews.com/2015/swc–anniversary/.

6. Davis, "How Baylor Got into the Big 12."

7. Theresa Bartos Drewell, "Interview with Author," dated August 5, 2011.

8. John T. Montford and Debbie Montford, "Interview with Author," dated July 13, 2016.

9. Matthew Henry, "Questions Emerge as Signs Point Toward Tech System," *Lubbock Avalanche-Journal,* December 22, 1996, retrieved on July 13, 2016, from: http://lubbockonline.com/news/122296/question.htm.

10. John T. Montford, "A Bill Entitled to Be an Act Relating to the Creation of the Texas Tech University System," Senate Bill No. 215, February 6, 1985, Regular Session of the 69th Legislature, Texas Legislative Reference Library.

11. John T. and Debbie Montford, "Interview with Author," dated July 13, 2016.

12. Ibid.

13. Ibid.

14. "Building No. 387—Southwest Collection/Special Collections Library," Drawing Flat File, Texas Tech University Physical Plant, Office of Engineering Services, retrieved on August 20, 2015.

15. "Article III. Agencies of Public Education [as portion of Senate Bill No. 5]," May 21, 1993, Regular Session of the 73rd Legislature, Texas Legislative Reference Library, 668.

16. Joe D. McKay, "Interview with Author," September 19, 2016.

17. Douglas Mann, "Interview with Author," September 13, 2016.

18. Theresa Bartos Drewell, "Interview with Author," dated March 29, 2013.

19. Mann, "Interview with Author."

20. Hellmuth, Obata, & Kassabaum, Inc., *Campus Master Plan*

(Lubbock: Texas Tech University and Texas Tech University Health Sciences Center, February 6, 1998), 10, 16.

21. "CW24. Campus Master Plan," Board Minutes, November 7, 1997 meeting, Texas University System Board of Regents.

22. Joe D. McKay, "Interview with Author," September 19, 2016.

23. Mann, "Interview with Author,"

24. "Doug Hensley, "Lubbock's Triumphs and Troubles of the '90s," *Lubbock Avalanche-Journal*, December 30, 1999, retrieved on September 6, 2014, from: http://lubbockonline.com/stories/123099/loc_123099088.shtml.

25. "Bricks and Mortar Report," October 2005 Edition, Texas Tech University System Facilities Planning and Construction, 35.

CHAPTER 19. MAELSTROM

1. Michael A. Ellicott, "Interview with Author," September 22, 2010.

2. Ibid.

3. Ibid.

4. Joe D. McKay, "Interview with Author," September 19, 2016.

5. "Inside TxDOT: Marsha Sharp Freeway," Texas Department of Transportation Website, retrieved on December 11, 2017, from: https://www.txdot.gov/inside-txdot/projects/studies/lubbock/sharp-freeway.html.

6. "Texas Tech University, Robert H. Ewalt Student Recreation Center, Lubbock, Texas," [Project Brief], *SchoolDesigns,* retrieved on March 16, 2017, from: https://schooldesigns.com/Project-Details.aspx?Project_ID=1514.

7. Conversation between Michael Shonrock and Robert Sabbatini [Overheard by Author], "North Campus Gateway District Plan," February 5, 2008.

8. William L. Adling, "Interview with Author," September 5, 2017.

9. Michael Reis, "Limestone Creates a Focal Point at Texas Tech," *Stone World,* March 1, 2005, retrieved on March 29, 2017, from: http://www.stoneworld.com/articles/83311-limestone-creates-a-focal-point-at-texas-tech

10. Robert Duncan, "A Bill Entitled to be An Act Relating to the Creation of the Texas Tech University System," Senate Bill No. 1088, offered April 23, 1999, Regular Session of the 76th Legislature, Texas Legislative Reference Library.

11. "Enhanced Logos Unveiled," Accessed from General Archived Stories at: https://texastech.com/news/1999/8/17/undefined on 24 August 2019.

12. "Fall Enrollment Since 1925," Texas Tech University Office of Institutional Research, last modified on October 4, 2017, retrieved from: https://www.depts.ttu.edu/irim/ARCHIVE/ENR/FALLENRL.php.

13. Sarah Self-Walbrick, "North Overton 20 Years Later: McDougals Say Nation's Largest Privately Funded Urban Renewal Effort Now Complete," *Lubbock Avalanche-Journal,* January 26, 2019, retrieved on February 2, 2019, from: https://www.lubbockonline.com/news/20190126/north-overton-20-years-later-mcdougals-say-nations-largest-privately-funded-urban-renewal-effort-now-complete.

14. "Enhanced Logos Unveiled," Texas Tech Athletics [Press Release], August 17, 1999, retrieved on November 20, 2017, from: https://texastech.com/news/1999/8/17/undefined.

15. Editorial, "Bush Library Trial Balloon Deflated," *Lubbock Avalanche-Journal,* Online edition, March 20, 2005, retrieved on April 2, 2017, from: http://lubbockonline.com/stories/032005/ran_032005029.shtml.

16. David Miller, "Interview with Author," dated April 6, 2017.

17. Elliott Blackburn, "Coalition Unveils Site for Bush Library Bid," *Lubbock Avalanche-Journal,* Online edition, August 23, 2005, retrieved on April 1, 2017, from: http://lubbockonline.com/stories/082305/loc_082305032.shtml.

18. David Miller, "Interview with Author," dated April 6, 2017.

19. Ibid.

CHAPTER 20. ELECTRA

1. Bergen Evans, *Dictionary of Mythology* (New York: Dell Publishing, 1970), 79.

2. Hugh Best, *Debrett's Texas Peerage* (New York: Coward-McCann, 1983), 122–124.

3. Ibid., 129–131

4. Ibid., 125

5. Bobby Weaver, "Interview with Electra Waggoner Biggs," Oral History, Texas Tech University Southwest Special Collections, November 27, 1978.

6. Telegram from Amon G. Carter to John Young [Student Band Master, Texas Technological College], dated October 29, 1926.

7. Jerry Flemmons, *Amon: The Texan Who Played Cowboy for America* (Lubbock: Texas Tech University Press, 1998), 172–173.

8. Bobby Weaver, "Interview with Electra Waggoner Biggs," Oral History, Texas Tech University Southwest Special Collections, November 27, 1978.

9. Best, *Debrett's Texas Peerage*, 126.

10. H. Allen Anderson, *Handbook of Texas Online*, "MASHED O RANCH [#1]," retrieved November 30, 2017, from: http://www.tshaonline.org/handbook/online/articles/apm01.

11. Ruth Horn Andrews, *The First Thirty Years,* (Lubbock: Texas Tech Press, 1956), 285–286.

12. Ibid., 286–287.

13. Robert Metzger, ed., *My Land Is the Southwest: Peter Hurd Letters and Journals* (College Station: Texas A&M University Press, 1983), 374–375.

14. Nolan Ellimore Barrick, "Interview with Author," October 25, 2009.

15. John T. Montford and Debbie Montford, "Interview with Author," July 13, 2016.

16. Ibid.

17. "Public Art Collection—Texas Tech University," 3rd ed., retrieved on April 6, 2018, from https://www.texastech.edu/fpc/public-art/walking
-tour-booklet/FLASH/index.html.

18. Amanda Castro-Crist, "Glenna Goodacre Announces Retirement with Sculpture Gift to Rawls College," *Texas Tech Today,* September 9, 2016, retrieved on April 7, 2018, from https://today.ttu.edu/posts/2016/09
/glenna-goodacre.

19. John T. Montford and Debbie Montford, "Interview with Author," July 13, 2016.

20. Ibid.

21. Ibid.

22. "Past Winners," Professional Grounds Management Society website, retrieved on December 2, 2017, from: https://pgms.org/green-star-awards
/past-winners/.

23. "University and College Grounds (Large) Honor Award—Texas Tech University," Professional Grounds Management Society website, retrieved on December 2, 2017 from: https://pgms.org/texas-tech
-university/.

24. Scott Slemmons, "Texas Tech Public Art Program Named One of Ten Best," *Texas Tech Today,* May 2006, retrieved from: http://today.ttu.edu/posts/2006/05/texas-tech-public-art-program-named-one-of
-ten-best.

25. Michael S. Molina, Theresa Bartos Drewell, et. al., *Lubbock Campus Master Plan 2014 Update,* 1st ed. (Lubbock: Office of Facilities Planning and Construction and the Texas Tech University Press, 2015), 68, 86, 88.

CHAPTER 21. SAINT CLIFFORD'S CATHEDRAL

1. "Full SWC Football Role Seen by 1961," *Lubbock Avalanche-Journal*, May 13, 1956, 1.

2. W. L. Stangel Oral History, Interviewed by David Murrah and Etta Lynch, January 19, March 7, 16, 1973, tape 6. Southwest Collection/Special Collections Library, Texas Tech University.

3. Ruth Horn Andrews, *The First Thirty Years* (Lubbock: Texas Tech Press, 1956), 331.

4. Randy Sanders, ed., *Greatest Moments in Texas Tech Football History* (Birmingham, AL: Epic Sports, 2001), 53.

5. "Stadium Damaged by Fire," *The Toreador,* vol. 18, no. S–1, June 2, 1944, 3.

6. "Board Minutes," March 30, 1946, meeting, Texas Technological College Board of Directors, vol. 6.

7. Correspondence from W. L. Stangel to F. S. Oldt, August 5, 1947.

8. Andrews, *The First Thirty Years*, 68.

9. William G. McMillan Jr., "Interview with Author and Mike W. Moss," February 2, 2011.

10. Ibid.

11. "1394. Stadium Enlargement Study," Board Minutes, April 13, 1957, meeting, Texas Technological College Board of Directors.

12. "1728. Stadium Contract," Board Minutes, June 3, 1957, meeting, Texas Technological College Board of Directors.

13. Nolan Ellimore Barrick, "Interview with Author," December 18, 2010.

14. "September 2, 1954—Ten Thousand People Watch as the Captured German Submarine U–505 Is Hauled Across Lake Shore Drive," *Connecting the Windy City,* retrieved on October 25, 2017 from: http://www.connectingthewindycity.com/2017/09/september-2-1954-u-505
-crosses-highway.html

15. McMillan, "Interview with Author and Mike W. Moss."

16. "W. G. McMillan Dies; Services Set," *Lubbock Evening Journal,* October 28, 1958, 4.

17. Barrick, "Interview with Author."

18. Construction photograph dated March 15, 1958, Parkhill, Smith & Cooper, Inc.

19. Barrick, "Interview with Author."

20. "Stadium Press Box Concrete Pouring Expected to Begin," *The Toreador,* July 23, 1959, 2.

21. "1960 Texas Tech Red Raiders Schedule and Results," Sports Reference CFB, retrieved on December 3, 2017 from: https://www.sports–reference.com/cfb/schools/texas–tech/1960–schedule.html.

22. Barrick, "Interview with Author," October 25, 2009.

23. McMillan, "Interview with Author and Mike W. Moss."

24. Stephen Faulk, "Interview with Author," dated August 29, 2016.

25. Ibid.

26. John T. Montford and Debbie Montford, "Interview with Author," July 13, 2016.

27. Faulk, "Interview with Author."

28. Michael A. Ellicott, "Interview with Author," September 22, 2010.

29. Faulk, "Interview with Author."

30. "Jones AT&T Stadium East Side Expansion," Facilities Planning and Construction: Projects: Texas Tech University, retrieved on November 19, 2017, from: http://www.texastech.edu/fpc/projects/project-status.php?project=08-40&entity=TTU&status=completed.

31. Catherine McKee, "Work Begins on Jones Expansion, Video Scoreboard," *The Daily Toreador,* January 21, 2013, retrieved on October 22, 2017, from: http://www.dailytoreador.com/news/work–begins–on–jones–expansion–video–scoreboard/article_4782f3de–6425–11e2–82ee–0019bb30f31a.html.

32. "Texas Tech Reveals $185M Athletics Facilities Makeover," *Amarillo Globe–News,* August 29, 2014, retrieved on October 22, 2017 from: https://www.amarillo.com/article/20140829/NEWS/308299656.

33. Jerry Fawcett, "Telephonic interview with Author," December 3, 2017.

CHAPTER 22. SPANREN

1. Dr. Donald Clancy, Course lecture [Heard by Author], "Financial and Managerial Accounting," December 2, 2002.

2. "$155M New Business Center Coming to UT McCombs School of Business," Stacy Blackman Consulting, September 12, 2012, retrieved on October 15, 2017, from: https://www.stacyblackman.com/blog/155m-new-business-center-coming-to-ut-mccombs--school-of-business/.

3. J. H. Elliott, *Imperial Spain, 1469–1716* (New York: St. Martin's Press, 1964), 155–156.

4. "Plaza de Vázquez de Molina Square," Spanish National Tourism Website, retrieved on December 10, 2017, from: https://www.spain.info/en_US/que-quieres/arte/monumentos/jaen/plaza_de_vazquez_de_molina.html.

5. Michael S. Molina, "Interview with Author," March 11, 2016.

6. Ibid.

7. Ibid.

8. Michael S. Molina, Theresa Bartos Drewell, et. al., *Lubbock Campus Master Plan 2014 Update,* 1st ed. (Lubbock: Office of Facilities Planning & Construction and the Texas Tech University Press, 2015), 12.

9. "Table 14: Expenditures for Research and Development—Texas Public Universities," Research Expenditures: September 1, 2003–August 31, 2004, Texas Public Universities and Health-Related Institutions, Texas Higher Education Coordinating Board, April 2005, 28.

10. "Office of the Vice President for Research—2016 Annual Report," retrieved on December 4, 2017, from: https://www.depts.ttu.edu/research/metrics/annual–report–archive.php.

11. Al York, "Interview with Author," March 5, 2017.

12. Molina, "Interview with Author."

13. Robert D. Waller, "Texas Tech University System Endowment Continues Growth in Support of Students and Faculty," Press Release, Texas Tech University System Office of Institutional Advancement, retrieved on February 3, 2019, from: http://www.give2tech.com/news/article/texas-tech-university-system-endowment-continues-growth-in-support-of-students-and-faculty/.

14. George Watson, "Bayer CropScience, Texas Tech University Open Seeds Innovation Center," *Texas Tech Today,* September 2, 2015, retrieved on November 29, 2017, from: http://today.ttu.edu/posts/2015/09/bayer-cropscience-texas-tech-open-seeds-innovation-center#prettyPhoto.

15. "Fall Enrollment Since 1925," Texas Tech University Office of Institutional Research, last modified on October 4, 2017, retrieved from: https://www.depts.ttu.edu/irim/ARCHIVE/ENR/FALLENRL.php

CHAPTER 23. FINIS CORONAT OPUS

1. Michael S. Molina, Theresa Bartos Drewell, et. al., *Lubbock Campus Master Plan 2014 Update,* 1st ed. (Lubbock: Office of Facilities Planning and Construction and the Texas Tech University Press, 2015), 86–89.

2. Parkhill, Smith & Cooper, Inc., "Proposed Exterior Rendering of North Façade—Academic Classroom Building," November 10, 2000.

3. Dr. Tedd Mitchell, speech given during informal question-and-answer forum, "2018 Annual State of the System Luncheon," October 16, 2018.

4. "Campus Master Plan," University of San Diego Office of Facilities Management Website, last updated on July 18, 2017. Retrieved from https://www.sandiego.edu/facilities/master-plan.php.

5. "New Mexico State University Master Plan 2017-2027," NMSU Facilities and Services and Office of the University Architect, October 2017, 9.

6. "National Research University Fund Eligibility: A Report to the Comptroller and the State Legislature," Texas Higher Education Coordinating Board, February 2013, 3, 5.

7. George Watson, "Bayer CropScience, Texas Tech University Open Seeds Innovation Center," *Texas Tech Today*, September 2, 2015, retrieved on November 29, 2017 from: http://today.ttu.edu/posts/2015/09/bayer-cropscience-texas-tech-open-seeds-innovation-center#prettyPhoto.

8. Chris Cook, "Texas Tech Achieves Tier One Carnegie Designation," *Texas Tech Today*, February 2, 2016, retrieved from: https://today.ttu.edu/posts/2016/02/tier-one-carnegie-designation.

9. Molina, et. al., *Lubbock Campus Master Plan 2014 Update*, 4–9, 86–88.

10. John Zerwas, "A Bill to Be Entitled an Act Relating to Authorizing the Issuance of Revenue Bonds to Fund Capital Projects at Public Institutions of Higher Education." House Bill No. 100, March 3, 2015, Regular Session of the 84th Texas Legislature, Legislative Reference Library, 12.

11. Michael S. Molina, "Interview with Author," March 11, 2016.

12. Molina, et. al., *Lubbock Campus Master Plan 2014 Update*, 86–88.

13. Molina, "Interview with Author."

14. Gary Cudney, "Industry Insights," April 2014, Carl Walker, Inc., retrieved on November 6, 2016, from https://carlwalkerconstruction.com/publications/.

15. Matt Dotray, "VA Moving Forward on Plan for New, $12.3M Lubbock Clinic," *Lubbock Avalanche-Journal*, October 3, 2018, last updated on October 3, 2018. Retrieved from https://www.lubbockonline.com/news/20181003/va-moving-forward-on-plan-for-new-123m-lubbock-clinic.

16. Lindsey M. Howden and Julie A. Meyer, "Table 2. Population by Age and Sex: 2000 and 2010," *Age and Sex Composition: 2010*, US Department of Commerce Economics and Statistics Administration, US Census Bureau, May 2011.

17. Correspondence, Johann Wolfgang von Goethe to Johann Peter Eckermann, March 23, 1829.

EPILOGUE. A REQUIEM FOR TEMPLES AND TITANS

1. Carl Abbott, *The Great Extravaganza: Portland and the Lewis and Clark Exposition*, 3rd ed. (Portland: Oregon Historical Society Press, 2004), 56.

2. Bertram Grosvenor Goodhue, *The Architecture and the Gardens of the San Diego Exposition* (San Francisco: Paul Elder and Company, 1916), 8–9.

3. "Today in History: Centennial of the Panama–California Exposition in San Diego," *People's World*, July 27, 2013, retrieved on November 29, 2017, from: https://www.peoplesworld.org/article/today-in-history-centennial-of-the-panama-california-exposition-in-san-diego/.

4. Romy Wyllie, *Bertram Goodhue: His Life and Residential Architecture* (New York: W. W. Norton & Company, 2007), 188.

5. Ibid., 192.

6. Ibid., 193.

7. Douglass Shand–Tucci, *Ralph Adams Cram: An Architect's Four Quests* (Amherst: University of Massachusetts Press, 2005), 520.

8. Ibid., 522.

9. Ibid., 521.

10. Victoria Kastner, *Hearst Castle: The Biography of a Country House* (New York: Harry N. Abrams, 2000), 183.

11. "Rare Books: Coronelli Globe," Texas Tech University Southwest Collection/Special Collections Library Home, last updated on March 2, 2019, retrieved from: http://swco.ttu.edu/rare_books/Coronelli.php.

12. Victoria Kastner, "Arthur Byne, Mildred Stapley Byne, and the Spanish Colonial Revival," (Master's Thesis, University of California Santa Barbara, 1989), 20.

13. Manuel Nieto Cumplido, "Bell-Tower of the Mosque-Cathedral [English Guide Brochure]," Cabildo Catedral de Córdoba, 2015 Printing.

14. Bernard Bevan, *History of Spanish Architecture* (New York: Charles Scribner's Sons, 1939), 133.

15. José Juste Ballesta and Eduardo Barceló de Torres, "El Plan Director de la Catedral de Sigüenza," Instituto del Patrimonio Histórico Español, del Ministerio de Educación, Cultura y Deporte, 1998, 64, 74–75.

16. José María San Luciano, *El incendio y destrucción del Archivo*

General Central – Alcalá de Henares, 1939, (Madrid: Domiduca Libreros y Lema Ediciones, 2009), 76–78.

17. Mildred Hedrick Fender and Ames Fender, AIA, "Interview with Author," November 29, 2009.

18. "Gone but Not Forgotten: 25 Years of City Memories," *Houston Business Journal*, September 29, 1996. Last updated on September 30, 1996, and retrieved from https://www.bizjournals.com/houston/stories/1996/09/30/focus2.html.

19. Mildred Hedrick Fender and Ames Fender, AIA, "Interview with Author," November 29, 2009.

20. Lynn Whitfield, "Caprock Chronicles: Elo J. Urbanovsky: Early Architect of the Texas Tech Campus," *Lubbock Avalanche-Journal*, last updated on December 8, 2018, https://www.lubbockonline.com/news/20181208/caprock-chronicles-elo-j-urbanovsky-early-architect-of-texas-tech-campus.

21. "Unsolved Murders," web slideshow, *Lubbock Avalanche-Journal*, last modified on June 6, 2013, retrieved from http://lubbockonline.com/slideshow/2012-06-13/unsolved-murders.

22. Nolan Ellimore Barrick, "Interview with Author," December 18, 2010.

INDEX

Page numbers in *italics* refer to illustrations.

Publication of this book was made possible
by the generous support of The CH Foundation
and Parkhill, Smith & Cooper.

A DOMINO FACTVM ESTISTVD